PERSPECTIVES OF THE SILENT MAJORITY: AIR POLLUTION, LIVELIHOOD AND FOOD SECURITY

COMMUNITY PERSPECTIVES IN ENVIRONMENT & DEVELOPMENT

Prof. Amitava Mukherjee Ph. D. was educated at Ranchi University, Ranchi; Rice University, Houston and at University of South Florida, Tampa. He researched at Rice University, Houston; Stanford University, Stanford; London School of Economics, London and the School of Oriental and African studies, University of London, London. Dr. Mukherjee is currently the Executive Director of Development Tracks in Research Training and Consultancy, a knowledge enterprise in New Delhi and is consultant to various UN agencies and international organisations in and outside India. He has written and lectured extensively on issues of hunger, food security and poverty almost worldwide, including at the UN. He has over two dozen books and numerous papers to his credit. His contributions to micro-level planning, participatory development, food security and hunger are internationally recognized.

Community Perspectives in Environment & Development-2

Perspectives of the Silent Majority : Air Pollution, Livehood and Food Security

Indepth studies through PRA methods on community perspectives in urban and peri–urban areas of Varanasi and Faridabad, India

AMITAVA MUKHERJEE

CONCEPT PUBLISHING COMPANY, NEW DELHI -110059

Originally published by
Ashgate Publishing Limited,
Grower House, Croft Road,
Aldershot,
Hampshire GU11 3HR
England

Ashgate Publishing Company
131 Main Street
Burlington, VT 05401 - 5600 USA

Ashgate website ://http:www.ashgate.com

ISBN 81-7022-985-5 (Series)
ISBN 81-7022-987-1 (Vol. 2)

South Asian Edition 2002

South Asian Edition
Published and Printed in India by
Ashok Kumar Mittal
Concept Publishing Company
A/15-16, Commercial Block, Mohan Garden,
NEW DELHI-110059

Phones : 5648039, 5649024
Fax : 091-11-5648053
Email : publishing@conceptpub.com

Dedicated to the village communities of Faridabad and Varanasi, who paticipated in this study and made it possible.

Contents

List of Charts, Boxes and Figures

Figures

List of Tables

Glossary of Indian Terms

Terms	**Meaning**
Aganwadi	A government child welfare day care centre where children upto the age of 5 receive free food and health check up.
Baithak	Living room.
Bajra	A coarse cereal.
Banga	Disease afflicting buffaloes. It affects the feet which get swollen.
Baroo	A type of weed which looks similar to jowar and is found mostly in jowar fields.
Barsam	Fodder sown in winter.
Basti	Ward or colony in a village organised mainly on the basis of caste/religion.
Bathua	A weed.
Bigha	Measure of Land: 5 Bigha = 1 acre.
Biswa	Measure of Lnad: 5 Biswa = 1 acre.
Burela	Another name for dhola.

Chepa	Tiny white insects which suck juice out of leaves in cabbage, bajra, mustard and sugarcane. Has a sticky texture.
Chhedak	Any caterpillar that bores holes. It is also called dhola/burela.
Chitli	A worm that eats vegetable roots.
Chula	Oven or stove made out of mud which uses wood, animal dung etc. as fuel.
Congress Grass	A weed having small white flowers. Also called parthenium.
Dhencha	Medium sized fodder plants sown in summer.
Dhola	Caterpillars that bore holes.
Fatinga	A grass hopper.
Galagotu	Disease found in buffaloes. It chokes buffaloes to death
Gander	A general term for caterpillars.
Gram Samiti	A village co-operative society.
Gram Sewak	An appointee of the Block Development Office for supervising development work in the village. He/She looks after 3 villages.
Gurchawa	A disease which results in wilting and crippling of leaves.
Hara Kira	Small green caterpillar.

Harwawa	A disease which turns leaves yellow.
Jhansi	A cluster of small caterpillars (pest).
Jhulsa	A disease resulting in wilting and blackening of leaves.
Jowar	An inferior cereal used also as fodder.
Kanduwa	A disease which affects the ear-rings of wheat and turns them black.
Kasba	A village which is the centre of rural growth having a population of 7000 or more.
Kateli	A medium sized tree-weed which has thorns.
Katui	A pest which cuts down paddy ear-rings.
Kirona	A caterpillar.
Koria	Crippling of leaves and plants like a leper. The fruits of the affected plants look deformed.
Lalrii	Red coloured small sized pests which can fly. It eats leaves of leafy vegetables.
Machchi/Makhi	House-fly.
Mandi	Wholesale market.
Morya or Gurchawa	A disease which wilts and cripples leaves especially in chilies and tomatoes.
Muhalla	Wards/Colony.
Najla	Ailment: running nose, headache nose burning.

Nakshatra	A constellation.
Nilagai	Blue bull.
Pankhi	Any pest which can fly.
Pradhan/Sarpanch	Village Head, usually elected to the village level unit of governance.
Rani Jai (Ghan Jai)	A weed similar in looks to wheat and whose seeds are like wheat grains, though slightly black in colour.
Safed Moondi	A weed having small seeds (coriander type), mainly found in wheat fields.
Sambar	A kind of deer.
Sati	Small sized weeds which mainly grow in bajra fields.
Soondi	Small sized caterpillar found in paddy leaves. It sucks the sap.
Telchatta	Small sized pest which can fly. It sucks juice out of mustard pods and cauliflower.
Tidda	A current variant of locust which is small in size.
Tiddi	Large sized locust (the earlier variant).
Tikuli	A beetle that sucks juice from leaves of vegetables mostly found in summer.
Titri	A small white moth which sucks milk from paddy ear-rings.

Months of the Year in the Indian Calendar

Vernacular Month	Corresponding Period in Roman Calendar
Baisakh	Mid-April to Mid-May
Jeth	Mid-May to Mid-June
Asard	Mid-June to Mid-July
Sawan	Mid-July to Mid-August
Bhado	Mid-August to Mid-September
Kuar*	Mid-September to Mid-October
Kartick	Mid-October to Mid-November
Aghan	Mid-November to Mid-December
Poos	Mid-December to Mid-January
Magh	Mid-January to Mid-February
Fagun	Mid-February to Mid-March
Chait**	Mid-March to Mid-April

Notes: *In some villages called Aswin. ** Also spelt as Cheth

Introduction: Community Perspectives

I. About the Silent Majority

This is an exercise in learning from the voices of the communities living in villages, near urban areas.

It is a book primarily to learn from what communities have to say on their well-being and livelihoods and is, therefore, an attempt to record and register as much as possible what communities say. The data and information have been written as far as possible, as a transliteration of the language in which it was spoken and presented to us. That is its uniqueness. There is no other book, which does that. The analysis is in our own language and to keep the general tenor of the presentation consistent, throughout the book, it is not written in a racy style.

II. The Prelude

Agriculture in urban and peri-urban areas of Haryana and Uttar Pradesh plays an important role not only as a source of livelihood but also in supplying food grains, vegetables, pulses, milk, fruits and other agricultural produce to urban and peri-urban communities and markets. It constitutes a major source of income and livelihood both for those who own land in and around such areas and for those offering their labour for employment. The range of food grains, pulses, cereals, vegetables and milk, produced by farmers in such areas are in part for self-consumption and in part for sale in the market. Such produce from agriculture helps in not only supplying essential commodities in the food chain but also in stabilising prices and markets and in maintaining stocks.

Air pollution has a major impact on productivity and efficiency of wo/man and nature and pose as a serious health hazard. The most talked about impact is the health impact of air pollution leading to higher levels of morbidity, premature mortality and cases of chronic bronchitis and other respiratory infections.

Box 1
Air Quality

"Air pollution can be described as substances put into the air by the activity of mankind into concentrations sufficient to cause harmful effects to health, property, crop yield or to interfere with the enjoyment of property. The main sources of air pollution in India are automobiles, thermal power plants, industries, agriculture, quarrying, and also natural process."

Source: Indira Gandhi Institute of Development Research: *India Development Report.* 1997

III. This Research

III.1. The Scientist's View

The impact of air pollution on crop yield and agriculture is an important field of inquiry but it is a relatively new area of research in India. Within this new area of research, the views of the communities residing in such polluted localities are of great significance for it is they who feel the brunt of the impact of pollution, more often than not caused by someone else, in their livelihoods and quality of life.

The costs of such pollution loaded on to the communities, almost forcibly and without either consultation or consent, are not easy to cope with. Some of these costs are direct costs while others are hidden and indirect, not visible at the first instance. Amongst the direct costs borne by the communities is the reduction in crop yields and decline in agricultural production. Scientific evidence shows that different pollutants cause different kinds of impacts on agriculture, crops and vegetables. The impact of air pollution on crops has been dealt with exhaustively in the literature on air pollution. Their analysis of the sensitivity of different crops to different kinds of air pollution, particularly sulphur dioxide, fluoride, ozone and acid rain puts the entire debate into perspective. Among the crops sensitive to air pollution of different kinds are rice, wheat, barley, maize, soybean, carrot, beans, radish, pea, potato, tomato and onion. Most interestingly it is pointed out:

> Not only may pollutant gases interact with one another, they may also encourage or suppress the growth of various pests and pathogens, so increasing in certain cases the amount of crop damage that would occur if only the gas or the pest or pathogen were present (*Conway and Pretty 1991*).

Mixture of pollutants may also produce "synergistic or antagonistic" effects. It is also possible that one pollutant may pre-dispose or desensitise a plant to the effect of the other. However, it is currently not possible to draw any robust conclusion about the type of interaction that will happen when a given crop is subjected to a particular combination of pollutants.

III. 2. Issues, Questions and Problems Investigated

The present study is to learn about the relationship between agriculture in urban and peri-urban areas and the phenomena of industrialisation/ urbanisation, particularly air pollution as perceived and viewed by the farmers. The present study may be taken as presenting the other perspective, the *farmers' perspective*, both women and men, who are most affected by industrialisation, urbanisation and the consequent rise in pollution, in relation to crops, crop yields and agriculture and finally hunger.

The farmers in presenting their perspectives, gave extremely important insights into some related issues such as the role of agriculture in their livelihoods, the nature of agricultural constraints, the impact of air pollution on health status and quality of life and the support systems for addressing the problems of the farmers. This study has attempted to capture these insights.

Taking an overall view of the matter, the present study is an exercise in learning from local communities about impacts of pollution on crops, crop yield, agriculture and ultimately on their well being, especially in urban and peri-urban areas. This is of *fundamental importance*.

III.3. The Nature and Character of Research

A series of fieldwork based on farmers' perspective was carried out in selected urban and peri-urban areas during the period August 1998 to November 1999. The fieldwork was geared towards listening to primary stakeholders - women and men farmers in urban and peri-urban areas about their agricultural activities, practices and constraints. The sphere of agriculture broadly included crop and vegetable cultivation and livestock raising. Field investigation also included the impact of agricultural constraints on agricultural production, livelihood and health with focus on environmental problems arising from industrialisation and urbanisation. The field research explored the support system for agriculture, the role of local institutions in order to study their effectiveness and farmers' perspective on suitable ways for capacity building of such institutions.

Box 2
Whose Reality?

"Anyone concerned with the agricultural research and extension.....can hardly fail to be thrown back to the questions basic to the agricultural professions:

- Whose criteria and priorities count?
- Whose knowledge?
- Whose modes of learning and analysis?
- Whose tests, experiments, observations, assessments?
- Whose reality counts?

The logic and realism of this new professionalism deserve promotion more than ever. Decentralisation, diversity and empowerment of the poor become key values to focus effort. Direct and personal facilitation in the field and learning from, with and by farmers, is invested with professional prestige."

Source: *Misquoted* from Robert Chambers, "*Foreward*" in Ian Scoones and John Thompson (eds.): *Beyond Farmer First* (London: Intermediate Technology) 1994.

Some of the issues addressed in the field under the research were as follows.

- Role of agriculture and constraints faced by farmers.
- How important is urban and peri-urban agriculture to them?
- Understanding the issues of air pollution from local communities' perspective.
- How significant is the impact of air pollution in agriculture?
- How does it compare with other agricultural constraints?
- What policy issues emerge from such community perspectives?
- How effective are the local institutions and support system for the farmers?
- What is the health status of local communities and what is its relationship with industrialisation and urbanisation?
- What more can be done in this regard?

III.4. Field Inquiry

Field research was undertaken at two sites in India, Faridabad and Varanasi. Micro level information was generated on the research topic through participatory rural appraisal (PRA) methods in selected agro-based villages of Faridabad and Varanasi located near industrial areas. A participatory approaches (PA) team undertook such field research periodically during the crop year 1998-99. Altogether 13 villages of Faridabad and 14 villages of

Varanasi were covered,[1] selection of which was primarily based on scientific sites with different types of air pollution.[2]

The field inquiry was based on community interactions using Participatory Rural Appraisal (PRA) methods. The researchers carried out participatory field study. Gender was mainstreamed into the fieldwork for approaching local community and learning about different perspectives (e.g. those of men/woman, old/young, rich/poor) in the communities undertaken for the study.

Box 3

Some Participatory Approaches of the 1980s and 1990s

Abbreviation	Full Form
AEA	Agroecosystem Analysis
BA	Beneficiary Assessment
DELTA	Development Education Leadership Teams
D&D	Diagnosis and Design
DRP	Diagnostico Rural Participativo
FPR	Farmer Participatory Research
FSR/E	Farming Systems Research/Extension
GRAAP	Groupe de recherche et d'appui pour l'auto-promotion paysanne
MARP	Methode Accelere de Recherche Participative
PALM	Participatory Analysis and Learning Methods
PAR	Participatory Action Research
PD	Process Documentation
PLA	Participatory Learning and Action
PPA	Participatory Poverty Assessment
PRA	Participatory Rural Appraisal
PRAP	Participatory Rural Appraisal and Planning
PRM	Participatory Research Methods
PTD	Participatory Technology Development
RA	Rapid Appraisal
RAAKS	Rapid Assessment of Agricultural Knowledge System
RAP	Rapid assessment Procedures

RAT	Rapid Assessment Techniques
RCA	Rapid Catchment Analysis
REA	Rapid Ethnographic Assessment
RFCA	Rapid Fertiliser Consumption Assessment
RFSA	Rapid Food Assessment
RMA	Rapid Multi-Perspective Appraisal
ROA	Rapid Organisational Assessment
RRA	Rapid Rural Appraisal
RRA	Relaxed Rural Appraisal
SB	Samuhik Brahman
TFD	Theatre for Development
TFT	Training for Transformation

The *outputs* from the study were several Research Findings by the individual Participatory Assessment Teams (in some cases there were one person teams as well) running into hundreds of pages of text, photographs, charts, drawings, maps and many other participatory outputs. Add to this field notes. The *outcome* was a study synthesizing the learning and research findings from the villages covered under field study at Varanasi and Faridabad, published as the companion volume entitled "Alternative Perspectives on Livelihoods, Agriculture and Air Pollution".

IV. The Studies

IV.1. The Rationale

The process of consolidation and synthesizing of separate research reports running into hundreds of pages of text and hundreds of pages of field notes, diagrams, pictures and anecdotes, into one compressed report of decent size and length is a difficult proposition. It has many advantages: it is readable, it became precise, it is focussed and above all is actionable. An inherent characteristic of such consolidation is ruthless selectivity. Much useful and insightful data and information had to be sacrificed in the interest of brevity. In research of this nature, where the perceptions of the villagers were sought to be captured, such selectivity can kill the richness of information and learning emanating from such a detailed participatory study. Each human formation is unique. It has its own history of struggle. It has its own usage, customs, practices, percepts and environment. A consolidated research, by design and definition, can not be expected to bring out all these dimensions. It was, therefore, felt that some of these villages need to be studied in depth, to support and enrich the final outcome of the study, articulated in the consolidated report.

With that end in view, therefore and in order to bring out unique individuality of the villages, in depth studies of individual villages were carried out. The in depth studies were expected to not only cull out the uniqueness of the villages, and to document how the people perceive their problems and suggest solutions, but were also expected to bring on record details of tables, diagrams, maps and figures drawn up by the villagers. Because it was not possible to go into such details, in an aggregated research report of findings for all the villages in the two districts taken one with the other. These then are the rationale for these in-depth studies.

IV.2 Selection of Villages

Of the twenty-eight villages studied, it was considered necessary to have in depth studies of a select number of villages. As a rule of thumb, out of field covered at least 15 percent of the villages should be the subject of the in depth studies. Thus it was decided to prepare in depth studies of 5 villages. Villages were chosen at random, the only consideration being that they should be from both the states and should conform to the principle of contiguity, to draw meaningful conclusions. Accordingly, Tikri and Chandpur in Varanasi, and Sagarpur, Kadhaoli and Uncha Goan in Faridabad were taken up for the in depth studies. This selection as it turned out later was extremely helpful and did provide a wide canvas of diversity in circumstances prevailing in the villages.

Tikri and Chandpur were from the Backward State of Uttar Pradesh in the district of Varanasi and both are, *ipso facto*, vulnerable to such air pollutants as ozone, SO_2, and NO_2. The similarity ended there. Tikri has a homogenous livelihood system, Chandpur has a heterogeneous livelihood pattern. Tikri is away from the Road; Chandpur is right on the Grand Trunk Road. Tikri is less urbanised than Chandpur. Landholding pattern in Tikri is of a moderate average size; the average landholding in Chandpur is very small. Both these villages have just stepped into the Green Revolution syndrome.

Similarly if we look at the villages in Fridabad, there are marked divergences and similarities. These villages lie at the heart of the Green Revolution belt of India, unlike the Varanasi Villages and are in the vicinity of one of the fastest growing industrial townships in India. Uncha Gaon is a municipal town and more urbanised than both Sagarpur and Kadhaoli. Uncha Gaon produces in the main vegetables, but the other two grow mainly wheat, paddy, jowar and bajra as their principal crops. While Sagarpur and Uncha Gaon are predominantly Jat dominated, Khadaoli is predominantly Muslim inhabited; that is, there are strong religious, cultural and economic differences between the inhabitants of the two sets of villages.

All these have afforded a unique opportunity to look at the perspectives of people very dissimilarly situated.

IV. 3. The Objectives of the In-depth Studies

Building in depth studies from the elements of an extensive participatory research can be dicey. The wealth of data can often lead to chaos and mental cataclysm. Too much analysis can lead to paralysis. In order to avoid the pitfalls, a set of issues and questions were agreed upon based on the experience of the research outputs. These questions were agreed upon in consultation with the International Institute for Environment and Development, London and the Imperial College of Science, Technology and Medicines, University of London, London. Thus the in-depth studies were designed to seek in general answers to the following sets of questions.

a. Learn about the Importance of Agriculture to the People Living in the Urban and Peri-urban Areas

Cropping Pattern

(i) What are the crops grown?
(ii) What is the cropping pattern?
(iii) What is the intensity of cultivation?

Agricultural Practices

(iv) What changes in cropping pattern and agricultural practices have taken place, if any?
(v) Why have the changes taken place, if at all?
(vi) What changes in yield of crops have taken place?

- Seasonal and historical trends.
- Farmers' response to declining yield, if any.

Spatial

(vii) Are there spatial differences in yields or crop quality?

Inputs

(viii) What are the inputs to agriculture and the cultivation process?
(ix) What are the agricultural inputs and how does the economics of the input work out?
(x) Who supplies the inputs and who provide the extension services regarding new seeds, pesticides and fertilisers?

Class

(xi) Who are the landowning and the landless groups?
(xii) Are there any variations of the type of land used by different farmers groups?
(xii) Is there any overlap between landownership with produce ownership?
(xiv) Are there migrant labourers in agriculture and migrant leasees?

Gender

(xv) Is there a difference in the tasks carried out by men and women?

(xvi) Is there any variation noticeable with age or caste group?

Significance

(xvii) What is the significance of agriculture in urban and peri-urban areas in terms of:

- employment (full time and part time).
- food security.
- income.
- others.

(xviii) In what ways does food production interact with other household activities?

(xix) What proportion of total household or village income is derived from agriculture?

b. Constraints to Agricultural Production and People's Response

(xx) What are the constraints for agricultural production?

(xxi) What are their impact?

(xxii) What factors influence the constraints?

c. Air Pollution

(xxiii) What are the perceived impacts of air pollution?

(xxiv) Is dust pollution from industrial areas/roads linked with a particular stage of cropping calendar?

(xxv) What changes in types of pests, pest population and past damage have been perceived spatially and historically?

d. Injury to Crops

(xxvi) Any visible injury to crops?

(xxvii) To what extent is leaf injury perceived to be caused by air pollution?

(xxviii) What happens to injured crops: consumed, sold, used as fodder or dumped?

e. How Do People Deal with Constraints to Agricultural Production

(xxix) How do farmers tackle perceived constraints: through changed practice? Organised action? Through existing organizational structures?

(xxx) If constraints can not be removed at the local level, whether farmers approach higher authorities? If yes, how do they do so?

(xxxi) What modalities are used to influence constraints for agriculture?

(xxxii) What are the resources on which basic attempts to influence are executed: money, caste/kinship, information/knowledge, legal rights, public trusts, political friends etc.?

(xxxiii) What are the skills, merits and resources perceived as necessary to determine success or failure of efforts to remove the constraints?

(xxxiv) what are the impact of industrialization?

V. Methodology for the Case Study

These in depth studies were built upon the material already collected during the field research. It could be the primary data collected by the researchers, their report(s) and the secondary data they have gathered. The participatory researchers had collected a large amount of data through a range of participatory tools. Mapping, drawings, time lines, historical transects, transects, seasonality analysis, ranking scoring, activity calendars, food calendars, and focussed group discussions were liberally used. In several cases, the researchers had recorded their own observations which proved very useful. Photographs collected by the researchers gave a face to a lot of the dry prose that emanated from loaded hours of fieldwork.

Use was also made of other published materials that were available on the villages and subject under study. Government publications were also used. Discussions held with experts who have knowledge of the areas and issues, gave valuable insights. Finally the author's personal knowledge of the economy of the areas under reference greatly helped to provide the conceptual framework necessary to bind the in depth studies into a coherent whole.

Given the nature of participatory research carried out and the materials collected, it was not possible to provide answers to all the issues listed above. Answers were sought within the framework of the original project and data limitations to which the original project was subject to also apply to this analysis. These limitations are listed partially in *Ray* (1999), *Jayaswal* (1999) and *Joshi* and *Bist* (1999), who conducted the Participatory Assessment in the field.

Thus in the in depth studies, while most of the issues listed above have been dealt with, on some issues the discussion is more intense that on others, depending on what the villagers' perceptions were and what were their priorities. If the villagers did not perceive any issue as important, such as chemicalisation of agriculture, by nature of things, the discussion on the subject has been limited. There was no attempt at "inventing facts", but to present and interpret what the villagers perceived about their livelihood systems, their problems and solutions and their well being. The time utitlised in the preparation of these in depth studies was tight. There is scope to expand and enrich these studies further, which is reserved for a future venture.

Each in depth study has been prepared as a stand alone in almost every respect, except for minor cross reference. The reader can read any one case study from each of the two districts and the Chapter on analysis of the villager's perception, without losing the essence of the findings of the in-depth studies. This has its own downside as well, which are too obvious to detain us. Those readers who may be persuaded into reading all the in-depth studies may find that there are similarities in the interpretations of facts and data, and the manner of presentation. This is expected and bound to happen because there are incredible amounts of similarities in the conditions prevailing in the villages under reference. And then there are, additionally, unusually large amounts of commonalities in the perceptions of the villagers as well. Such commonalities and similarities are particularly pronounced amongst villages *inter se* within the same State.

VI. A Caveat

It is important to underscore that open-ended participatory inquiry can generate asymmetric data depending on community perspectives and priorities. In the present study, field inquiry based on generic checklist of issues has been relatively open-ended and hence, by default, space has been created for considerable data asymmetry in the research topics considered for the study. However, this has not been a hindrance in evolving sufficiently broad generalisations for public policy debates and public action. Rather it has been an opportunity to flag community perspectives in the way that they have been voiced and also reflect their relative priorities as perceived by different village groups.

VII. Thanks and Disclaimer

In the preparation of this work I had benefited from the discussions I had on some of the issues with Dr. Y.K.Alagh, Hon'ble Member of the Parliament (Rajya Sabha) New Delhi; Dr. S.R. Hasim, Member Planning Commission, New Delhi; Prof. V. M.' Rao, Bangalore and Dr. A. N. Sharma, Acting Director, Institute for Human Development, New Delhi. To them I am thankful. My thanks are due to Sudipta Ray, Meera Jayaswal, Batindri Jena, Hema Joshi and Sunita Bist for all the good work they carried out at the field and brining out the outputs in time.

I am thankful to the Libraries of the Jawaharlal Nehru University, Delhi and of the British Council division of the British High Commission, New Delhi. My best thanks are due to Dr. (Mrs.) Neela Mukherjee, who coordinated the study at the India-end, for her support.

This study was conceived and led by Imperial College of Science, Technolgy and Medicines, University of London, London and the International Institute for Environment and Development, London. They deserve our deep thanks.

This study would not have been possible without generous funding. Funds for this research was provided by the DFID of the Government of United Kingdom. They are very sincerely thanked.

On behalf of all of us—the Researchers, Imperial College, London, International Institute for Environment and Development, London, the Co-ordinator and my personal behalf—I thank the villagers of all the villages studied for their time and resources expended, courtesies extended and kindness shown, to make this learning possible.

The errors that are there are all mine.

References

Chambers, Robert: *Foreward* in Scoones, Ian and John Thompson (eds.): *Beyond Farmer First* (London: Intermediate Technology) 1994.

Conway, Gordon and Jules Pretty (1991): *Unwelcome Harvest* (London: Earthscan).

Jaiswal, Meera: *Second Round of the Study on Impact of Air Pollution on Agriculture in Urban and Peri-Urban Areas of Faridabad* (Ranchi: Ranchi University) 1999, mimeograph.

Joshi, Hema and Sunita Bisht: *Report on Impact of Air Pollution on Agriculture in Urban and Peri-Urban Areas* (New Delhi; National Institute of Urban Affairs) 1999.

Ray, Sudipta: *Participatory Field Research Report: Impact of Air Pollution on Agriculture in the Urban and Peri-Urban Areas of Varanasi* (New-Delhi) 1999. Mimeograph.

Ray, Sudipta: *Impact of Air Pollution on Agriculture in Urban and Peri-Urban Areas of Faridabad, Field Report-Round II* (New Delhi) 1999, mimeograph.

UNDP (1992), Human Development Report (New Delhi: Oxford University Press).

UNDP (1996), Report on Human Development in Bangladesh, A Pro-Poor Agenda, volume 3, United Nations Development Programme, Dhaka.

Notes

1. The names of the Faridabad villages are Kadhaoli, Sagarpur Uncha Gaon, Baroli, Pali Kasba, Chandawali, Jajru, Pyala, Sahupura, Sahapur Kalan, Sumper, Sohtai and Malerna. The names of those villages covered in Varanasi are Chandpur, Navampura Kala, Seer Govardhanpur, Sarai Dongre, Lohta, Chitaipur, Nathupur, Tikri, Maraon, Maheshpur, Adityanagar, Karamanbir, Nuaon and Tarapur.
2. The villages for community interactions were selected based on sites where the scientists were experimenting on this impact under the project. Such selection of villages was refined and amended in consultation with village communities.

1 The Processes

I. Introduction

These indepth studies were a part of the project on "Impacts and Policy Implications of Air Pollution on Crop Yields in Developing Countries", Funded by DIFD's (Government of UK) Environment Research Programme and led by The T.H. Huxley School at the Imperial College of Science, Technology and Medicine, London and the International Institute for Environment and Development, London. Before we look into the individual studies, it would be useful to have a brief description of the process followed in the different villages, in the participatory sessions. This will put the discussion in perspective. Since no one process or method is correct in a participatory approach, all of them have some lessons to offer. We leave it to the readers to draw their own lessons from experience.

II. A Note on Participatory Methodology of Village Chandpur, Varanasi

Village Chandpur was subject of study by two sets of researchers. A two-person research team (TPRT) from National Institute of Urban Affairs, New Delhi comprising Ms. Hema Joshi and Ms. Sunita Bist first studied this village in and around November 1998, and then a one-person research team (OPRT) comprising Ms. Meera Jayaswal studied the village a second time around the same time. The two teams studied different segments of the village, called Bastis or Hamlets.

The research teams took Chandpur as the given area for study and did not go into the reasons for its selection. The village was one of the scientific sites of Government Agriculture Farm, where levels of sulphur dioxide (SO_2), nitrogen dioxide (NO_2) and ozone are high, is situated inside this village. It is a village adjacent to an industrial estate and therefore, prone to damages caused by polluting matter released by the industies in the industrial estate. The TPRT chose to study Patel Basti which is one of the six Bastis (Hamlets) of Chandpur, the reasons being relatively higher percentage of people engaged in agriculture, cultivation of vegetables and the size of the population not too large in the village, which will facilitate a participatory study. OPRT chose Naipurwa Hamlet for its study.

The methodology followed by TPRT included at first a meeting with the Village Pradhan and Block Development Committee Member, to appraise him of the intention of TPRT and to introduce themselves. On the first day the TPRT got an overview of the village and held discussions with a wide cross-section of the people. The Basti to be studied was then decided upon in consultation and with the agreement of the villagers. A visit of the chosen Basti, viz., Patel Basti, was made as a preparatory effort for next day's study. A broad overview of the Basti was obtained and the time for participatory study of the Basti on the following day was agreed upon with the villagers. From the second day onwards group discussions and personal interaction with the community together with participatory methods such as time line, historical transects, mapping, seasonality diagramming, health calendar etc. were used.

The methodology followed by the OPRT was slightly different. The OPRT on the first day of the study, per chance met up with a young lad of the village, named Chhotu, who turned out to be a key informant. Chhotu of his own volition accompanied OPRT in its visit through the hamlets of the villages and provided a "running commentary" on the village situation. The first method used by OPRT was participant observation to learn first hand about the kinds of crop and vegetables grown in the village as also some of the insects that visit the standing crops. On the first day after learning from the key informant that most of the men in the village were out in the towns during day time to earn a wage, and were not available once the sun went down as they busied themselves in the liquor shops which abound aplenty near Chandpur, OPRT decided to call it a day and fixed up with Chhotu a time the following morning for continuing with the study.

On the second day the study began, after completing some preliminary formalities including intoduction of the OPRT and the objective of the study, with a participatory session with a group of women and their children in Naipurwa. Considerable time was spent on ensuring that no undue expectations were raised and in allying doubts that clouded the minds of the gathered women. Discussions with key informants, Ms. Pratima and Maina Devi, were very instructive. This took a good part of the forenoon and a hour or so early in the afternoon and since the women had to return to their work by then, the study was adjourned for the day. After agreeing with the women to return to the learning session the next day, OPRT prepared to leave the hamlet. On the way back the OPRT met up with a group of elderly citizens who seemed to more than welcome the study (they already knew about the OPRT) and they agreed to spare some of their time with OPRT. Thus in the afternoon, participatory discussions were held with senior ctitzens of the hamlet. Seeing the composition of the group of elderly persons, historical transect and other methods were attempted and the transects/tables so emerging were interviewed, to gain an understanding of how the significant variables have behaved over the years.

OPRT picked up the thread on the third day from where it had left the women the day before and began with participatory discussions with the women. This was followed by historical time lines, mapping, transects, ranking, food calendar, health calendar, seasonality diagrams etc. All diagrams, charts and transects were discussed with the villagers.

Generally field notes were taken and reports prepared subsequently. But in a few cases in order to capture the richness of the discussion, with the permission of the villagers, details of discussion have been recorded verbatim.

III. Participatory Methodology for Study of Village Tikri

Village Tikri was one of the several villages chosen for the study on the "Impacts and Policy Implications of Air Pollution on Crop Yields in Developing Countries". The fundamental objective of the researchers in Tikri was to investigate people's perception on the issues involved, through participatory methods. There were two one-member teams of researchers.

The Village Pradhan of Tikri was approached on the first day by both the research teams, as a key informant to gather preliminary information about the village and to seek his permission to undertake the participatory study of the village under his "charge".

The information provided by the Pradhan formed the basis of selecting the Morya, Malah and Dherabir Bastis (out of 13 Bastis) of village Tikri for participatory study. Tikri being a very large village it is not possible to study the whole village as one unit. Choosing Bastis as units of study for participatory analysis also made eminent sense because, as we shall see while reviewing the settlement pattern later, the village is highly heterogeneous and each Basti of the village is organised along community lines, the communities being taken as synonymous with castes. Team One proceeded to Malah Basti and Team Two proceeded to Morya Basti.

Team One

Team One followed a series of discrete steps.

A Panchayat member from Malah Basti, Channu led the researcher to Malah Basti, which was the Basti of the fisherfolk and was situated about 2 kms away from the Pradhan's house. To begin with, rapport building with the community, followed by semi-structured interview engaged the researcher for the rest of the day.

Because Malah Basti was at a considerable distance from the Village interior and the lesser number of working hours that the short winter days permitted, it was decided not to press on with the investigation in Malah Basti. Instead, the Yadav Basti, the Basti of Milkmen/Milk Vendors, was selected. Rapport building with the Yadavs was the first step taken.

A partial seasonality analysis was also done with the women's group.

In order to have a fair view of the livelihood pattern of the landed class, who tilled the land they owned themselves, Dherabir Basti was also chosen for the study. A seasonality analysis was partially completed with the men's group. To contrast this with the livelihood system of landowners who did not till the land themselves, Chowdhurian Basti was included into the ambit of analysis. In Chowhurian Basti, seasonality analysis and historical transect were completed with the community with a mixed group of men and women. Seasonality analysis and historical transect were left incomplete in the first round of the investigation as the community had little time to spare, given that they were pre-occupied with harvesting paddy, sowing of wheat and winter vegetables. The court cases and the restricted number of working hours available during short winter days also necessitated shortening the day's work.

The investigation was then shifted to the Mahato Basti, a community of traditional farmers. A round of rapport building was inevitable. The Mahatos gave an account of the seasonal changes in their lives and their historical background on which their present status stood. The Mahatos being traditional farmers, had no inhibition in outlining the constraints faced by agriculture in their Basti. In the second round of the field work, the discussion on transects, sesonality analysis etc. with the men's group that was initiated in the first round, was taken to its logical conclusion.

Harijan Basti was made a part of the study and was studied in detail, because Harijans constituted 50 per cent of the total population of, the village and they are the ones who worked on the lands of the landowners as labourers. The women's group carried out seasonality analysis and historical analysis. The men's group was also engaged in historical analysis. The women's group in the Yadav Basti outlined the constraints faced by agriculture.

A mixed group of villagers assembled at the Pradhan's house to carry out a historical analysis and stage-wise loss of wheat due to different constraints faced by wheat farmers as also a cost benefit analysis of the industrial estate.

Team Two

Team two arrived at Kanhaiya's house (house of the father-in-law of the Pradhan). The team was introduced to two adolescent boys who were apparently students of Banares Hindu University. For about an hour, the team accompanied by these adolescent boys visited all the houses of the Basti, only to be discover that most of them were latched from outside. It was soon clear that most of the women and men were out in the fields, as it was time for deweeding the vegetable fields. It was an inopportune time to try any participatory session with these people. The team nevertheless requested the villagers if it was possible to have their time and attention for the proposed study. On their suggestion, on the following day a meeting was agreed at 10 a.m. in the village and one Sri Amarnath's house was the agreed venue for the meeting.

The research team arrived at the venue at the appointed time the next day and found that two villagers were awaiting her arrival. They were perched on a chouki, a wooden cot. Soon eight more people arrived and made themselves comfortable on the choukis. They already knew about the purpose of the meeting. The team introduced itself and explained the purpose, of the visit, though they had prior knowledge about it. The assembled gathering then introduced themselves. Various aspects of the village life were analysed through participatory methods. The process continued till 2 p.m., when the villagers decided to call it a day, with the understanding that they would resume their analysis the following morning.

At around 3 p.m. the research team could gather a group of women who agreed to spare their time. To make the discussion specific and relate their lives to months, the women used symbols to identify months in the Indian system of calendar, viz., lunar months. Then the analysis of village life proceeded. This included an analysis of agricultural operations, food security, livelihood, constraints to agriculture and so on.

The different topics discussed and the methods used are detailed below:

List of Topics Discussed and Methods Used

Topics	Methods Used
Livelihood Activities	Participatory discussion, scoring and pie diagram
Role of agriculture in livelihood	Participatory discussion
Criteria for socio-economic groupings	Participatory discussion
Income, expenditure and savings: monthwise	Pie diagram
Food pattern during various months	Seasonality analysis
Farming system	Time-lines
Crops grown	Time-lines and pie diagram
Yield	Time line
Inputs in agriculture	Time line
Returns from agriculture and other livelihood	Participatory discussion
Nature of constraints faced by agriculture	Participatory discussion
Constraints and problems of agricultural production	Participatory discussion
Prioritizing constraints	Scoring and ranking
Impact of industrial area on livelihood of households and on agriculture, health and livestock	Participatory discussion
impact of air pollution on agriculture and human health	Analysis of the villagers perception on air pollution
Livelihood in agriculture and others	Seasonal calendar

IV. A Note on the Methodology and Process of Participatory Assessment in Sagarpur

Village Sagarpur, district Faridabad was subject of study by two sets of researchers. A two-person research team (TPRT) comprising Dr. Meera Jaiswal and Ms. Sudipta Roy first studied this village in and around August 1998, and then both the researchers of the team studied the village, separately, a second time around November the same year. The two teams studied the same segments of the village, called Patyat Muhalla and Hawelliwalle Muhalla, in the first round, whereas during the second phase of the study, one of the researchers added Baghail Hamlet and Ita Bhatti Colony as well, for participatory learning.

The TPRT approached the village on their own without any prior notice to the village. As they approached the village, they saw a group of villagers sitting in the Baghel Baithak (village community centre). They met the group and introduced themselves to them and explained to them the object of their visit, that they wished to study Sagarpur, to learn from them about their lifestyles, community life, village and its surrounding environment, and agriculture in particular. The group of villagers was receptive to the idea and in turn introduced themselves the members of the TPRT. The villagers then briefed the TPRT about the overall situation in the village and provided them with basic data relating to their village, which are detailed in the body of the report. Based on this discussion, TPRT initially chose the two Muhallas for study, viz., Patyat and Hawelliwalle Muhallas, that is, the Muhallas predominantly of the Brahmins and Jats respectively.

The group then led the TPRT to the two chosen Muhallas and introduced them to the residents of these wards and Muhallas. In both the Muhallas open air community centres were chosen for interacting with the community as it is easier to assemble people at a place where people by habit assemble. Due to customs and socio-ecocnomic reasons it was not possible for the women to interact with the TPRT in the presence of their men folk. TPRT, therefore, decided to interact with the women separately in one of the participating woman's house. This helped the TPRT to elicit free and frank views from the women. Participants in both the locations included men and women who were engaged in agriculture.

The TPRT took the age profile of the participants into account for using different methods. People in the age group between 16 and 25 years were requested to participate in the occupational preference ranking and the senior citizens, aged between 55 and 80 years, were participants in historical analysis. Those belonging to the age band of 18-50 years participated in seasonality analysis, criteria scoring and cost benefit analysis.

Patyat Muhalla has a population of around 400, in 50 households. The farmers are in the main small and medium farmers, dominated by Brahmins. The agricultural fields of this Muhalla are adjacent to the brick kilns along the southern fringe of the village and Bharat Petroleum's LPG Filling Plant in Pyala lies to its northwest. Faridabad's Industrial Area is 8 kms to its north.

The other Muhalla, Hawelliwalle Muhalla, is about the same size as Patyat Muhalla, with 50 households and about 400 people. This is a village of Jats, mainly medium and large farmers. The agricultural fields of this Muhalla are adjoining to Village Sunper, which lies to the North East of Sagarpur. Its fields are 6.4 kms from Faridabad Industrial Area.

During the second phase of the study two more Muhallas were added: Ita Bhatti Colony adjoining the Brick Kilns in Sagarpur, which is inhabited by workers of the brick kilns, and Gareria Muhalla, inhabited mostly by other backward castes.

V. A Note on the Participatory Approaches Adopted by the Research Teams

Village Kadhaoli, was subject of study by two sets of researchers, as in case of Sagarpur. A two-person research team (TPRT) comprising Dr. Meera Jaiswal and Ms. Sudipta Roy first studied this village in and around August 1998, and then a member of the same team studied the village a second time around November same year. The two teams studied the same segments of the village, called Bisa or Ward.

The research team took Kadhaoli as the given area for study. However, it was chosen for study because the village is within 6 kms west of the Scientific Study Group's reference site; the village has four polluting factories; an area near the village has been acquired by the Government of Haryana for developing an industrial sector, sector 29 of Ballabgarh; it has a predominance of Muslims; it grew predominantly what is called "food crops"; around 1 per cent of the population works in the gulf countries and its has 90 per cent cemented roads and only 10 per cent bricklaid ones.

The TPRT arrived at village Kadhaoli for the first time in August 1998, in the midst of Kharif season. They found their way to the Panchayat Bhawan, on the advice of, and led by, some children, where they fortunately met the Panchayat (local level elected body) Members including the Sarpanch. The members of the TPRT introduced themselves and explained to the Panchayat Members the purpose of its visit. TPRT sought permission of the Panchayat to carry out participatory research. The Panches were happy that the TPRT were there to study their village.

The Sarpanch volunteered to take the TPRT through the village. The members of the research team first went on a transect walk, covering Aat Bisa and then covering Barha Bisa, the two wards of the village. During the transect walk the Sarpanch introduced the researchers to other villagers en route, some of whom also joined in the walk. It is on the basis of information gathered during this walk that the TPRT chose, with the participation and consent of the people, to study Aat Bisa and Ganje Muhalla of Barha Bisa.

Aat Bisa was selected because it formed that part of the village, which had agricultural land running parallel to and adjoining the road. This was considered helpful in determining the impact of pollution on livelihoods as roadside fields, adjoining houses and structures are exposed to higher levels of pollution, particularly air pollution than interior parts of the village. The houses and the fields in Aat Bisa are also nearer to the pharmaceutical company of village Kelly, on the other side of the road dividing the two villages, two rubber factories, and the plastic factory apart from the one cement brick kiln in Kadhaoli itself. The landowners in Aat Bisa were medium sized and large farmers, and grew a variety of crops.

Ganje Muhalla, in Barah Bisa ward was chosen by the villagers as the other site, situated away from the road and hence away from the polluting sources. Though Ganje Muhalla lies in the interior of the village, some of its fields faced a National Thermal Power Corporation (NTPC) Thermal

Plant located in the adjacent village, Samayur which lies to the North of Ganje Muhalla. The inhabitants of Ganje Muhalla are considered by the villagers to be less prosperous than those of Aat Bisa and are predominantly a Muhalla of small and marginal farmers.

A social map was prepared by the villagers, outlining the livelihood strategy of each household. The researchers had semi-structured interviews with male and female groups separately in Barah Bisa and in Aat Bisa which greatly helped them to learn about the importance of agriculture to the village economy. The historical transect with the elder citizens of Aat Bisa was designed to learn the changes that have visited Kadhaoli over the last fifty years in matters of role of agriculture, farming systems, farming practices, yield, quality of agricultural produce and agricultural constraints. Ranking and scoring was done on the constraints facing agriculture. Seasonality analysis separately with men and women's group formed an integral part of the study, to analyse how their (men's and women's) workload and way of life have gyrated over the twelve months of a typical year. Joint walks in the fields to learn about the visible impact of pollution on the standing crops were organised.

A second round of study was initiated in 1999, which was a one-person research team. The second round of study concentrated on the constraints faced by the farmers in growing wheat, impact of pollution on agriculture and map out the health status of the men and women over a year. Scoring of constraints and of the different ailments that trouble the farmers were particularly emphasized.

VI. A Note on the Process followed in Uncha Gaon Municipal Township

Uncha Gaon is situated approximately 4.3 kms South East of Faridabad old industrial area and 1.34 from Ballabgarh industrial area. It came under the Faridabad Nagapalika (Municipality) in 1985, the year in which land was acquired by Haryana Urban Development Authority for the Ballabgarh residential complex.

Uncha Gaon being an municipal area, is exposed to vehicular traffic and dust pollution due to its location right on the road. Uncha Gaon has the look and feel of a town as well as of a village. On both sides of the road you have rows of shops including liquor shops (called wine shops), hotels, chemists and studios.

The inner area of Uncha Gaon is called *Gola Neem*, resembles a village and is divided into smaller hamlets. The inhabitants have knowledge of agriculture and many of them are agriculturists and have considerable experience of cultivation. Uncha Gaon is divided into five hamlets or Muhallas. Inhabitants of three of the five Mukhallas, viz., Ahir, Saini and Sahupura Roadside Muhalla, have agricultural lands and cultivate their own land. Quite a few of the inhabitants work as agricultural labourers. Generally the *Malis* of Saini hamlet grow vegetables and the *Ahirs* of Ahir Muhalla cultivate wheat during winter (Rabi) season and jowar during rainy (Kharif) season.

VII. Developing the Bond in a Tea Stall

The Researchers arrived at the locale, Uncha Gaon, expecting pretty much of what they experienced in their earlier forays in Sagarpur and Kadhaoli. They were in for a big surprise. Not only was Uncha Gaon no village, but the social and economic environments were markedly different. The small open roadside tea stalls that greeted them in Sagarpur and Kadhaoli were all gone. In their place were restaurants, with formal furniture, notwithstanding their unseeming looks. The social capital of small groups of people found in the other villages was not visible here. They found it difficult to locate any group which had more than two people and who were at once knowledgeable about agriculture. Fields were visible. The participatory assessment researchers could see crops. Cultivators were noticeable. The researchsers started looking for farmers who would participate in the participatory sessions.

Ultimately one of the residents helped the researchers to reach one of the Muhallas, namely, Saini Muhalla. This was the oldest ward or hamlet of Uncha Gaon. The researchers were hoping to locate some farmers here.

They were led to a small tea stall. A few elder citizens of the ward were sitting. The first contact with farmers was established.

The process began. The researchers introduced themselves. They explained to the senior citizens that the purpose of their visit was to learn from them more about the village and their lives. The group of senior citizens seemed to welcome the idea. They in their turn introduced themselves and disclosed that they have been farmers since their childhood. They knew what farming was and what it meant. The ice was broken.

The senior citizens gave some idea to the researchers about Saini Muhalla: there were about 500 people in 150 households, around 80 per cent of whom were engaged in agriculture. Since the senior citizens were giving a whole lot of information, the researchers thought it would be better to focus the interface better. The researchers, therefore, wanted to streamline the discussion and so enquired of the villagers present in the tea stall whether they could join them for a group discussion on a voluntary basis, on agriculture. This did not go down well with the villagers present there. Discussing agriculture with outsiders was a felony. They refused to co-operate and got agitated that agriculture was sought to be discussed. It took the researchers some time to win over the villagers' confidence.

It was soon discovered that because Haryana Urban Development Authority was on a land-acquisition spree in Uncha Gaon, the villagers mistook the researchers as being Government functionaries, out there to elicit information for use by the Government. This was not acceptable, since the villagers had little land for cultivation and any further intrusion was not acceptable to them. The researchers ultimately succeeded in pacifying the group. In the meanwhile younger people joined the group and this helped ease the situation. This made the group quite big as well. To avoid further dislocation the group was divided into two: one of the researchers sat with one group in the tea stall and the other went out to the fields with a second group. Both the groups had a mixture of young and old alike, though the number of people participating in the discussion kept on changing, with fresh entries and exits.

A range of methods were used. This is summarised below:

List of Topics Discussed and Methods Used

Topics	Methods Used
Livelihood and constraints	Participatory discussion seasonality analysis
Role of agriculture in livelihood	Participatory discussion
Criteria for socio-economic groupings	Participatory discussion
Income, expenditure and savings: monthwise	Participatory discussion
Food pattern during various months	Seasonality analysis
Agricultural practices	Historical transect
Crops grown	Participatory discussion seasonality analysis
Changes in farm produce	Historical transect
Returns from agriculture and other livelihood	Participatory discussion
Nature of constraints faced by agriculture	Participatory discussion/ranking/ scoring
Constraints and to agricultural production	Seasonality analysis
Ranking of agricultural constraints	Scoring and ranking
Impact of industrial area on livelihood of households and on agriculture, health and livestock	Participatory discussion
Graded scoring of health problems	Scoring

VIII. Concluding Remarks

This chapter is not a process documentation. The discussion has been included to provide an idea of how the process was followed in different villages by the different researchers, indicating that there is no one correct way of doing things. There are varieties in both methods and processes. These varieties in methods and processes provide the rich mosaic to the participatory exercises.

Location Sketch Map of Villages in Faridabad

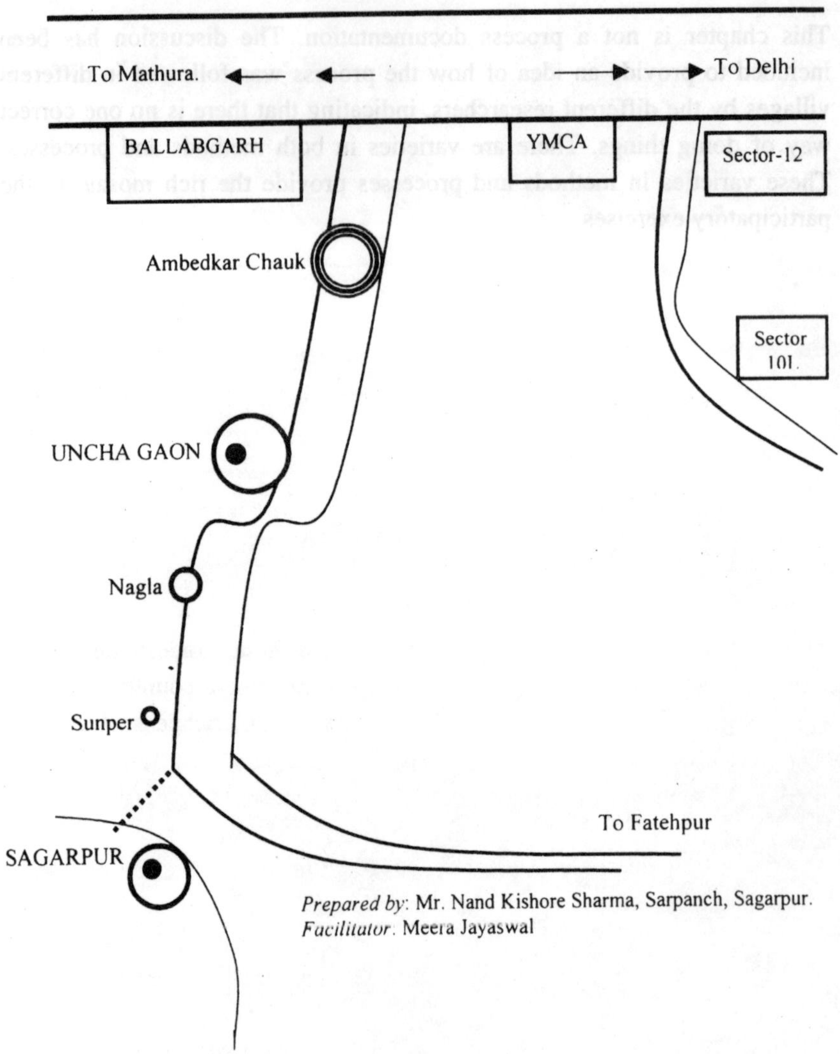

Prepared by: Mr. Nand Kishore Sharma, Sarpanch, Sagarpur.
Facilitator: Meera Jayaswal

2 A Perspective from an Under Developed State: Village Chandpur, Varanasi

I. Introduction

Varanasi

Chandpur Village lies in the district of Varanasi, which is the home of the ancient and holy city of Banares, known in ancient literature as Kashi, venerated and inhabited by the Hindus, Muslims, Jains and the Buddhists alike. In education, art, culture, religion, trade, crafts and commerce, Varanasi holds a special place in Indian history. It has a commanding view of the mighty Ganges, on whose banks the city of Banares and the district of Varanasi have thrived for centuries.

Varanasi lies in the eastern part of the State of Uttar Pradesh, known for its role in Indian political history, size (if it were to be a country, it would have been the seventh largest country in the world), richness of culture, history and of course, poverty. It is one of the states, which has seen a rise in poverty levels during the last decade (*Sen and Patnaik*, 1997; *Sen*, 1996). Uttar Pradesh has also given India eight of its Prime Ministers.

The principal sources of employment and occupation of the people in Varanasi are agriculture, medium and small scale industries, diesel locomotive works of the Indian railways and a spattering of heavy industries such as the Bharat Heavy Electricals, agro-processing units and agro-based industries.

The following landholding pattern for Varanasi gives an impression of the situation at hand.

Table 1 Landholding Pattern in Varanasi

Size of Holding	Number of Holdings
Less than 1 hectare	552565 holders
1 to 2 hectares	47619 holders
2 to 3 hectares	11608 holders
3 to 5 hectares	7276 holders
More than 5 hectares	2627 holders

Thus 89 per cent of the farmers hold 1 hectare or less of land and 96.5 per cent of the farmers own 2 or less than 2 hectares of land. There are two main cultivating seasons, Kharif and Rabi, with a relatively insignificant winter season.

The total area of Varanasi district is 4035.01 sq. kilometers, having a population of 3,7,82,949. The literacy rate is 65.36 per cent, which is higher than the national average and much higher than the state average of 41.6 per cent. The district is divided into four blocks, viz., Harhua, Araji Lines, Chirai Gaon and Kashi Vidyapeeth. Chandpur Village, which is the subject of our study, falls within the territorial jurisdiction of Kashi Vidyapeeth Block.

Kashi Vidyapeeth Block

Kashi Vidyapeeth Block consists of around 129 villages of which 122 are inhabited, and they are organised into 13 Panchayats, the smallest unit of governance (Local Self Government). The occupational structure of the inhabitants of the block exhibit an overwhelming preponderance of labourers and agriculturist and agricultural labourers: 49 per cent of the total population is main workers, 14 per cent are cultivators and about 6 per cent are agricultural labourers. Most of the farmers are small and marginal farmers.

Chandpur Village

Chandpur is a village situated in Kashi Vidyapeeth Block in the District of Varanasi, which forms part of Eastern Uttar Pradesh. It lies on the north west corner of the block, situated to the north of the famous grand trunk road connecting Calcutta to Delhi and then to Pathankot (and earlier to Peshawar, now in Pakistan) and to the south of the main railway trunk route, connecting Calcutta with Delhi. The influence of these major transport systems on the village is significant. It is also eight kms from the holy city of Varanasi and only one kilometre from the block headquarters, which also influences the way people perceive well being and the appropriateness of the trade and vocation which they practice.

II. General Information

Chandpur has a population of 5332, with 49 per cent females and 51 per cent males. The sex ratio in Chandpur compares favourably with the sex ratios in Uttar Pradesh and India, which are less flattering. The literacy rate is 60 per cent for males and 30 per cent for the females. That is, of the total population, about 55.5 per cent are literate, which is slightly below the national average, though the state average is 47 per cent. (The disaggregated literacy rate for the state is 62 per cent for men and 28 per cent for women.) This is somewhat surprising given that the village has a primary school, a co-educational school and two Junior High Schools, one for girls and the other for boys. Being near a major urban centre, the villagers have access to a Post Office, modest healthcare facilities, a Kisan Kendra, State Agricultural Farm and Bank.

The village has several sources of water, including 10 hand pumps, two wells and two pump sets for irrigation. Despite these sources of water, dependence on rain for agriculture seems to be very high.

There are several industrial establishments in and around the village. It has biscuit factories, saree printing firms, confectioneries, banares beeds factory and the Agra fan factory. Some of these firms are not strictly polluting but all cause some disturbance or the other to the social, economic and ecological environment of the village. The industrial estate situated to the east of village with over 100 factories has considerable influence on the mind set of the villagers, on the ecology, environment and economy of the village.

The village, like many Indian villages, particularly the large ones, is divided into separate hamlets: there are five such Hamlets (called Bastee in local parlance) viz., Barbaspur, Naipurwa, Yadav Basti, Sonak Bastee, Harijan

Bastee. These Bastees are of different sizes ranging from a population of about 50, to one with a population of 2000, in Chandpur. The people are a mixed lot with Harijans (the lower castes), Scheduled Castes, Yadavs (milk-mongers), Patels (businessman and petty traders). The distribution of population amongst different caste groups is as given below.

Caste	No. of Families	No. of People
Patel	182	3932
Scheduled Castes	8	150
Harijans	20	250
Yadavs	45	1000
Total	255	5332

The structural composition of the population has an impact of the kind of trade, vocation or profession practised by the villagers, for in the context of UP, the caste to which a person belongs often determines the means of livelihood she/he pursues, particularly for the men.

In the context of Chandpur, the Patels (the majority population) can be divided into two groups. One, the group of Patels (about 62 per cent) are engaged in agriculture and vegetable cultivation as their primary means of livelihood, and have animal husbandry and wage employment as their secondary means of livelihood. Two, the remaining 38 per cent or so of Patels have wage employment as their primary source of livelihood, and engage themselves in agriculture and casual labour as the secondary sources of income. Villagers belonging to scheduled castes have vegetable vending and daily wages as their means of livelihood. Those belonging to the Harijan community work both as daily wage earners and as agricultural labourers. Daily wage earners suffer from instability of wages they receive for most of the time they are not the "price setters"; they are wage takers: they have to work for whatever is on offer. They suffer all the disadvantages of the informal sector (*Mehta, 1997*). The Yadavs are the ones primarily engaged in animal husbandry, mostly bovine wealth.

III. Importance of Agriculture to the People of Chandpur

Given the composition of the population, it is not surprising that the people have a large number of livelihood systems in place, both on-farm and off-farm. Agriculture and agricultural labour, weaving (Saree), birdi (indigenous cigarettes made out of tobacco wrapped in tendu leaf) making rudrax (a kind of natural beads) garland making and jewellery making, and auto-rickshaw driving. However, since almost every segment of the population take up agriculture as a primary occupation or a secondary occupation or work as agricultural labourers, agriculture forms a very important element in the mosaic of alternative means of livelihood pursued in Chandpur village. This pattern is consistent with the caste composition of the village. Agriculture is the most important but not the only means of livelihood. The following Tables 2 and 3 illustrate the position.

These tables warrant a few comments. The percentages in Columns 3 of both Tables 2 and 3 do not add up to 100 per cent because the categories of people engaged in different livelihood systems are not unique; they overlap. Let us take Table 2. About 80 per cent of the people are engaged in agriculture, powerloom and handloom jointly. Several of these people would also be engaged, for instance, as daily wage earners when they do not have work either in cultivation/harvesting or powerloom/handloom. That is, people are engaged in multiple livelihood activities.

Table 2 Livelihood Activities Estimated by Men in a Hamlet of Chandpur

Serial No.	Livelihood Activities	Population Involved (per cent)
1	Agriculture, Powerloom and Handloom	80
2	Stitching and Agriculture	60
3	Daily Wage	40
4	Farm and Agricultural Work	25
5	Transport Sector Labour etc.	04
6	Auto Driving	04
7	Vegetable Hawker	02
8	Petty Shop	02
9	Electric Repairer	04

Village Analysts: Nawarangi, Budhram, Ramjatan Patel and Santlal.
Facilitator: Ms. Meera Jayaswal.
Date: 13.11.98.

Table 3 Livelihood Activities by Women's Group in a Hamlet of Chandpur

Serial No.	Livelihood Activities	Population Involved (per cent)
1	Birdi Making	50
2	Rudrax Garland Making	50
3	Agricultural Labourers	30
4	Powerloom	30
5	Ganzee Stitching	40
6	Cultivator	20
7	Transport Related Business	06
8	Service	02
9	Tailoring	02

Village Analysts: Reeta Devi, Rampati Devi, Dhandai, Hirwati.
Facilitator: Ms. Meera Jayaswal.
Date: 12.11.98.

From the foregoing, men consider agriculture as their most important activity as it along with powerloom and handloom engage upto 80 per cent of the villagers, but from women's perspective, the most important means of livelihood are off-farm activities, namely, Birdi making and Rudrax garland making, each of which employs 50 per cent of the population, with agricultural labour occupying only the third rank, in which 30 per cent of the people are engaged. This difference in perspective, between men and women is significant and is partially influenced by the way in which men and women are partitioned into these occupations.

Trade and petty business is also very important as a source of livelihood but wage employment seems to be the next most important source of livelihood after agriculture. Nearly 7 per cent of the people work in Government Offices and in firms on regular employment and around 30 per cent work as daily wage earners in different sectors including construction, transport, birdi making and in saree printing establishments etc.

If one were to look at the land use pattern, it seems consistent with the importance of agriculture. Of the total land 56 per cent is used for agricultural purposes, of which 63 per cent only is irrigated. About 5 per cent land is under orchard cultivation and about 38.9 per cent put to "other" uses. The percentage of land which is fallow and which is degraded is very small: 0.12 and 0.18 per cent respectively.

In terms of importance of agriculture as a source of income the following information extracted from a pie-chart prepared by the villagers provides some confirmation of our inference.

Sources of Income	Percentage of Income
Family Agriculture	30 per cent
Wages as Casual Labourers	25 per cent
Trade/Business	35 per cent
Regular Employment	10 per cent
Total	100 per cent

Source: Villagers Patel Basti as shown to Ms. Hema Joshi and Ms. Sunita Bist.

Of this income, expenditure looks astonishing: 25 per cent is spent on food, 25 per cent on consumption of liquor, 15 per cent on health, 10 per cent on education, 15 per cent on litigation and 10 per cent on others. This pattern of expenditure has serious implications for the village including its impact upon the social capital, state of health, literacy and food security of the villagers.

Box 2.1
Vintage of Agriculture

"Family agriculture as a form of subsistence is one of the oldest activities known to humanity. It represents a structure that has produced wealth."

David G. Francis in *Family Agriculture, Tradition and Transformation* (London: Earthscan) 1994.

If we go by the percentage of people who are engaged in family agriculture as depicted by Tables 2 and 3, which is about 80 per cent, the fact that agriculture is the source of only 30 per cent of income, indicates, prima facie, that in terms of income generation, agriculture is not a very profitable venture. This is true even in case of agricultural labourers. The local people come to work as agricultural labourers only as a second choice, because wages in this sector is lower than in alternative avenues of employment. Whereas in factories in the adjoining industrial estate, in saree printing and in construction work, a male worker makes Rs. 50, Rs. 100 and Rs. 100 per day, respectively, he earns no more than Rs. 40 per day in agriculture. Similarly women folk who earn Rs. 35, Rs. 50 and Rs. 100 per day, from factory work, Saree printing and construction work respectively, can earn no more than Rs. 25 per day in cash and in kind in the fields during cultivation and harvesting operations. However, the importance of agriculture has to be judged not only from the standpoint of its utility as a source of income but from a much broader perspective. Importance of agriculture in the lives of the people of Chandpur, lies in that it not only provides employment opportunities but also makes valuable contributions towards food security for the people (may be for part of the year), cash income as also fodder for its livestock. It is this total picture which should inform any inference about the importance or otherwise, of agriculture in the life of Chandpur.

Box 2.2
Agriculture and Food System

"Agriculture is the bed rock of the food system. In developing countries agriculture, humankind has modified and continues to modify the working of the biosphere. Agriculture techniques were developed in place of hunting and gathering to provide more managed, secure food supplies..."

Geoff Tansy and Tony Worsley in *The Food System, A Guide* (London: Earthscan) 1995.

IV. Cropping Pattern

Apparently a system of poly-culture prevails in the agricultural sector though crop diversity is declining. A fairly large number of crops used to be grown in the years of the yore, and a large number of them were grown until recently. Of late the number of crops grown in Chandpur has dwindled quite rapidly. In Chandpur the crops currently grown during Rabi and Kharif are as shown in Table 4.

Table 4 Crops Grown During Rabi and Kharif, Village Chandpur

Rabi (January-April)		Kharif (July-October)	
Crops	**Amount of Land Used (in Bighas)**	**Crops**	**Amount of Land Used (in Bighas)**
Wheat	25	Paddy	15
Vegetables	5	Maize	1
Cauliflower	6	Cauliflower	4
Gram/peas	1	Lentils (arhar)	0.5
Potatoes/onions	2	Jowar	3
Spinach/fenugreek	1	Brinjal	2

Source: Semi-structured interview with villagers by Ms. Hema Joshi and Ms. Sunita Bist.

Farming community in Chandpur consider vegetable cultivation as part of agriculture. In the two seasons, wheat and paddy are the principal crops. During both these seasons, vegetable cultivation, notably cauliflower is common. Most of the cereals (wheat, rice, maize, jowar) are for consumption at the household level. The vegetables are grown primarily for sale in the nearby markets. Food needs other than what is produced at the village level are satisfied from purchases in the open market. The principal crops are wheat, paddy and cauliflower, all other crops are being produced only at the margin.

Since, irrigation is limited and there is dependence on rains for agriculture, the cropping pattern is guided by the rainfall pattern. During (Kharif season) the monsoon months, starting from end June, cultivation of paddy is evident. This is followed by maize. Generally these two crops are grown concurrently on different kinds of land depending on moisture retention: paddy in low lands which retains a lot more moisture, and maize in uplands that retain less moisture. During Rabi season, wheat is cultivated, along with vegetables and green gram/green peas. In both the seasons, there is a mixture of food crops and cash crops, with food crops occupying a larger share of cultivable land.

V. Intensity of Cultivation

Since agriculture is *predominantly* rainfed, the intensity of cultivation is not very high. Only one principal food crop is harvested in each of the two seasons: paddy in Kharif and wheat in Rabi. Except for cauliflower all other crops/vegetables (radish, spinach, fenugreek, green grams, green peas, potatoes, brinjals, onion, garlic, lentil) grown are seasonal, which indicates that the inhabitants of Chandpur depend more upon the bounties (or niggardliness!) of nature than on new technology for their out put. The villagers are satisfied with one crop per season (Kharif and Rabi) from their agricultural lands, with vegetable production on a limited scale during the intervening winter. Cultivation during the winter season is limited. But while in the 1940s and in the 1950s and the 1960s as well, farmers were happy cultivating only during Kharif and Rabi seasons when they ploughed with bullock and the hoe, now with the introduction of tractors they have begun cultivating in the winter as well. The frequency of cultivation has increased, because the farmers explained, it was no longer necessary to rest the animals.

Different crops are grown but the practice of cultivating the same land several times over does not seem to have caught on. This has as much to do with poor state of extension services and incentives to produce more of agricultural crops, as to the fact that alternative means of livelihood elsewhere are available. The nearness of the village to a major urban centre of Varanasi and the industrial estate has helped in the process, which somewhat reduces the importance of agriculture as a source of livelihood.

VI. Agricultural Practices

VI. 1. Changes in Cropping Pattern and Agricultural Practices

The kinds and number of crops grown have been fairly dynamic. Over the years, there have been significant changes. While in the forties, the principal crops were barley, bare, sawa, sugarcane and vegetables, during the fifties wheat, paddy, peas, bengal gram, maize and red gram, began to be cultivated, and cultivation of *barley* and *sugarcane* was *discontinued.* That is, there was a diversification in production, between the 1940s and the 1950s. From the 1960s, this diversification lost its sway and the number of crops being cultivated got reduced to paddy and wheat besides vegetables. The trend continues till today, through the 1970s and 1980s. The cropping pattern has, therefore, seen substantial changes over the years but has stabilised during the 1990s. The transect at Table 5 is revealing.

Interestingly the transect reveals that two concurrent processes were in operation. One, the *cropping pattern* was changing and two, the *yield* was also changing. If we look at Table 5, the yield increased quite dramatically during the 1960s and then again fell during the 1970s, and continued at that level throughout the 1980s and 1990s. In 1988 there was a sharp drop in yield both for paddy and for wheat. Though the yields in the 1988 were higher than those obtaining in the 1950s, it is a cause for concern, unless one is prepared to treat it as an aberration. This is significant and needs further investigation.

The village has partially mechanised its cultivation. Whereas in the 1940s, 1950s and 1960s, ploughing was predominantly with bullocks and hoe, in the 1970s and thereafter, use of tractor has become the norm. As a consequence, the number of draught animals owned by the farming community has dwindled significantly, which contributed to a reduced need for fodder and hence a negative preference for crops which yielded high percentage of fodder, namely, barley. The use of tractors has also contributed to the noticeable increase in frequency in cultivation. While in the 1940s, land was cultivated only once, during 1950s and 1960s it went up to two: once, during the monsoons and then again during winter. However after tractors entered the fray the cultivators till their land thrice: during Kharif (the monsoons), during winter and during Rabi (the post-winter season). The historical transect at Table 5 reveals the position.

Table 5 Historical Transect of Main Crops and their Yield in Naipurwa Hamlet, Chandpur Village by Men's Group

Decade	Principal Crops	Yield (Quintal/Acre)
1940s	Barley, Bare,	0.4
	Sawa,	0.5
	Sugarcane,	
	Vegetables.	
1950s	Wheat,	3.5–4
	Paddy,	3.5–4
	Peas,	2.4–2.5
	Bengal gram,	2.4–2.5
	Red gram,	3.5–4
	Maize.	2.4–2.5
	Barley discontinued.	
1960s	Wheat,	16–18
	Paddy,	
	Vegetables.	16–18
1970s	Wheat,	10
	Paddy,	10–12
	Vegetables.	
1980s	Wheat,	10
	Paddy,	10–12
	Vegetables.	
1990s	Wheat,	10
	Paddy,	10–12
	Vegetables.	
1998	Wheat,	10
	Paddy,	
	Vegetables.	08

Village Analysts: Mohan Patel, Rajendra Prasad, Dhanilal, Shyamdayal Patel.
Facilitator: Ms. Meera Jayaswal.

The substitution of animal power by mechanical power (tractor) in agriculture has not been uniform all through the period from 1940s to 1990s. There has been a gradual and steady increase in the rate of substitution as a result of which the households of Chandpur have reduced their bovine wealth from 10 pairs in the 1960s to a meagre 1 pair in the 1990s. Significantly, during the 1960s, the number of bullocks held per household increased from an average of 7 pairs in the 1950s to 10 pairs. This is because with the introduction of new varieties of seeds, fertiliser and irrigation water, farming expanded rapidly in the 1960s requiring more animal power and hence higher holdings of bullock. Thus Chandpur pressed into operation the "new technology", with the traditional bullock and the wooden plough. But then the same rapid expansion in agriculture could not be sustained in the subsequent decades and the farmers discovered that they no longer require such a large contingent of animals. The introduction of farming by tractors further reduced the use of animals for farming. The Chandpur farmers, thus, reduced their animal holdings per family.

Table 6 Historical Transect of Farming Systems and Livestock in Chandpur Village: Men's Group

Serial No.	*Decade*	*Method of Ploughing*	*Frequency of Cultivation*	*Kinds of Livestock*	*No. of Bullocks*
1	1940	Bullock	One	Bullock, Cow, Goat, Buffalo	5-6 pairs per family
2	1950	Bullock	Two: Winter and Rainy	Bullock, Cow, Goat, Buffalo	7 pairs per family
3	1960	Bullock	Two: Winter and Rainy	Bullock, Cow, Goat, Buffalo	10 pairs per family
4	1970	Tractor	Three	Bullock, Cow, Goat, Buffalo	6 pairs per family
5	1980	Tractor	Three	Bullock, Cow, Goat, Buffalo	2 pairs per family
6	1990	Tractor	Three	Bullock, Cow, Goat, Buffalo	1 pair per family

Village Analysts: Mohan Patel, Rajendra Prasad, Dhanilal Singh, Shyamdayal Patel.
Facilitator: Ms. Meera Jayaswal.
Date: 11.11.98.

VI. 2. Why Have the Changes Taken Place?

We are reviewing a period in our economic history which saw rapid changes in every direction. Changes were many and some with quite far reaching consequences, such as mechanisation of agriculture and the introduction of "new technology", to which we made a brief reference above. A tentative answer to the questions relating to changes in cropping pattern and yield in Chandpur is best provided by time line drawn by the senior citizens of Naipurwa Hamlet of Chandpur village which bears repetition here as Table 7.

In the 1960s, new variety of seeds came, improved variety of wheat was introduced, lift irrigation through pumpsets and electrification of the pump sets commenced. There was a sharp rise in productivity in wheat and paddy we saw in Table 5 earlier. This sharp rise in productivity in wheat and paddy during the 1960s, was clearly due to the introduction of new varieties of seeds as also the introduction of pump sets for irrigation. This also marked a significant change in the mind set of the people, depending on the sky for succour. Thus, not only did they resort to improved variety of wheat and paddy seeds, as opposed to traditional varieties of seeds, but also shifted their dependence from "Raingods" to their own ingenuity of making water available through pump irrigation. The use of chemical fertilizers also started *(Joshi and Bisht, 1999)*. However, after the initial spurt in yield due to "new technology", in the 1960s, the yield fell as the chemical composition of the soil changed, no further improved varieties of seed were introduced and the extension work could not keep pace with changing times. The initial spurt during 1960s in much higher yields was lost during 1970s and in the subsequent decades. The use of HYV seeds, chemical fertilisers and pesticides etc., has adverse consequence which, has been noticed in several parts of the country. These adverse impacts have been called the "Yellowing of the Green Revolution" or classified as the "Violence of the Green Revolution" (*Shiva, 1991*). These were not mentioned by the farmers of Chandpur.

Table 7 Time Line: Historical Events as Recalled by the Senior Men of Naipurwa Hamlet of Chandpur Village

Decade	Year	Events
1940s	1942	Flood in River Baruna; bridge washed away
	1947	India wins Independence
	1947	Single Stage coach started from Vitari to Morai
1950s	1950–51	Locust attack
	1959–60	Transportation by truck started
	1959–60	Birdi making unit started
	1959–60	Reinforced Concrete Construction (RCC) of houses started
1960s	1962	New varieties of seeds introduced
	1964	New wheat variety (RR21) started
	1969	Electric supply started
		2-3 pump sets introduced
1970s	1972–73	Tractor introduced
	1975	Four new pump sets introduced
	1975	Sardar Ballab Bhai Cross Road (Chaumahani) constructed
	1976	Torrential rain leading to damage of crops (in November-December) which lasted for 7 days
1980s	1981(?)	Rudrax garland making unit started
1990s	1990	School constructed

Village Analysts: Mohan Patel, Rajendra Prasad Singh, Dhanilal, Shamdayal Patel.
Facilitator: Ms. Meera Jayaswal.
Date: 11.11.98.

The decision of the farmers to discontinue barley and sugarcane was mostly economic. In case of barley the farmers found that the proportion of chaff was very high, which had no use as the number of cattle-heads with the farmers had dwindled, culminating in the substitution of draught power by mechanical power of the tractor in 1972. There was also a change in the taste of people: they no longer liked the taste of barley and the new taste of wheat allured the people to make a shift in consumption in favour of consuming wheat. As regards sugarcane, the farmers decided generally to discontinue it because of a large variety of reasons. Firstly, the production cycle is such that land apportioned to sugarcane got occupied throughout the year, disabling the farmers from using the same land for wheat or other crops. Secondly, there is an increase in pest attack ('Deemak' in local language or white-ants) resulting in loss of crop yield. Finally, since the village is near or on a main road, theft of sugarcane caused considerable loss to farmers. Although forcible harvesting of crops is a common feature in many parts of the state but theft of sugarcane is easier and requires little expertise unlike in cases of wheat or paddy.

It is to be noted that the variety in principal crops have come down to three or so, because of major shifts in yields in other crops. Green peas, for instance, used to be grown earlier with traditional variety of seeds but with the introduction of improved variety of seeds, the productivity fell so dramatically that the villagers abandoned the crop altogether. The production of jowar has stopped because it has been replaced by a cash crop, namely, cauliflower. Jowar gets ready for harvest in October-November, if it is sown in August, whereas cauliflower seedlings have to be planted in September-October. Since income from growing cauliflower is much higher than what jowar could provide, villagers have opted for the former. This trend has been buttressed by the fact that people no longer like the taste of jowar. Cultivation of lentil (arhar) has been almost abandoned in the last 10-12 years because of its high vulnerability to pest attack and also because the same land on which arhar used to be cultivated competed with wheat as a crop. Given that people have a preference for wheat as a staple food crop, vis-à-vis arhar which, is not a staple, arhar got pushed out. This may have adverse effect on nutritional security as well as the palate and variety in the diet of the villagers, but that is another matter to which we shall come later in the study.

If we see the changes in farming in Chandpur over the years, it is clear that agriculture has moved from Zero External Input Agriculture (ZEIA) in the 1940s to Low External Input Agriculture (LEIA) in the 1960s and then it is tending towards High External Input Agriculture (HEIA) in the 1980s and 1990s. As farming in the 1980s and 1990s has tended to become more dependent on sourcing from outside Chandpur, farming has come to use more of resources that are not always renewable. Internal resources are "inherently renewable and thus have the potential to be used on a 'sustained' basis, indefinitely, through ecologically sound methods of farming" (*Conway and Barbier, 1990*).

Since agriculture in Chandpur has become dependent on external resources, much of it is not provided as a "free good", implying that the farming households must buy them and hence must generate a surplus of production, cash or whatever else of value to exchange for external resources. And the cost of acquiring these resources and their supply channels are rarely controllable always by the farmer household. This has at least three cost implications in terms of open costs, hidden costs and real costs.

The transition from ZEIA to LEIA and eventually to HEIA, has made agriculture a high *open* cost venture because the farmer has to buy the inputs. There is little of the resources required which is free of charge. Thus the cost of farming operation has gone up so much so that it has put sustainability of agriculture (not of the peasants) in doubt. One explanation for this sudden upward rise in input costs, according to us, lies in the implementation of the structural adjustment programme of the IMF-World Bank, consequent cut in subsidies (real or virtual) and the general rise in prices, all of which have jacked up input costs sharply. It is anticipated that with globalisations and full implementation of the TRIPS Agreement of the WTO, which is lurking round the corner, the cost of these inputs will rise further. (See *Third World Resurgence*, 1999 for a series of detailed discussions on the issues.) The several fold increase in yield seen in the 1970s will no longer be possible.

The transition from ZEIA to HEIA has also made a noticeable impact on the *hidden* cost of operation. The increase in fossil fuel use to keep outputs high, also means more energy consumption. Shift from ZEIA to HEIA has led to substitution of manual labour and animal power by tractors, threshers and pumpsets (either diesel or electric) that we saw, which implies that external energy sources have substituted energy sources found in the household and the community. All this along with use of fertilisers, which is mostly NKP, agriculture has become very energy intensive in Chandpur. Although we have no estimates of how much is the total energy inputs to agriculture due to the use of fertilisers (NKP), pumpsets and tractors in Chandpur but in third world countries these amongst themselves consume more than 90 per cent of total energy inputs for farming. For India as a whole there is one estimate that 10-20 per cent increase in yields following mechanisation, costs an additional 43-260 per cent more in energy consumption. In Punjab, farms in a class 14-25 hectares use three times as much direct energy per hectare as farmers smaller than 6 hectares (*Singh and Miglani, 1976*). The following Table is interesting.

Low input comparison	**High input comparison**	**Amount of extra yield for high input**	**Amount of extra energy consumption for high input**
	State of West Bengal in Eastern India		
Bullock, rice	Power tiller, rice	+ 8 per cent	+ 200 per cent
Bullock, rice	Tractor, rice	+ 13 per cent	+ 43 per cent
Bullock, wheat	Power tiller, wheat	+ 12 per cent	+ 74 per cent
Bullock, wheat	Tractor, wheat	+ 6 per cent	+ 89 per cent
	State of Uttar Pradesh in North India		
Bullock, rice	Mechanised rice	+ 20 per cent	+ 45 per cent
Bullock, wheat	Mechanised wheat	+ 29 per cent	+ 138 per cent

Source: *Singh and Singh*, 1976.

A look at the above table reveals that in case of West Bengal, by transiting from growing rice using bullocks to plough, to the system of using power tillers, farmers have reaped an extra yield from high external input of 8 per cent whereas the additional energy needed for the high input is 200 per cent. Similarly transition from bullock-wheat to power tiller-wheat, resulted in extra yield for high input of 6 per cent but increase in extra energy was 89 per cent. In case of Uttar Pradesh, movement from bullock-wheat to mechanised-wheat leads to yield increase of 29 per cent as against extra energy consumption of 138 per cent. Similarly for other forms of cultivating rice and wheat. Thus, as farming moves from traditional methods of cultivation to mechanised or partially mechanised agriculture, yield increases, but at the same time, increases in energy consumption are steep. In percentage terms, the increases in energy requirements far outstrip the increases in yield. The differentials in yield increase and extra energy requirement depends on local conditions and micro-level environments. Since we do not have data specific to Chandpur, we can only draw a general conclusion that the movement from

ZEIA to HEIA has increased the energy intensity of farming. We have to add to this the hidden cost of lost soil nutrients.

In high external input agriculture, entails a lot of *real costs*. Even where there is no direct monetary outgoing to acquire a resource, there may be real cost incurred by the farming household. The most obvious examples, of real costs, are time expended in obtaining seeds and other inputs from local distributors in Varansi or block headquarters; time expended in fetching diesel for pumpsets (in case the pumpsets are not electricity operated); chasing the State Electricity Board employees for various reasons and loss of crops when any of the inputs are either not available or not available in time.

Box 2.3

Synthetic Fertilizers and Soil Nutrition

"The import of synthetic fertilizers to the field cannot compensate for the loss of exported nutrients. Synthetic farming gives a high initial income, not because of inherent productivity of the technology but because the soil fertility is being mined. With continuous mining, yield and income decreases even with increasing synthetic fertiliser use. If the harvest goes to towns where the sewage is recycled, the fertility is at least shifted to another locality. But if the sewage is dumped into the sea the fertility is lost. It is worst if the harvest is exported from the country. The lost fertility, equivalent to the export of topsoil, represents a loss in the natural resource capital of the land."

Source: *Asking the Earth Farms, Forestry and Survival in India* (London: WWF) 1990.

VI. 3. Changes in Yield of Crops

- Seasonal and historical trends
- Farmers' response to declining

If we look at Table 5, it would be apparent that there is a historical trend. From column 3 of the Table, it seems that productivity was quite modest in the 1950s and then came in the 1960s, the era of improved variety of seeds, use of chemical fertilizers and irrigation water. In the 1960s, yield per acre of wheat jumped from an estimated 4 quintal per acre to 16 quintal per acre. Similarly for paddy. The yield in case of vegetables also increased quite dramatically in the period under review but how much from the earlier base is not clear. After the initial jump in yield for wheat, paddy and vegetables in the 1960s, the yield showed considerable decline in the 1970s: yield for wheat per acre came down to 10 quintal per acre, and yield per acre of paddy came down to 10-12 quintal per acre. Thereafter, the yield seems to have stabilised as a plateau at the 1970s level, barring that in the year of investigation, 1998 when yield from paddy has declined further due to bad weather but this has to be treated as an one-off aberration for the present. If one were to draw a graph of the yield of Chandpur, the trend is of an inverted 'V', with a longish flat portion attached to the right hand segment of V.

If we look at Table 8 below we get some idea of yield in Patel Basti which is more or less in the same vein as trends in yield noticed in Naipurwa Basti depicted in Table 5. In Patel Basti though we have no timeline data yet the yield reached its peak in the 1960s, and then in 1998 it shows a marked decline. For instance from an yield of 37.5 quintals of wheat per acre, the yield fell to 12 quintal per acre. The story is the same for maize and green peas and for all other crops that continued to be cultivated in 1998.

VII. Spatial Differences

Are there Spatial Differences in Yields or Crop Quality?

There is no difference in yields or crop quality within the village. Since the village is relatively small, it is difficult to isolate pockets within the village, which could exhibit difference in yield or crop quality. The cropping pattern in Patel Basti Hamlet of Chandpur is as in Table 8.

If we compare Tables 5 and 8, in both Patel Basti and in Naipurwa Hamlets, the principal crops are currently wheat and paddy. While in

Naipurwa Hamlet the villagers grow vegetables as cash crops in addition to the two food crops, in Patel Basti, instead of only vegetables the villagers grow jowar and maize along with green peas. The area and yield of jowar and maize are insignificant in the overall scheme of agriculture in the village. Granted that, the evidence does suggest that there is little variations in cropping pattern in different parts of the village.

Table 8 Cropped Area and Yield in Patel Basti of Village Chandpur

Crop	1960 Area Under Cultivation (Bigha)	1960 Yield Per Acre in Quintals	1998 Area Under Cultivation (Bigha)	1998 Yield Per Acre in Quintals
Wheat	10	37.5	25	12
Barley	25	12	–	–
Sugarcane	20	600	–	–
Green gram	5	12	–	–
Green peas	15	13.5	0.05	1.5
Paddy	10	6	15	15
Jowar	20	3	5	1.5
Arhar (lentil)	10	6	0.5	3
Maize	10	18	1.00	9

Source: Primary Data collected by Ms. Hema Joshi and Ms. Sunita Bisht as reported in *Report on Impact of Air Pollution on Agriculture In Urban and Peri-Urban Areas*, NIUA, New-Delhi, 1999.

VIII. Agricultural Inputs

VIII. 1. Cultivation Processes

The cultivation process is different for the two main seasons. For Kharif, the principal crop is paddy with which we shall deal in a bit of detail.

- The process starts in *May-June* every year. A small piece of land (called Beehengardhi) is chosen as a nursery in which paddy seedlings are grown. Farmers generally grow their own seedlings.
- In *June-July* once the monsoons set in, cultivation starts and by and large the farmers concentrate solely on paddy. It is a multiple step operation. First the fields are ploughed, usually twice or thrice. Farmers have found that yields are better in fields, which are repeatedly ploughed. Then the lumps of earth that ploughing yields are broken down, called "Karha". This is followed by "Kurhol", for puddling. Once this is completed, the paddy seedlings are uprooted from the "Beehengardi" and transplanted on to the fields. The ridges of all the fields are repaired. The first dose of fertilizers and/ or some manure is applied. As a secondary activity, the farmers plant brinjals, tomatoes, bottlegoud, pumpkin and "seeam", a kind of bean, mostly in kitchen gardens.
- In *August and September* deweeding becomes necessary, usually more than once depending on the need. These are the months most appropriate for the second/third doses of fertilizers and limited amount of manure, after deweeding is completed, depending upon the capacity of the farmers to bear the expenses.
- During *October-November*, we have the big harvesting season. Paddy is harvested and post harvest operations like threshing, winnowing, dehusking and pounding follows.
- Once the harvesting of paddy ends, green grams are sown in *October-November*. Now is the time for the farmers to sow potatoes, radish and cauliflower.
- During *November-December*, potato fields are tilled and readied for sowing vegetables. Cauliflower seedlings are transplanted and radish is harvested. This is the period when early variety wheat is sown. A moderate quantity of green peas are also sown and seedlings of onion are planted. Generally farmers procure onion seedlings from outside their farms.

- *December-January* are the months when attention is concentrated on wheat just as undivided attention is given to paddy cultivation during June-August. The wheat fields are tilled once again, deweeding is carried out and fertilizers are applied. Fields are irrigated.
- During *January-February*, a second round of irrigation is applied to the *early-variety* wheat. This is also the time when *late-variety* wheat is sown. The second dose of fertiliser is applied to *early-variety* wheat fields. Green peas, sown in the months of November-December, are now harvested. The first harvest of potatoes (sown in *October-November*) is reaped.
- *February-March* is the time for the third round of irrigation to be provided to the *early-variety* wheat. In case flowering starts, another round of fertiliser is applied. A second round of green peas is harvested. Irrigation is applied to onion fields.
  March-April is again harvesting season. Wheat is harvested. Onion and garlic are harvested. Green gram is also harvested.

During all these months, minor vegetables are harvested by the villagers. Since they are very small in quantity no significance is attached to them, except that such crops are for sale in the market and not for self-consumption at the household level. The cultivation process is involved for paddy and wheat cultivation, requiring tilling, weeding, applying irrigation and fertilizers and a lot of incidental activities in keeping the fields intact and protecting the crops from damage due to animal and human trespassing.

There is no significant use of use of herbicides, insecticides or pesticides. While deweeding is done to obviate the need for use of herbicide, no apparent steps are taken to take care of the problems of either pests or insects, except for minor applications of *Gamaxine (sic)* and *Dalidal (sic)*. The practice of soil testing is non-existent and there is no technical way of deciding both on the quantum and kind of chemical fertilizers that need to be used for different crops in the different fields during different seasons. Since the number of animals has dwindled over the last few years availability and hence application of manure and compost are limited. This could possibly have led to an imbalance in the chemical composition of land leading to a fall in yield during the 1980s and 1990s, after the initial spurt in the 1960s. This requires further investigation. Though improved varieties of seeds have been introduced, the agricultural processes remain the traditional ones, except for the substitution of animal power by mechanical power in ploughing the agricultural lands.

VIII. 2. Agricultural Inputs and Economics of the Inputs

From the cultivation process discussed above the inputs into agriculture sought by the farmers of Chandpur can be easily deduced. Clearly the inputs would come in the nature of "public" good or "free" good, such as soil fertility, sunshine, rains; and some in the nature of purchased inputs: be they seeds, fertilizers/manure, water and water lifting devices, labour and tractor. The nature of agricultural inputs has changed over time, which is consistent with various trends we have noticed earlier. As agriculture moved from greater diversification to lesser diversity (refer to Table 5) and as Chandpur saw the introduction of "new technology" in a limited way, agriculture moved from LEIA (Low External Input Agriculture) to HEIA (High External Input Agriculture). What impact this movement had on sustainability, one cannot say for sure, but agriculture in Chandpur has become so much more dependent on outside for its continuance.

In the 1940s, the inputs in agriculture were livestock dung and green manure, bullock available in the village, irrigation by the wheelbarrow, traditional variety of seed saved from earlier year's harvest and local, mostly family labour. There was no use of insecticide, herbicide and pesticides as there were none of the pests, weeds and diseases found now, or at least the villagers did not perceive their presence. In the 1950s, the same trend continued except that some chemical fertilizers (Chand Brand) came into use.

In the 1960s, green manure and animal dung got substituted by calcium, ammonia (urea), potash dye, ammonium chloride and irrigation by bullock drawn wheel burrows were replaced by pumpsets and in came *Gamaxine (sic)* as a few insects were noticed. By the time Chandpur came in the 1970s, use of local seeds literally vanished and improved variety of seeds came in: Jaya, Mansuri, Saket and P-4 in the case of paddy, and RR-21, K-68, Kalyan-2003, MRP-102 and UP-262, in the case of wheat. These were all imported varieties. The incidence of insects increased significantly and application of *Dalidal (sic)* started.

As Chandpur entered 1980s, inputs to agriculture remained unchanged from the ones used in the 1970s, except that amongst the varieties of paddy cultivated, jaya was discontinued due to its long gestation period and Pant-4 introduced. In case of wheat, Meelwi 37, 34 and 6, supposedly "disease resistant", came into use along with the other varieties. The infestation of insects increased even more. An insecticide called *Roger (sic)* came into use along with *Gamaxine* powder *(sic)*. In the 1990s the position remained unchanged.

It is significant that over the years, not only did Chandpur 'import' seeds and fertilizers and insecticides, from outside, but it even started hiring labourers from Mahuadih, and tractors from Kiraktarpur. Diesel had to be brought from nearby towns for the diesel pumpsets and electricity was tapped from the rural electrification programme of the Uttar Pradesh State Electricity Board. It is also significant that as agriculture became HEIA from LEIA, the vulnerability of the farming system in Chandpur increased significantly. The dispersal of risks due to a diversified cropping pattern was no longer available.

With a high level of external inputs, cost of production in agriculture has risen very significantly and at times it may even be not enough for the farming family to be above the poverty line defined as Rs. 11500 per annum per household (of five members). The economics of agriculture, in one of the Hamlets (Yadav Basti) of Chandpur worked out by the villagers is shown in Table 9.

In Column 13 of Table 9 the net returns are per season. Since cultivation and harvesting of several crops/vegetables overlap, it is difficult to calculate the net return to the farmer per month. If we look at the size of holdings, small farmers are no longer viable. The landholding pattern in Patel Basti, a typical Hamlet of Chandpur is as in the table that follows.

No. of Families	Landholding
10	Landless
8	Less than 0.16 Acre
9	0.16-0.33 Acre
4	0.33-0.5 Acre
0	0.5-0.66 Acre
8	0.66-1 Acre
2	1-2 Acre(s)
1	2-2.66 Acre(s)

Source: The table has been drawn from the primary data collected by Ms. Hema Joshi and Ms. Sunita Bisht and reported in *Report on Impact of Air Pollution on Agriculture In Urban and Peri-Urban Areas*, NIUA, New-Delhi, 1999.

The number of landless in India is 11 per cent and in Uttar Pradesh it is 4.9 per cent. The number of marginal and small farmers in Uttar Pradesh stands at 68.01 per cent and 18.52 per cent respectively according to NSS of the 48th round (*NSSO, 1997*). Given this background, the general situation of landholding in Chandpur is, therefore, little worse than Uttar Pradesh as a whole.

Table 9 Agricultural Return per Acre in Yadav Basti, Chandpur

Crop	Cost of preparing Land	Quantity of Seed	Cost of Seed	Quantity of Fertilizers	Cost of Fertilizers	Person days of Labour	Cost of Insecticide and Irrigation	Other costs such as Transport cost	Output per acre	Total cost	Return per acre	Net Profit
(1)	(2)	(3)	(4)	(5)	(6)	(7)	(8)	(9)	(10)	(11)	(12)	(13)
Wheat	Rs. 850	50 kg	Rs. 400	—	—	30 day @ 30/ day= Rs. 900	Rs. 80 plus cost of 21 hours irrigation = Rs. 315	Rs. 150	12 Quintals	Rs. 2645	Rs. 700 per quintal which is Rs. 8400	Rs. 5755

(1)	(2)	(3)	(4)	(5)	(6)	(7)	(8)	(9)	(10)	(11)	(12)	(13)
Paddy	Rs. 1000	25 kg	Rs. 200	DAP 100 kg and Urea 200 kg	Rs. 900 plus Rs. 800	46 days @ Rs. 30 per day = Rs. 1380	25 kg = Rs. 250	Rs. 150	15 quintal	Rs. 4680	Rs 800 per quintal = Rs 12000	Rs. 7320
Maize	Rs. 200	18 kg	Rs. 100	Urea 50 kg	Rs. 200	10 days @ Rs. 30 per day = Rs. 360		Rs. 100	10 quintal	Rs. 960	RS. 200 per quintal = Rs. 2000	Rs. 1040
Bajra	Rs. 200	5 kg	Rs. 30	Urea 30 kg plus DAP 50 kg	Rs. 200 plus Rs. 450	15 days @ 30 per day = Rs. 450	—	Rs. 50	1.5 quintal	Rs 830	Rs 600 per quintal = Rs. 900	Rs. 70
Caulif-lower per 5 Biswa	Rs. 1050	100 gm	Rs. 80	Urea 10 kg and DAP 10 kg	Rs. 130	18 days @ Rs. 30 per day = Rs. 240	Rs. 15 plus Rs. 450	Rs. 200	4000 pieces approximately	Rs. 2165	Rs. 4 per piece = Rs. 16000	Rs 13835 *per Biswa*
Radish per 5 Biswa	Rs. 1235	250	Rs.	—	—	10 @ Rs. 30 per day = Rs. 300	Gam-Powder = Rs. 50 plus irrigat-ion cost of 20 hours = Rs. 300	Rs. 200	500 kg	Rs. 1785	Re. 6 per kg = Rs. 3000	Rs. 1215 *per Biswa*

Clearly the landholdings are very small and hence agriculture as a source of livelihood all by itself is ruled out. Then significantly enough the cultivation of cash crops is far more profitable than cultivation of food crops (paddy and wheat in particular) which partly explains why people are shifting from food to cash crops. Because of small size of landholdings, diseconomies of scale operates in the cultivation and harvesting of food crops and hence they are not as profitable as one would have liked them to be.

In Table 9, it may be mentioned, credit as input in agriculture has not been shown separately. Credit is used by villagers in different amounts and doses, and hence cost of credit should be added to reflect true cost of cultivation, which has not been done.

VIII. 3. Who Supplies the Inputs and Who Provide the Extension Services Regarding New Seeds, Pesticides and Fertilizers?

In the agricultural operation, as we saw, there is a high component of external inputs. There is no fixed source from which the farmers access agricultural inputs. And the sources are varied. Seeds are procured from the government seed farm as their first choice, but not all the farmers get such seeds, usually certified. Such of those farmers, who can not obtain seeds from the seed farm, buy seeds from local traders and from shops in the adjoining township. Tractors are hired in from nearby villages and fertilizers are also brought in the open market, though the block development office is suppose to provide fertilizers and the government provides substantial amounts of subsidy for fertilizers. Pump sets are owned by some farmers but the not so fortunate ones also hire pumpsets from nearby villages. The cost of operation of the pumpsets works out to Rs. 5 to Rs. 25 per hour in case of owned pumps and Rs. 15-40 per hour in case of hired sets, depending on whether it is a diesel or an electric pump. Part of the labour is also hired from outside the village, namely, Mahuadih at the rate of Rs. 30 per day. They even buy manure from nearby villages, given that the number of animals in the village itself has dwindled down and hence the village no longer produces whatever little manure is used in cultivation. There is no extension service available. In fact it is a well known fact that though a huge retinue of extension workers are on the rolls of the Government, most of the extension workers, including the Village Level Workers (VLWs) have no budgetary allocation to travel for providing extension services. Chandpur is also a victim of this unfortunate situation.

Box 2.4
Input Suppliers: A Farmer's Best Friend?

With developments of more capital intensive agriculture, farmers increasingly relied on outside supplies to provide their tools, buildings, fertilisers, seeds and foodstuffs. Most of these supplies have grown to become huge conglomerates, often servicing a global market and taking a global view of their business. They can be divided into four groups:

- Agro-chemical industries provide fertilisers and biocides (toxic substances designed to kill animals or plant pests and called more specifically pesticides, herbicides, aphicides and fungicides).
- Seed producers and feed manufacturers provide seeds for planting and feedstuffs for intensively reared livestock and supplements for more extensively reared livestock.
- Biomedical companies provide drugs for prophylactic use in intensive farming for vaccination and curative purposes.
- Equipment and energy companies provide farm machinery and fuel to power it.

Input suppliers have a strong interest in maintaining markets for inputs to intensive agriculture….It is the interest of these suppliers, rather than farming, environmental or other interests, that is driving the move into bio-technology.

Source: Geoff Tansy and Tony Worsley: *The Food System* (London: Earthscan) 1995

IX. Class Issues

IX. 1. The Landowning and the Landless Groups

From a discussion of the class composition of the village, it is apparent that the Patels are the landowning class generally. The Harijans and the

Scheduled Castes are the landless classes. If we take the case of Patel Basti, for instance, people would categorize villagers in the hamlet as falling into three classes. One, those who own large chunks of land, have a stable job, have either rented out a house or part thereof and /or have some form of transport business. There are 8 such families and they are considered upper income group. Two, there are others who own a small piece of land for agriculture, and also have alternative sources of income such as rental from house let out, petty shop etc. There are 21 such families and they are considered middle income group. Then there is the third category, who own no land but work on leased-in land as share-croppers and depend for most of their needs on daily wages. There are 13 such families and they are considered as falling in the low income class. Land ownership is decidedly the critical element in classification of villagers, or what may be called "wealth ranking".

IX. 2. Overlap Between Landownership with Produce Ownership

Given the caste composition and the class composition of the village population, there is considerable overlap between land ownership and produce ownership. The cultivators are mostly owner-cultivators. Only a small percentage of cultivators are share-croppers. For instance in Patel Basti Hamlet only 13 families out of a total of 42 families are sharecroppers (or "Bataidars"). In Chandpur the share-croppers are concealed tenants, because by law, tenancy, which includes share-cropping, is banned (*Kripa Shankar, 1999*). The concealed tenants are worse-off than the non-concealed ones. The redeeming feature, however, is that the tenants in Chandpur being sharecroppers, share their produce with the landlords, which means the landlords also share the risks involved. Unlike the other two forms (fixed cash rent and fixed produce rent, also called "Danabandi") the risks are all borne by the tenants for whether there is crop or not, the tenant has to pay the agreed fixed rent.

It is also a fact that the Yadavs who own most of the Bovine wealth in the village and make a living out of animal husbandry, own the produce and have control over the same.

Table 10 Schedule of Wages Payable

Wages per Day	Rs. in Village	Rs. in Town
For Men		
On daily wages in construction activity	70	80
Mason	110	110
Saree weaving*	60	–
Stitching	50	–
Transport sector work: driver etc.	100	–
Auto rickshaw driving	100	–
Vegetable vending	50	–
Working in petty village shop	50	–
For Women		
Agricultural labour	30	–
Deweeding	30	–
Paddy harvesting	30	–
Threshing	30	–
Wheat harvesting	30	–
Transplanting	30	–
Birdi making**	8	–
Rodrax garland making***	15	–

* Wage received per Saree is Rs. 600 and it takes 10 days to weave one Saree.

** Women are paid on piece rate basis. For 100 Birdis, Rs. 16 is paid and it takes a person a day to make 50 Birdis.

*** For 90 garlands, the total wage payable is Rs. 50. It take about three days to make 90 rudrax garlands.

Village Analysts: Nawarangi, Budhram, Ramjatan Patel, Santlal.
Facilitator: Ms. Meera Jayaswal.
Date: 13.11. 98.

IX. 3. Migrant Labourers in Agriculture and Migrant Leasees

From the available data, the existence of migrant leasees can not be detected. If we look at the history of the village, one finds a steady increase in the number of households. Part of this is due to increase in population and part of it is on account of outsiders migrating to the village, particularly on account of the establishment of the industrial estate. But those who have been attracted by the industrial estate are semi-skilled workers, labourers, transport workers and other service providers. It did not attract cultivators. In fact it could not because returns from agriculture are unattractive vis-à-vis earnings from employment in the industrial estate. Hark the figures in Table 10.

With this schedule of compensation package, it is does not make sense for migrants to come to Chandpur as migrant cultivators as leasees. There are migrant labourers but they generally commute from nearby villages and do not migrate in the sense of settling down in the village even if during the cultivation and harvesting season. Generally, the experience and data reveal that migration is from the rural to the urban areas in search of better prospects of employment, and rarely from rural to rural areas and none from urban to rural areas. The reason being, the poverty of one village is hardly attractive to those who live in poverty in another area. Our villages, dependent on land and agriculture, do not offer employment opportunities of the kind and scale that appears reasonably good to induce influx of migrants from other villages. In fact in most of agriculture, there is disguised unemployment. Therefore, from first principles, migration into a poor village like Chandpur is unlikely.

X. Gender Issues

From the schedule of wages at Table 10, it is clear that men and women carry out different sets of activities. In case of off-farm systems of livelihood, women are mostly engaged in "inside-home" employment opportunities and men are employed in "outside-home" employment. While men are in construction work, auto-rickshaw driving, transport sector and other service activities, requiring them to travel out of their homes and even village, the women are confined to home based employment such as birdi making and rudrax garland making. Some of this division of work is on account of opportunities available and some of it also conditioned by social circumstances.

In terms of agricultural activities, there is also a clear division of tasks. While men do the ploughing, puddling, carrying seedlings and irrigating the fields, women are engaged in transplanting, deweeding, harvesting, threshing and in carrying crops from the fields to their home as headloads. This is a broad classification and is not watertight, as men also lend their hand in transplanting seedlings, harvesting and threshing, while women are seen to irrigate their fields and help in carrying seedlings. This is particularly so because agriculture is a family enterprise and it being rainfed, all the family resources have to be mustered while the rains last.

On the whole, however, the workload of women is more than that of men. Women continue to shoulder the responsibilities of fetching drinking water and fuelwood, process and cook food, bear and rear children, wash and clean in the households. They also look after the aged and the disabled. The workload is even more if account is taken of the maintenance functions under women's charge, such as tending the bullocks and providing them with fodder and, of post harvest operations, to which we have not paid much attention.

Box 2.5
Gender and Distribution of Work

Women work longer hours than men in most countries of the world. And often carry a disproportionate share of the burden of coping with poverty....A comparison of time use for women and men in rural and urban communities reveal that women spend an average of 20 per cent more time relative to men working in rural areas and six percent in urban areas......This difference is often a result of women's reproductive roles, their greater responsibility for agricultural work in family-owned farms, and barriers to entry in urban markets.

Source: United Nations Development Programme: *Human Development Report*, 1995

XI. Significance of Agriculture

We have already discussed the importance of agriculture in the context of employment and sources of income. Suffice it to reiterate that villagers of Chandpur are engaged in agriculture either tilling their own land or working on others' land as sharecroppers or as agricultural labourers. Share-cropping is one of the forms of tenancy: fixed cash rent and fixed produce being the other two.

However, a majority of the people do not depend upon agriculture solely for their livelihood, either as owner cultivators or as wage labourers. They are engaged in other on-farm or off-farm activities to support their life. For instance, it provides 150 days of employment to 50 labourers in Patel Basti. The situation is not dissimilar in other Hamlets of Chandpur.

The importance of agriculture for food security in a predominantly agricultural society, can not be overemphasised. Food security means that there is enough food in the system, that people have the purchasing power to access food, that people have the ability to access the food, that the food available is culturally acceptable and that the food so available has adequate nutritional value for a healthy life.

If we accept the above concept of food, role of agriculture in food security is important but not overwhelming. Take the case of Patel Basti. Wheat produced in the hamlet meets the requirement of wheat for the villagers for 4-5 months in a year. Paddy harvested can meet the needs of paddy of the villagers in the hamlet for 3-4 months. Maize and bajra produced is enough to meet the needs of the villagers for 8-10 days and 1-2 months respectively. And all the villagers do not grow all the crops. Thus the food produced meets about half the quantity of food necessary. For the rest of the food needs people buy food from the open market. Food produced in the village is culturally acceptable and given the employment opportunities outside of agriculture, available in and around Chandpur, the people have the requisite purchasing power to access food. Apparently people do not suffer starvation but existence of relative hunger is discernible. Take the case of Naipurwa women as revealed by the food calendar produced by the women of the hamlet as reproduced in Table 11.

If we look at Table 11, it is significant that the women have started the food calendar from the month of June-July (Ashar) and ends it in May-June (Jeth). This is because June-July is the month when the main cultivation season (Kharif) starts and it is associated in the psyche of the people as being the start of the process of food production. If we look at column 3, it is manifest that the women suffer from various degrees of hunger throughout the year. But their hunger is at its peak during the very hot summer and wet monsoon months, namely, months of Baisakh (April-May), Jeth (May-June), Asarh (June-July), Sawan (July-August) and Bhado (August-September). That is, the women survive on unwholesome meal for 5 months. Only with the advent of Kuar (September-October), once harvesting of some pulses start, and the poor earn some wages, that they have some nutrition and palate in the food intake by way of pulses and vegetables and this lasts for the five months from Kuar to Magh (mid-September to mid-February). During Fagun and Chait (mid-February to mid-April) pulses become scarce in the diet of the poor, until it vanishes in Baisakh (mid-April to mid-May).

Table 11 Food Calendar Prepared by the Women of Naipurwa Hamlet, Chandpur Village

Months	Financial Condition	Food Intake	Serial Number
Asardh (June-July)	Loan for purchasing seeds, from the village headman or the money lender	One meal of few chapatis and salt or chilly paste or some inexpensive vegetables	1
Sawan (July-August)	Take loan for purchasing food	One meal of few chapatis and salt or chilly paste or some inexpensive vegetables	2
Bhado (August-Sept)	Take loan for purchasing food	One meal of few chapatis and salt or chilly paste or some inexpensive vegetables	3
Kaur (Sept -Oct)	Income starts from sale of vegetables and from working as agricultural labourers	The same diet as in Bhado but intake of pulses and vegetables start	4
Kartick (Oct -Nov)	Income from vegetable sale and birdi/rudrax garland making	The same diet as in Kaur	5

Months	Financial Condition	Food Intake	Serial Number
Aghan (Nov -Dec)	Income from vegetable sale and birdi/rudrax garland making	Milk supplement is added to diet	6
Poosh (Dec -Jan)	Income from vegetable sale, work in fields and birdi/rudrax garland making	Same as in Aghan	7
Magh (Jan-February)	Income from vegetable sale and birdi/rudrax garland making	Same as in Poosh	8
Fagun (Feb - March)	Reduction in income from vegetable sale. Income from birdi/rudrax garland making is sustained	Same as in Magh but intake of pulses get reduced	9
Chait (March-April)	Income from non-agricultural work Income from wages earned in harvesting wheat	Same as in the month of Fagun but the intake of pulses gets further reduced	10
Baisakh (April-May)	Income from non-agricultural work Income from wages earned in harvesting wheat	One meal of chapatis and salt or chilly paste or inexpensive vegetables	11
Jeth (May-June)	Take loan for food at 10 per cent per month	One meal of chapatis and salt or chilly paste or inexpensive vegetables	12

Village Analysts: Rampati Devi, Dhandai Devi, Rita Devi.
Facilitator: Ms. Meera Jayaswal.
Date: 12.11.98.

The food intake is at its worst for the women during the months when they have to work the hardest: the summer and monsoon months for these are the months when they get to work in their own fields as also on wage employment in others' fields. These are also the months when the women expend a lot of energy in taking care of the sick, for during these months various kinds of disease afflict the poor, to which we will come later.

If we look at Columns 2 and 3, then a high degree of correlation between income and food intake is apparent. During the months of Jeth, Asarh, Sawan and Bhado (mid-May to mid-September) the women survive on loans for their food intake. Only when their income from sale of vegetables and wage earnings improve, do they include pulses and even milk in their diet.

On the whole then, people do not have food security all through the year, though they do not suffer from chronic hunger. Under nutrition and malnutrition of women are clearly made out. That the same holds true for the men can not be inferred straight away, because of the social fact of gross disparity in intra-familial distribution of food, flowing from disparity in intra-familial distribution of power, where the male member(s) dominate. However, given the wage rates, the employment rates and yield from agriculture we have discussed earlier, it is unlikely that men would have food security throughout the year, though they would be better-off than women. This is particularly so when about 25 per cent of total village income is expended on consumption of liquor.

Additionally Chandpur did not have access to much of common property resources, "micro-environments" (See *Chambers, 1992* for definition) and forests to support their food consumption. Food gathered from forests and CPRs have played a dynamic role is reducing hunger during hunger periods (see *Jodha, 1990; FAO, 1983, 1984, 1986*). Unfortunately the villagers of Chandpur did not have that benefit and whatever food producing CPR they had in the village were destroyed to produce commercial crops, to which we will come later.

Though not strictly related to the role of agriculture in food security, food security of the people could have been better ensured if the expenditure on health (15 per cent) and education (10 per cent) could have been more, and expenditure on liquor and litigation been less. Food security depends a great deal upon not only food production, distribution and access to food as also nutrition of food, but on general access that people have to basic education and primary health care (*Sen, 1995*).

In view of the role that women play in food production, there is no specific evidence available from the study that could pinpoint how far and in what ways food production and household activities interact. But if we re-examine the kinds of activities in which women are involved, it is apparent that food production is carried on as concurrent set of activities along with other household activities. Generally in this part of the world and certainly in eastern Uttar Pradesh, as we mentioned earlier, women are responsible for collecting fuelwood, fodder and potable water; carry out post-harvest processing of crops; processing and cooking food at home; looking after animals and most importantly bear and nurture children. The scheme of managing things within the household is so organised that the entire set of activities necessary for food production, is built into it as its integral part. No specific comments are possible beyond these general remarks.

Box 2.6
What Food?

Give me neither poverty nor riches,
Feed me with food convenient for me.

Proverbs, Ch. 30, V.8.

XII. Constraints to Agricultural Production and Community's Response

XII. 1. The Constraints for Agricultural Production

Though agriculture provides a substantial chunk of food needs of the people and provides employment and income to many in the village, it is not without problems. The constraints perceived by men and women are different and not surprisingly so: men find only six major constraints but the women would have us believe that there are ten constraints. Reference is invited to Tables 12 and 13.

Table 12 Constraints to Agriculture in Naipurwa Hamlet, Chandpur Village

	Men Group		Women Group	
Constraint	**Scoring**	**Priority**	**Scoring**	**Priority**
Jhulsa	***3	5	*****5	6
Angarwa	***3	5	*****5	6
Flies	********8	3	******6	5
Change in Climate	*********9	2	*******7	4
Insects	******6	4	*********9	2
Gharroj (Nilgai)	**********10	1	**********10	1
Rats	Not rated	Not Prioritised	********8	3
Tunki	Not rated	Not Prioritised	*******7	4
Conta-minated Water Reservoir	Not rated	Not Prioritised	*******7	4
Adolescent Boys	Not rated	Not Prioritised	*******7	4

Note: The stars indicate the number of bengal grams placed by the villagers against each of the constraints to indicate the relative severity of the constraint in their village context.

Village Analysts: Reeta Devi, Rampati Devi, Sabitri, Gulabi, Kalo Devi and Sunita Devi.
Facilitator: Ms. Meera Jayaswal.
Date: 16.11.98.

Both men and women in Naipurwa Hamlet, Chandpur village, consider the attack by nilgais as their biggest problem. Nilgais being a protected animal (it is a species of deer) they cannot be killed and because the forest cover which is their natural source of food and habitat, has been considerably depleted, these animals come down to neighbouring villages in search of food. According to women, insects are the second biggest problem while men think change in climate as the next big problem. While the climatic change has made rainfall less and less consistent with the cultivation and harvesting seasons and hence has injected an element of uncertainty about availability of water, in time, insect attack destroys crops in the field as well as in the granaries. Both have similar effect of reducing food availability and of reducing saleability of marketable agricultural produce.

If we look at Village Chandpur as a whole, the picture is a little more complex but consistent. The constraints are uncertainty, irregularity and maldistribution of rainfall, non-availability of irrigation in time, pest and insect attack on crops, non-availability of manure/fertilisers, non-availability of good quality seeds, small size of holdings, non-availability of seeds and fertilizers at fair prices, lack of agricultural labourers, problem of electric supply, non-availability of agricultural credit institutions, non-availability of credit in time and high rate of interest, lack of co-ordination amongst Government functionaries connected with agriculture, lack of extension and training, effluent discharge from the industrial establishments, lack of animal power and machines (read tractors) for use in agriculture, attack by nilgais, floods, attack of white ants, distance between agricultural lands and human habitation, high irrigation charges and frost bites.

These constraints can be classified as falling under four broad categories.

Environmental and Situational Constraints: uncertainty, irregularity and maldistribution of rainfall, small size of holdings, non-availability of irrigation in time, effluent discharge from the industrial establishments, floods etc.

Agro-Biological Constraints: non-availability of manure/fertilisers, non-availability of good quality seeds, attack by nilgais, frost bites, pest and insect attack on crops, attack of white ants etc.

Socio-Economic Constraints: non-availability of credit in time and high rate of interest, high irrigation charges, lack of animal power and machines (read tractors) for use in agriculture, problem of electric power, lack of extension and training, non-availability of seeds and fertilizers at fair prices, etc.

Administrative and Managerial Constraints: distance between agricultural lands and human habitation, lack of co-ordination amongst Government functionaries connected with agriculture etc.

All the constraints have been ranked by the small and medium sized farmers of Chandpur. For the small and medium farmers, of all these constraints, insect and pest attacks are the most formidable ones. Uncertainty, irregularity and maldistribution of rainfall are deemed as the second and third most difficult constraints respectively. The medium sized farmers consider frostbite as the third most important problem. For the small farmers, the second most intractable constraint, is small sized holdings, while the medium sized farmers consider small holdings as their fourth most important constraint.

If one were to take a broad picture from the ranking of the problems, the major problems faced by agriculture in Chandpur are insect and pest attack, frostbite, irregularity and maldistribution of rainfall and small size of holdings. Of these, insect and pest attacks have been ranked as *Numero Uno*.

XII. 2. What are their Impact?

The exact nature of the impact of all of these constraints on agricultural productivity is hard to assess but the impact of insects and pest can be found out in fair amount of details. *Jhulsa* attacks paddy and spinach when the crop is about a month old, leading to yellowing of the plants and preventing formation of the grain. As a result, in case of paddy hit by jhulsa, more of chaff than grain reaches the granary. It can cause up to 50 per cent loss in yield. *Angarwa* attacks cauliflower and other minor vegetables like bottle gourd, leading to premature falling off of leaves and fading of the roots. It can cause extensive damage but the extent of damage depends upon the severity of the disease. *Flies* attack paddy just when the flowering starts. This restricts formation of the grains in the pods and can be very damaging. The extent of damage varies in proportion to the number of flies that attack a particular crop. *Insects* like bhurilwa (stripped blackish-yellow caterpillar) are generally attracted to cauliflower, radish and spinach. And this has been happening for the last 7 years or so. These insects nibble away the leaves leading to output from the crops either withering away totally or their fruits being stunted and small. *Tunki* is a disease identified by the women which attacks garlic and onion plants.

Once Tunki sets in, the leaves and stems of the plants start shrinking ultimately affecting the roots. Since these are tuber crops, the shrinking of the root leads to crop loss as the bulbs either gets deformed or they shrink in size. According to the people the estimated loss is up to 90 cent reduction in yield.

Contaminated water from the reservoir is a peculiar problem unique in many respects to Chandpur. It does not affect the crops because the water from the reservoir is not used for irrigating agricultural lands, but the diseases that it causes in human beings wreck havoc. Through percolation channels, the contaminated water of the reservoir pollutes ground water used for drinking purposes, leading to jaundice (hepatitis) and the breeding ground that it provides to the mosquitoes, leads to widespread attack of malaria. Ultimately these diseases lead to a severe decline in the ability of the people to contribute to productive activities in agriculture and leads to loss of valuable productive person days.

The uncertainty of climatic conditions, and change in climate, have had adverse effects on the overall agricultural scenario. *Frost* damages potatoes, green peas and tomatoes during December, January and February, the coldest months of the year. Frosts can affect crops at any stage in the cropping cycle. This has been particularly noticeable during the last 7 years. Then comes the big menace of the *nilgais* herds, which not only graze crops but also trample them. The estimated loss of crops from attacks by nilgais is about 15 per cent per annum and this has been happening from the last 6 years or so.

XII. 3. What Changes in Types of Pests, Pest Population and Past Damage have been Perceived Spatially and Historically?

All of these constraints have not been with Chandpur forever. Some have been there for long while others have appeared recently. The constraints are of varying vintage. The evidence available of the pest attack and of the attendant damage is based on the recall of the community. *Jhulsa* attack started about 5 years back. *Angarwar, flies* and *rats* emerged in Chandpur about ten years ago. The uncertainty in climate is a more recent phenomenon of about 2-3 years. The problems posed by *insects* and *nilgais* have assumed serious proportions over the last 5 years or so. *Contaminated water* has been a problem for the villagers for the last 5 years, but they have not been able to do much. *Tunki* is the most recent addition to their problem, having started 2-3 years back. Thus, the constraints faced by agriculture in Chandpur have increased over the years: while 10 years ago the major constraints were of *angarwa, flies and rats*, about five years ago *jhulsa, insects* and *nilgais* got added to the list of constraints. *Tunki* and *change in climate* got further added 2-3 years ago. The extent of loss that these constraints taken one with the other, have caused could not be ascertained, except as indicated in the previous section, though these have been significant, ranging from 15 to 50 per cent loss in crops from some of these constraints.

XIII. Air Pollution and Industrialization

XIII. 1. What are the Perceived Impacts of Air Pollution and the Impact of Industrialization?

In Chandpur, though the brick kilns have closed, fruit production has dropped and soil is damaged but the chemical effluent in the form of wastewater, from industrial estate and Saree printing units have made 10 bighas of land barren. The villagers are aware of the adverse effects of emissions from the brick kiln (Chandpur village) on mango (blackening in colour, lessening of its sweetness etc.), on papaya (lessening of its sweetness) and on neem tree (making the leaves yellowish and weakening its twigs and small branches). There is little or no awareness of the adverse effects of air pollution in the hamlets of Chandpur, possibly because there was no primary pollutant near-by.

There are visible injuries to crops but not necessarily from air pollution. The field researchers did find at least three kinds of visible injury to crops. Cauliflower is affected by *angarwa* disease; *Angarwa* attacks spinach and damage caused to standing paddy crop by infestation of *flies*. Beyond that it is difficult to say much and there is no evidence to directly link these injuries to air pollution.

However, the community perceives that the establishment of the *industrial estate* has caused perceptible damage to their environment and well-being. There has been a loss of a large chunk of agricultural land due to effluent discharge from the industries of the estate and substantial portion of agricultural land has been usurped for non-agricultural purposes including construction of residential dwelling. Since population has increased, this reduction in area under cultivation, has been a cause of further fragmentation of land holdings, which has, in turn, accentuated the problem of small landholding pattern in the village. The pest and insect attacks on the crops are on the increase, and this is consistent with what was perceived by the community as discussed above. The introduction of chemical fertilizers has adversely affected the quality of the soil and in some cases erstwhile agricultural land has even been rendered uncultivable. The spurt in construction of residential dwellings has led to conversion of large chunks of agricultural land into wasteland due to excavation of the soil required for brick making.

The brick kilns have visibly affected horticulture in the village. Mango and guava trees no longer bear fruits as a result of pollution from the brick kilns and the industrial estate. Mango trees shed their flowers before they bear fruits. As a result, at least 5 Bigha of orchard has been cleared of fruit trees and the land so cleared, has been re-deployed for vegetable cultivation, which again is not free from pest and insect attack. In whatever fruit bearing trees that remain, there is a marked increase in white-ant attack over the last 10 years or so. The nearby ponds no longer provide "Singara", a kind of nutritious fruit-bearing weed, due to contamination of their water. To that extent, supply of a kind of food from common property resources has been cut off (see *Mukherjee, 1994, 1996; Mukherjee and Mukherjee, 1997, 1999* on the importance of CPR in food security). Most important the community perceives that the impact of the industrial estate has been most damaging on the social environment. With new firms being established in the industrial estate, workers from "outside" who have migrated to the village have disturbed the social equilibrium.

Alcoholism and prostitution are seen as on the rise as a consequence of the influx of outsiders.

There in no indication about any particular stage when dust pollution affects cropping calendar. Generally since both Kharif and Rabi crops are grown, pollutants from industry and road would affect cropping calendar for almost six months. That is, throughout the two seasons, except during the monsoons when rains reduce/eliminates dust.

XIII. 2. Impact on Health

Villagers complained of increased incidence of coughs, skin disease, stomach enlargement, and eye disease in children in the last 15-20 years. Increases in incidence of skin disease, TB, gastric ulcer in adults, especially in women were also reported. In Chandpur the rise in incidence of malaria is a notable development in its health status (50 persons affected during last June/July) due to breeding of mosquitoes in stagnant water without proper drainage facilities. The women group said that pneumonia had become endemic for the last.7 to 8 years and at least 100 children were affected last year, of which 10 children died. Health problems of villagers caused by jaundice, gastritis (on the rise over the last 7 to 10 years supposedly due to contaminated food), frequent body ache and mild fever in elderly people, cough, cold, asthma (25 per cent of adult and almost every old men and women suffer in silence for they think that the disease is incurable and medicines provide temporary relief), have been clearly articulated. Amongst the diseases affecting children (taking 20-25 days for recovery and an expenditure of Rs. 6000 to Rs. 7000), increase in incidence of pimples all over body caused due to mosquito bites (50 per cent of children were suffering at the time of field research), ear disease with pimple in the ear and pus flowing, and nagging cold and cough were mentioned.

The impact that pollution has on state of health of the villagers be best assessed through the health calendar prepared by the villagers as at Table 13.

Table 13 Health Calendar of Patel Basti, Chandpur

Diseases	*Less than 10 years old*	*10-25 years old*	*Above 25 years old*	*Months when intense*	*Since when*	*Treatment: what and where?*	*Notes and causes*
Cough	60 per cent	20 per cent	15 per cent	Sept. to Dec.	Since more than 10 years	Private doctor out of the village	Due to change in climate & from smoke/ smog from G.T. road
T.B.	—	—	2 persons	—	10-12 years	Outside the village	Neglig- ence & alcoholism
Eye problem, weak eyesight and watery eyes	8 persons	—	5 per cent	—	5-6 years	Private doctor in the village	Smoke & from malnutri- tion
Swelling of stomach	75 per cent	—	—	—	12 years	No treatment	Eating of soil
Diarrhoea and vomiting	50 per cent	5 per cent	2-3 per cent	Summer years	8-9	Private doctor in the Village	Heat and unhygie- nic food
Stomach ache	—	—	50 per- cent men and 80	Through out the year but more during summer	5-6 years	Private doctor in the village	Unhyg- ienic food

Diseases	*Less than 10 years old*	*10-25 years old*	*Above 25 years old* per-cent women	*Months when intense*	*Since when*	*Treatment: what and where?*	*Notes and causes*
Append-icitis	—	—	4 persons	—	2-3 years	Private doctor at Varanasi	Neglig-ence in food habits
Skin disease	1 person	1 person	1 person	—	5-6 years	Private doctor in the village	Hereditary and tradi-tional medicines
Philaria	—	—	3 people	—	12 years	No treatment	—
Malaria	50 per cent	25 per cent	25 per-cent	July to Sept.	8-10 years	Private doctor in the village	Cause by garbage and mosquito breeding in the village
Pneu-monia	75 per-cent of child-ren below 5 years age	10 per-cent	—	Sept. to Feb.	15-20 years	Private doctor in the village	During winter and during change of season

Village Analysts: Reeta Devi, Rampati Devi, Sabitri and Gulabi.
Facilitator: Ms. Meera Jayaswal.
Date: 17.11.98.

According to residents of Naipurwa, weakness, fever and bodyache cause considerable distress to them. Men rank asthma, weakness and fever and body-ache as the diseases that cause greatest disturbance in the family. Women, however, perceive the flowing ears and pneumonia as the two major disturbing elements in their family life. Differences in perception spring from the fact that men and women view impact of disease from different perspectives. Diseases which prevent men from working outside their homes, have been rated as causing the greatest distress, by men's group. Diseases which render children sick (who are cared for by the women) are rated as most distressing by women, because they are the ones who look after the children, whether ill or healthy, at home.

This disease calendar of Patel Basti, as also the discussion with Naipurwa, is striking in two respects. *One*, the majority of the diseases afflicts children and this was explained by the villagers as being caused by pollution owing to the G.T. Road, along which the village and its school are situated. *Second*, the villagers suffer from a larger number of diseases now than say 5 years ago or so. For example, asthma, appendicitis, skin diseases, stomach-ache, ear and eye problems have afflicted the community since last 5-6 years. The community did associate some of these diseases, particularly those afflicting the children as being caused by pollution created by heavy vehicular traffic on the GT. Road.

XIII. 3. How Do People Deal with Constraints to Agricultural Production?

The responses of the people to cope with the constraints to agriculture are varied.

In case of *Jhulsa/Jhulswa* and *Angarwa,* the affected plants are uprooted. Thus affected crops like paddy, spinach, cauliflower and bottlegourd, are dumped as waste and are neither sold in the open market nor consumed at home, for the simple reason that they are not consumable once infested with insects/pests/disease. For dealing with *flies and insects,* the farmers sprinkle *gamaxin powder (sic)* and spray *rogar (sic).* The attack by nilgais is dealt with by physically guarding the crops during the relevant period, day and night. Rat poisoning is resorted to by the cultivators to get rid of rats but with limited success.

When improved variety of seeds is not available from the Government seed farm, they procure the same from the open market. Since they lack financial resources to fund their operations, the farmers borrow money from the village money lender(s) at exorbitant rates of interest. The problem of erratic rainfall caused by climate change is partly circumvented by lift irrigation through use of diesel and electric pumps.

There is virtually no response to a whole list of other constraints, including paucity of credit, non-availability of seeds and extension services, lack of co-ordination amongst Government Departments dealing with agriculture, lack of irrigation facilities, problem of electric supply, and most significantly, the pollutants discharged by the industries in the industrial estates. It appears than Chandpur has resigned itself to suffer these constraints and deal with whatever is possible at the community level.

In matters of health, the villagers seek the help of private practitioners both in the village and outside the village, including in Varanasi. There is no effort on the part of the community to avail of the services of Government Healthcare facilities. If we recall, the infrastructure available in the village does include a Government Healthcare outlet but the community apparently does not access the available health facilities. This also explains that the villagers spend about 15 per cent of their income on health, which is equal to 50 percent of what they spend on their food, and this for a poor community is an exceptionally high percentage of expenditure. There is no mention of any preventive and promotive health care being accessed. Thus the coping mechanism of the villagers, with their problems of health, as in the case of agriculture, is dependent upon their own resources and effort.

Farmers do not approach higher authorities, if the constraints cannot be removed at the local level.

If we see the coping mechanisms farmers adopt, the modalities are clearly based on self help, as it were. Be it improved variety seeds, credit, irrigation or pest attack, they try and deal with them in their own way. There is no organised action to deal with the problems at higher levels. Thus it is not possible to conclude what are the resources on the basis of which basic attempts to influence are executed such as money, caste/ kinship, information/knowledge, legal rights, public trusts, political friends etc. Similarly one can not say what skills, merits and resources are perceived as necessary to determine success or failure of efforts to remove the constraints.

XIV. Conclusions

From the above discussion the following broad conclusions are possible.

1. Agriculture is an important source of livelihood for the people but may not be categorized as the most important. It provides nearly 30 per cent of village income and provides food for about 4 months. The crops grown are a combination of food and cash crops (in the form of vegetables). Villagers generally have a diversified means of livelihood and do not depend upon any one means of livelihood for sustenance and survival. For example, those who are engaged in agriculture are also engaged in some alternative means of livelihood.
2. Agriculture has become High External Input Agriculture, from Zero External Input Agriculture, even as late as in the 1940s. Though agriculture is still polyculture, crop diversity has declined markedly. These changes have made the farmers vulnerable to both external shocks and to internal risks. Since, agriculture has become high external input agriculture in the 1960s, 1970s, 1980s and the 1990s, agriculture has become a high cost operation venture and the vulnerability of the farmers to external shocks so much more significant.
3. The Industrial Estate near the village has opened up job opportunities for the job seekers, but these job opportunities have not necessarily always gone to the villagers alone, because lot of people from outside have come to Chandpur to take up employment in the Industrial estate under reference. The industrial estate has also disturbed the social capital of the village.
4. There are a large number of constraints faced by the villagers in their agricultural operations, including pest and insect attacks. Cultivators have some system of coping with these based on their

own resources and knowledge. Non-existence of Extension Services and paucity of vital agricultural inputs such as improved variety of seeds, timely irrigation, credit and fertilizers are serious constraints but there is no effort on the part of the community to deal with these beyond what is possible within the community. There are certain constraints like uncertainty/irregularity of rainfall and climatic changes which are way beyond the community's capacity to solve. The output of horticultural products, particularly mangoes and guava, has been reduced to nil, in an area famous for these two fruits in terms of both quantity and quality.

5. Diseases, pests and insects that attack crops have increased over time. The same is true of diseases afflicting human beings. As in the case of agriculture, the community copes with their health problems and tackle health hazards within the confines of their own community and resources. The existence of the State seems to be overlooked by the villagers in their fight for survival, may be because the quality of the care available in Government outlets are so poor that it fails to inspire confidence in the people or that they only exist in paper.
6. The role of the established State institutions in the life of the community is limited and the villagers also do not seek out these services whatever the reasons. The exceptionally high level of yield in the 1960s achieved was by the use of "new technology", viz., use of fertilisers, improved variety of seeds and irrigation. With the increase in yield has come a large number of pests, diseases and insects. The response of the community to remove these pests, insects and diseases has been use of insecticides, pesticides and what the farmers called "killer medicines". There are a large number of constraints to agriculture. The response of the community to remove those constraints has been minimum. There are established institutions to provide support to agriculture, but they are, in the perception of Chandpur farmers, dysfunctional. There is no extension service available and there is no demand for such extension service as well. There is need for state intervention urgently despite the new age of downsizing the state.

Box 2.7
Role of the State

"……..reducing or diluting the state's role can not be the end of reform story. Even with more selectivity and greater reliance on the citizenry and on private firms, meeting a broad range of collective needs and more effectively, will still mean making the State's central institutions work better. For human welfare to be advanced, the state's capability—*defined as the ability to undertake and promote collective action efficiently*—must be increased."

Source: *World Development Report* (Washington D.C.: The World Bank) 1997.

7. Pollution has increased. But the co-relation between pollution and injury to crops is not perceived. Leaf injuries to crops are visible and the insects/ diseases, which cause such injuries, are known but that they are due to air pollution, is not established.
8. There are gender discriminations and gender injustice, and both in terms of leisure/entertainment and workload, the dice is loaded against women.
9. Chandpur has food security for four to five months in a year for people belonging to lower SES. For rest of the year, people suffer from various degrees of hunger. Hunger for the people of Chandpur is at its peak during the months of Jeth (May-June), Asarh (June-July), and Sawan (July-August). The hunger months correspond with the months when people have to work the hardest and have the highest workload.
10. Pollution is perceived to have adverse impact on the state of health in Chandpur.

Figure 1: Map of Chandpur

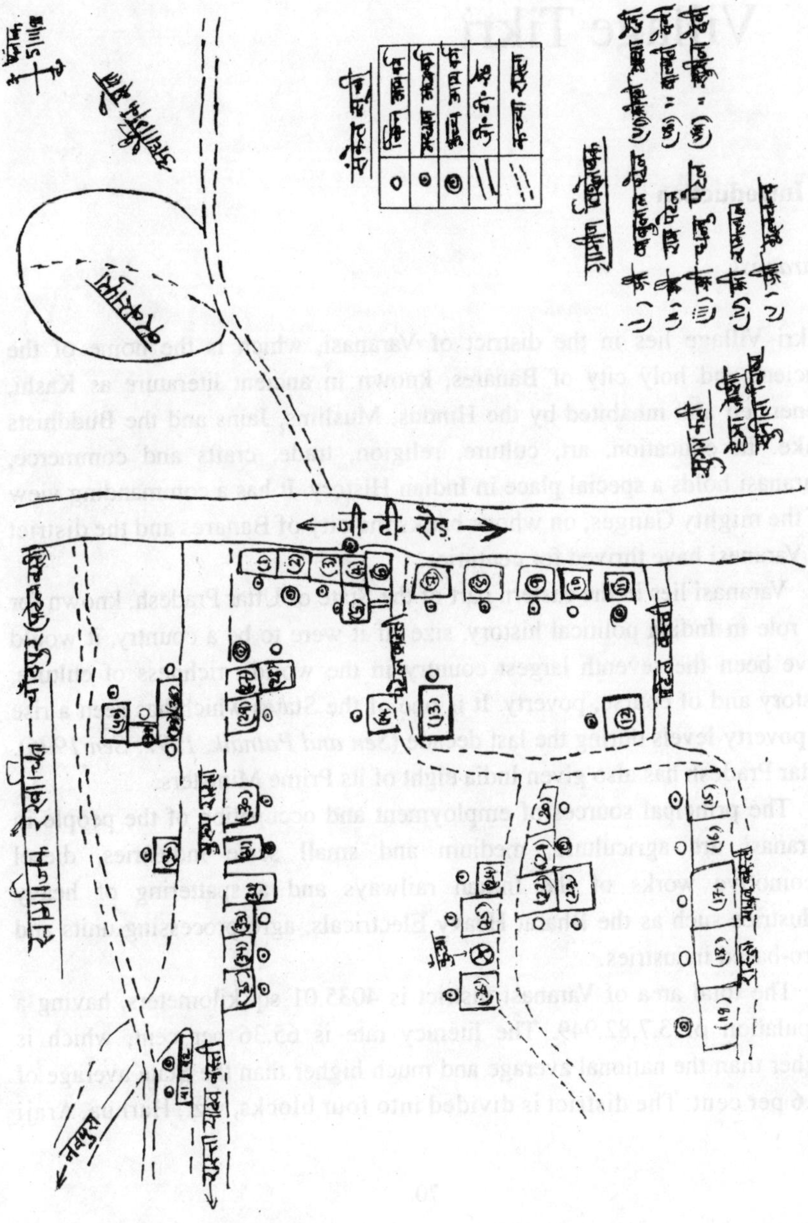

3 A Second Perspective from an Under Developed Region: Village Tikri

I. Introduction

Varanasi

Tikri Village lies in the district of Varanasi, which is the home of the ancient and holy city of Banares, known in ancient literature as Kashi, venerated and inhabited by the Hindus, Muslims, Jains and the Buddhists alike. In education, art, culture, religion, trade, crafts and commerce, Varanasi holds a special place in Indian History. It has a commanding view of the mighty Ganges, on whose banks the city of Banares and the district of Varanasi have thrived for centuries.

Varanasi lies in the eastern part of the State of Uttar Pradesh, known for its role in Indian political history, size (if it were to be a country, it would have been the seventh largest country in the world), richness of culture, history and of course, poverty. It is one of the States which has seen a rise in poverty levels during the last decade (*Sen and Patnaik, 1997; Sen 1996*). Uttar Pradesh has also given India eight of its Prime Ministers.

The principal sources of employment and occupation of the people in Varanasi are agriculture, medium and small scale industries, diesel locomotive works of the Indian railways and a spattering of heavy industries such as the Bharat Heavy Electricals, agro-processing units and agro-based industries.

The total area of Varanasi district is 4035.01 sq. kilometers, having a population of 3,7,82,949. The literacy rate is 65.36 per cent, which is higher than the national average and much higher than the State average of 41.6 per cent. The district is divided into four blocks, viz., Harhua, Araji

Lines, Chirai Gaon and Kashi Vidyapeeth. Tikri Village, which is the subject of our study, falls within the territorial jurisdiction of Kashi Vidyapeeth block. Agriculture in Varanasi is mostly peasant agriculture. The following landholding pattern for Varanasi gives an impression of the situation at hand.

Table 1 Landholding Pattern in Varanasi

Size of Holding	Number of Holdings
Less than 1 hectare	552565 holders
1 to 2 hectares	47619 holders
2 to 3 hectares	11608 holders
3 to 5 hectares	7276 holders
More than 5 hectares	2627 holders

Thus 89 per cent of the farmers hold 1 hectare or less that 1 hectare of land, and 96.5 per cent of the farmers own 2 or less than 2 hectares of land. There are two main seasons, Kharif and Rabi, with a relatively insignificant winter season. The villagers of this village, like villagers of Chandpur generally seemed content from two principal cropping seasons. We will revert back to the subject again later in this chapter.

Kashi Vidyapeeth Block

Kashi Vidyapeeth block consists of around 129 villages of which 122 are inhabited, and they are organised into 13 Panchayats, the smallest unit of governance (local self-government). The occupational structure of the inhabitants of the block exhibit an overwhelming preponderance of labourers and agriculturist and agricultural labourers: 49 per cent of the total population are main workers, 14 per cent are cultivators and about 6 per cent are agricultural labourers. Most of the farmers are small and marginal farmers.

II. General Information

Tikri Village is situated on the banks of the Ganges, at a distance of 12kms from Block Head Quarters, Kashi Vidyapeeth and 6 kms from the Banares Hindu University. It has a total population of 3400, with an unusual sex ratio of 1:1.

Tikri is organized into 13 Bastis or wards: Mahato Basti, Yadav Basti, Chowdhurian Basti, Dherabir Basti, Malah Basti, Tisra Basti, Sato Patti Basti, Brahmin Basti, Maurya Basti, Telyiyan Basti, Atari Basti, Naale Par Basti and Bari Basti. The names of the Bastis indicate that most of the Bastis are organised more or less along caste lines: Harijans (Chamars, Lohars etc.), Mauryas, Mahatos (predominantly vegetable growers), Yadavs (milkmen), Chowdhury, Malah (fisherfolk), Bhumiyars, Brahmins, and Telyia (oilmongers) live in separate Bastis of their own. The village is decidedly a Hindu village. Tikri has been declared as an "Ambedkar Village" and hence has at least 50 per cent of the people belonging to Scheduled Castes.

From a socio-economic perspective, the structural composition of the population of Tikri is remarkably self sufficient in skills: it has farmers, vegetable growers, milkmen, blacksmith, cobblers, fishermen, priests, oilmongers and the landed class. People belonging to different castes are interrelated to each other through exchange of goods and/or services, resources and social interactions. The social and economic interactions between villagers are based on occupational structure. The community in Tikri has almost every skill required for weaving and sustaining the social fabric of a civilised society. That society got fragmented along these lines for different sets of reasons is another matter (*Srinivas, 1955*).

The total area of the village is 1300 acres, of which 100 acres is under orchard, 50 acres is waste land and 50 acres is covered by human habitation. The area under orchard is significant since Varanasi and its adjoining areas are famous for fruits, notably, mangoes and guava. The area under waste land is also alarming, because Tikri is situated right on the Ganges, which makes the soil extremely fertile as the river brings alluvial soil from the higher reaches of the Himalayas. However, the villagers explained that 50 acres of land has become barren because of repeated attacks by Nilgais and hence the villagers have abandoned the land, leading to barrenness and degradation.

The village has four primary schools and two middle schools. It has a health sub-centre in addition to a mother and child centre ("Jachcha Bachch Kendra"). It has a branch of a bank and a Kisan Sewa Kendra is also located in the village. There is also a Post Office. In terms of social overheads, therefore, Tikri is relatively well endowed. (See *Shariff 1999* for a comparative picture.) This does not, however, seem to have any impact on the village: the literacy rate is only 40 per cent though the state average is 47 per cent, 62 per cent for men and 28 per cent for women. And the average number of children per households is 4-6, which indicate non-accessing of health facilities for family planning in general. The general trend in Uttar Pradesh, which has about the lowest contraceptive prevalence rates, for both the termination method and the spacing method *(NSSO, 1992)* conforms to this picture.

Part I. Importance of Agriculture to the People of Tikri

Livelihood

Though Tikri is a large village and is near the urban agglomeration of Banares, the means of livelihood available to the villagers are limited mainly to agriculture, employment either as agricultural labourers or as employees in the service sector and as milk vendors. The traditional professions in which specific groups specialised, are on the decline. The distribution of the population of Tikri amongst various means of livelihood is given in Table 2.

Table 2 Livelihood Activities of Village Tikri

Serial No.	Livelihood Activities	Population Involved (per cent)
1.	Agriculture and Milk Vending	10
2	Agriculture and Labourer	20
3	Agriculture and Services	10
4	Agricultural Labourers	30
5	Out Migrated (Emigrants)	30

Village Analysts: Sushil, Uday Nath, Murli Singh, Meera, Phulwati.
Facilitator: Sudipta Roy.
Date: 2.11.98.

The number of inhabitants dependent on agriculture, partly or wholly is a hefty 70 per cent, which is a shade above the national average of 69 per cent for the country as a whole, according to the last census operations. Incidentally for India, around 70 per cent (give or take 2 per cent) of the people in India have been dependent on agriculture throughout the 20th century, since the 1901 Census, though there is a noticeable declining employment intensity of agriculture (*Singh and Dash, 1999*). In Tikri the picture is same with the additional feature that except for the agricultural labourers (30 per cent of the villagers) others who depend upon agriculture as their primary source of livelihood, all have a secondary means of livelihood as well: either as milk vendors, or as labourers or as providers of services. As a matter of fact only 5 per cent of the villagers have only one source of livelihood; 26 per cent have two; 32 per cent have three; 26 per cent have 4 and 11 per cent have 5 means of livelihood. Within the system of adopting multiple means of livelihood, some people pursue several of these options concurrently while a handful are pursued consecutively at different times in the year. This means that agriculture does not by itself provide subsistence and sustenance throughout the year, to all the villagers, particularly so because many of the farmers (in the district of Banares 96.2 per cent own 2 or less than 2 hectares of land) are small and marginal farmers or tenants. We will deal with the issue again while discussing the economics of agricultural operations in Part V later in this Chapter. The landholding pattern in Tikri is a reflection of the situation obtaining in Varanasi district. The picture looks like Table 3.

Table 3 Landholding Pattern in Tikri

Landholding size	Percentage of Population	Definition
Nil	15	Landless
Less than I.5 Bigha	40-45	—
1.5 to 3 Bighas*	30	Small and Medium Farmers
Above 3 Bighas*	10-15	Large Farmers

****1 Acre is equal to 1.5 Bighas.***

Village Analysts: Kanhaiya Lal, Mangal Singh and Channa.
Facilitator: Sudipta Ray.
Date: 2.11.98.

The picture that Table 3 gives us is that of a village of small and marginal farmers. The number of landless in Tikri compares favourably with the macro picture, the percentage of landless people in India being 11 per cent and in Uttar Pradesh being 4.9 per cent. The number of marginal and small farmers in U.P. stands at 68.01 per cent and 18.52 per cent respectively according to NSS of the 48th round (*NSSO, 1997*). The general situation of landholding in Tikri is, therefore, little worse than Uttar Pradesh as a whole.

Except for the inhabitants of Teliyan Basti, all other Bastis have cultivators. Farmers of Sato Patti, Tisra Patti, Chowdhurian Patti and Dherabir Basti are large or middle sized farmers. The rest of the cultivators are small and marginal farmers. Significantly, only 25 per cent of the cultivators are owner-cultivators. The other 75 per cent are either owner-tenants or pure tenants and the system of landlordism and absentee landlordism, are fairly widespread. The Malahs, Harijans and Yadavs are generally all tenants. This is consistent with the fact that 30 per cent of the inhabitants of Tikri have migrated out of the village and land belonging to the emigrants (some of them) are cultivated either by the landless as pure tenants or by small and marginal farmers (who have 'spare capacity') as owner-tenants. And people belonging to upper castes, namely the Mauryas of Mauryan Basti, Bhumiars of Tisra Patti, Bhumiyars of Sato Patti, Brahmins of Brahmin Patti and Chowdhurys of Chowdhurian Patti, also do not cultivate their landholdings themselves and lease out their land for cultivation to tenants of both varieties.

The tenancy is either on fixed cash rent of Rs. 100 per Biswa per annum, or on share-cropping basis, where the produce is shared in the ratio of 50:50 between the landlords (owners) and the tenants, with landlords providing no input save the temporary usufructory rights on the land to the tenants. All tenants are *hidden tenants* because by law tenancy is forbidden in Uttar Pradesh, whether on the basis of sharecropping or fixed cash rent or fixed output rent (*Kripa Shankar, 1999*). Tikri is a classic example of the reality being far removed from percepts and of a blatant non-implementation of laws that are progressive and pro-productivity.

The total livestock population in Tikri is about 4000 of which the majority are owned by the Yadavs. Of these 60 per cent are buffaloes, 30 per cent are cows/ox and 10 per cent goats. Each Yadav family owns about 20-25 buffaloes. The Yadavs are the ones who sell milk in partial fulfillment of their livelihood needs, which also explains the large size of the herds they own. The large animal population in Tikri, the villagers indicate, is explained by the fact that cultivation is still not mechanised and animal power provides the bulwark of energy required in farming.

Milk vending is also important for the Yadavs as it is a traditional occupation handed down to them for generations. Sale of milk is also part of the livelihood of the Chowdhurians, the difference being that they, unlike the Yadavs, do not sell milk in the nearby township but sell it to the Yadavs who in turn sell the milk to retail buyers in the city. The Yadavs are thus both milk producers and milk traders. The price of milk charged by the Yadavs is constant at Rs. 10-11 per litre in the town throughout the year. The Chowdhurians sell the milk at differential rates: Rs. 14 per litre inside the village and Rs. 22 per litre in the town during *summer* months; and at Rs. 12 per litre inside the village and at Rs. 18-20 per litre during *winter* months. That is, the Chowdhurians modulate the prices of milk according as its supply gyrates: when supply is higher during winter (due to various reasons, including higher productivity and greater availability of green fodder) the prices are lowered; when supply shrinks during the blistering summer months, the prices are hiked. Buyers are prepared to pay a higher price (100 per cent more in the case of the town) for the milk supplied out of Chowdhurian Basti than that supplied by the Yadavs. The price differential being on account of much higher fat content of milk from Choudhurian Basti, making it more suitable for commercial use such as churning butter, manufacturing ghee or making sweatmeats. The higher fat content in milk from milch animals of Chowdhurian Basti is because these animals are stall-fed.

Women work as agricultural labourers, birdi makers and bead necklace makers. Some of these women, especially from the Harijan Basti, are also in the flesh trade. These women prefer to work inside their homes in case their menfolk have sufficient income to take care of the families' needs. Men prefer to work outside the village, in the towns. Working with contractors is the preferred option for those offering their services for a wage because of continuity of service and stability of income. Daily wage earners feel hamstrung by the inflexibility in working environment in jobs available on daily wages and suffer from instability of wages they receive, for when they get to negotiating their daily wage, they are wage takers most of the time. They suffer all the disadvantages of the informal sector (*Mehta, 1997*). Wages earned by different classes of workers are given below in Table 4.

Table 4 Schedule of Wages Payable

Wages per Day	**Rs. in Village**	**Rs. in Town**
For Men		
On Daily Wages	40	80
Mason	100	120
Service	200	
Artificial Pearl Making	Rs. 2 per dozen. Per day Rs. 4-6	
For Women		
Kordai	20	
Deweeding	20	
Paddy Harvesting	7-8 kg Paddy plus a frugal lunch/Rs. 20 p.d.	
Threshing	20-25	
Wheat Harvesting	7-8 kg Wheat plus frugal lunch/Rs. 30 p. d.	
Transplanting	30	

Village Analysts: Amarnath, Pannalal and Ashok Morya.
Facilitator: Meera Jayaswal.
Date: 3.11.98.

Wages earned by men are higher by a wide margin than wages earned by women. The wage differential is explained in part by differences in the nature and content of work done by men and women. Men are generally in semi-skilled work (such as masonry, driving auto-rickshaws) whereas women are in unskilled jobs (like kodai, deweeding, harvesting). And where men engage in unskilled work, such as artificial pearl making, their wage earnings fall dramatically.

The difference in work done by men and women, and the employment structure *per se* of the village mirrors the traditional "inside-home" and "outside-home" syndrome. Most of the employment opportunities for the women are inside their homes whereas most of the employment opportunities for the men are outside their homes. The wage differentials between men and women and also between work in the village and in the towns is significant. The wage rates are more during Rabi season than in Kharif, because, *inter alia*, during Rabi the farmers grow potatoes and with the soil being sandy, the labour input is significantly higher and consequent demand for labour is higher. Additionally, during Rabi, because land brought under wheat cultivation is much higher than in Kharif when the farmers cultivate paddy, demand for labour is pushed up and with it wages rise.

There has been a dramatic change in the livelihood pattern over the last few decades. While in the 1940s, Tikri was predominantly an agrarian society, in the late 1990s, there is a craze for service sector: the less educated seek blue collar jobs on daily wages, the relatively well educated seek jobs with the Government. A section of the Harijan, like the Chamars (cobblers), are no longer interested in their traditional profession as it lacks social respectability. The Lohars (blacksmith), however, continue to practice blacksmithy. Though Malahs would still like to persist with their traditional profession of fishing as a secondary source of income, they fail to do so as the increasing pollution of Ganges has reduced fish breeding. In consequence the Malahs face secularly declining diminishing returns from fishing.

There has been a significant change in the labour market as well. In the 1940s, bonded labourers were a common sight in Tikri, and the Harijans were mostly confined to working within the confines of the village. The situation has changed since. In the 1970s, more particularly during the latter half of the decade, Harijans started moving out of the village in search of work. By the 1980s men stopped working as agricultural labourers, leaving the field for the women only. The attitude of the upper caste has also changed, as they could no longer find all the labourers to complete their tasks, and the practice of hiring labourers from lower castes slowly got acceptance.

Box 3.1

The Ganges—Pure or Polluted?

Myth has it that the goddess Ganga descended to earth in the form of a river, the Ganges, to purify the souls of the 60,000 sons of the ancient King Sagara, who had been burned to ashes by an enraged ascetic......If Ganga originally came to bring salvation to Sagara's 60,000 sons, the poor goddess has ended up with a burden 10,000 times greater than she bargained for. Supporting a staggering 400 million people along its 1560-mile course, the Ganges forms the most populous river basin in the world,....

Today there are more than 29 cities, 70 towns and thousands of villages along the Ganges's banks, depositing nearly all their sewage—more than 1.3 billion litre a day—directly into the river. Another 260 million litre of industrial waste are added to this by the hundreds of factories along the river's banks. All this waste enters the river largely untreated. To the raw sewage and factory effluents are added the runoff from more than 6 million tons of chemical fertiliser and some 9000 tons of pesticides. And the Ganges serves as the final resting-place for thousands of Hindus, whose cremated ashes or half-burned corpses are put into the river for spiritual rebirth.

The result is deeply ironic: the ancient symbol of purity and cleansing has become a great open sewer along much of its length. When the 15th Century poet Kabir wrote of the Ganges, "hell flows along that river, with rotten men and beasts", few would have believed that his impious lament would one day prove so prophetic. But under the 20th century pressures of burgeoning population and industrial growth, the Ganges's cleansing capacity cannot keep up. Toady, in the basin of half a billion souls, purification and pollution swim together in unholy wed lock.

Source: Payal Sampat: *The River Ganges' Long Decline*, Worldwatch, Vol. 9, No. 4, 1996.

Part II. Cropping Pattern

What are the Crops Grown and What is the Cropping Pattern?

There are three cultivation seasons, two major and one minor:

- Summer season from Baisakh to Sawan (mid-April to mid-August) is a minor season;
- Kharif (the monsoon season) running from Bhado to Kartik (mid-August to mid-November) is one of the major seasons and
- Rabi season from Aghan to Chait (mid-November to mid-April) is the most important agricultural season for Tikri.

The principal crops grown during Kharif is paddy, bajra and fodder at the margin. During Rabi, the principal crops cultivated are wheat, vegetables and spices such as ginger, garlic, chilli, fenugreek and coriander. The summer season is of no major significance since only some sundry vegetables are grown such as ninwa (snake gourd), bitter gourd, bottle gourd, cucumber, kakri (another species of cucumber, longer and thinner in shape with a thick outer skin) sugar baby, kohra (pumpkin), lady's finger and moong (a kind of lentil).

The principal crop during Kharif is paddy and the principal crop during Rabi is wheat. The area-wise cropping pattern is as in Table 5.

Table 5 makes an interesting reading. First, Rabi is the major season for the villagers in terms of the area cultivated: only 5 per cent remain fallow. During Kharif as high as 30 per cent of the land is left fallow. Second, in a predominantly rice eating area, wheat is the major crop being cultivated on 90 per cent of the land. Paddy being the second principal crop, is grown on only 30 per cent of land under the plough. Maize, jowar, and bajra are the other coarse cereals produced, but on less than 20 per cent of land. Third, agriculture in Tikri is dominated by food crops and the concept of cash crops has caught on only in the 90s: Potato, cauliflowers, tomatoes etc. are grown for sale in the market during Rabi and that too on only 5 per cent of the land with other vegetables notably brinjals. This is quite surprising given the proximity of Tikri to a major city like Varanasi where a ready market for such crops flourish. The villagers pointed out that cultivation of peas, and maize in particular, have lately increased because of a reduction in the predation by nilgais (an endangered species of large deer).

Table 5 Area-wise Cropping Pattern in Tikri

Kharif (Monsoon)	**Kharif (Monsoon)**	**Rabi (Winter)**	**Rabi (Winter)**	**Summer**	**Summer**
Crop	*per cent of Area*	*Crop*	*per cent of Area*	*Crop*	*per cent of Area*
Paddy	30	Wheat	90	Vegetables	10
Bajra	20	Vegetables: cauliflower, potato, brinjal and spinach	5	Fallow	90
Maize, jowar, bajra, peas, sesame	20	Fallow	5		
Fallow	30				

Source: From field notes of participatory discussion with farmers of Tikri by Sudipta Ray and Meera Jayaswal held on 2.11.98, 3.11.98 and 8.11.98.

The selection of crops is dependent on a number of factors. While most people said that the choice of crop is a function of labour involved, good income, yield and total cost of production, some (Chowdhurys) point out that vulnerability of the crop to disease is an additional factor that influence their decision in this regard. For instance, whether they would grow mustard or not is influenced by the fact that mustard flowers were prone to maho, if the winter days are predominantly cloudy.

What is the Intensity of Cultivation?

Generally during all the three seasons, only one crop is grown on most of the land. It is only during winter that on parts of cultivable land, the villagers grow vegetables, like potatoes in the first round and then plough the land a second time round for growing wheat, along with other lands exclusively deployed in wheat cultivation. Despite being located on the fertile banks of Ganges, the diversity of crops grown is nothing to write home about and the intensity of cropping is not out of the ordinary. Generally, availability or non-availability of water determines cropping intensity, but with no such constraint apparent both in terms of rainfall received and irrigation facility in Tikri, it is intriguing as to why there has been so little diversity and intensity in crop cultivation.

Part III. Agricultural Practices

What Changes in Cropping Pattern and Agricultural Practices have taken Place, if any?

It is important to put in perspective the general socio-economic and political changes that have been faced by the villagers in Tikri, to better appreciate the changes in cropping pattern and agricultural practices. The historical transect by the villagers of Mahato Basti, which is reproduced as Table 6, gives a graphic account of these changes.

Table 6 Time Line: Historical Events as Recalled by Men of Mahato Basti Hamlet of Tikri Village

Period	Events	Cropping Pattern	Agricultural Practices	Crop Care	Agricultural Constraints
1940s	Flood in the village	Bajra, barley, paddy (in limited	Ploughing by ox, irrigation by moat	Yield 4-5 maunds per bigha	Flood from the Ganges

Period	Events	Cropping Pattern	Agricultural Practices	Crop Care	Agricultural Constraints
		quantity), wheat (in limited quantity), gram, peas, & chili (as speciali-sation)	Organic manure in use Traditional seeds used		
1950s	Middle school Started	Same as in 1940s	Aluminum sulphate introduced Tubewell installed for irrigation	Yield 8-10 maund per Bigha	Tirri pest attack on Jowar Kanduwa attack on wheat Flood caused damage
1960s	Brick houses const-ructed	Increased wheat and paddy Cultivation of vegetables like potatoes started	Irrigation by pumpsets fertilisers, new-hybrid seeds and pesticides introduced Tractors came	Same as in 1950s	Gurchawa disease in chilies
1970s	Irrigation canal construc-ted Washed away by floods	Moong, barley, peas grams, chilies, pigeon peas, bajra and sunui dominated cultivation Wheat as second fiddle	Same as in the 1960s	Same as in 1960s, farmers to stop its cultivation	Gurchawa disease in chilies forced

Period	Events	Cropping Pattern	Agricultural Practices	Crop Care	Agricultural Constraints
1980s	Outbreak of measles Increase in fertiliser use Famine in 1986-87 Bank opened	Intensive wheat cultivation overtakes all other crops Cultivation of moong, barley, gram, peas and chili reduced	Same as in the 1970s	Yield 10-15 maunds per bigha	Nilgais damage crops. Rats damaged crops. Diseases like hardwa, jhulsa and gurchawa affecting crops
1990s	1995: Vaccination on mass scale Girl's School started 1997: Metaled roads laid 1998: Hails before Diwali	Wheat, peas, potatoes, paddy, ninua (snake gourd), cauliflower, tomatoes etc. jowar cultivated for fodder only	Same as in the 1980s Weedicides introduced in the farming of wheat	Yield 12-14 maund per bigha for wheat and 10-12 maunds per bigha for paddy	Nilgais and rats damaged crops. Diseases like hardwa, jhulsa & gurchawa, as also pests like dhola and hazari affecting crops**.

**Note that these are the major constraints indicated by the farmers. There are other constraints which they narrated during the analysis and prioritisation of agricultural constraints.

Village Analysts:	Pratap Narain, Hiralal, Radheysham, Ramesh Kumar Patel, Bahadur Patel, Munnalal, Ashok, Krishan.
Facilitator:	Sudipta Roy.
Dates:	2.11.98 and 8.11.98.

In the sixty years covered by the Historical Transect, Tikri has seen major changes generally and in the agricultural sector in particular. In this changing scenario, there are four landmarks in this flow of agricultural history: one, the introduction of Aluminum Sulphate in 1950s and the installation of tubewells for irrigation in the same period: two, the commencement of mechanisation of ploughing and irrigation through use of tractors and pumpsets respectively, introduction of hybrid variety seeds and the beginning of extensive use of fertilisers and of pesticides, in the 1960s; three, for two decades, the 1970s and 1980s, there has been no change in farming systems and four, in the 1990s the substitution of manual weeding by weedicides and proliferation of crops with high salability.

1940s was a decade of indigenous system of farming of zero external input (ZEIA). The 50s was still low external input agriculture (LEIA). Come the 60s, the romanticism of the "new-technology" swamps Tikri, and the entire farming system becomes driven by external inputs: the farmers of Tikri arrived at the age of high external input agriculture (HEIA). And it continues to be so since then until the 1990s, when HEIA was further intensified with the introduction of weedicides. This has also meant that over the years as Tikri migrated from ZEIA to HEIA, the cost of cultivation has gone up perceptibly: whereas in the 1940s and a good deal in the 1950s, much of what was necessary for farming was supplied by the resources of the farmers and by community/common property resources, by the time Tikri stepped into the "new-technology" era of the 1960s, most agricultural inputs used in Tikri had to be bought by the farmers (at prices determined by the market forces) from outside the village. Community and farmers' control over supply of inputs, as a consequence, got substantially diminished in the bargain. If the full implementation of the TRIPS Agreement of the WTO is carried out (which will indeed be the case) then the control of much of what the farmers of Tikri are using as inputs will go into the control of multi-national corporations.

Box 3.2
Strategic Silence

Many farmer-first promoters acknowledge that they are well aware of the points put forward by their critics, but claim they have chosen to remain silent on them for strategic reasons....Recent commentaries and policy statements by some of the most influential thinkers and agencies in the field reveal just how little impact these farmer first arguments have had on some quarters in conventional agricultural research and extension (TAC, 1993). For example, Norman Borlaug (1992), the Nobel Laureate and plant geneticists, writing on the state of agriculture in Africa, has declared:

> Development specialists...must stop 'romanticizing' the virtues of traditional agriculture in the Third World. Moreover, leaders in developing countries must not be duped into believing that future food requirements can be met through continuing reliance on....the new, complicated and sophisticated 'low-input low-output' technologies that are impractical for farmers to adopt.

Would a more theoretically rich and politically sophisticated argument about knowledge, power, research and extension help convince sceptics such as Borlaugh that there is no simple 'techno-fix' just as there is no simple 'participation-fix' to the agricultural problems of the world's resource-poor farmers? We believe it would, particularly if it is accompanied by realistic methodological and institutional alternatives.

Source: Ian Scoons and John Thompson in *Knowledge, power and agriculture—towards a theoretical understanding* in *Beyond Farmer First* (London: Intermediate Technology) 1994

The agricultural practices have had significant influence on the cropping pattern. Because agriculture became HEIA, yield, income and cost of cultivation became the dominant determinants in deciding what crops would be chosen for cultivation; not taste, not cultural acceptability, not nutritional value, not staying power, not even tradition. There are five phases in the cropping pattern:

- Through most of 1940s and 1950s a wide range of crops were grown: bajra, barley, some paddy, some wheat, grams, chilies, peas and the like. There was an unfailing sign of poly-culture and crop diversity.

- In the 1960s, the "new-technology" in agriculture had its influence on Tikri and cultivation of wheat and paddy was increased, and other crops slipped down the ladder of importance. Vegetable cultivation was carried out for sale in the adjoining towns and not for consumption at the household level. It is worth underscoring that paddy and wheat were the two crops in which improved variety of seeds were made available, use of fertilisers was encouraged (read subsidised), and irrigation facilities were provided (and subsidised including credit from the Banks!).
- Then came the 1970s, when again a wide variety of crops (barley, chili, pigeon peas, grams, pea, bajra and sunui) came to be cultivated. Wheat was cultivated but on a limited scale. Again productivity remained at about the same level as was the case in 1960s.
- By the time we come to the 1980s, intensive cultivation of wheat had begun and cultivation of barley, chili, peas and grams fell considerably. This the villagers explained was because the use of fertilisers rendered the soil unsuitable for cultivating these crops. The non-existence of improved variety of seeds in some of crops, such as barley, led to a reduction in farming them. And then the predatory attacks by the nilgais made life for those farmers who cultivated these crops somewhat more difficult.
- In the 1990s, wheat became the dominant crop and those vegetables which had higher commercial value, such as cauliflowers, potatoes, onion, and ninwa came to be included in the cropping pattern, to the exclusion of others. Jowar was still cultivated, not as food crop but for fodder. The yield of wheat increased to 12 maunds per bigha and that of paddy was recorded at 10-12 maunds per bigha.

This chronology of events also indicates that after the seventies, agriculture made a shift towards greater market orientation and less towards meeting household needs.

Why have the Changes taken Place, if at all?

Implements: The most significant change seen by the villagers is the use of implements for ploughing. The introduction of tractors for cultivation was a big change, but farmers still prefer the good old ox and wooden plough, though it costs more to plough the fields that way. The reason being, ploughing the traditional way uproots the weeds completely and helps sunshine and air to penetrate deep into the soil. Most important, the old combination of ox and plough constitute an appropriate technology for Tikri, with most of its cultivators classified as small and marginal farmers, since they enable the farmers to cultivate smaller plots, where tractors can not be operated.

Agricultural Practices: The observed changes in agricultural practices have been caused by several factors. First was the technological change. As supply of improved variety seeds (wheat and paddy) was made possible, as lift irrigation became available and as use of chemical fertilisers was encouraged, the farmers responded to these moves, though not necessarily with higher yield. The farmers apparently did respond to incentives and to technological breakthrough. The use of chemical fertilisers in a village with nearly 4000 animals and the consequent availability of free manure in large quantity, was a surprising change. However, the villagers explained, the use of fertilisers was also "needs driven" because animal dung which used to be available as manure was diverted to alternative use as fuel. The shortage of fuelwood consequent upon loss in bio-mass production and deforestation, had the ultimate effect of diverting animal dung from manure to fuel. Second, the practice of growing of a large number of crops was abandoned because of degradation of soil caused by over/wrong use of chemical fertilisers. The use of fertilisers was not scientifically administered and without support of extension services, which adversely affected soil fertility. Third, the decrease in the forest cover which led to shortfall in supply of fuelwood, also forced the farmers to change the cropping pattern. With the decrease in forest cover, nilgais lost a better portion of their natural source of fodder and therefore, intruded into human habitations in search of food. This brought the predation of the nilgais to the doorsteps of the farmers, who could not deal with these animals the way they would normally deal with these predators, because these were endangered species and killing nilgais is banned. Finally, the change in the employment opportunities and the rise in wages/salaries (which we will discuss later) induced people to leave agriculture and migrate to towns.

What Changes in Yield of Crops have taken Place?

(a) Seasonal and historical trends
(b) Farmers' response to declining yield, if any?

Looking at Table 6 one gets an idea of the changes in yield, indicated by the villagers, of their principal crop, namely, wheat. During the 1940s, the yield was unusually low at 4-5 maunds per bigha. It rose during the 1950s to about 10 maunds and it remained at that level during the next two decades. In the 80s there was a jump to 10-15 maunds per bigha and remained at more or less that level during the 1990s. In Table 6, since people were trying to portray a whole range of changes, they restricted the information on yield to their principal crop, wheat. A better picture emerges from the historical transect of yield drawn up the men of Tikri, which is reproduced as Table 7.

Table 7 Historical Transect of Main Crops and their Yield (Maunds/Acre) in Tikri Village

Main Crops	1940s	1950s	1960s	1970s	1980s	1990s
Monsoon (Kharif) Crops						
Paddy	10	10	20	40	45	50
Maize	30	40	40	50	50	40
Pearl millet (bajra)	10	10	20	25	20	15
Red gram (arhar)	12	12	12	6	3	1
Green gram (moong)	5	5	10	—	—	—
Urad	5	5	10	—	—	—
Kodo	5	5	10	—	—	—
Utalia	5	5	—	—	—	—
Rabi Crops						
Wheat	10	10	20	45	45	50
Barley	10	10	5	—	—	—

Main Crops	1940s	1950s	1960s	1970s	1980s	1990s
Bengal gram	10	10	5	—	—	—
Bare	10	10	5	—	—	—
Peas	10	10	5	2	—	—
Alsi	2	2	2	—	—	—
Mustard	3	3	3	2	1	0.50

Village Analysts: Pannalal, Kanhaiyalal, Laxman Mourya, Musseram and Chhatanki..
Facilitator: Meera Jayaswal.
Date: 6.11.99.

Table 8 Historical Transect of Vegetable Yields (Maund/Acre) by Men of Tikri

Main Vegetables	1940s	1950s	1960s	1970s	1980s	1990s
Potato	150	150	150	200	200	250
Chilies	5	5	5	—	—	—

Village Analysts: Pannalal, Kanhaiyalal, Laxman Mourya, Musseram and Chhatanki.
Facilitator: Meera Jayaswal.
Date: 6.11.98.

If we compare Tables 7 and 8, clearly there has been changes both in terms of diversity and yield. The number of Rabi crops got reduced to 2 in the 1990s, from 7 in the 1940s, 1950s and 1960s. It came down initially to 3 in the 1970s and then from the 1980s it got to 2. Similarly in case of Kharif crops, from a basket of 8 crops grown in 1940s, by the time Tikri reached the 70s, the basket had only 4 crops, a pattern that continues today. Similarly with vegetables, as only potatoes are grown as the main vegetable. Reduction in crop diversity means, that distribution of risk has also shrunk and the vulnerability of the farmers to natural or man made calamity has increased. It has led to the abandonment of several time tested practices known to the community such as crop rotation which is possible when a large number of and different kinds of crops are grown, for restoration of soil vitality and reduce the risk of failure (See *Murakami* 1991; *Wijewardene,* 1994).

Prior to 1960s (pre-new-technology or "Green Revolution" days), the villagers explained, they practiced crop rotation, field rotation, mixed cropping, rotational grazing and applied green manure to ensure better yield from farming. Field rotation and rotational grazing were complementary activities: fields were left fallow deliberately for restoring nutritional strength of the soil and allowing animals to graze on fallow fields, a process which also naturally manured the fields from animal droppings. Depending on the nature of the crops, farmers cultivated crops in a series sequence to ensure that subsequent crop replenished nutrients used by the earlier one. And in some cases, crops were cultivated concurrently in the same field for reasons similar to crop rotation. For instance, mustard and wheat were farmed concurrently. Grass was grown in the arable areas, to be ploughed back into the same fields to manure them. After the 1960s (post-new-technology or "Green Revolution" days), these systems lost out to the use of chemical fertilisers, improved variety of seeds etc. These had several adverse consequences in several parts of the country classified as the "violence of the Green Revolution" (*Shiva*, 1991) though these were not mentioned by the farmers of Tikri.

Nevertheless yield did show distinct changes. Take the case of paddy. With the onset of new-technology in the 1960s, the yield jumped by 100 per cent and then again by another 100 per cent between 1960s and 1970s: Paddy yield increased from 10 maunds per acre in the 1950s to 50 maunds per acre in the 1990s. Thereafter, the increase in yield has been more modest. In case of wheat the pattern is similar. Yield jumped up from 10 maunds per acre in the 1950s to 20 maunds per acre in the 60s and then to 45 maunds per acre in the 70s and then it more or less stabilised at that level till date. In this case too, yields seem to have responded to the introduction of new-technology. As a matter of fact all crops grown during Kharif have recorded remarkable growth in yield. For Rabi, it is different. Except for wheat which has shown remarkable increase in yield as well, all other crops have recorded a secularly falling yield, with decline in yield from peas being most dramatic: from 10 maunds per acre in the 1950s, it has come down to 2 maunds per acre in the 1970s.

The variation in yields has also been influenced by the variations in the quality and kinds of agricultural inputs applied by the farmers. A detailed discussion of this aspect will be made in the section on agricultural inputs below. Suffice it to say for the present that farmers of Tikri indicated that prior to 1960s yield was low because there was total dependency on Monsoons for water, which often betrayed the farmers. After the introduction of the pumpsets, water supply was guaranteed through assured irrigation. The system of field rotation prior to 1960 also meant that some fields would be deliberately left uncultivated, which resulted in lower returns to the farmer from agriculture per year. The older system of farming may have been more sustainable but was poorer in terms of yield per acre.

Part IV. Agricultural Inputs

What are the Cultivation Processes?

The cultivation process is different for the two main seasons. For Kharif, the principal crop is paddy. The cultivation process is as under;

- The process starts in *May-June* every year. A small piece of land (called "Beehengardhi") is chosen as nursery for growing seedlings. Farmers grow their own seedlings.
- In *June-July,* once the monsoons set in, cultivation starts and by and large farmers concentrate solely on paddy. It is a multiple step operation. First the fields are ploughed, usually two to three times. Then the lumps of earth are broken down, called "Karha", followed by puddling, through a process called "Kurhol". Once puddling is completed, paddy seedlings are uprooted from the "Beehingardi" and transplanted on to the fields. The ridges of all the fields are repaired. The first dose of fertilizers and/or some manure is applied. As secondary activity, farmers plant brinjals, tomatoes, bottle goud, pumpkin and "seam", a kind of bean mostly in kitchen gardens.
- In *August and September* deweeding operation is carried out, usually more than once depending on the need. These are the months during which second/third doses of fertilizers and limited amount of manure are applied, after deweeding, depending upon the capacity of the farmers to bear the expenses.

- During *October* we have the big harvesting season. Paddy is harvested and post harvest operations like threshing, winnowing, dehusking and pounding follows.
- Once the harvesting of paddy ends, green grams are sown in *October-November*. During these months the farmers sow potatoes, radish and cauliflower.

(vi) During *November-December*, potato fields are tilled. Cauliflower seedlings are transplanted and radish is harvested. This is the period when early variety wheat is sown. A moderate quantity of green peas is also sown and seedlings of onion are planted. Generally farmers procure onion seedlings from outside their farms.

(vii) *December-January* are the months when attention is concentrated on wheat just as undivided attention is given to paddy cultivation during June-August. The wheat fields are tilled once again, deweeding is carried out and fertilizer is applied. Fields are irrigated.

(viii) During *January-February*, a second round of irrigation is applied to the *early-variety* wheat. This is also the time when *late-variety* wheat is sown. The second dose of fertilizer is applied to *early-variety* wheat fields. Green peas sown in the months of November-December, is now harvested. The first harvest of potatoes (sown in *October-November*) is reaped.

(ix) *February-March* is the time for the third round of irrigation to be provided to the *early-variety* wheat. In case flowering starts, another round of fertilizer is applied. A second round of green peas is harvested. Irrigation is applied to onion fields.

(x) *March-April* is again harvesting season. Wheat is harvested. onion and garlic are also harvested. Green gram is also harvested.

The perception of men and women about the seasonality of agricultural activities differ in some detail. This is best illustrated by the two activity calendars prepared by men and women separately for Morya Hamlet, Tikri Village. The Activity Calendar is at Table 9.

Table 9 Agricultural Activity Calendar

Men's Description		Women's Description	
Months	**Activity**	**Months**	**Activity**
Jeth (May-June)	Sowing paddy seeds	Jeth (May-June)	—
Asard (June-July)	Paddy transplantation (women only)	Asard (June-July)	Paddy transplantation. Sowing vegetable seeds.
Sawan (July-August)	Paddy transplantation (women only)	Sawan (July-August)	Paddy transplantation. Sowing vegetable seeds.
Bhado (August-September)	Sowing and planting spinach (women only)	Bhado (August-September)	Deweeding paddy and vegetable fields. Vegetable transplantation.
Kaur (September -October)	Sowing cauliflower seeds	Kaur (September -October)	Deweeding paddy and Vegetable fields. Vegetable transplantation.
Kartick (October-November)	Sowing wheat seeds	Kartick (October-November)	Paddy harvesting, threshing and carrying to storing place. Deweeding vegetable fields. Harvesting matured vegetables. Sowing potato.
Aghan (November-December)	Sowing cauliflower and spinach	Aghan (November-December)	Paddy harvesting, threshing and carrying to storing place. Deweeding vegetable fields. Harvesting matured vegetables. Sowing potato.

Men's Description		**Women's Description**	
Months	**Activity**	**Months**	**Activity**
Push (December -January)	Sowing seeds of late variety wheat	Push (December -January)	Deweeding vegetable farms. Land preparations for wheat cultivation. Gathering matured vegetables.
Magh (January -February)	Sowing seeds of late variety wheat	Magh (January -February)	Deweeding vegetable farms. Wheat cultivation. Gathering matured vegetables.
Fagun (February -March)	Wheat harvesting (women only)	Fagun (February -March)	Deweeding wheat fields
Chait (March -April)	Wheat harvesting (women only)	Chait (March -April)	Wheat harvesting. Carrying wheat grains for storing. Cleaning wheat farm.
Baisakh (April-May)	Sugarcane plantation	Baisakh (April-May)	Wheat Harvesting. Carrying wheat grains for storing. Cleaning wheat farm.

Village Analysts: Amarnath, Ashok, Pannalal Morya for analysis by men.
Village Analysts: Kusum Devi, Anita, Jali and Urmila for analysis by women.
Facilitator: Dr. Meera Jayaswal.
Date: 5.11.98.

The cultivation processes for paddy and wheat are quite involved, requiring tilling, weeding, applying irrigation and fertilizers and a lot of incidental activities in maintaining the fields intact and protecting the crops from damage due to animal predation and human trespassing etc. Men and women have a division of functions on who does what. Naturally men's group and women's group chose to describe different activities. Because men were eager to highlight what they saw were the more important elements of the agricultural processes, and women highlighted what they thought were more critical elements in farming practices, there are differences in activity calendars prepared by men's and women's groups.

In the above description, there is no mention of the use of use of either herbicides, or insecticides or pesticides. This does not imply that there is no application of these in Tikri; it only emphasizes the fact that in terms of effort and time required to apply these "medicines", they do not constitute a very important set of activities. We will discuss more of it while discussing constraints.

While deweeding is done to obviate the need for use of deewicide no apparent steps are taken to take care of the problems of either pests or insects, except for minor applications of *gamaxine (sic)* and *dalidal (sic)*. The practice of soil testing is non-existent and there is no technical way of deciding upon both, the quantum and kind of chemical fertilizers that need to be applied to different crops. Since the number of animals has dwindled over the last few years that we discussed earlier, availability and hence application of manure and compost are limited. This has possibly led to an imbalance in the chemical composition of land, resulting in a fall in yield during the 1980s and 1990s, after the initial spurt in the 1970s, as noted earlier. This requires further investigation. Though improved varieties of seeds have been introduced, the agricultural processes remain the traditional ones, except for the substitution of animal power by mechanical power in ploughing the agricultural lands and use of pumps for irrigation.

What are the Agricultural Inputs and how does the Economics of the Input Work out?

The agricultural inputs being currently used by the farmers as also as they were used over the years is described in the historical transect of inputs as reported in Table 10. The economics of agricultural inputs would be different for different crops. For the sake of brevity, we will discuss the economics of agricultural inputs in relation to paddy and wheat, the principal crops of the Kharif and Rabi Seasons, of milk vending and vegetable cultivation. Reference is invited to Tables 11, 12, 13, 14, and 15.

Table 10 Historical Transect of Agricultural Inputs in Tikri

Decade	Wheat Seeds	Paddy Seeds	Potato Seeds	Fertilisers/ Manure etc.	Irrigation	Disease	Medicines
1940	Local	Local	Local	Dung, Green (Savai)	Bullock	No	No
1950	Local	Local	Darjeeling	Dung, Green (savai)	Bullock	No	No
1960	Imported (Mexico)	Imported	Darjeeling	Chemical (chand) Brand-Sindri	Pumpset	Very few	No
1970	Imported Malwi 34 Malwi 36 RR 21	Pant 4 Saket 4	Local	Alumi-nium Sulphate, Zinc and Potash	Pumpset	Increased	Yes Gamaxine (sic)
1980	Imported Malwi 34 Malwi22 RR 21, RR 2003	BHU	Local	Aluminium Sulphate Zinc and Potash	Pumpset	Increased	Gamaxin and Dalidal (sic)
1990	Imported Malwi 234, 236, 2003 and Malwi 2285	BHU	Imported	Urea, Dye, Potash, Calcium, Sulphate, Zinc	Pumpset	Very high	Gamaxin and Dalidal and Roger (sic)

Village Analysts: Pannalal, Kanhaiyalal, Laxman Morya, Musseram, Chhatanki. *Facilitator*: Meera Jayaswal. *Date:* 6.11.98.

Table 11 Return from Agricultural Operation Per Biswa Paddy: (1 Biswa = 0.16 Acre)

Inputs	**Rate or Cost Per Unit**	**Quantity Used**	**Total Cost**
Seeds	Rs. 100 per kg	1 kg	Rs. 100
Fertilisers			
Dye	Rs. 40 per kg	1 kg	Rs. 40
Potash	Rs. 5 per kg	5 kg	Rs. 25
Urea	Rs. 4 per kg	15 kg	Rs. 60
Deweeding	Rs. 20 per day per person	6 labourer for 1 day	Rs. 120
Harvesting	Rs. 20 per person per day	5 labourer for 1 day	Rs. 100
Threshing	Rs. 20 per person per day	3 labourer for 1 day	Rs. 60
Kutai (Dehusking)	Rs. 25 per quintal	**	Rs. 60
Total Cost	—	—	Rs. 555
Yield	2 quintals Paddy = 1 quintal Rice	Rs. 1700 per quintal of Rice	Rs. 1700
Net Return	—	—	Rs. 1700-Rs. 555 = Rs. 1145

Note: This table does not include the cost of ploughing as it is provided by family labour.

Village Analysts: Amarnath Morya, Ashok Morya and Pannalal Morya and others.
Facilitated by: Ms. Meera Jayaswal.
Date: 3.11.98.

Table 12 Return from Agricultural Operation: Vegetables

Net Return	***Period***	***Total Net Return***
Rs. 1000 per Month	Six Months	Rs. 6000

Village Analysts: Amarnath Morya, Ashok Morya and Pannalal Morya and others.
Facilitated by: Ms. Meera Jayaswal.
Date: 3.11.98.

Table 13 Return from Agricultural Operation Per Biswa: Wheat (1 Biswa = 0.16 Acre)

Inputs	Rate or Cost Per Unit	Quantity Used	Total Cost
Seeds	Rs. 12 per kg	3 kg	Rs. 36
Fertilisers			
Dye	Rs. 8 per kg	5 kg	Rs. 40
Urea	Rs. 4 per kg	5 kg	Rs. 20
Potash	Rs. 5 per kg	3 kg	Rs.15
Ploughing	Rs. 20 per ploughing	4 times	Rs.80
Harvesting	Rs. 30 per person per day	5 labourer for 1 day	Rs. 150
Threshing	Rs. 25 per maund	6 maenad	Rs.150
Irrigation	Rs. 10 per hour	8 hours on three occasions	Rs. 240
Total Cost	—		Rs. 731
Yield	6 quintals Wheat	Rs. 700 per quintal of Wheat	Rs. 1680
Net Return	—	—	Rs. 1680-731 = Rs. 949

Note: This table does not include the cost of ploughing as it is provided by family labour.

Village Analysts: Amarnath Morya, Ashok Morya and Pannalal Morya and others.
Facilitated by: Ms. Meera Jayaswal. *Date*: 3.11.98.

Table 14 Return from Agricultural Operation: Milk per Buffalo

Expenditure Head	Rate; Sale/Purchase Price	Total
Fodder 6 kg per day	Rs. 3 per kg	Rs. 3 times 6 times 30 = Rs. 540
Grass/oil cakes etc.	—	Lump Sum Rs. 300
Total cost	—	Rs. 840
Milk yield 4 liters per day	Rs. 11 per liters.	Rs. 11 times 4 times 30 = Rs. 1320
Net return		Rs. 1320 less Rs. 840 = Rs. 480
Imputed labour costs	Rs. 20 per day for 20 days	Rs. 600
Final net return	—	Rs. 120 (Net Loss)

Note: This table does not include the cost of ploughing as it is provided by family labour.

Village Analysts: Amarnath Morya, Ashok Morya and Pannalal Morya and others.
Facilitated by: Ms. Meera Jayaswal. *Date:* 3.11.98.

If we summarise these tables, it is apparent that:

- Return per annum from paddy farming is Rs. 1145 per biswa, from wheat farming it is Rs. 949 per biswa, from vegetable cultivation it is lump sum of Rs. 6000 per annum average.
- For those engaged in dairy business, they earn Rs. 480 per month per buffalo, without taking into account their labour cost.
- For those engaged in artificial pearl making they earn Rs. 1800 per year.
- Assuming that a person is employed for 15 days a month, the earnings from daily wages for men is Rs. 7200 per year, whereas women would make about Rs. 3600 per year.
- If a person is gainfully employed with a regular employer the person earns Rs. 6000 per month or Rs. 72000 per year.

From the cultivation process discussed above the inputs into agriculture sought by farmers of Tikri can be easily deduced. Clearly some inputs would come in the nature of "public" good or "free" good, such as soil fertility, sunshine, rains; and some in the nature of purchased inputs: be they seeds, fertilizers/manure, insecticides, pesticides, water and water lifting devices, labour and tractor. The nature of agricultural inputs has changed over time, which is consistent with various trends we have noticed earlier. As we noted earlier agriculture moved from greater diversification to lesser so, and as Tikri saw the introduction of "new technology", agriculture moved from ZEIA (Zero External Input Agriculture) to LEIA (Low External Input Agriculture) and then to HEIA (High External Input Agriculture). What impact this movement had on sustainability, one cannot say for sure, but agriculture in Tikri has become much more dependent on outside sources for inputs into farming. In the process agriculture has become much more expensive. In the 1950s, the inputs in agriculture were livestock dung and green manure, ox available in the village for ploughing, irrigation by the wheelbarrow and harvesting rainwater, traditional variety of seed saved from earlier year's harvest and local, mostly family labour.

There was no use of imported seeds, chemical fertilisers, insecticide, herbicide, weedicides and pesticides, or at least the villagers did not perceive their presence. But as the external content of agricultural inputs increased so did the cost of operation. A comparison of the net return from growing paddy and wheat and milk vending with the wages earned and the salaries received (as set forth in Table 16), gives an indication of why the younger generation move out of the village and absentee landlordism is on the rise. The movement of agriculture from ZEIA to HEIA also means that the vulnerability of the farmers of Tikri to external shocks has increased, and their and their community's control over the supply of quality agricultural inputs has been nearly extinguished. The increased vulnerability of agriculture to external shocks could play havoc with the lives of farmers. Indeed, if we see Table 21 it is apparent that farmers are already experiencing constraints to agriculture on account of poor supply of electricity, adulterated fertilisers and spurious insecticides. That is, the farmers are dependent upon Uttar Pradesh state electricity board to run their pumps for irrigation; on the fertilizer companies and their dealers for supply of nutrients to the soil; the insecticide companies and their dealers for tackling the problems of plant diseases and on seed manufacturers for supply of seeds. If the current phase of globalisation is taken to its logical end, which probably will happen, farmers in Tikri will be rendered dependent upon transnational companies and their dealers for supply of many more of their inputs, adding to not only costs but other externalities associated with such dependence. When we add to the picture, facts about dwindling diversity of crops, any hope of preventing Tikri farmers from widely diffusing risks of farming is likely to be turned into a nightmare. Farming is not only more risky but also more open to disturbance due to external shocks.

As farming in the 1980s and 1990s has become more dependent on sourcing from outside Tikri, farming has come to use resources that are not always renewable. Internal resources are "inherently renewable and thus have the potential to be used on a 'sustained' basis, indefinitely, through ecologically sound methods of farming" (*Conway and Barbier, 1990*). Seeds saved from earlier harvests, manure from animal dung, irrigation by wheel and bullocks/buffalo and harvesting rain water, ox and the wooden hoe for ploughing, and of course family labour are all renewable. They have the inherent property of being used on a sustainable basis through ecologically sound methods of farming. This is not the case with HEIA currently practiced.

Table 15 Schedule of Wages Payable

Wages per Day	**Rs. in Village**	**Rs. in Town**
For Men		
On daily wages	40	80
Mason	100	120
Service	200	
Artificial pearl making	Rs. 2 per dozen. Per day Rs. 4-6	
For Women		
Kordai	20	
Deweeding	20	
Paddy harvesting	7-8 kg Paddy plus a frugal lunch	
Threshing	30	
Wheat harvesting	7-8 kg Wheat plus frugal lunch per day	
Transplanting	30	

Village Analysts: Kusum Devi, Anita , Urmila , Jali, Amarnath Morya, Ashok Morya and Pannalal Morya and others.
Facilitated by: Ms. Meera Jayaswal.
Date: 4.11.98.

Since agriculture in Tikri has become dependent on external resources, much of it is not provided as a "free good", implying that the farming households must buy them and hence must generate a surplus of production, cash or whatever else of value to exchange for external resources. And the cost of acquiring these resources and their supply channels are beyond the control of farming households. This has at least three cost implications as in the case of Chandpur, in terms of open costs, hidden costs and real costs.

The transition from ZEIA to LEIA and eventually to HEIA, has made agriculture a high *open* cost venture because the farmer has to buy most of the inputs to agriculture as in the case of Chandpur.

The transition from ZEIA to HEIA has also made a noticeable impact on the *hidden* cost of operation for agriculture in Tikri as in the case of Chandpur.

High external input agriculture, it is important to note entails a lot of *real costs*. Even where there is no direct monetary outgoing to acquire an input, there may be real cost incurred by the farming household. The most obvious examples are the time used for obtaining seeds and other inputs from local distributors in Varanasi or Kashi Vidyapeeth Block Office; time expended in fetching diesel for pumpsets (in case the pumpsets are not electricity operated); chasing the Uttar Pradesh state electricity board employees for restoration of power when power failure occurs etc. and loss of crops when any of the inputs are either not available or not available in time. Because in case of HEIA, farmers have no control over prices and supply of inputs, the impact of increased real costs is substantial. The uncertainty it injects adds to the problems of peasant farming.

And then this transition also means chemicalisation of agriculture. Right from different kinds of chemical fertilisers and to some extent insecticides/pesticides applied directly to the fields and used elsewhere, agriculture has come to include in its inputs a whole range of chemicals. The impact of such chemicals on soil chemistry may not be currently perceived as important in Tikri. Nevertheless it requires attention for agricultural history in different parts of the country is replete with instances where such a transition has caused damage to land leading to fall in productivity, a phenomenon poetically called "Yellowing of the Green Revolution".

Part V. Class

Who are the Landowning and the Landless Groups?

While discussing the structural composition of the population of Tikri and the importance of agriculture in Tikri we have briefly touched upon these issues. The pattern of settlement in the village is a clear indication of landowning and the landless classes. Tikri is a multi-caste village and caste composition of the village gives a fairly good approximation of the landless and land-owning groups. In Tikri, generally, the Telys, Harijans, Chamars, Lohars, Malahs and the Yadavs comprise the landless people and many of them are hidden tenants. As mentioned above, about 15 per cent of the people in Tikri are landless. These are the people who are categorised as belonging to scheduled castes (SC) and other backward castes (OBC). The upper castes comprising the Brahmins, Bhumiars, Mauryas, Chowdhurians and inhabitants of Dherabir Basti are the landowing classes. Many of the emigrants also own lands but do not till their own lands. Tenants cultivate landholdings of emigrants.

Is there Any overlap Between Landownership with Produce Ownership?

With such a neat classification of landless and landowning lasses, it is easy to see that there is some overlap between landownership and produce ownership. The landowning people do not cultivate all the land they own and they lease out their land. It may be recalled that 75 per cent of the people in Tikri are some form of tenants and, only 25 per cent of the population are owner cultivators. There are five kinds of tenancy systems and land-produce ownership pattern found. Firstly those who own and cultivate their land fully, have a complete overlap between landownership and produce thereof. They have in Amartya Sen's terminology endowment entitlements. Secondly, those who own land but have leased it out on share cropping ("Bataidari"). These people have exchange entitlement. In this case there is 50 per cent overlap between landownership and produce, because under the tenancy agreement, output is shared between the tenants and landlords (read landowners) on a 50:50 basis. Thirdly, we have those who own land but lease it out on fixed cash rent. There is, in these cases, no overlap between landownership and produce because the land owner is only entitled to an agreed fixed rent specified in monetary terms. The fourth category have to include those who own land but lease it out on fixed rent expressed as a fixed quantity of the produce ("Dana Bandi"). Here the overlap between land-ownwership and produce is only partial. The fifth category would have been the bonded labourers, who cultivated their own land without any right to the produce. It has been reported that bonded labour has been abolished and no longer tarnishes the image of Tikri, though there are reasons to believe that this may not be a true and fair account of the state of affairs. It needs further examination.

On the whole, there is, therefore, a continuum of convergence or overlap between land ownership and produce ownership, though law in Uttar Pradesh prohibits the divergence between land ownership and produce ownership as tenancy is illegal. But as in many other cases, the law is followed more in the breach than in its observance, and this makes all the tenants, concealed tenants.

Are there Migrant Labourers in Agriculture and Migrant Leasees?

Though there is considerable variation in the kinds of cultivators we have in Tikri, there is no evidence of migrant leasees or of migrant labourers in agriculture. With 15 per cent of the population landless and 89 per cent of the farmers, small and marginal, with plenty of "spare farming capacity", there is no dearth of agricultural labourer. The *prioritised* constraints identified in the different Bastis of Tikri also do not include lack of agricultural labourer as a major problem, though it is included in the first list prepared. However, during peak agricultural season, when demand for labour suddenly jumps up, temporary shortage of labour is experienced which is tackled by hiring labour from neighbouring villages/hamlets. Such shortages do not attract migrant labourers. As a matter of fact 30 per cent of the villagers are emigrants, some of whom in search of employment outside the village. Data on migration consistently reveal that throughout India, the migration is from the rural to the urban areas in search of better employment opportunities, and rarely from rural to rural areas and none from urban to rural areas. The poverty of one village is hardly attractive to those who live in poverty in another area to migrant. Our villages, dependent on land and agriculture, do not offer employment opportunities of the kind and scale that appears reasonably good to induce influx of migrants from other villages. Indeed in most of agriculture, there is disguised unemployment. Therefore, from first principles, migration into a poor village like Tikri is unlikely.

The situation is perhaps no different for migrant leasees as well, but there was no direct investigation of this issue. Since leasing of land for agricultural purposes is an illegal activity, it is easier for an insider to live as a concealed tenant, than for an outsiders. There are, thus, very strong negative incentives against migrant leasees.

Box 3.3
A Real Life Story of the 1930s from a Compassionate Hunter

"The hut is on the ridge of the high hill overlooking Mohan, and as I approached it along the level stretch of road running across the face of the hill, in turning a corner in a ravine where there is some dense undergrowth, I came on a woman filling an earthenware pitcher from a little trickle of water flowing down a wooden trough. Apprehending that my approach on rubber-soled shoes would frighten her, I coughed to attract her attention, noticed that she started violently as I did so; and a few yards beyond her, stopped to light a cigarette. A minute or two later I asked, without turning my head, if it was safe for anyone to be in this lonely spot, and after a little hesitation the woman answered that it was not safe but that water had to be fetched and as there was no one in the home to accompany her, she had come alone. Was there no man? Yes there was a man but he was in the fields ploughing, and in any case *it was the duty of the women to fetch water*."

Jim Corbett
While telling us his story of trying to Kill the Mohan Man Eater, in the Kumaon Hills of Uttar Pradesh.
"The Man Eaters of Kumaon" (Emphasis Added)

Part VI. Gender

Difference in the Tasks Carried out by Men and Women

That both men and women work hard in villages is a reality. Nevertheless the tasks performed by the two are different. We will discuss this issue here only in relation to agricultural activities and farming practices. It is almost an axiomatic truth in Indian villages, and in Uttar Pradesh in particular, that most of household activities, viz., cooking, cleaning, collecting fuelwood, collecting potable water, collecting fodder, child bearing and rearing, looking after the sick, disabled and the old at home, are the responsibility of the women. And this has remained virtually unchanged for centuries. They also participate in equal measure in agricultural operations along with men.

Let us refer back to Table 9. The first two columns are activities described by men and the third and the fourth columns are the agricultural activities described by women. In both cases, though details differ, yet the number of tasks carried out by women are more, even according to men. And this did not appear strange to them: the men were socially conditioned to believing that women have to do what they are doing. Men's thinking is also psychologically constructed to think that they do shoulder a fair share of their responsibility in the farms and in the households, and that there is no need to change the equilibrium.

Box 3.4
Male Bias

"Overcoming male bias is not simply a matter of persuation, argument, change in viewpoint in everyday attitudes, in theoretical reasoning, and in policy process. It also requires changes in the deep structures of economic and social life, and collective action, not simply individual action."

Diane Elson in *Male Bias in the Development Process,* 1991

If we read Tables 15 with Table 9, the division of work is clearly demarcated. Mason's work, work in the service sector, Pearl making etc. fall in the domain of male work. Ploughing of fields, applying fertilizers, irrigation, "Karha", "Khurhol", repairing of ridges, carrying harvested crops from the field to the granary ("Khalihan") and preserving seeds for next year's cultivation etc. are all primarily the work of men. As against this, Kodai, transplantation of seedlings, deweeding, paddy harvesting, wheat harvesting, threshing, winnowing, paddy husking and paddy pounding lie in the women's domain. In addition they work for supplementary income in Tikri on Garland Making etc., often late into the night. The figure (figure 2) drawn by the villagers of Morya Basti of Tikri, depicting the length of working hours for men and women separately, clearly bears this division of activities. The diagram brings home the fact that all our village folks are early risers: their day begins at about 4 a.m. and then for men it ends at sundown at about 6 p.m., but women work till almost midnight. Within this working day men have rest in the afternoon and then recreation and leisure during the evenings, but women have none of it. Not only are there differences in tasks carried out by men and women, but that there are differences in hours of leisure, entertainment, complexity and arduousness of the tasks as well. Always to the disadvantage of the women.

Part VII. Significance of Agriculture.

What is the Significance of Agriculture in Urban and Peri-urban Areas in Terms of: Employment (Part-time or Full-time), Food Security, Income and Others?

Employment The capacity/potential of agriculture to provide employment is unmistakable, given the composition of the village population, notwithstanding that 30 per cent of the people seek employment outside the village.

Classification of Poor In the circumstances of Tikri where people lease-out and lease-in land, *ipso facto* all inhabitants can not be food insecure. The poor people would be the ones who would probably be the real sufferers. It would be useful to refer to the classification provided by the villagers of Morya of those who were poor and those who were non-poor. They used five criteria to classify people as falling in three classes *Garib* (Low SES), *Kamate-Khate* (Middle SES) and *Amir* (High SES): size of land holding; condition of house and its physical facilities; economic status; facilities provided to their children and capacity to meet the expenses for "social function". Based on the above criteria the villages arrived at the classification of the inhabitants of Tikri as at Table 16.

Food Security We need not labour the point that the issue of food security concerns people belonging to Lower SES. Food Security will neither bother people belonging to Middle SES nor to Higher SES. We would, therefore, examine the issue of food security in the context of people belonging to Lower SES only. This does not, however, mean that all people belonging to Middle and Higher SES, are food secure. Because of disparity in intra-familial distribution of power and because of traditions and customs, in

Table 16 Characteristics of Low, Middle and High Socio-Economic Strata (SES) in Morya

Criteria	*Low SES*	*Middle SES*	*High SES*
Landholding	**Less than 5 Biswa**	**5 Biswa to 1 Acre**	**More than 1 Acre**
Condition of the house	Clay built. Single storied. No toilet, no latrine and bathroom. Only one room for one family. No source of drinking water.	Cemented. Single storied with latrine and source of water: well. Separate guest room ('baithak') and chauki (wooden cot).	Cemented. Well maintained, double-storied or more, house with handpump, well etc for drinking water, toilets, latrine, bathroom and 'baithak'.
Economic status	100 per cent dependent on daily wages to arrange for food.	Do not have to strain resources for meeting daily needs.	Economically very sound. Money lenders for middle SES and low SES people.
Employment	Daily wage earners. Agricultural labourers.	Cultivators, daily wage earners and milk vendors.	In service and/or in business.
facilities for children	Can not afford to send children to school. Children start working at an early age and help parents in their work.	Children are enrolled in local school.	Children are enrolled in "good" schools.
Capacity to bear expenses to meet social obligations	Cannot afford to bear expenses to meet social obligations associated with birth, marriage, death etc. survive on borrowings and charity during emergency such as illness, death etc.	Can partially bear expenses to meet social obligations out of own resources and partly out of borrowings.	Spend ostentatiously during social occasions.

Village Analysts: Indubala, Kamala, Urmila and Jali. *Facilitator*: Meera Jaiswal. *Date*: 11.11.98.

many households categorised as falling in middle SES and higher SES, there would be women and girl children suffering from food insecurity. For want of data we are not pursuing here that line of investigation.

Let us also state at the outset that food security is a complex issue and we ought to get the concept right before embarking on a discussion on the subject. The importance of agriculture for food security in a predominantly agricultural society, can not be overemphasized. By food security we mean there is enough food in the system, but also that people have the purchasing power to access the food so available, that people have the ability to access such food, that the food available is culturally acceptable to the people and that the food so available has adequate nutritional value for a healthy life.

If we accept the above concept of food, role of agriculture in food security is important but not overwhelming. Take the case of Morya Hamlet. Wheat produced in the hamlet meets its requirement for 4-5 months in a year. Paddy harvested can meet the needs of paddy of the villagers for 3-4 months. Maize and bajra produced is enough to meet their needs for only a few days. And all the villagers do not grow all the crops. Thus the food produced meets only a part of the quantity of food necessary for food security. For the rest of the food-needs people buy food from the open market.

There is no question that food produced in the village is culturally acceptable and given the employment opportunities outside of agriculture, available in and around Tikri, people do have the requisite purchasing power to access food. Apparently people do not suffer starvation but existence of differentiated hunger is discernible. The facts revealed by the food calendar produced by the women of Morya Hamlet as in Table 17 is instructive. If we look at Table 17, it is significant that the group of women have started the food calendar from the month of May-June (Jeth), possibly because May-June is the month when cultivation season (Kharif) starts and it is associated in the psyche of the people as the beginning of the process of food production. If we look at column 2, it is manifest that the women and men suffer from various degrees of hunger for a considerable part of the year. But their hunger is at its peak during the very hot summer and humid monsoon months, namely, months of Jeth (May-June), Asarh (June-July), and Sawan (July-August). That is, the women, men and children survive on one unwholesome meal per day for 3 months. As Bhado (August-September) comes, the nutritional value of food intake increases due to inclusion of vegetables harvested from their

Table 17 Food Calendar Prepared by the Women of Morya Hamlet, Tikri Village

Months	Food Intake	Serial Number
Asardh (June-July)	One meal of few chapatis and salt or chilli paste	1
Sawan (July-August)	One meal of few chapatis and salt or chilli paste Towards the end of the month, two meals are possible	2
Bhado (August-Sept)	One stomach filling meal of chapatis, vegetables and rice. Pulses very rarely	3
Kaur (Sept-Oct)	The same diet as in Bhado	4
Kartick (Oct-Nov)	Stomach filling meal of chapatis, vegetables and rice. Two meals	5
Aghan (Nov-Dec)	Stomach filling meal of chapatis, vegetables and rice. Two meals	6
Poosh (Dec-Jan)	Same as in Aghan	7
Magh (Jan-February)	Same as in Poosh	8
Fagun (Feb-March)	Same as in Magh but intake of pulses and costly items get reduced. Two meals	9
Chait (March-April)	Same as in the month of Fagun, but the intake of pulses gets further reduced	10
Baisakh (April-May)	Same as Chait	11
Jeth (May-June)	One meal of chapatis and salt or chilli paste	12

Village Analysts: Indubala, Kamala, Urmila, Jali.
Facilitated by: Meera Jayaswal.
Date: 11.11.98.

own fields. With the advent of Bhado (August-September), harvesting of some pulses also start, which enables people to have some pulses as well which further increases the nutritional content and palate in their food intake. The pattern of food intake in Kaur (mid-September to mid-October) is generally a continuation of the pattern obtaining in Bhado.

For the four months from Kartik to Magh (mid-October to mid-February) people earn handsomely, as this is the principal farming season, which they use in good measure to buy food. Thus daily intake of vegetables, bi-weekly or tri-weekly intake of pulses and some amount of milk, poultry, meat and fish, at least once a month, make the diet best during this part of the year. During Fagun and Chait (mid-February to mid-April) though people still manage two meals, the nutritional content of the food and their palate are considerabley diminished as the quantity of pulses, vegetables and milk steadily become scarce in their diet, until it vanishes by the end of Baisakh (mid-April to mid-May). Jeth, Ashar and Sawan are the real "hunger months" for the villagers. Table 9 read with Table 17, indicate that food intake is at its worst during the months when people have to work the hardest, namely, the summer and monsoon months. For these are the months when not only do they get to work in their own fields as also find wage employment in others' fields, but also work hard at home to deal with disease and sickness that visit the people during this part of the year.

The villagers of Bari Basti of Tikri also gave us their food calendar, which is in Table 18. They divide the year not in terms of months but in terms of farming seasons, viz., summer, rainy and winter. During summer months a typical food basket of the villagers in Bari Basti, contains pulses, chapatis and rice. They would have vegetables every alternate day. During the rainy season, their food basket improves and includes pulses, rice, chappati, vegetables every alternate days, and meat, fish or poultry once in two months. Every household would have two meals a day. When winter sets in, rice, pulses, vegetables and sometimes "Khichri" (a kind of heavy porridge) made of bajra make their meals. Though the food calendars of Morya and bari bastis are not comparable because different time frames have been used, nevertheless the general trends from both the food calendars have considerable congruence. The "hunger months" are about the same and the hunger months correspond with the period when the women have to work the hardest.

Table 18 Livelihood and Food Consumption Calendar by Women's Group, Bari Basti, Village Tikri

Season Summer	**Livelihood**	**Consumption**
(Chait, Baisakh, Jeth)	Work as agricultural labourers during harvesting of wheat and planting onion sapling.	Pulses, rice, chappati once a day. Vegetables every alternate days.
Rainy (Asardh, Sawan, Bhado,)	Sowing paddy. Women work as agricultural labourers. Work in deweeding (8 days), 10 days in transplantation of paddy. Harvesting 25-20 days.	Pulses, rice, chappati, every alternate days vegetables. Meat, fish and egg once in two months. Meals twice a day.
Winter (Kuar, Kartick, Aghan, Poosh, Magh and Phagun)	More work for men in town in early Kuar-Kartick. They are best months too. In the start of winter, work in harvesting paddy and bajra. Selling of vegetable by women.	Bajra chappati, rice, pulses, vegetables every day. Sometimes they eat khichri made of bajra.

Notes:

(i) Children only upto 2 years old are fed milk. Fruits consumption is rare unless available in village orchards or are gifted by guests.

(ii) Almost 50 per cent of he women in the ward makes bead-necklace initiated since mid-1980s by the Government under IRDP, which gives women an income of Rs. 25 per week.

Village Analysts: Savita Devi, Rits Devi, Shanti Devi, Urmila Devi, Shakuntala Devi, Dhanra Devi, Kimari Devi, Satti Devi, Sangeeta Devi, Phula Devi, Chamna Devi, Bindo Devi, Renu Devi, Chandrawati Devi, Sachho Devi, Rama Devi, Meena Devi, Arti Devi, Seema Devi, Prabha Devi, Kalawati.

Facilitator: Sudipta Ray.

Date: 31. 1. 99.

Interestingly there is a high-degree of correlation between income and food intake. Let us look at Tables 19 and 20 detailing income and expenditure of people in Morya Hamlet. Starting from Jeth (mid-May to mid-June), when the income is at the lowest, income starts rising from Asardh, when cultivation starts and employment opportunities expand. It peaks in Magh, and then it starts falling again to reach a fairly low level in Baisakh (mid-April to mid-May). This income comprise income from agriculture, sale of milk, daily wages earned by men and women separately and artificial pearl garland making by women, of which income from agriculture is the *smallest* component and daily wage is the *largest* constituent. Of these, while daily wages earned by women remain virtually constant throughout the year at Rs. 200 per month, wages earned by men remain at Rs. 400 per month for 6 months from Jeth to Kartik and then jumps up to Rs. 600 per month in Aghan, to remain at that figure till summer sets in, in Baisakh when it falls back to Rs. 400 per month. Income from garland making out of artificial pearl remains at a low ebb from Jeth till Bhado at Rs. 120 per month, and then picks up to reach Rs. 180 per month in Kaur and stays at that level till Baisakh.

Now look at Table 20. Aggregate expenditure of the people is made up of expenditure on basically three items: food, miscellaneous and social visit. Of these, expenditure on food is by far the largest chunk of the expenditure: it is about 66 per cent for Jeth and Asarh; 80 per cent for Sawan, Bhado and Kaur; 96 per cent for Kartik; above 80 per cent from Aghan to Chait and above 76 per cent in Baisakh. Expenditure on food rises in absolute terms also from Rs. 600 per month in Jeth to Rs. 1300 per month in Poosh, only to marginally decline in Chait and Baisakh. Thus the pattern of expenditure exhibit a copybook case of an under-developed economy, where expenditure on food consumption is unusually high. This rise in expenditure has a high degree of correlation with the incremental variations in income. Compare columns 7 and 1 of Table 19 with columns 1 and 5 of Table 20 and the picture will be clear. If we also compare last column of Table 19 with column 5, of Table 20, we see there is excess of expenditure over income during the summer months of Baisakh and Jeth and the wet month of Asardh. This is the time people get into debt as shown by column 6 of Table 20.

Table 19 Monthly Income of Low SES Families in Morya Hamlet, Tikri

Months	Daily Labour (Men)	Daily Labour (Women)	Garland Making	Selling Milk	Agriculture	Total
Jeth	400	100	120	100	—	620
Asardh	400	100	120	200	—	820
Sawan	400	200	120	300	50	970
Bhado	200	200	120	300	100	1120
Kuar	400	200	180	500	250	1330
Kartick	400	200	180	500	250	1530
Aghan	600	200	180	500	250	1530
Poos	600	200	180	400	250	1630
Magh	600	200	180	400	250	1630
Fagun	600	200	1809	400	100	1480
Chait	600	200	180	300	100	1380
Baisakh	400	—	180	300	—	1280
Total	5600	2000	1920	4200	1600	15320

Village Analysts: Amarnath Morya, Ashok Morya, Chatanki Morya, Panchan Morya.
Facilitator: Ms. Meera Jayaswal. *Date*: 5.11.98

Table 20 Monthly Expenditure of Low SES Families in Morya Hamlet of Tikri

Months	Expenditure				Loan
	Food	Miscellaneous	Social Visit	Total	
Jeth	600	200	100	900	500
Asardh	600	200	100	900	200
Sawan	1000	100	100	1200	200
Bhado	1000	100	100	1200	—
Kuar	1000	100	100	1200	—
Kartick	1200	100	150	1250	—
Aghan	1200	100	200	1450	—
Poos	1300	100	200	1500	—
Magh	1300	100	200	1600	—
Fagun	1300	100	200	1600	—
Chait	1200	100	100	1400	—
Baisakh	1000	150	150	1300	—
Total	12700	1500	1700	15900	900

Village Analysts: Amarnath Morya, Ashok Morya, Chatanki Morya, Panchan Morya.
Facilitator: Ms. Meera Jayaswal. *Date*: 5.11.98

Table 21 Constraints to Agriculture and Coping Strategies (Men Group) Morya Basti, Tikri

Constraint	Months	Affected Plants	Stage Most Affected	Symptoms	Extent of Damage	Damaged Since (Years)	Farmers' Response
Low Electricity Supply	Asar-Kuar	Wheat, paddy	Early Stages	Plants dry up	40-50 per cent	2-3	Generator hiring
Nilgai	Always	All Crops	All Stages	Graze, stampede	25-30 per cent	10	Boundary walls and hutments in fields
Dhola Pest	Kartick Aghan	Spinach, cauliflower, brinjal	All Stages	Hole in leaves	75 per cent	4	Pesticides
Demak Pest	Always	Chilies, brinjal, sugarcane, wheat	Starts damaging 15-20 days old plants	Roots are spoilt	20-25 per cent	15	Watering roots during plantation

Machhi Pest	Kuar	Paddy	While ear of corn start milking	Grains do not form	10-15 per cent	1	Gamaxin powder, falidal are sprayed
Bhanjh rog (plant disease)	Always	Chili, brinjal, tomato	1-2 months old	Many branches come	20-25 per cent	5	Pesticide
Gur Chawa (leaf roll)	Always	Chili, brinjal, Tomato	Always	Leaves curl	15-20 per cent	5	No solution
Galwa pest	Ashar-Bhado	Spinach, cauliflower, tomato	Very young plants; spinach	Crops are littered and spoilt	80-90 per cent	4-5	No solution
Jhulsa pest	Always	Brinjal, potato, spinach, gourd, pumpkin	One month old plant	Plants die	10-15 per cent (This year 90 per cent)	15	Pesticides

Constraint	Months	Affected Plants	Stage Most Affected	Symptoms	Extent of Damage	Damaged Since (Years)	Farmers' Response
Maho Pest	Fagun	Brinjal, Potato, Spinach, Gourd, Pumpkin	A month old plants, when flower comes	Plants especially flowers are laced with insects	15-20 per cent	10	
Ukatha Pest	All Year	All crops except paddy	All stages	Dry up in the afternool	50-60 per cent	6-7	Nothing
Kabra Pest	Asar	Paddy/ Wheat	15 days old plants	Yellowing of plants	50-100 per cent	2	Zinc save damage upto 50 per cent
Khadra Pest		Suran		The sides dry up	20 per cent	5	Nothing
Weeds (Gehu ka Mama)	Aghan to Magh	Wheat	All stages		Depends on no. of plants	4-5	Uproothing and use of herbicide. Saves only 20 per cent

Constraint	Months	Affected Plants	Stage Most Affected	Symptoms	Extent of Damage	Damaged Since (Years)	Farmers' Response
Change of weather	All year	All crops	All stages	—	—	2	
Scattered land	—	—	—	—	—		
Adulterated fertilisers	—	—	—	—	—	5	
Duplicate medicines for killing insects	—	—	—	—	—	5	
Rats	Poos to bai-sakh	All crops	All stages	—	Depends on the no. of rats	5	Rat poisoning, but saves only 10%
High quality seed not available	Jeth to Sawan; poos, magh	Paddy, wheat	—	Low yield	20 per cent	2	Use local seeds

Constraint	Months	Affected Plants	Stage Most Affected	Symptoms	Extent of Damage	Damaged Since (Years)	Farmers' Response
Shortage of labourers	Asar, sawan, fagun, chait	Paddy, wheat	Paddy plantation and wheat harvesting	—	10 per cent	2	Hire at higher rates from other places

Village Analysts: Vijay Kumar Morya, Ajay Kumar Morya, Subhas Kushwaha, Kamaresh Morya, Shiv Kumar Morya, Satya Prakash Morya, Shankar Morya.
Facilitator: Ms. Meera Jayaswal.
Date: 8.11.99.

Table 22 Constraints to Agriculture and Coping Strategies (Women Group) Morya Basti, Tikri

Constraint	Months	Affected Plants	Stage Most Affected	Symptoms	Extent of Damage	Damaged Since (Years)	Farmers' Response
Nilgai	Whole year	All crop	From 6" height to last stages	Graze	75 per cent	10	Boundary walls Guard all night
Plant disease	Whole year except years of excess rain, hot and winter	All crops	All stages	Spoil	Depends on severity of the disease	10	Medicines
Weeds	Whole year	All crops	Growing stage	Consume nutrition of the crop	1 per cent	10	Deweeding

Constraint	Months	Affected Plants	Stage Most Affected	Symptoms	Extent of Damage	Damaged Since (Years)	Farmers' Response
Acute shortage of money	—	Paddy/ wheat	—	—	—	—	Loan arranged
Heavy workload	—	—	—	Females become weak. They cannot work in fields	—	—	—
Scarcity of land	—	All crops	—	—	—	—	—
Lack of irrigation water	Summer	Vegetable	All stages	Plants	75 per cent	5	Arrange pumpsets
Rats	All months except rainy	All crops	All stages	Cuts	50 per cent	20	Rat

Village Analyst: Kamla Devi, Urmila Devi, Jali, Fulra Devi. *Facilitator*: Ms. Meera Jayaswal. *Date*: 8.11.98.

On the whole then, people do not seem to have food security throughout the year, though they do not suffer from chronic hunger. Under-nutrition and malnutrition, of women is clearly made out. Incidentally in many parts of the country, people who suffer from food insecurity of the variety we see here, resort to satisfying a part of their hunger by collecting, gathering and hunting food from secondary sources of food (*Mukherjee, 1994, 1997; Mukherjee and Mukherjee, 1997, 1999*) viz., common property resources, forests, and "micro environments"(Chambers, 1993). In case of Tikri that option is also closed. There is none of these present here. The guava orchard and the mango orchard in the village have been cleared to raise crops etc., because apparently yield from these trees had declined so sharply that retaining them was of little value.

In what ways does Food Production Interact with Other Household Activities?

Though all the people in Tirkri do not have food security all the time, nevertheless food production occupies a major part of the working hours of both men and women. As we saw, since most of the household activities, namely, cooking, cleaning, collecting fuelwood, collecting potable water, collecting fodder, child bearing and rearing, looking after the sick, disabled and the old, are the responsibility of the women and women also perform a whole range agricultural operations, an interaction between these two sets of activities is inevitable. Reference is invited to Tables 9 and 15, from which it is clear that certain tasks are only performed by the women and since the household chores are also the responsibility of women, there is *ipso facto* a good deal of interface between food production and household activities. However, very few of the households chores are complementary to agricultural activities. In fact the two sets of activities compete for allocation of time from the men and women. If one were to take account of post-harvest operations, the interface between household activities and food production will be more pronounced.

Part VIII. Constraints to Agricultural Production and Community's Response

What are the Constraints for Agricultural Production?

There are several constraints to agriculture. Men and women have different perceptions about these constraints. Refer to Tables 21 and 22. Broadly one can classify these constraints as falling into three groups as perceived by the farmers of Morya. These are environmental and situational constraints, imposed by either nature or by the fact that the farmers have these conditions as given parameters; Agro-biological constraints, imposed by life forms such as pests, insects and weeds and finally socio-economic, imposed by social and economic structures, processes and policies. The details are discussed below. The constraints to which agriculture is subject to are perceived differently by men and women. This is in part explained by the fact that men and women perform different agricultural task in the farming process and hence they articulate those constraints which they encounter most.

These are as follows.

- *Environmental and Situational Constraints*: change in climatic conditions leading to uncertainty/irregularity of rainfall, small size of holdings, scattered land, etc. *The women added scarcity of land as an additional problem.*
- *Agro-Biological Constraints*: weeds, diseases like Banjh Rog, pests (Dhola, Deemak, Machhi-Flies) and insect attack on crops (Gur Chawa-Leaf-Roll, Galwa, Jhulsa, Maho, Ukatha, Kabra and Khadra), attack by white ants and rats etc. *The women perceive that the problem of attacks by nilgais needs to be addressed.*
- *Socio-Economic Constraints*: lack of electric power, non-availability of seeds and un-adulterated fertilizers, spurious insecticides and shortage of labour. Shortage of money and water for irrigation were added problems indicated by the women.

What is their Impact?

These constraints affected agriculture in Morya at various stages in the agricultural process. There was no stage, which was free from constraints but there were some constraints which affected agriculture throughout the year. Predation by Nilgais and plant disease like *Banj Rog* and also pest/insect attack like *gur chawa, jhulsa, deemak* (Whiteants) and *ukatha* always bothered the farmers in the cultivation process. There are other constraints, which, affect agriculture intensively during some months, like non-availability of seeds during Asard, Sawan, Bhado, Poosh and Magh. Shortage of labourer affect agriculture during Asard, Sawan, Fagun and Chait: to be precise during the cultivation and harvesting seasons when demand for labour reaches its peak.

Farmers were able to quantify in some cases the extent of loss or damage caused by these constraints. Problem of electric power reduces yield by 40-50 per cent. Nilgais damaged upto 25-30 per cent of crops, which the women placed as upto 75 per cent. Whiteants *(deemak)* and *machhi* (flies) damage nearly 20-25 per cent and 10-15 per cent of the crops respectively. When plant diseases strike, damage to crops could be anything between 15-20 per cent to even 100 per cent. Damages caused by different diseases are of the order of 25 per cent in case of *banj rog;* 15-20 per cent from *gur chawa;* 80-90 per cent from *galwa;* normally 10-15 per cent from *jhulsa* but in 1998 it was as high as 90 per cent; 15-20 per cent from *Maho;* 50-60 per cent from *ukatha;* 50-100 per cent from *kabra* and 20 per cent from *khadra.* Farmers estimate that loss on account of non-availability of good quality seed could be about 20 per cent and shortage of labour causes loss of about 10-15 per cent of agricultural produce. The women pointed out that lack of irrigation facility causes 75 per cent loss in crops, and rats were such a nuisance that a farmer could lose as much as 50 per cent of agricultural produce due to their infestation, although men thought it may not be possible to estimate the extent of damage suffered on account of rats.

The villagers were quick to point out that not all crops were subject to all the constraints. And all the constraints were not of equal importance. Men and women have different perspectives on the constraints. The constraints identified by men are in Table 21 and the constraints identified by women are in Table 22. It is apparent that in hamlets of Tikri, men have a much more detailed list of constraints than women, unlike what we find in other villages where it is the other way around.

Table 23 Ranking of Constraints in Morya Basti

Scoring By Women			Scoring By Men		
Rank	*Constraint*	*Group Scoring by No. of Seeds*	*Rank*	*Constraint*	*Group Scoring by No. of Seeds*
1w	Change of weather	**********10	1m	Heavy Work Load	**********10
2w	Plant diseases	********8	2m	Acute Shortage of Money	*********9
3w	Nilgai menace	*******7	3m	Scarcity of Land	********8
3w	Power problem	*******7	4m	Nilgai Menace	******6
4w	Weeds	******6	4m	Plant Disease	******6
4w	Spurious medicines for killing insects	******6	4m	Lack of Sufficient Water	******6
5w	Insects	*****5	5m	Weeds	*****5
5w	Adulterated fertilisers	*****5	6m	Rats	****4
6w	Rats	****4			
6w	Scattered land	****4			

Note: *m* denotes ranking by Men and *w* denotes ranking by women.

Village Analysts: Vijay, Ajay, Subhas, Komaresh and ShivKumar Morya for ranking by men. Kamala Devi, Urmila Devi, Jali, Fulra Devi for ranking by women.
Facilitator: Ms. Meera Jayaswal.
Date: 811.98.

And while the majority of the constraints identified by the men related to weeds, pests, insects, diseases, power and labour shortage, the majority of the constraints narrated by women relate to resource crunch. This is a significant difference. The women and men have accordingly ranked the constraints separately. Refer to Table 23.

At least one difference in perception warrants comments. Since most of the agricultural operations are carried out by women and they also take care of the household chores, we discussed earlier, the pressure of work is telling and for them, the work load is, naturally, the most important constraints. In contrast men consider climatic changes leading to erratic rainfall as the most important constraint. It is a reflection, in a sense, on gender justice and the prevalence of traditional concept of 'who does what' in rural households.

The community's response to these constraints is detailed later in this document.

What Changes in Types of Constraints, Pest Population and Past Damage have been Perceived Spatially and Historically?

Historical Differences The vintage of these constraints differ substantially. Some of these pests and constraints have been with the farmers for a long time while some others have cropped up in more recent years. Attack by Nilgais, *deemak, jhulsa, maho* and weeds have been perceived as constraints since last 10-15 years. Rats have been with the farmers for last 20 years, but *dhola, banj rog, gur chawa, galwa* and *khadra* have afflicted farming picture in Tikri for the last 5 years or so. *Kabra* arrived on the scene some 2 years back and machhis (flies) appeared on the farming scene for the first time in 1998.

Shortage of water is a problem that has troubled farming for the last 5 years, which is compounded by erratic rainfall on account of climatic change. That Tikri faces shortage of irrigation water due to erratic and lower rainfall, despite the country receiving good monsoons for ten years in a row, tell us that status of water being available for farming at the local level can be different from status of water availability at the maco-level. The constraints posed by climatic change, non-availability of quality seeds and shortage of labour have assumed problem proportions over the last two years. Similarly power shortage is a problem since last three years, caused on the one hand by shortage in power generation by Uttar Pradesh State Electricity Board and by increased demand for power with mechanisation of irrigation/agricultural operations.

Historically, therefore, there is a rise in the number of constraints faced by the farmers, notably the increase in plant disease and pests.

Spatial Differences There are different constraints being felt in different parts of the village. The women inhabitants of Yadav Basti perceive shortage of irrigation sources as their worst problem (scoring 10); *bhurila* pest (hairy caterpillar) and plant diseases (like *hardwa, gurchawa* and *jhulsa*) are their second most serious constraint (all scoring 8); *genhu ka mama* (pest) and *hara kira* (green caterpillar) are the other major problems (scoring 7). The women of Yadav Basti also perceive unseasonal rains, nilgai attack, *macchi,* hailstorm and rats, as the other major constraints to agriculture. This set of constraints has its own variation, but is quite similar to the constraints identified by women of Morya Basti, shown in Tables 21 and 22. These constraints are also of varying vintage: *genhu ka mama* arrived about 10 years ago after the PL 480 wheat was introduced into the village, followed by attack by nilgais since last 8 years. Rats assumed problem dimension about 7 years' back. Unseasonal rains, *macchis* and *hara kira* are the most recent additions to their list.

The men of Mahato Basti have their own story of constraints they face in farming. They too perceive shortage of water as their *numero uno* problem (scoring 10). They rank plant diseases *(gurchawa and jhulsa), hara kira* along with pests (like *katui, tikuli* and *bahadur kira*) as their second level problems (all of them scoring 7). Predation by nilgais and *uktwa* (a plant disease) are their next most important problems. The other constraints perceived by the men of Mahato Basti are *safra* and *hardwa* (plant diseases), *gandhi kira* (pest), and nature's attack in terms of hailstorms, frost and fog, which are substantially different from the constraints outlined in Table 21 by the men of Morya Basti.

There are inter-Basti differences, in perceived variations of damages caused by the constraints as well. The damages estimated are in the nature of what has been the general trend in the hamlets over the years. The perceived damages caused to crops by these pests, diseases and constraints in Yadav Basti and Mahato Basti, are somewhat at variance with the perceptions of the farmers. For instance the women of Yadav Basti felt that *bhurila* (hairy caterpillar) damages 25 per cent of produce. Farmers of Mahato Basti felt that nature's attack through hailstorms, frost and fog could cause losses of up to 100 per cent, 60 per cent and 40 per cent respectively, particularly to potatoes and cauliflower. *Safra* damages crop upto 30 per cent in case of peas, and 15 per cent in case of gram. *Hardwa* can destroy 20 per cent of paddy and inflict perceptible damage to wheat as well. *Gurchawa* and *jhulsa* can destroy from 75 to 100 per cent of chilies, tomatoes and brinjals. *Jhulsa* attack is more damaging. Pests *(katui, tikuli* and *bahadur kira)* can damage bitter gourd by 8 per cent, potato output by 25 per cent; a farmer could lose as much as 25 per cent of produce in case paddy is hit by *katui. Uktwa* affects peas and eat into it seriously causing even 50 per cent loss in output.

These variations in the kinds and extent of damages/loss to agriculture varies within the village. These variations are in part because different crops are grown by villagers in different parts and in part because of soil conditions, kinds of seeds used and above all the judgmental assessment and application of preventive measures.

Part IX. Air Pollution and Industrialization

Benefits

The people did perceive that industrialization has brought about significant changes to Tikri and in the lives of its people. The concept of industrialisation as applied in Tikri, is broader and encompasses urbanisation and growth of industrial establishments around Tikri, not necessarily in Tikri. The presence of an adjoining town, with growing population, helps farmers of Tikri to quickly take their vegetables to the market and sell them fresh which fetch better prices. Since farmers can transport their wares on their own, without involving any cost of transportation, the cost of production at the "market-gate" is lower, allowing them better margins. Similarly surplus milk which has no off-take in the village is easily marketed in the town without intermediaries. This ensures better price realization. The town also provides temporary employment to those willing to work, but unable to find work in Tikri. Availability of modern means of living in the town has helped improve the quality of life for those villagers of Tikri, who are rich enough to afford these goods.

On the social front, the nearness to the Town makes flow of information between Tikri and the Town so much easier and faster. The frequencies of people from Tikri visiting the town and people from the town coming to Tikri, are very high. This two way intense process, makes villagers in Tikri aware of development and keeps them abreast of what's happening around the world. The social interface between the town and villagers, has helped the Harijans to break away from the bondage of the landed classes, as they find work in the town. Awareness and economic independence and stability of income, imparted by employment opportunities opened by an urban agglomeration, have been the driving forces in bringing about social emancipation of Harijans. This mobility of the Harijans is remarkable, given the feudal culture of Uttar Pradesh. Harijan women also told us that they no longer need to work as labourers only in the houses of upper caste rich people, exposing themselves to exploitation. They work elsewhere depending on how well they negotiate their compensation. The stratification *per se* of society in Tikri, along caste lines, has also loosened up on account of these social exchanges and flow of ideas. As a consequence, upper caste people who earlier hesitated to employ lower caste people in their homes, have become more flexible on this score. In one sense untouchability of the earlier years have lost its "pristine glory" (*Rao et. al* 1999 arrive at similar findings).

Injury

The proximity of Tikri to Varanasi is, however, not an unmixed blessing. Increased population is polluting land and the Ganges by dumping garbage, often containing non-bio-degradable matter. Rapid urbanisation as a consequence of industrialisation in adjoining areas is leading to conversion of agricultural lands into lands for building houses. Rapid urbanisation and industrialization, have attracted migrant labourers from outside the state to the industries, denying the local people of the employment opportunities that they would otherwise have had. In the process, the migrant labourers who come to work in the industries, encroach village lands, giving rise to slums. Brick kilns have grown like mushrooms in and around Narottampur, an adjoining community, which in turn emits smoke that is harmful to crops, notably mangoes which now have black spots on them, have become smaller in size and at times have a tinge of bitterness.

Mining of sand along the banks of Ganges, has increased on account of the spurt in construction activity, which in turn has increased the movement of trucks and tractors transporting sand, along the road on which Malah and Dherabir Bastis of Tikri are situated. This has resulted in considerable increase in dust pollution, and the loose sand particles that blow out from these trucks and tractors, cause of major eye irritation to the villagers. Though no apparent cause could be pinpointed, the fat content in milk from the Bovine wealth of Tikri has declined. Some milk vendors felt, however, that fodder grown with urea could be one of the proximate causes.

What are the Perceived Impacts of Air Pollution? Any Visible injury to Crops Including Leaf Injury ? To what Extent is Leaf Injury Perceived to be Caused by Air Pollution?

Villagers in Tikri reported loss in yield of fruit from the orchard (mango) due to smoke coming from brick kiln. Loss in mango and berry yields due to the deposition of smoke etc. from the brick kiln in the neighbouring villages. Pollution from brick kiln was the only identified source of pollution. Tikri, did not report any increased pest attack (given the same seed variety in consecutive years) except for one ward where pest attack had increased (which had used different variety of seeds) over the years. The latter resulted in more pesticide consumption. The farmers thought that this was due to increased resistance to pests.

The impact of air pollution in Tikri looks like a non-issue. Of the constraints identified by the villagers in the 3 Bastis, none seemed *prima facie* to relate any of these constraints to air pollution. There is no perception amongst the villagers that air pollution has any bearing whatsoever on any of the pests, diseases and weeds causing loss or injury to crops, barring their effect on mangoes.

Leaf injuries are visible, but these were not perceived as being due to air pollution. Hairy caterpillar nibble away leaves and drive holes in them. When *gurchawa* affects crops like chilies, brinjals, tomatoes etc., their leaves roll up and twirl. When *galwa* affects spinach, cauliflowers and tomato plants, their leaves degenerate. When *jhulsa* attacks plants of brinjal, potatoes, turmeric, gourd, their leaves initially shrivel and then fall off. *Ukthaka* initially leads to drying up of the leaves, ultimately leading to drying up of the entire plant. It affects all crops other than paddy.

Villagers of Morya thought some of the identified constraints (like *Galwa*) could have been caused by change in climate leading to untimely rain and some due to deterioration of soil quality (*Gurchawa*). Shortage of water is not only due to erratic rainfall but also due to lowering of the water table resulting in lower volumes of water available from using pumpsets for irrigation.

Is Dust Pollution from Industrial Areas/Roads Linked with a Particular Stage of Cropping Calendar?

The villagers did perceive that there has been an increase in pollution and certainly in dust pollution due to different reasons. But the common perception of the villagers of the Bastis studied do not reflect any concern for dust pollution in relation to crops. They were concerned about health hazards arising out of air pollution such as the ones relating to plying of vehicles transporting sands through Tikri.

How Do People Deal with Constraints to Agricultural Production?

The people deal with the constraints to agricultural production on the basis of their indigenous knowledge and locally available resources and wisdom. Let us take the case of constraints faced in Morya. They deal with nilgais by erecting high walls around their fields, a strategy deployed by the relatively well off. To deal with hairy caterpillars, they spray and sprinkle pesticides. Whiteants are capable of attacking any time. Hence a close watch is kept at the vulnerable crops and on sighting the first sign of whiteants, insecticides are sprayed. When *bang rog* or infertility disease hits a crop, plants are uprooted. Since *gurchawa* is believed to have its origin in polluted soil, attempts are made to change the top soil and replace it by cowdung mixed with a moderate amount of urea. *Galwa* is perceived to have flourished due to untimely rain caused by a change in climatic conditions. There is, therefore, no coping mechanism devised to deal with *Galwa*. Tikri has no knowledge about the origin and causes of *jhulsa* and farmers have no clue about how to deal with it. There is no coping mechanism disclosed on tackling *maho, ukhatha and kabra*. The age old trick of dealing with rats by baiting them with poisoned food, continues to be popular. There is apparently no attempt to tackle problems of adulterated fertilisers, pesticides and insecticides. Similarly precious little is done to circumvent the constraint posed by non-availability of high quality seeds. The use of pumpsets has obviated the problem of lack of sufficient water but only partially and shortage of water for irrigation continues to bug farmers though apparently nothing is done to ensure better management of water resources.

The situation in Mahato Basti is identical. There is nothing that the farmers do to get rid of plant diseases like *gurchawa, jhulsa* and *ukthwa;* insect *hara kira* and *safra* disease. There is nothing that the farmers do to eliminate poor quality seeds; they have no protection against frosts and hailstorm. They sprinkle sulphur on the fields hit by fog. There is no response to shortage of water. The simple device of erecting boundary walls on fields to protect crop form nilgais seen in Morya, is also not used in Mahato Basti. There is a conscious attempt to kill pests like *katui, tikuli* and *bahadur kira* by spraying pesticides such as *endocile* and *dimocron. gandhi kira* seems to respond to sprinkling of BAC 10 per cent.

The picture in Yadav Basti looks familiar. Out of the 9 constraints that cause damage to agriculture in Yadav Basti, the farmers have found ways and means to tackle only one and partly to tackle two others. Rats are easiest to deal through rat poisoning and that is done. Some rich cultivators have started to use weedicides to tackle *genhu ka mama*, through uprooting of plants continue to be the preferred response to deal with *genhu ka mama.* Plant diseases, like *hardwa, gurchawa* and *jhulsa,* are sought to be eliminated by spraying some pesticides, but without much success. Nothing is done to clear other bottlenecks, including the one posed by shortage of irrigation sources.

It is against human sanctity to know a problems at hand but do nothing to solve them, particularly so when such problems cause injury, and harm their means of survival. That would be irrational behaviour. On first inspection one is left wondering if villagers in Tikri are being irrational. A deeper examination, however, reveals that there is nothing irrational in what they are doing. Since 75 per cent of the farmers are tenants and concealed tenants at that, they can be evicted at will. It is a known historical fact in this country, moreso in Uttar Pradesh, that concealed tenants are at the mercy of the landlords and they are subject to frequent evictions. As a result, the farmers (read tenants) only try to remove those constraints that require no long term investment. Tenants take those measures that do not involve substantial investments. Only where the tenants are recorded and do not face eviction at will of the landlord, will there be investments by tenants (See the case of West Bengal in *Sanyal et. al.* 1998). Otherwise the tenants only take short-term measure, involving small outlays, to improve yield in the very short run. Complete property rights are a prerequisite for efficiency in agriculture (*Kerr et. al.,* 1998). Even otherwise the tenants have very little incentive to improve the quality of the land because of non-economic considerations. This is brilliantly summed up by a Pancha Kol in Bajha Tola, Village Bahilpurwa, which is repeated here:

> Earlier we used to take land on lease. But Raja Bhaiya (Landlord) would constantly abuse us and when the demons were upon us, he would beat us. Later he uprooted our bast (locality). Now we prefer not to work for him. We live by cutting wood in the forests and selling it (*Rao, Sharma and Srivastav,*1999).

Thus our Tikri farmers try to make some half hearted attempts at taking care of some of the pests, insects and diseases by spraying and sprinkling, what they call "killer medicines", but they do not erect boundary walls to protect their crops from being grazed by nilgais. The boundary walls on fields noticeable in Tikri are on land tilled by owner-cultivators. They do not change cropping pattern as that requires considerable investment and enormous risk bearing. In any event since they only at best keep 50 per cent of the produce, after bearing the full variable cost of cultivation, they have little incentive, if at all, to improve the quality of land (which is someone else's asset) which they till as tenants. They are unwilling to bear capital cost of land improvement. As one farmer beautifully put it: "How can I keep money in a Post Office "Khata" which I can't withdraw". (In local language "Khata" is used to signify Account and Post Offices offer some Banking facilities). (See *Yugandhar et. al.* 1995, for a good discussion on tenancy, and incentives for land improvement.) They do nothing to improve the availability of water for irrigation as well, for that too involves substantial capital outlay.

The fact that these tenants are poor and mostly small and marginal farmers also leads to apathy of sorts. These farmers lack the required resources as well to remove the constraints. The availability and cost of credit for agriculture are major deterrents for even those who are prepared to risk the venture.

How do Farmers Tackle Perceived Constraints: Through Changed Practice? Organized Action? Through Existing Organizational Structures? What Modalities are used to Influence constraints for Agriculture?

The foregoing recital of farmers' responses gives an account of the nature and content of farmer's response to constraints. This leaves little additional scope to discuss how farmers tackle the perceived constraints except perhaps to conclude that the responses are short run and ad hoc. There is scant systematic response. There is no changed practice which, the villagers indicated. There is no organised action. Given the fact that most of the farmers are concealed tenants they can not take organised action.

There are organisational (read institutional!) structures, but none come to the help of these farmers, some poor and some not so poor, in overcoming the problems they face. Let us look at figure 3, containing a Venn Diagram. This diagram shows the importance and psychological distance, of different institutions to Tikri farmers. The pesticide shop and the seed shop are the nearest in mental distance to the farmers. Then comes in nearness is the co-operative, followed by the bhumiyars who supply hired pumpsets, hired tractors, lease out land and even credit, though at an exorbitant rate of interest. The Bank (Union Bank of India) is far away, as farmers from Tikri balk at the paper work involved in having a small loan, not to speak of a credit line sanctioned, and demand for collateral security of which they have none. The story is the same for the Village Headman. And the Kashi Vidyapeeth Block Office, under whose territorial jurisdiction Tikri falls, is furthest.

In terms of importance, signified by the size of the circles, Tikri farmers think the Pesticide and Seed Shops are of utmost importance, followed by the Kashi Vidyapeeth Block Office. The Bhumiars are next in importance. The Bank and the Village Headman are less important to them; Cooperative comes at the bottom of the scale. Thus though the Kashi Vidyapeeth Block Office is considered very important by the farmers, the Office is psychologically furthest from them, because it is neither approachable nor is it useful. This is tragic: Block Development Offices are suppose to provide all the extension services, ensure supply of seeds and fertilisers and provide ancillary support to agriculture. The Village Headman is also far away from the villagers and is of little material consequence. The Bank (a Nationalised Bank whose *raison d etre* is mass Banking with emphasis on agricultural credit as part of its priority sector lending) do not matter to the agriculturists for the reasons just mentioned. Thus the existing institutional structures are of no use to the community.

The fact that the farmers conceive of the Seed and Pesticide Shops, as being both most important and nearest to their psyche, is a consequence of agriculture becoming HEIA. The cultivators depend on outsiders for vital inputs, an issue which, we have already explored at length.

If Constraints can not be Removed at the Local Level, Whether Farmers Approach Higher Authorities? If yes, how do they do so?

There is no sign of approaching higher authorities to remove the constraints faced by agriculture. We saw that in many cases the farmers have made no attempt to remove the constraint at all. They have resolved what was possible and have behaved rationally in removing the constraints with their own resources. Thus far and no further. The nearest and most visible "higher authorities" for the farmers is the Kashi Vidyapeeth block development office. If that office is psychologically so far removed from Tikri, both by its demeanor and functioning, there is little hope that the farmers who need support would go any further up. It is also a matter of public history that the bureaucracy is insensitive to the needs of the poor in this country, which leaves the villagers unpersuaded into believing that approaching higher authorities would make their life any better. It is absolutely important to recognise that approaching higher authorities is not a costless affair. The poverty and deprivation that stalk the poor farmers of Tikri certainly makes them feel hamstrung by paucity of disposable resources to approach higher authorities. The low level of literacy, with literacy mostly concentrated amongst the relatively better off, is a major impediment to approaching authorities in the Sub-division or district headquarters.

Part X. Impact on Health

Of the two social sectors, health is a matter of concern in all our rural areas. Tikri is no exception to this general rule. Groups from Tikri (as in some other villages in the area, such as Maraon) pointed out the poor health of the villagers, especially the younger group, is partly because of increased consumption of fertiliser-based crops and poor food intake.

Tikri village highlighted pre-mature greying of hair, though no reason was ascribed. Some villagers thought that TB and asthma were hereditary diseases. A moderate increase in respiratory problems was reported from Tikri. As explained by the villagers, better accessibility of doctors as compared to earlier days, increased consciousness and knowledge of the ailments previously unknown. In Morya hamlet of Tikri village, one health problem is related to stomach trouble due to consumption and handling of grains to which insecticides and pesticides have been applied. In the same hamlet, some villagers get sores on different parts of the body, such as hand, head, face, stomach, legs etc. The disease starts with patches of swelling, increasing gradually in size and getting converted to open sores. It usually takes six months or more for healing. The treatment for the sore is expensive costing a minimum of Rs.500/- per month per person. Around 5 to 6 persons in the village have been affected by such swelling, reasons for which were attributed to atmospheric temperature and changes in weather.

In Morya halmet, the participants thought that they were getting weaker due to consumption of food grown with the help of fertilisers and pesticides, which lacked nutrients and could not provide strength. Consumption of such grains by livestock also lead to weakness in livestock. The milk yield of livestock has been adversely affected and the quality of milk had low level of nutrients. The villagers perceive that handling and consuming foodgrains laced with "killer medicines" (applied to get rid of insecticides and pesticides), cause stomach related problems.

Weakness is a common disease pointed out. This is associated again with consumption of foodgrains not grown organically. Fertilizers, and "killer medicines" applied to vegetables and crops of different varieties, and in increasing quantities, are the real problems. Such crops have a better appearance and farmers get better yields but their nutritional value is suspect. The lower than the required minimum consumption of food as disclosed by food calendars we discussed earlier, adds to the problem: it leads to mal-nutrition and under-nutrition, which in turn also contribute to exacerbate weakness in the villagers.

The sand particles let loose by trucks and tractors carrying sand from the banks of Ganges through Tikri cause *eye problems* for the villagers in the Bastis lying along the road.

Part XI. Conclusions

We may now try and summarise the main conclusions from the case study.

1. Tikri is a village where people depend predominantly on agriculture for their livelihood, some as owners-cultivators, some as owner-tenants, some as pure tenants and some as agricultural labourers. As many as 70 per cent people depend upon agriculture. Most of the cultivators are small and marginal farmers.
2. There is an unusually high number of tenants. Almost 75 per cent of the people are tenants. Since by law there can be no tenants most of the tenants are also concealed tenants. This has adverse effect on the quality of land, for tenants who can be 'evicted at will' as they are powerless and illegal, have no incentive to effect long term improvement to land entrusted to their care. They are only interested in increasing current yields.

3. Agriculture has become High External Input Agriculture, from Zero External Input Agriculture, even as late as in the 1940s. Though agriculture is still polyculture, crop diversity has declined markedly. These changes have made the farmers vulnerable to both external shocks and to internal risks.
4. There is an increase in productivity in 1990 vis-a-vis what obtained in the 1950s. Yields were at their highest in the 1960s but the high growth in yield achieved in the 1960s, could not be maintained in the subsequent decades. The exceptionally high level of yield in the 1960s was largely due to "new technology", viz., use of fertilisers, improved variety of seeds and irrigation.
5. With the increase in yield has also come a large number of pests, diseases and insects. The response of the community to remove these pests, insects and diseases has been use of insecticides, pesticides and what the farmers called "killer medicines". There are a large number of constraints to agriculture. The response of the community to remove those constraints has been minimum. There are established institutions to provide support to agriculture, but they are, in the perception of Tikri farmers, dysfunctional. There is no extension service available and there is no demand for such extension service as well.
6. Pollution has increased. But the co-relation between pollution and injury to crops is not perceived. Leaf injury to crops is visible and the insects/diseases which cause such injuries are known but that they are due to air pollution is not established.
7. There are gender discriminations and gender injustice, and both in terms of leisure/entertainment and workload, the dice is loaded against women.
8. There is food security for four to five months in a year for people belonging to lower SES. For rest of the year, people suffer from various degrees of hunger. Hunger for the people of Tikri is at its peak during the months of Jeth (May-June), Asarh (June-July), and Sawan (July-August). The hunger months correspond with the months when people have to work the hardest and have the highest workload.
9. Pollution is perceived to have adverse impact on the state of health in Tikri.

Figure 2: Comparison of Men's and Women's Working Hours in Moyra Hamlet, Village Tikri

Time of the day	Men's Work 		Women's Work 	
4 A.M.	• Gets up. • Goes to the market to sell vegetables.	***** ***** ***** *****	• Gets up. • Cleans house. • Prepares meals.	****** ****** ****** ******
6 A.M.	• Returns home. • Have breakfast.	***** ***** *****	• Cleans utensils • Eats.	****** ****** ******
8 A.M.	• Prepares for field work.	***** ***** *****	• Goes to vegetable farm	****** ****** ******
10 A.M.	• Does labour work.	***** ***** ***** *****	• Picks up matured vegetables.	****** ****** ******
12 Noon		***** ***** *****	• Deweeding vegetable Farms.	****** ****** ******
	• Have refreshments		• Lunch. • Garland stitching	****** ****** ****** ******
2 P.M.	• Does labour work	***** ***** ***** *****	• Harvesting of crops	****** ****** ******
4 P.M.		***** ***** ***** *****		****** ****** ******
6 P.M.	• Watches TV. • Chats with villagers	***** ***** ***** *****		****** ****** ******
8 P.M.	• Dinner	***** ***** ***** ***** *****	• Cleans utensils. • Prepares dinner. • Serves dinner to family members.	****** ****** ****** ******
10 P.M.	• Sleeps		• Makes garlands of artificial pearls	****** ****** ****** *****
12 midnight till 4 A.M.	• Sleeps		• Sleeps.	

Note: Shaded portion shows working hours. Blanks show leisure time and rest.
Facilitator: Meera Jayaswal.
Reproduction of diagram by the villagers of Moyra Hamlet, Village Tikri.

Figure 3: Diagram for Support System (Male Group) Mahato Basti (Hamlet)

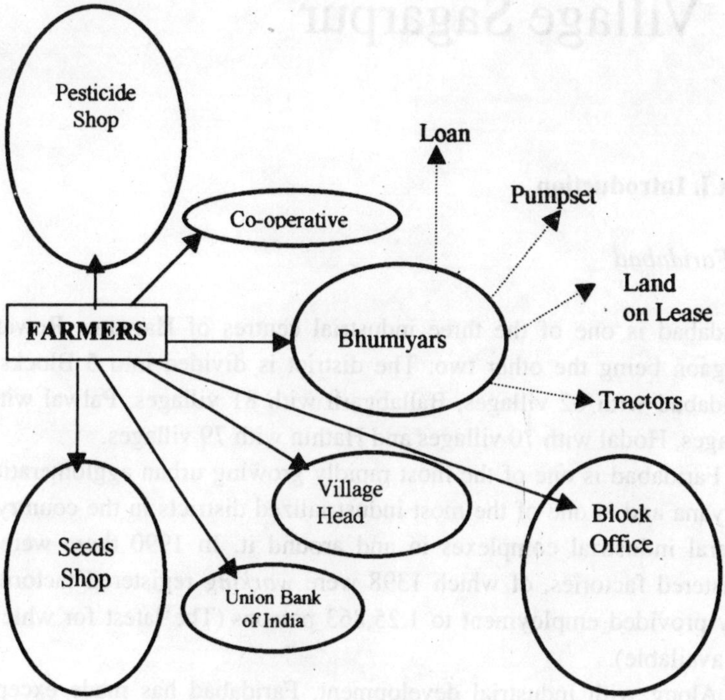

Notes: Village Analysts: Pratap Patel, Radhyeshyam, Hiralal, Ashok, Munnalal.
Date: 30.1.99.
Facilitator: Sudipta Ray.
The size of the circles indicates the degree of importance to the farmers in theory. The distance of the circles from the farmers indicates the level of support actually received by the farmers. Dotted arrows show the services provided by the Bhymiyar (money lender-landlord).

4 Perspectives from the Heartland of Green Revolution: Village Sagarpur

Part I. Introduction

I.1 Faridabad

Faridabad is one of the three industrial centres of Haryana, Rewari and Gurgaon being the other two. The district is divided into 5 Blocks, viz., Faridabad with 62 villages, Ballabgarh with 81 villages, Palwal with 122 villages, Hodal with 70 villages and Hathin with 79 villages.

Faridabad is one of the most rapidly growing urban agglomerations of Haryana and is one of the most industrialized districts in the country, with several industrial complexes in and around it. In 1990 there were 1647 registered factories, of which 1398 were *working* registered factories and they provided employment to 1,25,863 persons (The latest for which data are available).

Along with industrial development, Faridabad has made exceptional progress in the agricultural sector and lies at the heart of the Green Revolution belt of India. The progress in agriculture has been made possible by huge increases in agricultural production, improved irrigation, flood control measures and the introduction of the "new technology". The total area under High Yielding Varieties of foodgrains, such as bajra, maize, wheat and paddy during 1989-90 is of the order of 140, 000 hectares. High yielding varieties of wheat are grown in 98.3 per cent of the area under wheat cultivation; and high yielding varieties of paddy are grown in 77.8 per cent of the area under paddy cultivation. The major Kharif crops are bajra (cultivated over 19.8 thousand hectares) and barley (grown in 5.1 thousand hectares in 1989-90). The major Rabi crops are wheat, cultivated in 119.5 thousand hectares and barley, cultivated in 5.1 thousand hectares, as in 1989-90. Strides in animal husbandry and fisheries have also contributed significantly to the development of the district.

I. 2. Sagarpur

Sagarpur is predominantly a Hindu Village, approximately 8 kms west of Faridabad industrial area and 5.4 kms south west of Ballabgarh industrial area. It is spread over a total area of 4500 bighas of which 800 acres of land is earmarked for agricultural purposes. Sixty per cent of the people are engaged in agriculture.

Because Sagarpur lies in the close proximity to the industrial areas of Faridabad and Ballabgarh, it is vulnerable to pollution from large industrial establishments. Land has been acquired around the periphery of Sagarpur, viz., in the neighbouring villages of Sahupura, Malerna and Uncha Gaon for residential, commercial and industrial purposes, by the Local Development Authority. Sagarpur is under pressure of urbanisation and all the pollution that go with it. Along the northern border of the village is Pyala which houses the liquid petroleum gas bottling plant of Bharat Petroleum Ltd. and where another LPG Bottling Plant is being set up by Indian Oil Corporation, exposing Sagarpur to further sources of pollution. Sagarpur has the disadvantage of being nearer to, or home of, brick kilns: there are 17 brick kilns along its southern border; to the south of Sagarpur there are 3 other brick kilns, established about 5 years back, and to the west of Sagarpur is Asawati, where 2 more brick kilns are in operation for the last 4-5 years. In Jajru, due north of Sagarpur, National Thermal Power Corporation (NTPC) is setting up a Thermal Power Plant, covering an area of approximately 300 acres.

Sagarpur has two Anganwadis, and a dairy, established and managed by the women of the village. It has one high school, one recreation park (under construction), Gram Samiti in each ward to provide loans, a pond for pisciculture and 60 per cent metalled roads, all of which indicate that Sagarpur is well endowed in terms of infrastructure. The houses are all brick houses, have both electricity and piped water connections and an estimated 65 per cent of the households have television sets, indicating a good overall state of well being. With 93.6 per cent of the people literate and the average number of children per family being 5, the status of human development *prima facie* looks satisfactory.

The villagers, nevertheless, face a number of problems, which, are important to put the discussion of the village in perspective. There are six major problems listed and ranked by the women of Baghail Hamlet. In this list the problem of alcoholism among men ranks highest, scoring 10 points, followed by female illiteracy and shortage of money, both scoring 8 points. The list of ten problems prepared by women of Hawelliwalle and ranked by them, has unemployment and acquisition of land by Haryana Urban Development Authority as the "best" two problems, both scoring 10, followed by alcoholism in men, corruption and acute shortage of money, all three having been given a score of 6. The two rankings are reproduced in Table 1.

To isolate the major problems, as a rule of thumb (and obviously arbitrarily) we would consider a problem as acute, which has scored more than 5. Granted that, the problem rankings by the two sets of women, place alcoholism, shortage of money, illiteracy in women, unemployment, land acquisition, corruption and absence of hospital in the village, as the "best problems" of Sagarpur and there is a pattern to it. Women, being more circumspect about food for themselves and their family's livelihood, added two more best problems, viz., absence of compensation from the government for damage to agricultural produce caused by hailstorm and droughts and nilgais; and the inordinate delay in announcing the *minimum support prices* and the *procurement price* for wheat (and paddy) that Government of India customarily offers. These two additional problems highlight three issues: *one*, that the women are aware of crop insurance scheme of the Government and were a bit puzzled (angry!) that they were being denied their entitlements which explains all the noise about lack of compensation for damaged crops; *two*, that the price incentives of the Government of India is actually valued in as much as even the timing of their declaration is keenly watched by the farmers; *three*, that the Government has created, for good or bad, a dependency ("Mai Baap") syndrome, where the common people (read farmers) look up to the Government to solve all their problems.

Table 1 Problem Ranking by Women in two Hamlets of Sagarpur

Ranking by Women of Baghail			Ranking by Women in Hawelliwalle		
Problems	*Scoring*	*Rank*	*Problems*	*Scoring*	*Rank*
Drinking habit of men	**********10	1	Unemployment	********8	1
Illiteracy of women	********8	2	Land acquisition by HUDA	********8	1
Shortage of money	******** 8	2	Corruption	******6	2
No hospital in village	******6	3	Shortage of money	******6	2
Small land holding	*****5	4	Drinking habit of men	******6	2
Insufficient electric supply	****4	5	Low electric supply	***** 5	3
			Weeds	**** 4	4
			NTPC	**** 4	4
			Late fixation of wheat prices	****4	4
			No compensation for damaged crops	*** 3	5

Village Analysts from Hawelliwalle: Rajmati, Bhagwati, Prem and Pyari.
Village Analysts from Baghail: Prem, Shanti, Saroj, Phulwati.
Facilitator: Meera Jayaswal.
Date: 5. 4. 99.

A few words on unemployment are warranted. In a society where women do not seek employment, except self-employment of sorts, they are virtually totally dependent on men for all they need. Unemployment amongst men is, therefore, as much a problem for the women as it is for the men. With a high rate of unemployment, the paucity of money is an obvious consequence. Because men control resources, in the typically patriarchal society of Sagarpur, they expend a part of their resources on alcohol, adding a new dimension to the problem of shortage of money that the women face. Illiteracy among women is disempowering, which results in women adopting a line of least resistance to alcoholism perpetrated upon them by men. Significantly enough, except for problems of small size of holdings and weeds, ranked lower down in priority any way, none of the major problems perceived by women of Sagarpur, relate to farming *per se*.

Caste is not a problem in the village. The Castewise population of Sagarpur is in Table 2.

Table 2 Castewise Population of Sagarpur

Caste	Number of Households	Population
Jat	170	1000
Brahmin	50	400
Backward Castes	80	700
Harijans	100	900
Total	400	3000

Table 2 makes an interesting reading. The Jats and the Brahmins, the upper castes on the one hand, and the Harijans and the Backward Castes on the other, are equally represented in the village. The average household size is between 8.7 and 9. As such there is neither inter-caste variation in the size of the families, nor is there inter-caste variations in economic status, though there are variations in economic status within the castes *inter se*. The latter explains the former, at least partially.

The village is organised into 6 wards, or Muhallas, which are not strictly organised along caste lines but there is dominance of certain castes that is noticeable in almost all the Muhallas. The distribution of castes in the Muhallas is given in Table 3.

Table 3 Distribution of Castes and Muhallas

Muhallas	Number of Households	per cent of Population in Agriculture	Dominant Caste	Dominant Class
Hawelliwalle	50	95	Jat	Middle
Harijan	100	40	Harijan	Middle
Chawkiwalle	80	90	Jat	Middle
Hatewalle	50	95	Jat	Middle
Gareria/Baghail	50	90	Backward Castes	Poor
Patyat	50	90	Brahmin	Middle

There is also a colony of brick kiln workers called Ita Bhatti Colony, inhabited by brick kiln workers, within a distance of 50 yards from the brick kilns.

The definition of class classification adopted by the villagers are non-monetary, but expressed in monetary terms. They first defined the boundary classes, in a three tiered class system, and then deduced the middle class. Households having less than 1 acre of land or are landless and some member of the households works as a labourer, the total monetised value of whose annual income ranges between Rs. 18000 and Rs. 20000, are considered poor. Households possessing land in excess of 14 acres with one or two of its members working in either government sector or the private enterprises, the monetised value of their total income exceeding Rs. 40,000, are considered rich. All other households are classified as falling in the what the villagers call the "middle class". The rich constitute 15-16 per cent of the population. Obviously enough, land holding and employment in the service of the Government have a special place in psyche of Sagarpur: poultry, dairy, trade, commerce, self employment and traditional occupation are nowhere in the class mapping in the villagers. What then is the landholding pattern?

The landholding pattern in Sagarpur is at Table 4.

Table 4 Land Holding Pattern

Size of Farmers/ Farm Size	Percentage of Population	Muhallas
Marginal Farmers/1-1.5 Acres	75	Most of Harijan Muhalla
Small Farmers/2-4 Acres	8	All
Medium Farmers/4-8 Acres	5	All
Large Farmers/8-20 Acres	2	All
Landless	10	All

The landholding pattern is clearly marked by the preponderance of the marginal farmers, with the landless as the next biggest class. If we see Tables 3 and 4, all large farmers are not in the "Rich" category: households owning 8-20 acres of land (large farmers) and have at least one or two of their members in service are rich. The poor are obviously the landless, because the marginal farmers too have 1-1.5 acres of land, whereas, by definition a poor household has no land or land measuring less than 1 acre.

Part II: Livelihood

II. 1. The Livelihood Pattern

The livelihood system in the village is evident from the livelihood map prepared by the men's group in Patyat Muhalla and from the group discussions. For the purposes of mapping the livelihood system in Sagarpur, the villagers elected to take account of the livelihoods of people (men) above the age of 18 only. The information provided looks like Table 5.

The villagers did not chart out the livelihood pattern of women, because women do not work outside their homes and family fields, other than running the small dairy in the village established and managed by the them. The familiar distinction between "inside-home" and "outside-home" tasks/ jobs are deeply entrenched in the village, despite the high literacy rate. Incidentally, the fact that both the Muhallas studied are dominated by upper castes, who consider it a dishonour for the women to work outside their family, has brought out the dichotomy even more sharply. We will deal with it again while dealing with issues relating to gender later in this study.

Table 5 Occupational Structure

Occupation/Source of Income	Patyat Muhalla	Hawelliwalle Muhalla
People with more than 1 source	21 per cent	25 per cent
HH with more than I source	29 per cent	30 per cent
People highly dependent on agriculture	21 per cent	27 per cent
People highly dependent on industry	15 per cent	10 per cent
In Government service	28 per cent	25 per cent
In business related jobs	06 per cent	05 per cent
Labourers	10 per cent	08 per cent
Selling milk	50 per cent	70 per cent
Unemployed	20 per cent	25 per cent
Total adult males	60	75

Table 5 has percentage of people in each category of occupation. Because some people are in two or more occupations concurrently, they figure in all the occupations in which they are engaged. The table does not distribute the total population (in the relevant age group) into different occupations, which is why the percentages in each column do not add up to 100.

People have a variety of occupations and they are by and large mainly distributed in agriculture, Government service and industry. Only 21 percent of the people are in agriculture. And there are few, if at all, pure agriculturists in the village. Agriculture is perceived by the villagers, as a part time occupation and income from agriculture is considered supplementary income. For instance, those who work in Government Offices and in business establishments take leave and return to Sagarpur during both cultivation and harvesting seasons. Similarly, selling milk is also considered a source of supplementary income and there are no professional milk vendors, like the "Yadavs" or the Gujjars.

While nearly one fifth of *individuals* have two or more sources of income, about one third of *households* have more than one source of income. Thus there are more households with more than one source of income than individuals with more than one income source. Because all individuals are part of some household or the other, and individuals constitute households, this seemed a little confusing. The villagers recognise the distinction between individuals and households. The villagers distinguished between "household occupation" and "individual occupations". Agriculture and selling milk are household occupations as everyone in the household has her/his distinctive role cut out in these occupations, whereas working in government or business or as labourers, are individual occupations where other members of the household have no role. This explains why it is important to show separately the percentage of people and percentage of households with more than one source of income.

The general pattern of livelihood is about the same in both the Muhallas. Government Service is the most preferred option. Agriculture is not. This is interesting for a relatively well off village, in the heart of the Green Revolution belt. Unemployment rate is very high, 20-25 per cent and selling milk is very popular, engaging 50 per cent and 70 per cent of the people in Patyat and Hawelliwalle Muhallas respectively, indicating that a high demand for milk exists in and around Sagarpur. Thus the psyche and characteristics of Sagarpur reflect the character of a typical middle class urban area: craze for job security and craze for Government jobs; high rate of unemployment; reluctance to soil their hands in agriculture, probably a flip side of feeling educated and high demand for milk. This needs further probing, particularly the decline in the interest in agriculture.

If we take all the livelihood systems pursued in Sagarpur, they form part of the larger hierarchy of agro-ecosystems shown in figure 4 (*Conway, 1987*). If we consider the totality of the hierarchy of the agro-ecosytems, then the villagers gave us an account of the systems from village level and below. In terms of figure 4, the villagers are not generally engaged in gathering hunting and handicraft manufacture; only a few are in off-farm employment and trading systems. Agriculture remains at the heart of the livelihood system in Sagarpur, though a fairly large section of the population has more than one source of livelihood. Within the farming system, the inhabitants rely partly on livestock system in its paddock variety (they are no herdsmen) and more fully in cropping system, involved in the field and the crop.

Table 6 Changes in Wheat Crop Shown by Men's Group, Patyat Muhalla

Decade	Change in Yield per acre	Change in Size	Change in Quality	Change in Colour
1940-50	3-4 quintals	Big	Good	Golden
1950-60	6 quintals	Big	Good	Do
1960-70	6 quintals	Big	Good	Do
1970-80	16 quintals	Relatively smaller	Not sweet	Yellow
1980-90	16 quintals	Do	Not that sweet	Do
1990-99	14 quintals	Small and thin	Taste deteriorating	Do

Village Analysts: Suresh Gautam, Kamal, Nand Kishore Sharma, Shamevir, Puran Singh, Dhirendra, Shivchandi, Charanjit Lal, Ashok Gautam.

Facilitator: Sudipta Ray.

Table 7 Historical Transect Prepared by Men's Group, Patyat Muhalla

Decade	Livelihood	Industry	Farming System	Cropping Pattern
1940-50	99.5 per cent in agriculture and rest in Azad Hind Fauz or caste based occupation	None	Irrigation by rehant; organic manure; ploughing with bullocks; harvesting with sickle; own seeds, rains for water	Jowar, gram, sugarcane, wheat (less), bajra, barley
1950-60	97 per cent in agriculture and rest in caste based occupation or army	Escort and Bata	Same as in 1940-50	Same as in 1940-50
1960-70	92 per cent in agriculture; 20 per cent in milk vending; 1 per cent	Gadore Co.	Tubewell and canal irrigation; country seeds; tractor for ploughing; organic	Same as in 1950-60, but sugarcane and paddy

Decade	Livelihood	Industry	Farming System	Cropping Pattern
	in military service; 1 per cent in industry and rest in caste based occupation. 2 per cent unemployed		manure	introduced
1970-80	Agriculture: 85 per cent; industry: 2 per cent; labourers: 4 per cent; Government Service: 2 per cent; milk selling: 30; per cent; unemployed 4 per cent; traditional caste-based occupation: 1 per cent		Tubewell and canal irrigation; HYV wheat seeds; tractor for ploughing and harvesting; chemical fertilizers, pesticides.	Main Rabi Crop: Wheat. Main Kharif Crop: Bajra. Gram stopped
1980-90	Agriculture: 75 per cent; industry: 5 per cent; Government Service: 2 per cent; milk: 30 per cent; unemployed: 10 per cent; labourer: 6 per cent; business: 2 per cent and milk: 35 per cent	Payala's LPG Bottling Plant	Same as in 1970-80	Same as in 1970-80, but sugarcane declined. Mustard introduced.
1990-99	Agriculture: 60 per cent; milk: 40 per cent; Government Service: 2 per cent; labourer: 10 per cent; unemployed: 25 per cent and traditonal caste based work: 2 per cent	17 Brick kilns in the village NTPC's plant in Jajru	Same as in 1970-80	Wheat main Rabi crop. Main Kharif crop; Jowar (for fodder) and paddy. Some vegetables

Village Analysts: Suresh Gautam, Kamal, Nand Kishore Sharma, Shamevir, Puran Singh, Dhirendra, Shivchandi, Charanjit Lal, Ashok Gautam.

Facilitator: Sudipta Ray.

II. 2. Changes in Livelihood Pattern

Sagarpur being nearer to the heart of the industrial hub of Faridabad has seen several changes in its social, economic and agricultural structure. These shifts all have all left their mark on the livelihood pattern of the villagers. The historical transects with mens' group in Patyat and Hawelliwalle give a total picture of the dynamics of structural changes in livelihood pattern experienced by Sagarpur over the last half a century or so. These transects are in Tables 6, 7, 8 and 9.

The villagers volunteered additional information that cotton cultivation declined in the 1980s because of small size of holdings, and mustard cultivation was discontinued in the 1990s because of the high risk involved. They also said that sugarcane cultivation was discontinued due to drying up of demand for the same from Palwal Sugar Mill (due to some problem) which brought sugarcane from Sagarpur.

Table 8 Historical Transect by Men's Group in Hawelliwalle Muhalla

Decade	Livelihood	Industry	Farming System	Cropping Pattern
1940-50	98 per cent in agriculture and rest in caste based occupation or in the army	None	Irrigation by rehant; organic manure; ploughing with bullocks; harvesting with sickle; own seeds, rains for water	Jowar, pulses gram, sugarcane, wheat (less), bajra, barley
1950-60	95 per cent in agriculture and rest in caste based occupation or army	Escorts and bata	Same as in 1940-50	Same as in 1940-50

Decade	Livelihood	Indu-stry	Farming System	Cropping Pattern
1960-70	90 per cent in agriculture; 20 per cent in milk vending; 3 per cent in military service; 1per cent in industry and rest in caste based occupation. 2 per cent unemployed. Teaching 1 per cent	Gadore Co.	Tubewell and canal irrigation; country seeds; tractor for ploughing; organic manure	Same as in 1950-60, but paddy introduced on commercial basis
1970-80	Agriculture: 80 per cent; industry: 2 per cent; labourers: 6 per cent; Government service: 2 per cent; milk selling 30 per cent; unemployed 5 per cent; traditional caste-based occupation: 3 per cent		Tubewell and canal irrigation; HYV wheat seeds; tractor for ploughing and harvesting; chemical fertilizers, pesticides.	Main Rabi Crop: Wheat. Main Kharif Crop: Bajra. gram stopped.
1980-90	Agriculture: 70 per cent; industry: 6 per cent; Govt. service: 3 per cent; milk: 70 per cent; unemployed: 10 per cent; labourer 6 per cent; business: 1 per cent and milk: 35 per cent	Pyala's LPG Bottling Plant	Same as in 1970-80	Same as in 1970-80, but mustard declined and cotton stopped.

Decade	Livelihood	Industry	Farming System	Cropping Pattern
1990-99	Agriculture: 60 per cent; milk: 95 per cent; Govt. service: 2 per cent; labourer: 10 per cent; unemployed: 16 per cent and traditional caste based work: 2 per cent. industry 40 per cent. labourer 10 per cent.	17 brick kilns in the Village. NTPC's plant in Jajru	Same as in 1970-80	Wheat main Rabi crop. Main Kharif crop jowar (for fodder) and paddy. Some vegetables

Village Analysts: Harchandi, Mohan Singh, Balbir Singh, Ram Swaroop Singh, Rishal Singh, Nathu Ram, Dharamveer, Sant Singh.

Facilitator: Sudipta Ray.

Table 9 Historical Transect by Men's Group, Hawelliwalle Muhalla. Changes in Wheat Crop

Decade	Change in Yield per acre	Change in Size	Change in Quality	Change in Colour
1940-50	Less because of two droughts	Big	Good	Golden
1950-60	6-8 quintals	Big	Good	Do
1960-70	6 -8 quintals	Big	Good	Do
1970-80	16-18 quintals	Relatively smaller	Not sweet	Yellow
1980-90	16-18 quintals	Do	Not that sweet	Do
1990-99	14-16 quintals	Small and thin	Taste deteriorating	Do

Village Analysts: Harchandi, Mohan Singh, Balbir Singh, Ram Swaroop Singh, Rishal Singh, Nathu Ram, Dharamveer, Sant Singh.

Facilitator: Sudipta Ray.

If we examine Tables 6,7,8 and 9, few trends are discernible:

Agriculture, which absorbed over 98 per cent of the total population of Sagarpur in the 1940-50, has gradually lost its pre-eminence. It now supports no more than 60 per cent of the population, which is below the national average of 70 per cent, a magic figure that has been a part of Indian rural landscape since 1901 Census operation. The economy of Sagarpur, nonetheless, remains greatly dependent on agriculture for its survival and sustenance.

As agriculture declined in importance, selling milk gained in prominence: from almost nil in the 1940-50, it now engages almost 40 per cent of the total population of Sagarpur, as a secondary source of employment and a supplementary source of income.

With the flux of time as new industries moved into the vicinity of Sagarpur, people diversified their livelihood pattern: from a purely agrarian economy in the 1950s, Sagarpur has moved into an economy where service sector has become important, industry has absorbed a chunk of the people, and demand for pure labourers has increased.

This diversification in livelihood and demand for labourers as also services could not absorb all the additional hands that were either added to the labour force or those who were released from agriculture, consequent upon its mechanisation. This showed up as large number of unemployed: 25 per cent in Patyat and 16 per cent in Hawelliwalle. This difference in the number of unemployed in the two Muhallas is understandable: because Hawellewalle Muhalla had the large farmers of the village and richer people, they are less likely to be unemployed. Unemployment is higher among the poor than among the non-poor.

There has been several changes in the yield pattern and in the inherent quality of agricultural produce, as shown by Tables 6 and 9. We are not discussing these important changes for the present as they would form part of our discussion later in this book, in the context of changes in cropping pattern and yields.

Part III: Importance of Agriculture to the People

III. 1. Decline in Interest in Agriculture

The decline in agriculture as an occupation is obvious and for an agrarian economy it is a serious issue. In order to probe the issue further the groups of villagers identified their current sources of income for the village and gave a rough estimate of income earned from each of them by the villagers as also indicate alongside each sources of income, the percentage of population engaged in them. Onlookers who (initially not part of the participating groups) also chipped in from time to time and enriched the study. The groups then ranked their preferences for each of the occupations in the next five years and the percentage of population who, they anticipate, would join the respective occupations.

Tables 10 and 11, are categorical that there is an overwhelming preference to move out of agriculture and seek more and more of jobs in the government. Business cr petty shop come rather low down the preference scale. Significantly, there is no mention of any off-farm occupation except selling milk. There is no mention of any traditional trade or occupation. There is no special category of work for women. There is no cottage and village industry in the village.

On the face of it, it might seem that with the current process of liberalisation, government would shrink, and with it government jobs, and the people of Sagarpur may come to grief. This is, however, not the case in reality. Most of the people who work for the government, are either in police or military. (The Jat Regiment of the Indian Army is known for its valour and contribution to the upkeep of the country's territorial integrity.) These services are least likely to shrink in the foreseeable future, given the geo-politics of the sub-continent.

The decline of interest in agriculture is on account of a combination of factors, foremost among which is the high cost of cultivation and of shortage of power and water for irrigation. Erratic rain and equally depressing ground water level, poses big problems for agriculture (see Column 6 of Tables 10 and 11). The preference for government service stems from the promise of job security and lucrative compensation package both during service and after retirement that it holds out. The breakdown of the joint family system and the consequent pressure on the earning member(s) of the family (the male member) to earn more for better education and to provide even better facilities for the children, have added new dimensions to the attractiveness of migration out of agriculture into the job market. This has important lessons to learn: the farmers judge the well being of a family from the quality and number of facilities provided to their children. Children are valued and their welfare is taken as an index of a household's well being.

The preference for milk selling as a source of income, is both due to returns and due to the anticipated rise in demand for milk consequent upon, current and potential, urbanisation in and around Sagarpur, viz., Sahupura, Malerna and Uncha Gaon. Large tracts of land have been acquired, as we mentioned earlier, by the local development authority, for setting up residential, industrial and commercial complexes, in these areas.

Table 10 Estimated Percentage of Population in Different Occupations Shown by Men of Patyat Muhalla

Livlihood Options	*Caste-wise Population*	*Class-wise Population*	*Per cent People in Future*	*Per cent People currently*	*Reason for Decline/increase in Interest*	*Current Income*
Milk	All	All	20	50	Expensive feed. Unremunerative milk prices. Loss due to death of animals. Absence of veterinary services.	Rs. 2500 in winter and Rs. 1700-1800 p.m. in summer

Livlihood Options	*Caste-wise Population*	*Class-wise Population*	*Per cent People in Future*	*Per cent People currently*	*Reason for Decline/increase in Interest*	*Current Income*
Agriculture	Mostly Jats	Land-owners		21	Power and water problems. Erratic rains. Small sized holdings. High cost of inputs. Lack of capital.	Rs. 5000 from wheat p.a.
Industry	All	Middle and Upper	20	15	Hard work and less income than from Govt. jobs. Accidents. Education required.	Rs. 1000-2000 p.m.
Govt. service	All	Middle and Upper	100	28	Less strenuous. Mostly in police and army. Compensation and retirement benefits good. Job security.	Rs. 4200 p.m. starting salary
Shop	All	Middle and Upper	10	6	Demand for goods due to TV and nearness to town. Women prefer village shop.	Rs. 800 p.m.
Tempo	Mostly Jats	Middle and Upper	20	—	Increasing number of commuters to and from town.	Rs. 2000 p.m. Loan available at EMI Rs. 500

Livli-hood Options	*Caste-wise Popu-lation*	*Class-wise Popu-lation*	*Per cent People in Future*	*Per cent People currently*	*Reason for Decline/increase in Interest*	*Current Income*
Tractor	Mostly Jats	Middle and Upper	10	—	Renting tractors give good return	Rs. 400-Rs. 500 p.d.
Cart	Hari-jans	Poor	0	—	Falling demand	Rs. 50-100 p.d.
Donkey	Praja-pats	Poor	0	—	Used only for carrying building materials through lanes	Rs. 50-100 p.d. for 10 days per month
Labourer	Hari-jans/ Backward Castes.	Poor	0	10	Only during harvesting months and in contract job for construction	Rs. 80 for men and Rs. 60 p.d. for women for 4-5 months

Note: For making comparisons easy, Column 5 in Table 10 above, is derived from Table 5, and was not shown by the villagers during the exercise of occupation preference ranking.

Table 11 Estimated Percentage of Population in Different Occupations (Men of Hawelliwalle)

Livlihood Options	*Caste-wise Population*	*Class-wise Population*	*Per cent People in Future*	*Per cent People currently*	*Reason for Decline/increase in Interest*	*Current Income*
Milk	All	All	100	70	Women can take care of animals in their absence. Growing milk demand. Supplementary income.	Rs. 2500 in winter and Rs. 1700-1800 p.m. in summer
Agriculture	Majority Jats	Landowners	60	27	Power and water problems. Erratic rains. Small sized holdings. High cost of inputs. Unable to grow vegetables.	Rs. 5000 from wheat p.a. 10 per cent
Industry	All	Middle and Upper	50		Ranked below Govt. jobs. Education required. Insecurity. Better than agriculture as gives monthly income unlike annual income from agriculture.	Rs. 1000-2000 p.m.

Livlihood Options	*Caste-wise Population*	*Class-wise Population*	*Per cent People in Future*	*Per cent People currently*	*Reason for Decline/increase in Interest*	*Current Income*
Govt. Service	All	Middle and Upper	100	25	Compensation and retirement benefits good. Job security. Children get job in case of death and wife gets pension. Compensation in case of accident.	Rs. 4200 p.m. starting salary
Shops truck, tempo, tourist vans	All	Middle and Upper	60	5	Demand for consumer goods due to TV and nearness to town. Women prefer village shop. No timing. Time for children's development. But risky.	Rs. 800 p.m.
Labourer	Harijans/ Backward Castes	Poor	0	8	Only during harvesting months and in contract job for construction, liable to be terminated any time.	Rs. 80 for men and Rs. 60 p.d. for women for 4-5 months.

Notes: As in case of Table 10, for making comparisons easier, Column 5 in Table 11 is derived from Table 5, and was not shown by the villagers during the exercise of occupation preference ranking.

Village Analysts: Krishan Singh, Rajvir Singh, Om Prakash Sharma, Udai Bir, Bacchu Singh.

Facilitator: Sudipta Ray.

There are differences in Table 10 and 11. These differences are due to the customs and traditions of the two dominant castes. The Jats in Hawelliwalle are all for selling milk, but the Brahmins are less so inclined (100 per cent vis-à-vis 20 per cent). In fact the Brahmins of Patyat anticipate that there would be a fall in the percentage of people engaged in selling milk. They have assigned various reasons including loss due to death of animals to the tune of Rs. 15000-20,000, and the absence of support facilities like veterinary services and feed. The same is not true of the Jats of Hawelliwalle, who anticipate that all the Households in the village will take to milk selling as it could be managed by the women and supported by anticipated growth in the demand for milk.

A Jat farmer explained this difference in perception. According to him, the women in Brahmins families are less adept in dealing with buffaloes (lack the requisite technology!). The Jats of Hawelliwalla are proficient. This makes a lot of difference, both in terms of caring and saving buffaloes, and output. Secondly because the people of Patyat are mostly small and medium farmers, vis-à-vis large Jat farmers of Hawelliwalle, the formers' output of fodder for their bovine wealth from their own fields is insufficient to see them throughout the year. Brahmin women do not go out to fetch fodder walking long distances. It is against their grain. Villagers of Patyat are thus forced to buy feed, which is expensive and adversely affects the cost structure of milk production. This is where the Brahmins of Patyat lose out to the Jats of Hawelliwalle.

It is significant that only Harijans, Prajapats and other backward castes are anticipated to participate in the work force as labourers and as cart and donkey operators, transporting goods, involving arduous physical labour (see last three rows of Table 10 and last two rows of Table 11). Whereas in mechanised transportation of goods that do not involve much of physical strain, like tempo, tractor etc., the Jats are anticipated to be the major players. This reflects two phenomenon: one, an attitude of mind where certain category of tasks are considered as of lower status and hence are separated for those in the lower strata of the community; second, access to the requisite resources. The mechanised system of transporting goods requires a large outlay. Only Jats have command over such resources, being large farmers and rich. The availability of credit to Harijans, Prajapats and other backward castes, from Gurgaon Gramin Bank, is also doubtful, because in the villagers' perception, they are the ones traditionally viewed as non-Bankable; they lose out as they hardly have anything to offer as collateral to secure their loans.

III. 2. Crops Grown and Cropping Pattern

Tables 6, 7, 8 and 9 gives a fair account of the crops grown and the cropping pattern of Sagarpur. Reference is invited to last column of Tables 7 and 8 in particular. There are two seasons: Rabi and Kharif (Monsoon). Actually it should be enumerated the other way round: Kharif and Rabi, for one following the other. But given the importance of Rabi, the villagers prefer to discuss Rabi first and then Kharif. The main crops during Rabi are the two varieties of wheat (the early and the late varieties), of which the early variety is grown both for household consumption and sale in the market to non-government buyers. The main Kharif crops are paddy and jowar (as fodder). A more recent interest in growing vegetables (potatoes, radish and carrot) is noticeable, owing to demand for vegetables in the neighbouring markets, which industries have helped to build.

Wheat is by far the most important crop. When the researchers visited the village during the second round of the study they could see only wheat standing all over the fields. The women expressed the importance of wheat by a diagram, which is figure 5 of this chapter. Wheat is cultivated in 15 Annas of land (that is, 84 per cent, for in the pre-metric system of currency denomination, 16 Annas made one Rupee) and vegetables and mustard are cultivated in only 1 Anna (or 6 per cent) of land. Men are more precise. According to them, wheat is cultivated in 99 per cent of land; Mustard on 0.5 per cent and vegetables such as barseem on the remaining 0.5 per cent land. The net result is that most of the villagers engaged in agriculture have placed reliance on wheat as their best bet in farming.

We mentioned there are two varieties of wheat cultivated, an early variety and a late variety. The early variety is cultivated in 70 per cent of the cultivable land and late variety is grown on the remaining 30 per cent of land. There is a difference in yield between the two varieties: the early variety yields more by about 2 quintals per acre than the late variety. But farmers opt for the late variety for growing wheat as a second crop on land, which they cultivate to grow Jowar and bajra as their first crops, and these crops are not ready for harvesting in time for sowing the early variety of wheat.

Harvesting of wheat is in three phases. First class yield comes from the first phase of the crop usually harvested in the first week of April. The grains are very good, are bought by people for personal consumption and fetches higher price by a margin of Rs.100 per quintal over the price normally fetched by ordinary wheat. This is the harvest, which is also stored for household level consumption. The second crop is harvested in the second week of April, which yields ordinary grains. This is the harvest, which is sold to the Government at the declared procurement prices (we will talk more about these prices later), for the public distribution system run by the government. The crop, which is harvested in the third week of April, yields green crops, usually used as livestock feed. The last crop is of poor quality because of late sowing, insufficient water and poor quality seeds. By growing the third grade wheat, the farmers actually try to minimise their loss, for otherwise their land will remain fallow.

III. 3. Intensity of Cultivation

Though cultivation and farming in Sagarpur is mostly from canal and lift irrigation since 1960-70, intensity of cultivation remains mono cropping. The farmers cultivate their land once during each of the two principal seasons, with some overlap. The farmers look upon agriculture as a supplementary source of livelihood or at least one among the principal sources of livelihoods. The farmers are engaged, along with agriculture, in either selling milk, or serving the government or working for business and so on. Generally, farmers have three crops: Wheat in Rabi; and paddy and jowar (for fodder) during Kharif. Wheat among these three is by far the most important crop. A look at the total cropping scenario tells us that Sagarpur is moving further away from multiple cropping to annual cropping (*Boserup*, 1993 has identified several stages in agriculture). There is application of chemical fertilisers in various doses, based on gut feeling and experience of farmers, in the absence of proper extension service.

III. 4. Changes in Cropping Pattern

We take the decade 1940-50 as the point of departure and Tables 7 and 8 as reference evidence. See the last columns of these Tables. In the decade, a large number of crops were cultivated, though it is difficult to reconstruct the percentage of arable land on which each crop was grown. The crops were a mixture of staple, coarse cereals, lentils, pulses and sugarcane (for only jaggery). The main crops were coarse grains (barley and bajra) and grams. Most of the crops grown were for consumption in the households in the village. Farming was both subsistence and sustenance activity. By growing a mosaic of crops, the farmers not only diffused their risk of failure, on account of loss due to attack by pests, insects, droughts, floods, disease or whatever, either singly or in some combination, but also ensured that their households had a basket of food which contained fibre, nutrition and protein: carbohydrates, cereals and pulses.

In 1960-70, winds of change began to sweep Sagarpur. Some of the crops were viewed with less of interest. By the time Sagarpur reached 1970s, paddy was introduced, and so is sugarcane. In the next decade, as HYV seeds gained ground, wheat remained the only main Rabi crop and bajra held on as the main Kharif crop. Cultivation of gram stopped. In the decade 1980-90, mustard cultivation took roots as a cash crop in the hope a high return, but at the same time, cultivation of cotton was reduced because the small size of landholdings rendered them unsuitable for cotton cultivation.

As of now (1990s) farmers in sagarpur are left with wheat and a sprinkling of mustard, and some vegetables on an experimental basis, as principal Rabi crops to grow. Wheat is grown both for household consumption and for sale in the market; vegetables are, in the main, for sale. The high risk of cultivating mustard dissuades the farmers from continuing with their fascination for mustard. The "Yellow Revolution" of the government is not taking roots. Sugarcane also is dropped from the list of crops grown as the sugar-mill in Palwal, within whose catchment area Sagarpur falls, has fallen into bad days and no longer buys sugarcane from Sagarpur. During Kharif, paddy constitutes the main crops, with Jowar grown for fodder. In terms of variety and diversity, there is a marked reduction, to which extent, the capacity of the farmers to diffuse risk is pruned. This trend of reduction in crop variety and increase in risks borne by the farmer is, curiously enough, in keeping with the trends seen world-wide (see *Pimbert,* 1993; FAO; 1993, *Soetomo* 1992; *Fowler et. al.* 1990). For instance in India itself more than 30, 000 varieties of rice were grown, of which an estimated 10 cover 75 per cent of the area under rice cultivation.

As we move from the 1940-50 into the last decade of this century, Tables 7 and 8 brings us near the truth that the mosaic of crops grown in Sagarpur has turned dull. From several crops of different values and uses and nutrition, the present day crops grown, are basically three: Wheat, paddy and jowar (as fodder). This reduction in diversity of crops signals a movement away from poly-culture towards standard monoculture. It signals reduction in palate and nutritional value of the food consumed in Sagarpur households. The crop grown in the farms can provide basically only carbohydrates and a modicum of fibre in terms of some vegetable, as most of it is for sale. It also indicates that whereas in 1950s and 1960s much of agricultural operations were for ensuring self-sufficiency in *food*, in 1990s the emphasis seems to be more on self-sufficiency in *income*. There is a movement from growing crops to meet food requirements of households and of the community, to growing crops for the market's consumption and for money. Importantly enough, this marks a shift in the rural mindset and this shift in the mindset has bearing on the social and political environment in the village.

We have to add here that it is no one's position that a mixture of crops is better than mono/bi-cropping. Much depends upon the local conditions and the characteristics of the crops themselves. However growing a large number of crops has its advantages, backed by decades of farmers' experience. For instance, pest infestation frequently gets reduced in inter-cropping, because of various factors including the difficulty faced by pests to locate a host plant (*Risch, Andow, Altieri 1983*). "Host plants are more widely spread and so harder to find; one species may trap a pest or one specie may repel a pest; and/or predators may be attracted. Weeds are more likely to be suppressed by mixtures" (*Pretty, 1995*).

III. 5. Changes in Agricultural Practices and Reasons for the Changes

Changes in cropping pattern has been influenced by a chain of dynamic changes in farming practices. In 1940s and 1950s, we find agriculture as wholly rainfed. Agriculture is all about traditional practices in regard to seeds, water harvesting structures, soil nutrients and implements. It was a family affair. The farmers and the community are in total control of the inputs, barring rains where they are fully dependent upon nature's bounties (or niggardliness!). There is none of any inputs required to be imported from outside the village.

During 1960-70 mechanisation of agriculture starts taking roots: tubewells and tractors come to their own. In 1970-80, we see evidence of agriculture in Sagarpur exposed to full blown "new technology": hybrid or HYV seeds replacing traditional varieties; chemical fertilisers crowding out manure, insecticides and pesticides substituting pest and insect resistant seeds, along with tractors substituting for the bullocks and the wooden plough. Dependence on the vagaries of nature for water is curtailed for sure, but independence from the clutches of human beings is surrendered in the process. Farmers depend on seed companies/farms for their seeds; pesticide and insecticide companies (and their dealers) for pesticides and insecticides; Haryana State Electricity Board for their power and hence for water to irrigate their fields; Tractor Companies and their dealers for ploughing and the fertilisers companies and their dealers for replenishing soil nutrition. The control of the farmers and the community on inputs vital for their survival, is out of their hands.

It is often lost that this shift in farming practices also means that farming is now a High External Input Agriculture (HEIA) from Zero External Input Agriculture (ZEIA) during 1940-50 and then Low External Input Agriculture (LEIA) in 1960-70, as we travel through time. In the 1940s and 1950s agriculture was based on what the farmer and the community had: seeds, labour, bullocks, plough and the wooden hoe, manure and rains. In the 1980s and 1990s, agriculture has come to be based on inputs more from outside the households and the community: HYV seeds, pesticides, insecticides, chemical fertilisers, electricity, tractor power, tubewells and pumpsets. Thus whereas in the 1940s and 1950s, farmers could carry out their cultivation and farming, without demur or recourse, buying virtually nothing from outside his/her household, or at best only accessing inputs from the community, in the 1990s we are in Sagarpur where farmers buy virtually everything except for family labour from outside the household. Hark the information in Chart I below.

Chart 1

Farming in the 1940s and 1950s

Sourcing of Resources

Sun	Sources of energy for plant photosynthesis
Water	Rain and small/or small local irrigation schemes
Nitrogen	Fixed from air, recycled in soil organic matter
Other Nutrients	From soil reserves recycled in cropping system
Weed and Pest Control	Biological, cultural and mechanical
Seed	Varieties produced on farm save from previous year
Machinery	Built and maintained by farming households or in the community
Labour	Most work done by family members
Capital	Source is household and community, reinvested locally
Management	Information from farmers and local community

Farming in the 1980s and 1990s

Sourcing of Resources

Sun	Sources of energy for plant photosynthesis
Water	Large dams, centralised distribution, pumpsets, deep wells
Nitrogen	Primarily from applied chemical fertilisers
Other Nutrients	Applied from outside
Weed and Pest control	Chemical insecticides, herbicides and weedicides
Seeds	Hybrid, HYV or certified varieties purchased annually
Machinery	Purchased and replaced frequently
Labour	Family labour and hired labour. Labour hired for fixing pumpsets/tractors/threshers etc.
Capital	External indebtedness to banks, money lenders; resources leave the community
Management	From input suppliers, extension workers, agricultural experts

Francis and King (1988) provide a copybook case confirming the framework of "internal resources vs. external resources" this transition from ZEIA to LEIA and eventually to HEIA that the villagers of Sagarpur show us through Tables 6 to 8. We have compared the sourcing of resources in the 1940s and 1950s, vis-à-vis 1980s and 90s in Chart 1, which is self-explanatory.

In the Chart under reference, other than the source of energy for plant photosynthesis, almost everything has changed. It is true that there is yet to be a total conversion from one system to other, but the phenomenon of a very large amount of inputs being accessed from outside is setting in. There is little to doubt that. Thus farming in the 1980s and 1990s has become more dependent on sourcing from outside Sagarpur. Farming has in the process come to use resources that are not always renewable. Internal resources are "inherently renewable and thus have the potential to be used on a 'sustained' basis, indefinitely, through ecologically sound methods of farming" (*Conway and Barbier, 1990*). Water, nitrogen, other nutrients, seeds, machinery, weed and pest control are made available by using resources that are no longer renewable.

Since agriculture in Sagarpur has become dependent on external resources, much of it is not provided as a "free good", implying that the farming households must buy many of these inputs which were earlier free (e.g. water). Hence the farmers must generate a surplus of production, in cash or whatever else of value, to exchange for external resources. And the cost of acquiring these resources and their supply channels are rarely controllable always by the farming households. All these taken one with the other, has at least three cost implications: open costs, hidden costs and real costs.

The transition from ZEIA to LEIA and eventually to HEIA, has made agriculture a high *open* cost because the farmer has to buy the inputs. There is little of the resources required which is free of charge. Thus the cost of farming operation has gone up so much so that it has put sustainability of peasant agriculture in doubt and the high cost of external inputs is pinching the farmers lately. One explanation for this sudden upward rise in input costs, according to us, lies in the implementation of the structural adjustment programme of the IMF-World Bank, consequent cut in subsidies (real or virtual) and the general rise in prices, have jacked up input costs sharply. It is anticipated that with globalisation and full implementation of the TRIPS Agreement of the WTO, which is lurking round the corner, the cost of these inputs will rise further. Under the new patent laws, a patent holder will have patent rights for 20 years. Individuals and firms who would take out patents will not change the technology for as long as they could and this bodes ill for the farmers so keen to adopt new technology: technology will remain stagnant for a long time. The several fold increase in yield seen in the 1970s due to adoption of new technology will no longer be possible.

Box 4.1
What are TRIPS and its Impact?

"...........The agreement on Trade-Related Aspects of Intellectual Property Rights or TRIPS came into effect in 1995 under the World Trade Organisation (WTO). It affects such diverse areas as computer programming and circuit design, pharmaceuticals and transgenic crops. Although each country implements intellectual property rights laws at the national level, the TRIPS agreement imposes minimum standards on patents, copyright, trademarks and trade secrets. These standards are derived from the legislation of industrial countries, applying forms and level of protection of the industrial world to all WTO members. This is far tighter than existing legislation in most developing countries and often conflicts with their national interests and needs. Developing countries have been given until 2000 to adjust their laws; least developing countries until 2005.

The WTO's TRIPS agreement can be enforced through the integrated dispute settlement dispute settlement system. This effectively means that if a country does not fulfil its intellectual property rights obligations, trade sanctions can be applied against it—a serious threat."

Source: South Centre: *The Trips Agreement: A Guide for the South*, Geneva, 1997.

"Tighter intellectual property rights raise the *price of technology transfer*, and risk blocking developing countries out of the dynamic knowledge sector......."

UNDP: *Human Development Report*, Oxford University Press, 1999

The transition from ZEIA to HEIA has also made a noticeable impact on the *hidden* cost of operation. The increase in fossil fuel use to keep outputs high, also means more energy consumption. Shift from ZEIA to HEIA has led to substitution of manual labour and animal power by tractors, threshers and pumpsets (either diesel or electric) that we saw, which implies that external energy sources have substituted energy sources found in the household and the community. All this along with use of fertilisers, which is mostly NKP, means agriculture has become very energy intensive in Sagarpur. Although we have no estimates of how much is the total energy inputs to agriculture due to the use of fertilisers (NKP), pumpsets and tractors, in Sagarpur but in third world countries these amongst themselves consume more than 90 per cent of total energy inputs for farming. For India as a whole there is one estimate that 10-20 per cent increase in yields following mechanisation, costs an additional 43-260 per cent more in energy consumption. In Punjab, the neighbouring state of Sagarpur, farms in a class 14-25 hectares use three times as much direct energy per hectare as farmers smaller than 6 Hectares (*Singh* and *Miglani, 1976*). The following Chart 2 is interesting.

Chart 2 Input Output Comparison

Low input comparison	High input comparison	Amount of extra yield for high input	Amount of extra energy consumption for high input
State of West Bengal, in Eastern India			
Bullock, rice	Power tiller, rice	+ 8 per cent	+ 200 per cent
Bullock, rice	Tractor, rice	+ 13 per cent	+ 43 per cent
Bullock, wheat	Power tiller, wheat	+ 12 per cent	+ 74 per cent
Bullock, wheat	Tractor, wheat	+ 6 per cent	+ 89 per cent
State of Uttar Pradesh in North India			
Bullock, rice	Mechanised rice	+ 20 per cent	+ 45 per cent
Bullock, wheat	Mechanised wheat	+ 29 per cent	+ 138 per cent

Source: *Singh and Singh, 1976.*

In the above table, as West Bengal, transits from growing rice using bullocks for ploughing to tilling power tillers, extra yield for high external input is 8 per cent, whereas the additional energy consumption needed for the high input is 200 per cent. Similarly as the State transited from bullock-wheat to power tiller-wheat, extra yield for high input was 6 per cent but increase in extra energy was 89 per cent. The case of Uttar Pradesh is similar. As we see its movement from bullock-wheat to mechanised-wheat, yield increases by 29 per cent as against increase in extra energy consumption by 138 per cent. Similarly for other forms of cultivating rice and wheat in both the States, indicating that as farming moves away from traditional cultivation to mechanised or partially mechanised agriculture, yield increases, but at once, energy consumption increases steeply. Percentage increases in energy requirements far outstrip the percentage increases in yield. The differentials in yield increase and extra energy requirement depends on local conditions and environments. We can only draw a general conclusion that the movement from ZEIA to HEIA has increased the energy intensity of farming in Sagarpur.

In high external input agriculture, it is important to note entails a lot of *real costs*. Even where there is no direct monetary outgoing to acquire a resource, there are real cost incurred by the farming households to procure inputs. The most obvious examples are the time required in bringing seeds and other inputs from local distributors in Ballabgarh or Faridabad or Block Office. Time expended in fetching diesel for pumpsets (in case the pumpsets are not electricity operated) and chasing the Haryana State Electricity Board employees for restoration of power when power failure occurs etc. are other examples that come to mind. Loss of crops when any of the inputs are either not available or not available in time, because as we noted earlier, in case of HEIA, the control over prices and supply of inputs do not rest with the farmers and their community.

It is true that output has also increased but as we shall examine a little later, the increase in cost has outstripped the benefit of increased output. Small wonder, the villagers assigned high cost of agriculture as a reason why they want to migrate out of the sector. (Reference is invited to columns 4 of Tables 10 and 11.) In such a situation, HEIA always puts sustainability of agriculture in doubt.

And then this transition HEIA has also increased the chemicalisation of agriculture and the consequences for the health of land and of those who consume agricultural products are likely to be disturbing. Right from a variety of chemical fertilisers, to different insecticides, to different kinds of pesticides applied directly to the fields and seeds, agriculture has come to include in its inputs a whole range of chemicals. The impact of these on soil conditions may not be currently perceived as important in Sagarpur, but agricultural history in that part of the country is replete with instances where such a transition has caused damage to land leading to a fall in productivity, a phenomenon poetically called "Yellowing of the Green Revolution". Add to this the impact that consumption of food so grown might have on the general state of health in the village.

Box 4.2
Alternatives to Pesticide Use

Integrated pest management relies on such techniques as crop rotation and inter-cropping to inhibit the proliferation of weeds, pests and pathogens. Then there are biological controls, which rely on nature's own checks and balances. Natural predators are introduced to keep pest population to a minimum, or pest breeding is disrupted by the release of sterilised males.
Integrated pest management has produced good results in Brazil, China and India. In Soybean cultivation in Brazil, pesticide use has been reduced by 80 per cent over a seven-year period by introducing integrated pest management. In India, insecticide use has been cut by upto 50 per cent in Orissa through the integrated pest management practices.
Biological control has reduced mealy bug pests in bout 65 million hectares of land used for growing Cassava. Biological control has reduced Banana pest population in Costa Rica.

Source: Geoffrey Lean: *WWF Atlas of the Environment* (Oxford: Helican) 1992.

III. 6. Changes in Yields and the Reasons Therefore

Have such dramatic shifts had any impact on yields? We have to return for a while to Tables 6 and 9 once again. Since wheat is the principal crop grown and the world of farmers in Sagarpur revolves, as it were, around wheat, it is best to discuss variations in the yields in terms of how yield of wheat has varied. During 1940-50s, output of wheat per acre was 4 quintals only. During 1950-60 and during 1960-70, the yield increased to about 6 quintals per acre. In the next decade, 1970-80, once tubewells and tractors for irrigation and ploughing respectively, came into use, yield jumped up by almost 150 per cent: from 6 quintals an acre to around 16 quintals an acre.

This was also the decade, when Sagarpur got the taste of full blown "new technology". And it remained at that level in the 1980-90. This was the high noon of the Green Revolution, when HYV seeds, fertilisers, other chemicals, pesticides and assured irrigation were seen as doing the trick. These were the also the decades of when government of India began providing price incentives to farmers of wheat (and paddy) in terms of *minimum support price* (a "floor" price at which government would buy foodgrains if the market price fell below the stated price on account of higher production and consequent higher supply) and *procurement prices* (a "ceiling" price at which government would buy foodgrains from the farmers for meeting the demands of the public distribution system). Thus yield was responding to both changes in technology as also to the farmers' inclination to grow more in sympathy with price incentives offered by government of India. But the yield of the 1980s was not sustained in the 1990s. Yield per acre fell by as much as 12 per cent, to reach about 14 quintals per acre during the current decade.

During the years under review, not only did the villagers perceive yield change but the intrinsic quality of agricultural produce itself was perceived to have changed, in looks, shapes, sizes and tastes. Wheat changed in colour from golden yellow to reddish yellow, at the time HYV seeds were introduced. The shape of the grains changed from 'big' grains to relatively smaller grains in the seventies and then to "small and thin" grains in the 1990s. The good taste of the traditional variety also gave way to less tastier stuff during 1970-80. And the villagers note with concern than in recent years taste continues to deteriorate.

III. 7. Are there Spatial Differences in Yields or Crop Quality?

If we look at Tables 7 and 9 above, we have a fairly good idea of how decadal yield of the principal crop has behaved over the last 50 years or so. Both in Patyat and Hawelliwalle Muhallas the yield have been about the same. The variations are only marginal, more to do with how the two groups aggregated annual yields into decadal yield. The current yield of around 14-16 quintals per acre, is what is confirmed by official data in the area.

In terms of crop quality, taken by the texture, shape, colour and size of the grains, in both the localities, there is no variation. From big and golden coloured grains in 1940-50, to relatively smaller sized yellow coloured grains in 1970-80 and then to small sized thin grains in 1990s, are common to both the localities. The perceived changes in the taste of wheat they grow have also been seen in both Patyat and Hawelliwalle Muhallas. In 1970-80, inhabitants in both the Muhallas perceive that wheat no longer tastes as good as it used to in the earlier decades, and then during recent years, deteriorating taste of wheat is perceived in both the Muhallas.

Part IV: Constraints to Agricultural Production

IV. 1. What are the Constraints faced by Agriculture?

A review given by the villagers in Tables 6, 7, 8 and 9 above, of the sweep of changes that agriculture of Sagarpur has seen, points to certain crops being dropped from the agricultural map, due to reasons of, *inter alia*, small size of holdings or risks involved. It did mean that agriculture has faced constraints of different kinds over these years. The rationale for dwindling interest in agriculture set forth by the villagers also point to certain negative features of agriculture perceived. However, constraints faced by agriculture are perceived differently by different stakeholders. In this study the perceived constraints have been classified as those seen by men and women separately and by these groups in the two Muhallas separately as well. These constraints are ranked by the two groups of villagers, separately for the two Muhallas studied. These Constraint Rankings are at Tables 12, 13, 14 and 15.

The women of Patyat Muhalla have ranked the constraints in descending order of the magnitude of the problem, but there are no clear breaks: there is a continuum of gravity of the problems the constraints pose. And it is difficult to discern any logic underlying this gradation (though there is one) precisely because they did not provide any estimate of damage or loss in 5 out of 9 constraints ranked. But the women of Hawelliwalle Muhalla, have categorised the 8 constraints, ranked by them, into 4 clusters, each containing two constraints: shortage of power and locust, placed at the top priority bracket with a score of 10; whereas, *gandar* and *jai* categorised as the least troublesome constraints. The men also provide a continuum of ranking and do not give clear clusters of problems based on the intensity of harm caused.

The constraints ranked in descending order of magnitude of the damage/loss they cause, by both the women's group and the men's group include *shortage of power, locust, nilgais and termites*, as the constraints that cause most damage. Of the remaining constraints ranked by the women, the majority are weeds (5 out of 9 in Patyat Muhalla and 3 out of 8 in Hawelliwalle Muhalla). As against this most of the constraints ranked by the men are insects and pests (7 out of 14 in Patyat Muhalla, and 4 out of 9 in Hawelliwalle Muhalla). Women are the key actors in deweeding during both the seasons, Rabi and Kharif, and therefore, they recognise the constraints weeds put to agriculture and articulating them. Men on the other hand, because they have the assigned responsibilities of "outside-home" work, interact with outsiders and fetch "pesticides etc." to deal with pests. They are, therefore, keen to talk about pests than weeds and they do so in full measure. Men also find nature's contribution in the form of hail as a major constraint which women do not mention.

Though estimates of damage vary, from Rs. 2500 to Rs. 3000 per acre, all estimates by both men and women group place locust as the most damaging of the constraints and there are a host of animals and pests which cause damages running into thousands. The major constraints are pests, animals and shortage of power. The loss inflicted by weeds, rats and termites are all comparatively lesser and they are, therefore, ranked lower in the graded list of constraints by all groups. A rational response should, therefore, have been emphasis on removing the constraints caused by locusts, animals and pests. Weeds, rats and termites should have been lower down in the response agenda. If we see the responses (last column of Tables 12 and 13) it is surprising that farmers have tried to tackle basically the weeds. The measures taken to confront the problems caused by locust, animals and pest have been only marginal.

Table 12 Constraint Ranking by Men's Group in Patyat Muhalla

Constraints	Crops attacked	Effect	Cause and Relation-ships	Estimated loss (In Rs.)	Score	Stage when attacked	Measures
Locust (insect)	Jowar, bajra and maize	Eats away leaves (2-3)	Late rain or untimely rain	3000/acre	****** (6)	Youth stage	Spraying a very expensive insecticide at Rs. 800 per acre.
Batti (weed)	Paddy	Inhibits growth	Natural	No estimate	*** (3)	Infant stage	Uprooting
Termites (pest)	Wheat, jo, maize, bajra and jowar	Weakens roots and destroys grains	Dry winter and dry soil	1000/ acre	****** (6)	All stages	Pesticide at the rate of one bottle per acre. Price Rs. 200 per bottle
Power shortage	All crops	Reduces irrigation	Power to industrial area and towns	No estimate	****** **** (10)	All stages	No solution excepting borrowing tractor for irrigating.
Safed moondi (weed)	Wheat	Looks like wheat. Prevents growth of wheat (3)	unknown. Grows naturally	500/acre	*** (3)	Infant stage	None. Up-rooting for use as fodder

Rat	All crops with grains	Eats grains	—	—	** (2)	Matured stage	Rat poison
Chepa (pest)	Mustard, Bajra, Sugarcane	Eats leaves/ flowers (3)	Humid weather	1000/acre for Bajra, Total plants loss of mustard	***(3)	Young	None
Congress grass (weed)	All crops with grains	Stunts growth of crop	Came with american wheat	No estimate	***** (5)	Any stage	No solution
Safed kira (pest)	Wheat, Jo, Maize	Eats roots	Not known	250-300/acre	* (1)	Youth stage	None
Titri (insect)	Jowar, Bajra, Mustard	Eats leaves	Not known	100/acre	* (1)	Youth stage	None
Sati (weed)	Jowar, Bajra and Maize	Impedes growth	Less rain or dry soil	1000/acre	******(6)	Infant stage	Uprooting if less in number
Nilgai	All crop especially Mustard	Aggressive grazing in herds	Deforestation/ noise pollution	No estimate	*(1)	Any stage	No solution
Soondi (pest)	Paddy	Destroys leaves		No estimate	*****(5)	Young plants	Dimscron by large farmers
Hailstorm	Wheat/ Mustard	Damage crop	Natural	No estimate	*(1)	Any stage	No solution

Notes: ***# Perceived as future threat and animals fall sick after consuming locust invested Jowar leaves. Figures in parentheses in Column 3, indicates the vintage of the constraint.***

Village Analysts: Nirmal Kumar, Nand Kishore Sharma, Prahlad Singh, Haridutt Sharma, Girija Singh, Srichand Sharma, Dharmvir, Mukesh Kumar Sharma and Nannu Ram. *Facilitator*: Sudipta Ray.

Table 13 Constraints Ranking Men's Group of Hawelliwalle Muhalla

Constraints	Crops attacked	Effect	Cause and Relation-ships	Estimated loss (In Rs.)	Score	Stage when attacked	Measures
Power shortage	All crops	Reduces irrigation (5-6)	Govt. policy	No estimate	****** **** (10)	All stages especially infant	No solution
Nilgais	All crops	Grazes/ destroys crop	Deforestation and ban on killing	100 per cent loss of entire fields	*** (3)	All stages. Parti-cularly matured stage	No solution except driving them away
Locust (pest)	Jawor bajra, maize	Eats away leaves (2)	Dry weather and soil	2500/acre	*****(5)	Young Stage	No solution
Chepa (pest)	Mustard, bajra, sugarcane	Eats leaves and flowers	Wet climate	1000/acre for crops. 100 per cent in case of Mustard	**** (4)	Youth stage	No solution

Sāti (weed)	Jowar	Crops do not grow (2-3)	Late monsoon	1500/acre	*****(5)	Infant stage	Uprooting but difficult
Safed Mondi (weed)	Wheat	Stunts growth (2-3)	Unknown	1000/acre	****(4) Stage	Infant	Uprooting but difficult. Crop used as inferior fodder
Rani Jai	Wheat, jowar	Compete with wheat	Same as safed moondi	500-700 per acre	*** (3)	Matured stage	Same as in case of safed moondi
Termites	Wheat, jowar, bajra	Eats roots	Less rain	1250/acre	*****(5)	Any stage	No solution
Congress Grass (weed)	Wheat, mustard, jowar, bajra	Stunts growth of crop (3)	Came with imported wheat. In 1970s.	No estimate	***** (5)	Any stage but rapid during monsoons	No solution

Notes: Village Analysts: Kishan Singh, Rajvir Singh, Om Prakash Sharma, Udham Singh, Udai Vir, Bachu Singh.

Facilitator: Ms. Meera Jayaswal.
Date: 5.4.99.

Table 14 Constraint Ranking by Women's Group in Patyat Muhalla

Constraints	Crops attacked	Effect	Cause and Relation-ships	Estimated loss (In Rs.)	Score	Stage when attacked	Measures
Locust (insect)	Jowar, bajra and maize	Eats away leaves(2-3)	Unknown	No estimate	****** **** (10)	Youth	None except waiting for rain
Batti (weed)	Paddy	Inhibits growth	Natural	500/acre	*** (3)	Infant stage	Uprooting. Used as fodder
Power shortage	All crops	Reduces irrigation (3-4 years)	Government policy	No estimate	***** ***** (10)	All stages	No solution except waiting for rains to help
Safed Moondi (weed)	Wheat	Looks like wheat. Prevents growth of wheat. (3)	Unknown. Grows naturally.	No estimate	**** ***(7)	Infant stage	None. Up-rooting for use as fodder
Jai (weed)	Wheat	Stunts growth of crop.	Natural	500/acre	****** (6)	Infant Stage	Uprooted and fed to animals

Sama (weed)	Paddy	Stunts growth of crop	Unknown, may be natural	250-300	***(3)	Infant stage	Deweeding
Sati (weed)	Jowar, bajra and maize	Impedes growth (4)	Less rain or dry soil	No estimate	***** ***(8)	Infant stage	Uprooting if less in number
Nilgai	All crop especially mustard	Aggressive grazing in herds and sits on crops	Deforestation & noise pollution	No estimate	*****(5)	Any stage	

Notes: The numbers occurring in column 3 indicate the vintage of the constraints.
Village Analysts: Fulwati, Harmukhi and Kela.
Facilitator: Sudipta Ray.

Table 15 Constraints Ranking Women's Group of Hawelliwalle Muhalla

Constraints	Crops attacked	Effect	Cause and Relation-ships	Estimated loss (In Rs.)	Score	Stage when attacked	Measures
Power shortage	All crops	Reduces irrigation	Govt. policy	100 per cent	****** **** (10)	All stages especially infant crops	No solution
Nilgai	All crops	Grazes/ destroys crop	High growth in population	75-100 per cent loss of entire fields	****** (6)	All stages, parti-cularly matured stage	No solution except driving them away
Locust (pest)	Jowar, bajra, maize	Eats away leaves	Dry weather and soil	3000/acre	******* *** (10)	Young stage	No solution
Sati (weed)	Jowar	Crops do not grow	Late monsoon	1500/acre	**** *** (7)	Infant stage	Uprooting but difficult
Safed Mondi (weed)	Wheat	Stunts growth (2)	Unknown	1000/acre	****** (6)	Infant Stage	Uprooting but difficult Crop used as fodder

Jai	Wheat	Compete with wheat	Same as safed mondi	500 per acre	***** (5)	Matured stage	Same as in case of safed mondi
Termites	Wheat, jowar, bajra	Eats roots	Dryness soil/air	2000/acre	**** *** (7)	Any stage	No solution
Gandar	Paddy, vegetables jowar	Eats roots, leaves and stem	Unknown	800/acre	***** (5)	Matured stage	No solution

Village Analysts: Rajwati, Bhagwati, Vudya, Rajkali, Anguri.
Facilitator: Ms. Meera Jayaswal.
Date: 5.4.99.

IV. 2. Constraints to Growing Wheat

Since wheat occupies so much of the agricultural universe of Sagarpur, a discussion on the constraints to agriculture in the village without a discussion on the constraints faced by wheat would be incomplete. The villagers during the second round of investigation, also gave a separate analysis of the constraints that they face in growing wheat. During the second phase of the study on constraints faced in cultivating wheat, a new Muhalla, Garieria Muhalla (also called Baghail Muhalla) inhabited by backward castes was included in the study. This provided a perspective of backward castes on the issues at hand to be contrasted and compared with the perspective of the Upper Castes. Let us first see why wheat is grown in the scale that it is grown.

Box 4.3
A Natural "Weedicide"

In Tamilnadu, where farmers are troubled with grasses that look like rice, a purple-leaved variety of rice is sown every five years, although its yield is much lower than normal varieties. The seedlings can be easily distinguished and the weeds eradicated.

Source: Winin Pereira and Jeremay Seabrook in *Asking The Earth Farms, Forestry and Survival*

In the first instance the preference for wheat stems from the fact that it provides the villagers with their staple food. It is the ingredient for their main course, *Roti* or *Chapati* or *Parantha*. They like the taste of "Aata" (ground wheat) made of homegrown wheat. Growing wheat is convenient for farmers, as it is not very labour intensive, allowing them the liberty to pursue alternative occupations, as secondary to agriculture. They have the technology to grow wheat and there are price incentives as well. Thus, the farmers grow wheat to meet their consumption needs and to sell them in the *Mandis* (Market) to have cash to meet other needs of the households. Generally the villagers perceived the loss suffered by the farmers on account of the constraints common to growing wheat as being within the limits of their loss-absorbing capacity: about 6 per cent due to west-wind and an additional 4 per cent on account of other agents of damage, such as power shortage (2 per cent) and weeds, pests etc. (2 per cent). In 1998, the loss was actually half of the general trend: 2 per cent due to untimely rain; 1 per cent due to termites, weeds etc., and 2 per cent due to insufficient electric supply.

These advantages of cultivating wheat are then pitched against alternatives now left with the farmers and a choice made: growing mustard and vegetables. The risks involved are perceived as very great in cultivating mustard. In 1998, due to *chepa* attack, the farmers lost 90 per cent of their crop, though in 1999, as at the time of the study, there was no loss to mustard. As for cultivating vegetable, it is perceived as even more risky. While in 1998, untimely rain, insect attack and diseases, wiped out the yield, in 1999 though there is no such damage to crop production, there is glut in the vegetable market (precisely for the same reason). As a result the prices that vegetables fetch are absolutely unremunerative. There being no agro-processing plants and post harvest technology available to Sagarpur farmers, the vegetable growers have no way of holding on to their produce, till prices become remunerative. The figures 3 and 4 summarise the discussion. Additionally, the villagers perceived that they are still experimenting with vegetable cultivation, which is highly labour intensive and the technology for growing vegetables relatively new for them.

But this does not mean that cultivating wheat is all hunky-dory. As with all farming systems, Sagarpur's wheat growing is constrained by natural and man made factors. We have a summary of the constraints faced by wheat in the seasonality calendar prepared by women of Hawelliwalle in Table 16.

The constraints faced by wheat farmers are a combination of winds, birds, weeds and insects, on the one hand and shortage of power and good quality seeds on the other. The farmers' responses are mostly to deal with power shortage and weeds. One reason why not much effort is put into tackling other constraints is that the opportunity cost of dealing with them is more than the loss caused by the constraints, which as the villagers had earlier explained, was within their limits of tolerance, viz., 10 per cent. The villagers also make it clear that low quality seeds, power shortage and the dry west-wind are the major problems, of which the former two are policy related and can be tackled only through policy measures, at the Ministerial level. The problem of west-wind requires, as the villagers explained, development of shorter duration seeds, which ripen early before the west-wind blows, or varieties, which are resistant to west-winds. This again is an issue that lie in the public domain. Farmers near the brick kilns face additional constraints due to pollution, which we will discuss later in the section on impact of air pollution on agriculture.

In course of group discussion three more disincentives for cultivation, that did not surface in the Constraint Ranking exercise, came out as worthy of mention. First, the growth in population. In the introductory section earlier villagers told us that generally a household has 5 children. This means, with the passing of each generation, landholdings are partitioned among the sons, leading to fragmentation of land bequeathed from one generation to another. This fragmentation of land disfavours cultivation, particularly mechanised cultivation. Second, as a consequence of the first, whenever landholdings fall below one acre, it is no longer possible for a household of 6-8 members to feed itself by cultivating that piece and parcel of land. Farmers are, thus, forced to sell their land and go in for either salaried or self-employment. Vimla, one of the participants in the study, explained: "We have sold our one Kila land last year for Rupees two lakhs. My husband has started carpentry business. We are happy now". Third, Government's land acquisition programme, to meet the demands of rapid urbanisation, is a singular damper for farmers. Bhagawati of Hawelliwalle Muhalla suspects that most of their land will be sold off within next ten years, as land prices are rising rapidly because of urbanisation, and farmers, like Vimla, would be induced to sell off their holdings. She confided in one of the researchers: "I shall sell my land when the cost of one acre (Kila) will be Rs. 8 Lakhs. We all will migrate to Uttar Pradesh, across the river Jamuna. Land is inexpensive there; hence we shall buy at least 10 acres (Kila) of land. We will cultivate wheat there and do milk business".

It is interesting to note that the the number of constraints to agriculture (pests, weeds, insects and so on) have increased over time, as the number of crops grown has declined. Probably the farmers realised this but did not articulate the well known fact that growing crops in continual mono-culture or bi-culture leads inevitably to much greater pest, weed, disease, fertility and soil erosion problems than the mixed cropping systems (*Francis, 1994; Edwards et.al., 1993*). Though agriculture in Sagarpur has not yet turned into mono or bi-culture but the tendency is towards that limiting case. And together with that trend is an increase in constraints mentioned earlier. These have to be taken care, of or else tackling pests, weeds, etc. will be a farmer's nightmare.

IV. 3. What Factors Influence the Constraints?

Details of factors that influence the constraints are somewhat limited, viewed in the light of other details provided. Nonetheless the available data is sufficient to provide incisive insights. Attack of locust, according to the all the men's and women's groups in Sagarpur, is greatly influenced by timings of the monsoons. Delayed monsoon, leading to late rains, increases the danger of locust infestation considerably. Termites, for them, flourish in dry winter, and are attributable to dry soil and lower than normal rainfall (*Indian Express*, 24th September, 1999)

Sati weed has again been attributed to the late arrival of rains and use of chemical fertilisers. Termites, they think, women and men groups alike, were more visible during dry weather. Nilgais have strayed into human habitation and into farmers' fields as deforestation has robbed them of their natural source of food. And shortage of power, both the women's and men's groups thought, was caused by government policy of meeting undue demand on power put by towns and industry.

All groups consider all other constraints to be imposed by nature or the causes are unknown to them. None of the groups considered paucity of funds (credit) as a constraint to agriculture, though they had counted lack of money in the village, as one of the major general problems of them.

Table 16 Constraints Ranking in Wheat Cultivation by Women's Group of Hawelliwalle Muhalla

Month	Activities attacked	Constr-aints	Rank	Damage	Loss	Measures
Aghan	Land preparation First irrigation Puddling (palewat) Making field ridge Sowing seed	Crow Koko gilgila birds Poor quality seeds	2 6	Eat newly sown seeds	Rs.50 per acre	Install scare crow with bow and arrow
Poosh	Second irrigation One dose of fertiliser Application of weedicides	Giddar insects Termites Power shortage	1 8	Eat leaves and roots	At least Rs. 500	Medicines Generator for power
Magh	One dose of fertiliser Application of weedicides	Same as in poosh	1	Same as in Poosh	—	Medicines Generator for power
Fagun	Third irrigation Grains start forming	Kadwa disease	2	Grains become black	Same as in Poosh	None

Chait	Deweeding Fourth irrigation	Crow, Koko	2	Eat grains	Same as in Fagun	None
Baisakh	Fifth irrigation Harvesting, threshing, transporting, selling, repaying loan	West wind, rains, termites, birds	10	Plants dry up early and hence grains as well	Depends on how early the wind blows	None

Village Analysts: Rajwati, Pyari, Prem, Purandai.
Validated by: Kisanwati, Birpal Shyamwati, Mahesh.
Facilitator: Ms. Meera Jayaswal.
Date: 27.3.99.

Part V. Economics of Agricultural Operations

V. 1. What are the Inputs to Agriculture and the Cultivation Process?

It is best to start with the cultivation process and then summarise the inputs to agriculture. Reference is invited to seasonality analysis of agricultural activities done by men and women in Table 17.

From Table 17, the basic inputs to agriculture are: ploughing (tractor time), seeds, fertilisers, irrigation in several rounds and pumpsets; labour and of course land. There is no mention of any kind of pesticides, insecticides or weedicides.

The process of agriculture, in a normal year, that is a year not hit by disease and pests etc., is fairly straight forward, as is evident from column-2 of Table 17. There are 12 steps. In the months of Kartik and Aghan (mid-October to mid-December) land is ploughed for five times, of which two are wet ploughing, and then levelled. Successive steps that go on for 6 months in a row follow this. Land is then irrigated during the same months and puddles made. Aghan (mid-November to mid-December) is for fertilisers to be applied and seeds to be sown (wheat 1553, 2283, 2329, 2338). Sowing is done along with DAP (50 kg per acre). Then for four months, from Poosh to Chait (mid-December to mid-April), fields receive five rounds of irrigation, at the rate of one round per month except the month of Magh (mid-January to mid-February) when two rounds of irrigation, called Pokhara, are necessary. The first round of irrigation, called bhur, in Poosh is followed by application of weedicides. Each of the first three rounds of irrigation is accompanied by a dose of fertiliser, being 50 kg of urea per acre.

In Baisakh (mid-April to mid-May), when wheat is harvested and bundles made, as a preparatory step for the harvest to be taken for threshing. It is then threshed which occupies farmers for most of Baisakh. Jeth (mid-May to Mid-June), is the month for storing wheat for household consumption. The surplus is then taken to the market (called "Mandis") for sale either to the government at the procurement prices declared, or to other buyers and traders at the going market price.

Significantly farmers, neither women nor men, mention either use of pesticides or insecticides as a major activity. Use of these inputs is limited given the robustness of the crop against pest and insect attacks (cited by the farmers as one of the reasons for voting wheat as the most preferred crop) and even where such attack(s) come, the loss is small which farmers easily absorb.

V. 2. How Does the Economics of Input Work Out?

The economics of the inputs can be worked out by comparing the yield mentioned in Table 6 with the price of inputs. Instead of us doing the exercise, the villagers themselves provided estimates of returns from wheat, mustard and potato, which influenced their decision on the choice of crops. Their estimates are in Table 18.

Agriculture is *prima facie* not profitable. The preferred option is wheat cultivation, where for a household (family of 5-6 persons as women, men and children contribute all their labour in agriculture) the return is Rs. 4420 over a period of 6 months per acre, without adding the imputed cost of family labour, on an outlay of Rs. 4330, that is, the family earns from wheat cultivation Rs. 735.7 (approximately) per month per acre. However, if family labour cost is factored into it as additional outlay, even at the rate of Rs. 80 per day for 60 days, (one third of 6 months, assuming that farmers would work for no more than 2 months in agricultural operations during a wheat farming cycle) which works out to be Rs. 4800 for one person, there is a net loss of Rs. 360 per acre per year. And if this estimate is further refined by adding the cost of credit or the foregone interest on the outlay of Rs. 4330, at the rate of 5 per cent per annum (the rate of interest paid on savings bank account in banks and in the post offices, assuming of course that the farmers do not borrow while in practice they do borrow and only the opportunity cost of an alternative channel of investment has been imputed), and the land tax, cess and other exaction payable to the state, a further cost escalation is inevitable, on to the outlay already estimated. A farmer, in village Sagarpur, succinctly lamented: “Landowners do not have money; cultivation eats all of it”.

Table 17 Agricultural Process and Involvement of Men and Women

Activities	Months	Men's Work	Women's Work	Time taken (Days)	How do Men manage time	How do Women manage time
Ploughing and levelling (Mej & Jot)	Kartik Aghan	Plough by using tractors	Supervise whether entire field covered	8-10	Take leave from scheduled work	Additional to daily work schedule
Irrigation and puddling (Palewat)	Kartik Aghan	Use pumpsets	Supervise*	4-5	Take leave from scheduled work	Additional to daily work schedule
Apply fertiliser Sow seeds	Aghan	Apply fertilisers	Supervise*	4-5	Take leave from scheduled work	Additional to daily work schedule
First irrigation at 6 inch plant	Poosh	Use pumpsets	Supervise*	4-5	Work during night	Additional to daily schedule of work
Second irrigation on ear of corn formation	Magh	Use pumpsets	Supervise*	4-5	Work during night	Additional to daily schedule of work

Third irrigation on ear of corn coming out	Magh	Use pumpsets	Supervise*	4-5	Work during night	Additional to daily schedule of work
Fourth irrigation on grain formation	Fagun	Use pumpsets	Supervise*	4-5	Work during night	Additional to daily schedule of work
Fifth irrigation on hardening of grain	Chait	Use pumpsets	Supervise*	4-5	Work during night	Additional to daily schedule of work
Harvesting grains are ready	Baisakh		Harvest	6		Additional to daily schedule of work
Making bundles	Baisakh		Make bundles	1-2		Additional to daily schedule of work
Threshing	Baisakh	Using tractors		4-5	Take leave	Additional to daily schedule of work
Transporting to home and market	Jeth	Using tractors		1	Take leave	Additional to daily schedule of work

Note: * Supervision, according to the women, include ensuring the flow of irrigation water to all parts of the field.

Table 18 Estimate of Cost and Returns from Different Crops (Per Acre) and One Buffalo Per Day Prepared Jointly by Men and Women

Wheat		Mustard		Potato		Radish
Items	Costs (Rs.)	Items	Costs (Rs.)	Items	Costs (Rs.)	Costs per Kila (Rs.)
Ploughing	1000	Land preparation	1000	Ploughing and levelling	1000	1000
Levelling	70	Irrigation twice	250	Manure	300	800
Softening and irrigation	1000	Seeds 5 kg	500	20 kg seed	240	1000
Fertilisers	1200	"Medicines"	500	10 kg DAP	100	
Seeds (60 Kg.)	500	Yield 10 quintals	25000	Irrigation 10 hours twice	500	1400
Harvesting and transporting	1280			Labour		400
Threshing	480			Yield	15 kg	
Yield 35 Maunds.$	8750					

Total Cost	4330	Total Cost	2250	Total Cost	2140	4600
Total Return	8750	Total Return	25000	Total Return	15	1500
Net Return	4420	Net Return	22750	Net Return	(-)2125	(-)3100

Notes: $ indicates 35 maunds of wheat multiplied by Rs. 250, the rate at which wheat is sold.

Village Analysts from Lalait Basti: Nand Kishore Sharma, Dhirendra, Ashok, Puran.
Village Analysts from Baghail Hamlet: Parem, Riwari, Saroj, Shanti.
Village Analysts from Hawelliwalle Muhalla: Rajwati, Pyari, Bhagwali and Purandei. Dates: 3.4.99 and 5.4.99.
Facilitator: Meera Jayaswal. Meera Jayaswal.
Dates: 3.4.99 and 5.4.99.

However, if the farmers do not find employment in half of the six months required to raise wheat crop from *Mej* to pulling the grains into the households, then the net profit would be Rs. 4420 over a six-month period. Since in Kharif, the other crops are grown on much smaller scale and are less profitable, the annual income for a farmer's household from agriculture would be about just above Rs. 8840 per annum, assuming that the household had similar income in the Kharif season as well. This is below the "poverty line" for India. Shortage of money, small wonder, has been listed as the number 2 problem in the list of priority problem in Sagarpur, scoring 8 points (see Table 1).

If farmers opt for mustard, in place of wheat, the outlay is lower, and the return better. But the uncertainty and high risk associated with mustard cultivation are daunting. Farmers are deterred from venturing into growing mustard in lieu of wheat. Not that they have not tried, but with bitter consequences. For instance nearly 90 per cent of all mustard crop was lost in 1998 due to *chepa* infestation, as indicated earlier. The story of vegetable cultivation is new and in 1998, they lost out both in potato and radish, as there was a glut in the market, leading to a crash in prices.

These experiences and non-profitability of agriculture, have impressed upon villagers of Sagarpur the importance of serving either the government or the private sector. This provides at least a partial answer to the question of why people pursue multiple occupations. And this also provides a basis for validating the projections of how people would tend to move out of agriculture presented by the groups in Table 11 earlier.

Box 4.4
Process Underlying the Observed Trends

"The shift of the work-force away from agriculture and self-employment activities, can be understood properly only with reference to changes in the organisation of production in agriculture and manufacturing during the past two decades."

Source: *Alternative Economic Survey, 1996-97* (New Delhi: Delhi Science Forum)

Why do farmers still keep to farming? It is a mindset that plays a crucial role in farmers' satisfaction. Land is the farmers' primary asset and its utility as perceived by the farmers of Sagarpur lies not because it is the biological basis for agriculture, but also because it is of immense utility as the established basis of power. As an asset its value determines how much the farmers can borrow from the Gurgaon Grameen Bank. They are also aware that who controls the land and to whom the benefits from it accrue, have a bearing on their existence. And the tinge of pride in cultivating land they have inherited, cultivated by their ancestors (and perhaps "irrigated by their blood and sweat", as they say), helps them derive intangible utility from cultivating their own land. It is the mental satisfaction that they make a living out of their own land that keeps them going, and the comforting thought that all the while their capital (the value of the land) keeps on appreciating, sobers their urge to move on to greener pastures. Land is the source of employment and secure basis for supply of food and fodder. It gives them a foundation to build their social standing. What with the prevailing employment situation, the alternative avenues for employment have withered away. Farmers who even vaguely think about leaving agriculture, can foresee no alternative occupation that they could fall back upon for their subsistence and sustenance. Farming remains the last refuge.

V. 3. Who Supplies the Inputs and Who Provides the Extension Services Regarding New Seeds and Fertilisers?

Inputs in case of wheat cultivation are tractors, seeds, fertilisers, irrigation in several rounds, and therefore water and pumpsets; family labour; outside labour; and of course land. As we saw the year long agricultural operations are carried out by family labour. The farmers own tractors and there is inter-household hiring of tractors. The case is similar with pumpsets for irrigation. Farmers access other inputs from the open market. The existence of extension service in nowhere noticeable which is why farmers do not respond to a host of constraints they have identified, in Tables 12 to 16, all of which reflect absence of extension support. Even the use of fertilisers is uniform throughout the fields, with no soil testing and without concern for chemical imbalance of agricultural lands.

Part VI. Class Issues

VI. 1. Who are the Landowning and Landless Groups?

The division of the village into landowning and landless groups is not critical in Sagarpur. In the general description of the village in the introductory section it came out fairly well that most of the people own land. Table 3 indicates that except for the Harijan Muhalla, in all other Muhallas 90 per cent or more people are into agriculture. Table 3, read with Table 4, indicates that only 10 per cent of the people are landless, and that the Harijans are the landless class. They pursue their traditional occupation, which includes carting goods on donkeys and carts and working as labourers. Jats and Brahmins and some of the other backward castes are traditionally landowners and/or cultivators and farmers.

Sagarpur farmers also showed no signs of stratification in terms of who cultivated which crop or land. Generally all farmers cultivate, or are potential cultivators of, all the crops (wheat being the dominant) depending on several factors, including weather, soil conditions, resource availability and opportunity. It is not possible to draw any inference that some farmers exclusively grow wheat whereas others grow only vegetables and so on. Farmers *inter se* are not divided along caste or religious lines. It is only possible to identify different groups of farmers on one objective basis, viz., on the basis of landholdings: large farmers, medium sized farmers and small farmers.

The village land is most suitable for cultivating wheat. There is no direct evidence on the subject but, given the relative homogeneity of the farming community and the cropping pattern being what it is, variations in different in types of land used by different farmer groups are remote.

VI. 2. Is there any Overlap Between Landownership with Produce Ownership?

The issue of landownership and produce ownership is not very critical in Sagarpur. Most people are engaged in agriculture, except the Harijans who are in any case landless. Agriculture is for the most part a family enterprise. Those who own the land are the producers as well. There is no system of tenancy. Even those who work outside the village return to the village whenever required in the interest of farming. We may recall, men take leave for *mej, jot and palewat* and during threshing and marketing, while for irrigating their fields, they work at night.

Sagarpur farmers know that possession is 90 per cent title to land. To establish their possession on land, these farmers, prefer to till their own land and not lease them out. Leasing land is dicey business and can result in the land being recorded in the name of the tenant, who would enjoy usufructory rights until evicted in due course of law. This in reality is tantamount to land going out of the owner-farmer's control perpetually. The legal process in its civil garb is notorious for its delay and clumsiness.

The most overwhelming reason for absence of tenant, is the economics of farming itself. Recall Table 20 and the discussion following it. If wheat cultivation results in a net loss to the farmer, after factoring in cost of credit and imputed cost of labour, when the farmer has access to the full produce, what incentive will the tenant have if he can retain only half of the produce, after putting in as much resources and labour ? Given the general principle of sharing of produce between landlords and tenants in the ratio of 50:50, the gross return to the tenant cultivator would be half of Rs. 4420 for a 6 month period, that is, Rs. 2210 against an out lay of Rs. 4330, without including imputed labour cost (or wages foregone) plus imputed cost of credit. With such economics of farming, tenancy is not in the flovour of the month.

The owner cultivator incurs losses and continues to be in agriculture incurring losses as a part of its long run strategy of holding operations and maintaining possession. These farmers also operate on the expectation, we were told, that with the appreciation of land prices, consequent upon the industrialization of Faridabad and Ballabgarh 8 kms and 5.4 kms away respectively from Sagarpur, their asset value and net worth will increase in the long run, even though the incur short run losses from cultivating land. The tenant has no such long run incentive to cultivate at a net loss, as by definition he is only interested in the immediate run and the short run produce from the leased-in land, as most of the time he is a "tenant-at-will".

VI. 3. Are there Migrant Labourers in Agriculture and Migrant Leases?

Let us look at Table 17 once again. The farmers themselves and their families perform most of the steps in cultivation. There is very little input of labourers from outside the family. Where large farmers owning very large farms, the villagers pointed out, require additional person power, they hire labourers from within the village from amongst the Harijans and marginal farmers who have spare "cultivating capacity". As the women within the household manage most of other activities like looking after animals etc. and men partake the responsibility of milking large herds and in selling all household output whether in the village or outside, there is no scope for employing labourers. Hence migrant labourers are non-existent in the agricultural sector. Similar is the case of migrant leases and we have discussed the issue in the previous paragraphs. In any event the village itself suffers from an unemployment rate of 20-25 per cent (see Table 5).

Part VII. Gender

VII. 1. Is there a Difference in the Tasks Carried out by Men and Women?

In Sagarpur, we are talking about a community comprising Jats and Brahmins where boundary conditions of what women and men can do (and cannot do) are clearly demarcated. The dichotomy of "inside-home" and "out-side" home jobs, in this schema is distinct, about which a brief reference was made earlier.

If we look at Table 17, the tasks assigned to women are well demarcated. In wheat cultivation, the mainstay of agriculture, in Table 17, women supervise ploughing, levelling and puddling (*mej, jot and palewat*) and several rounds of irrigation. All the tasks of harvesting, and making bundles for threshing, involving 2 months of work are under the charge of women. Even when men are engaged in threshing with machines, the women make the smaller bundles out of the larger bundles to facilitate threshing.

It is to be noted that activities under women's charge are in addition to their traditionally assigned responsibilities, viz., fetching water, collecting fuel and fodder, feeding animals, cleaning and washing, bearing and rearing children, processing and cooking food for the households. And entertain their men folk, in some cases in drunken state. In case of men, for irrigating their land they work additional hours at night but for other operations like *mej, jot and palewat*; for threshing and for taking the produce to the *mandi* (market), they take leave from their normal routine. If one were to compute the workload of men and women on a comparative basis, from Column 5, Table 17, women are overloaded. And the workload has increased with larger output from the field following the introduction of the new technology. Noted observers have, therefore, commented that the induction of new-technology into agriculture has led to feminisation of work (*Ahmed, 1994*).

The division of labour amongst women and men, can also be categorized as being manual and mechanised. Most of the tasks assigned to the women require them to "soil their hands as it were", for they can only be manually performed, using simple implements like a sickle for harvesting, starting from supervising irrigation (which is arranging to have the water reach all parts of the field) to harvesting and making bundles for threshing. The tasks performed by men, viz., ploughing, irrigating, threshing and transporting, are all mechanised. In terms of effort and disagreeableness, women face a more arduous set of tasks.

The division of labour amongst women and men also has the colour of "inside-family" and "outside-family" syndrome. Women (other than Harijan women) are generally engaged inside their homes or own fields, most of the time along with male members of the households. They generally do not work for other farmers. Men on the other hand are primarily concerned with such of these activities which warrant interface with outsiders and movement outside their homes/fields. Arranging tractors, arranging irrigation pumpsets, threshing wheat and selling wheat both inside the village and in Ballabhgarh town, are tasks assigned to men.

The fact that men are responsible for selling the produce of the farming household family has a serious economic implication. Without any disparity in intra-familial disparity in power-relationship, the proceeds out of the sale of the produce should ideally be distributed amongst all members of the "production team", on the basis of some principle of allocation, such as proportion of labour contributed. However, in case of Sagarpur, because men *sell* the produce created out of family resources, the proceeds of the sale from such produce go to men. Though women, men and children all conjointly participate in generating the output, custody of income arising out of such output eventually rests with the men.

There is apparently no noticeable variation with age or caste group, barring that those belonging to the Harijan community who are generally landless. People belonging to Harijan community are not farmers. They have an altogether different economic and societal role cut out for them.

Part VIII. Significance of Agriculture

VIII. 1. What is the Significance Of Agriculture in Urban and Peri-Urban Areas in Terms of:

- Employment
- Food Security
- Income
- Others

Employment The significance of agriculture in the life of Sagarpur has been dealt with at length. In each of the six Muhallas of the village, baring the Harijan Basti, 90-95 per cent of the people depend on agriculture (Table 1). It is not only a source of income, it is also a source of employment, food and fodder as well. Agriculture providing employment to the women is particularly important. However, it is not the *only* source of income. As in many other similar villages in Faridabad, people pursue alternative livelihoods within the village and outside. There are farmers who work in establishments outside the village but attend to cultivation and harvesting whenever required. There are people serving in the government offices and in business establishments. Agriculture is the most important source of employment but not the only one.

Since much of agriculture is based on family labour, and demand for labour in agriculture at best of times is only seasonal, agriculture as a source of employment to those who depend solely on sale of their labour power is limited. This is the reason why Harijans, Prajapats and some people belonging to other backward castes, anticipate that they would prefer to get into the business of transporting goods using carts and donkeys.

Food Security The importance of agriculture for food security in a poor agricultural society, can not be overemphasised. Food security means that there is enough food in the system, that people have the purchasing power to access the food so available, that people have the ability to access such food, that the food available is culturally acceptable and that the food so available has adequate nutritional value for a healthy life.

In terms of food security, the data in terms of the problem prioritisation in Table 1, do not indicate availability of food as a problem or as a constraint to livelihood. Even the historical transects of the village nowhere indicates that insufficient food or hunger ever visited the community.

On the significance of agriculture, we noted that large, medium and small farmers (constituting 25 per cent of the population) were categorical about *storing* their produce for household consumption and then selling the remaining surplus to the government's procurement agency or in the *mandi* (market). We discussed earlier, that the first harvest during the first week of April, which yields the best quality grains is stored for household consumption and whatever is sold out of this first class crop, is also bought for domestic consumption. Only second class wheat is sold to the government. Food grown is deemed as the basis of life. The farmers give a high priority to food security. Thus there is some evidence indicating that food has the nutritional value, but we have no data on the adequacy or otherwise of the level of nutrition.

The case of the marginal farmers (constituting 75 per cent of the village population) stand on a different footing. Of the marginal farmers, those who owned less than 1 acre of land, would suffer from food insecurity, because for a family of 6-8 people, food grown on less than 1 acre of land will be insufficient to feed the family for a full year. Thus on the balance only 25 per cent of the villagers have assured food throughout the year.

The redeeming feature is the cropping pattern. The cropping pattern indicates that Sagarpur has migrated from ZEIA to HEIA and the diversity of crops has been on the decline, nevertheless, the principal crops grown are food crops, whether for household consumption or for marketing surplus. The only minor exception being vegetable cultivation, currently carried out on an experimental basis. Despite being near two major industrial centres and urban agglomerations, of Ballabgarh and Faridabad, Sagarpur has not migrated from food crops to cash crops. Their underlying concern for ensuring food for their households play, in their subconscious mind, a part in preventing the pull towards cash crops. This has policy implications to which we may turn later.

Income Agriculture as a profitable venture is in some doubt. However, stability and certainty of assured prices for their crops (read wheat) is not in doubt, particularly when they are assured every year of a *Minimum Support Price* and of a *Procurement Price* for wheat and paddy. These prices impart a degree of certainty to cultivating wheat and help reduce risks involved in farming. Growing vegetables and mustard are either not profitable or fraught with high risk of failure, without any price cover like the ones which growing wheat and paddy enjoys.

Food production is part of the overall life in Sagarpur. While activities in the chain of activities essential for food production, assigned to women, are carried out by them in addition to their daily schedule of work as in other villages in India. Men contribute their share, as determined by convention or consent, either by working at night or taking leave from their place of employment, if they are employed in regular employment, a situation similar to Kadhaoli. As seen elsewhere, women and men work for producing and processing food as part of their life style. Food production is perceived as an integral part of household activities and as a necessary condition for its continuance. In the absence of food in the households, the other household activities, in the villagers perception, will be difficult to pursue.

Part IX. Injury to Crops

IX. 1. Any visible injury to crops?

Constraints set out in the five tables, being Tables 12 to 16, spell out that visible injury to crops is noticeable. Grazing by nilgais, which featured in the constraints listed by all the groups, leaves brazen marks of injury on the crops. Locust attack, *chepa* infestation and hailstorm imprint visible signs of injury on the leaves and the crop. Termites nibbling away the plant roots, and *safed kira* eating roots of wheat and maize, all leave scar on the crops. The researchers, however, did not notice for themselves any visible injury. But there was nothing in terms of injury in the perception of the Villagers which, was due to air pollution. The visible and not so visible injuries to crops were, in the perception of the villagers, due to pests, insects, diseases and weeds, not due to air pollution.

IX. 2. To what Extent is Leaf Injury Perceived to be Caused by Air Pollution?

For the villagers in the village, length of wheat crops has shortened and there are lesser number of grains per wheat plant, which are relatively thin, perceived to be caused by dust from brick kiln that falls on the crops. The people of Sagarpur do not perceive that any of the leaf injuries (barring the ones mentioned by the residents of Ita Bhatti Colony) are indeed caused by air. Tables 12, 13, 14, 15 and 16, while specifying the causes of the injuries do not include air pollution as one of them. Most of them are natural, connected with rainfall or policy directed. The inhabitants of Ita Bhatti Colony only notice that on fields adjacent to the brick kilns, standing wheat have deposits of dust and dirt on them and the grains produced from such crops are smaller and thinner, due primarily to the hot blasts released by the kilns.

Crops injured are differentially treated. Insect infested and disease infested crops, which are likely to perpetuate the pest or the disease are uprooted and dumped. Crops affected by locust, *jai rani, safed moondi* and *asi* weeds are uprooted and, some of it, is used as inferior quality fodder. Crops infected with *sati* are uprooted and dumped, for even animals refuse to consume them. *Batti* invested crops are used as fodder. Grains affected by nilgai, *chepa* pest, hail and green locust are sold in the market for whatever remains of them. Generally injured crops are not consumed by human beings.

IX. 3. What are the Perceived Impacts of Air Pollution on Agriculture?

During the first phase of the study, air pollution did not figure in any of the discussions, diagrams, analysis and mapping. The first phase of the study indicates that women are apparently not aware of air pollution caused by industries.

During the second phase of the study, the research team did try to enliven the discussion with women's group of Hawelliwalle, by a leading question, on whether they know anything about kinds of air pollution. Pat came the reply: "Clean air and dirty air". "Clean air", they continued, "has no smell, no dust and no smoke". Then the women identified four sources, which are causing dirty air: smoke from vehicles, from factories, from brick kilns and from open drains and garbage. They also pointed out that the dust coming out of the brick kilns in the village, causes further uncleanness in the air. They perceived no damage to human beings, cattle and agriculture from air pollution. Neither does the smoke emitted by the factories harm agriculture or the herds of cattle they own. They perceived no harm to their crops and land from pollutants released from Ballabgarh and Faridabad as well. Only wheat and paddy cultivated on land adjacent to the brick kilns suffer from hot air released from the kilns. The nature and extent of damage is similar to the damage generally caused by hot westerly winds. Wheat grains from land adjacent to the brick kilns are thinner and smaller, which accounts for approximately a loss of 2 quintals per acre.

Where the density of smoke emitted from the factories is high, they believe, only the factory workers fall prey. They suffer from suffocation, cough and tuberculosis. The contamination released from the brick kilns harms human health, for residents adjacent to the brick kilns in the Ita Bhatti Colony, fall prey to asthma, persistent cough and ultimately tuberculosis.

Air contaminated by open drains and garbage dumps, is a cause of irritation but the group of women perceive this as harmless to crops and human beings. Nevertheless they are quick to volunteer information that mosquitoes that breed in the stagnant water of the open drains and garbage dumps, are a veritable menace: they not only cause malaria but also bite milch animals which reduces milk output by upto a litre per milking.

The interaction the research team had with the women's group during the second round of study revealed that fields adjoining the brick kilns have special problems. As water is difficult to draw in the vicinity of these kilns, cost of irrigation goes up dramatically by upto 100 per cent, from Rs. 100 per hour to Rs. 200 per hour, which compels the farmers to irrigate wheat fields only thrice or at the most four times, in place of the required 6 rounds of irrigation. The quality of crop suffers, the grains being thinner than in other parts of the village. Hot wind discharged from the kilns exacerbate the problem of crop drying up early due to west-wind. The dust from the movement of donkeys carrying goods to the kilns and the dust particles emanating from the kilns *per se* leave dust coating on the standing crops. As a sum total of all of this output of wheat per acre is reduced by 2-4 quintals

IX. 4. What Changes in Types of Pest, Pest Population and Past Damage have been Perceived Spatially and Historically?

The prevailing perception is that the number of pests and weeds are on the rise in recent years. Since the analysis was in terms of constraints, the discussion focused on constraints. Refer to Tables 12 to 16. In column 3, of the Tables, women and men have indicated by assigning a number, the vintage of the constraints. Locust, *safed moondi, chepa* and *jai rani* have plagued agriculture for the last 3 years or so. Termites have come in over the last 4-5 years. Nilgais are farmers nightmares since last 10 years or so. Shortage of power is creating problems ,since 5-8 years. Rest of the problems according them have been with them from before and in many cases the villagers did not specify the vintage as well.

If we consider Hawelliwalle, Patyat and Baghail Muhallas, and Ita Bhatti Colony as separate geographical entities, there are some minor differences in the vintage of the constraints faced by the two locations. But these differences are more matters of details and not of substance specific to location. For instance, the problems created by brick kilns have emerged after the establishment of brick kilns and affects only one of the four Muhallas studied. Similarly power shortage, is mentioned by the men of Hawelliwalle Muhalla, as a problem for last 5-8 years, whereas the men's group in Patyat mentions this as a problem since last few years. There are other examples as well like the vintage of the locust attack is given as 3 years, with intensity growing over the last two, by women's group of Hawelliwalle, but the women in Patyat place the vintage as 3-4 years. Since we are not looking at data having clock like precision but at general trends, these differences are of no material consequence.

Part X. How Do People Deal with Constraints to Agricultural Production?

X. 1. How do Farmers Tackle Perceived Constraints: Through Changed Practice? Organized Action/ Through Existing Organizational Structures?

We have dealt with the responses indicated by the groups to the constraints in Tables 12, 13, 14, 15 and 16 and the recital of farmers' responses gives an account of the nature and content of such responses. There is not much to discuss further on how farmers tackle the perceived constraints except perhaps to conclude that the responses are short run and ad hoc.

There is no systematic response. There is no changed practice which the villagers indicate and there is none of the organised action which we see in some other parts of the country and in the state, like the agitation for power supply at subsidised rates in Haryana. The villagers themselves point the latter fact out in the context of awareness about air pollution and its effects. Given the fact that 75 per cent of the farmers are marginal, they are dispersed, unorganised and take no organised action.

There are organisational (read institutional!) structures, but none apparently come to the help of these farmers, some poor and some not so poor, in overcoming the problems they face. The one sign of organised action that the villagers boast about is the recreational park. A formidable number of Neem, Banyan, Mahua, Sesam and other trees have been planted in a bid to clean the air.

X.2. If Constraints can not be Removed at the Local Level, Whether Farmers Approach Higher Authorities? If yes, how do they do so?

The role of the different arms of the state as perceived by the villagers is drawn in the Chapati (Venn) Diagram, being figure 8. The villagers perceive authorities at different levels.

First at the government (*ministerial*) level. They perceive that the Government's role should be "doing" role, viz., it should arrange for supply of seeds, medicines (read pesticides, weedicides, insecticides) and fertilisers at subsidised rates; prevent acquisition of agricultural land for non-agricultural purposes; arrange for credit to cultivators at low rates of interest and provide for compensation for loss incurred due to natural calamities and due to development work executed by the government like construction of roads, NTPC cabling etc.

Second at the Panchayat secretary and the sub-divisional magistrate's level (*sub-divisional level*). The villagers perceive her role to be a supporting role, viz., monitoring the functioning of the Sarpanch, so that development fund meant for the village is properly utilised, and suggest to government pro-farmer policies, such as providing compensation in case of loss incurred by the farmers for reasons cited above.

Third is the sarpanch level (*local level*). The villagers perceive her role as one of communicating their needs to the panchayat secretary and Sub-divisional magistrate.

Fourth at the level of local institutions: banks and credit society. The role of the bank and of credit society is perceived as purveyors of credit at low rate of interest.

But there is no sign of villagers approaching higher authorities to ameliorate their condition. We saw earlier that in many cases, farmers have made no attempt to remove the constraint at all. They resolve whatever is possible within their ways and means. And behave rationally in doing nothing in redressing the constraints that can not be removed solely with their own resources. The fact that Haryana Urban Development Authority (HUDA) is trying to acquire land in the village, has disheartened Sagarpur villagers. It has actually instilled a fear of dislocation in them. That the bureaucracy is not sensitive to the needs of the poor in this country is well established. It has left the villagers of Sagarpur into believing that approaching higher authorities would not in any way make their life easier, which is why they think that the government at the minister's level should provide such simple relief, as supply of affordable seeds, fertilisers, credit etc., subsidy for all of which is provided for in State budgets and should be theirs almost automatically. The Venn Diagram shows that the government's role at the *minister's level* is perceived very large, followed by the sub-divisional magistrate and panchayat secretary, and then the sarpanch of the village. But alas, it is not always possible, if at all ever, for villagers to deal with ministers in tackling their local problems. They remain unattended.

It is important to recognise that approaching higher authorities is not a costless affair. It costs time and money. It requires "endless reams" of paper work. The problems that stalk the poor farmers of Sagarpur certainly do not encourage them to approaching higher authorities in seeking redressal of their problems.

To influence constraints for agriculture neither money, caste/kinship, nor information/knowledge, nor legal rights, nor public trusts nor political friends are used. The farmers have neither of these. There are no public trusts. There are little of legal rights.

Part XI. Impact on Health

XI. 1. What are the Impacts of Industrialization?

The impact of pollution on the status of health in humans and animals, in Sagarpur, has been noticed. Eyesight getting affected amongst others by brick kiln emissions, rise in cases of TB and cancer; lethargy, greying of hair, breathing problems and fever especially among children, are some of the diseases indicated by the villagers. Like in Kadhaoli, mysterious death of buffaloes during the last two years in monsoon is perceived to be due to increased pollution. These issues were explored at the participatory sessions and the results are briefly discussed below.

Let us deal with that portion of the village which is most exposed to health hazard, viz., the Ita Bhatti Colony. The women of Ita Bhatti draw up a graded scoring of different health problems faced by the inhabitants of their colony. Refer to Table 19. The ranking of health problems in other parts of the village are in Tables 20 and 21.

Table 19 Graded Scoring of Health Problems in Ita Bhatti Colony (by Women's Group)

Health Problems	Scoring	Rank
Cough	**** 4	3
Fever and head ache	****** 6	2
Weakness	** 2	5
White discharge	**** 4	3
Breathing problem	******** 8	1
Tuberculosis	*** 3	4

Village Analysts: Prem, Saroj, Shanti, Pappi, Nirmala, Sunita, Sita and Rewati.
Facilitator: Ms. Meera Jayaswal.
Date: 4.4.99.

The range of diseases villagers suffer varies from serious to common ailments. But the women rank breathing problem as the most serious problem. Since they lived by the side of the kilns, which emitted dust and smoke, breathing problem is a natural consequence. Fever and headache are ranked second, followed by cough. The women take great pains to explain that they come to live in the colony for 9 months, from October to July, that is, from the end of the rainy season till the beginning of the next rainy season, which is when their health problems get aggravated. Their perception, therefore, is that the pollutants from the brick kilns are a health hazard.

The health problems in the other parts of the village are similar but more extensive. The health analysis and ranking of health problems in

Tables 20 and 21are a quick review of health status in Sagarpur.

The ranking has curious looks. TB, appendicitis and heart palpitation are at the bottom of the scale. Even cholera and diarrhoea are ranked last but one in this ranking, whereas "cough, cold and najla", are the top scorers. The villagers are aware of this apparent paradox. They explain that they rank those health problems as being gravest, which have visible external symptoms, which spare none and which interfere with the agricultural operations most; not their killing potential. Thus cough, cold and najla rank high. Malaria also does not discriminates between men or women or children, and hits them right in the midst of the cultivating season. TB, asthma and cholera are less restrictive in their impact on the immediate capability of the farmers to carry out their duties in the fields and hence are placed at the lower end of the ranking.

What the villagers of Sagarpur did not perceive is the impact of the use of pesticides, herbicides etc. (often called by villagers, "medicines") upon the farmers themselves, both from being exposed to them while spraying and sprinkling them and from consuming food laced with these "medicines". Health hazards due to pesticides, insecticides, herbicides have been well documented in other parts of the world (*Conway and Pretty, 1991; Dinham, 1993; Banerjee, 1984*) including the developing countries, and the available information is disturbing. There is reason to believe that such hazards do not spare our farmers and there is need to investigate the issue.

Box 4.5
Pesticides and Food

Organochloride pesticide residues are present in almost every food article that one buys in Bombay. Except for fruit and prawns, the per cent of other food samples containing residues….was appreciably high, ranging from 40 to 70 per cent…. The level of DDT and BHC in the body of the average Indian is among the highest in the world. The effect of this is as follows: "Since these pesticides have been shown to affect some of the enzymes of key metabolic pathways, and since they are stored in fat deposits and are biostable, their continued intake through food affect their health and well being".

Source: S. A. Banerjee :"Pesticides and Pollution" *in* Keemat, August, 1994

Table 20 Ranking of Diseases by Villagers, Hawelliwalle Muhalla, Sagarpur

Problems/Diseases	No. of Rajma Placed	Rank
Cough, cold and najla	**********	1
Malaria	******	2
Gastritis	***	3
Cholera, diarrhoea, vomiting	***	3
Asthma	***	3
Gallstone	***	3
Heart palpitation	**	4
Appendicitis	**	4
Tuberculosis	**	4

Village Analysts: Prandei, Bhagawati, Mukesh, Prem.
Facilitator: Ms. Meera Jayaswal.
Date: 4.4.99.

Part XII: Conclusions

There could be several minor and major conclusions drawn from the above discussion, some of which have been pointed out in the main text itself. It would nonetheless useful to draw the following broad conclusions.

1. Agriculture is an important source of livelihood in Sagarpur but may not be categorized as being the single most important. It provides stable village income and provides fodder and ensures food availability for the village. It is important to recognise that we are only dealing with the agro-ecosystems from village level and downwards. Any conclusion about it must be informed by the fact that the behaviour of the higher systems in such a hierarchy has not been readily discovered. This has serious consequences. Like in any other livelihood system study, each level in the agro-ecosystems hierarchy has to be analysed, and developed both in itself and in relation to how it interfaces with other levels, above and below and this totality of understanding has to used as the basis of framing development interventions.

Table 21 Health Analysis Hawelliwalle Muhalla, Sagarpur

Health Problem	Annual Incidence	Trend incurred in	Expenses Causes treatment	Perceived	Treatment
Malaria	Men and children	Increasing	Minimum Rs. 100	Mosquito bites	Treatment in Balabhgarh
Appendicitis	Men and women	Not known	Rs. 15000	Not known	Surgery in Faridabad
Cough, cold and najla	Women, children and men	Increasing10 years ago few were affected	Minimum Rs. 100 per occasion	Excessive heat and cold	Medical help sought if condition is acute
Gallstone	Women	Increasing	Rs. 5000	Over use of spinach, tea etc.	Surgery in Ballabgarh
Heart palpitation	Women	Increasing, 20 years ago there was no incidence	—	Tension	—
Gastritis	More men and some women	Increasing	At least Rs. 3000	By birth control measures for women	Private doctor

Tuberculosis	More men than in women	Same as before	At least Rs. 3000	Cough	Private Doctor
Cholera, vomiting and diarrhoea	Children and women	Increasing since last ten years	Minimum Rs. 2000		Treatment in extreme cases only
Asthma	More men and few women	Increasing	Minimum Rs. 1000		Treatment with private doctor

Village Analysts: Pursndei, Bhagawati, Mukesh, Prem.
Facilitator: Ms. Meera Jayaswal.
Date: 4.4.99.

The crops grown in Sagarpur, are mostly food crops, and that too predominantly wheat and paddy in the Rabi and Kharif seasons respectively. Only a moderate acreage is occupied by cash crops in the form of vegetables on an experimental basis but with discouraging results in 1998.

2. Villagers generally have a diversified means of livelihood and do not depend upon any one means of livelihood for sustenance and survival. For example, those who are engaged in agriculture are also engaged in some alternative means of livelihood like milk selling. There is some element of poly-culture still visible, despite dwindling diversity in the crops grown witnessed over the years. There is no apparent food insecurity for the large and medium sized farmers, who constitute less than 15 per cent of the households in the village. Marginal farmers, who constitute 75 per cent of the households in the village, face food insecurity where their landholding is less than one acre.
3. Agriculture is today High External Input Agriculture, from Zero External Input Agriculture, even as late as in the 1940s. This change has increased the farmers' vulnerability to both external shocks and to internal risks.
4. As agriculture gradually graduated to High External Input Agriculture in the 1960s, 1970s, 1980s and the 1990s, it has resulted in making agriculture a high cost operation and the vulnerability of the farmers to external shocks so much more significant. This is a deterrent to new entrants in the field and a disincentive for those in agriculture, to continue with the struggle. Agriculture is not seen as a profitable venture. Since we are concerned here with the perception of the villagers, one may not probe the issue further, but it has to be noted that a part of the problem lies in approaching agriculture as a profit oriented institution as opposed to life oriented structure. As such it is placed in the field of competition on this very narrowly defined basis. It has to be recognised that this is a partial analysis which is not cognisant of the vital aspects of sustainability of resource use, reproduction of competent personnel and maintenance of

biodiversity. There are similar dilemma confronting farming in many other parts of the world and the choices are similar (*Lobao, 1990; Francis, 1994*).

5. There is a dramatic increase in productivity in 1970 over the level obtaining in 1950s. Yields are seen to reach their highest in the 1970s and 1980s but the high growth rates in yield so achieved, could not be maintained in the 1990s. The exceptionally high level of yield in the 1970s was achieved by the use of "new technology", viz., use of fertilisers, improved (HYV) variety of seeds and irrigation.
6. The rapid industrialisation of areas around Sagarpur is opening up job opportunities for the job seekers, but these job opportunities are not necessarily always going to the villagers alone. The unemployment rate in Sagarpur is very high. About 20-25 per cent of the people are unemployed.
7. There are a large number of constraints faced by the villagers in their agricultural operations, including pest and insect attacks. None are, however, related to pollution in general and air pollution in particular. While pests, insects and diseases have caused more damage than weeds, most of the measures taken by the farmers to counter the constraints are restricted to eliminating weeds and bare minimum towards pests and animals. The cultivators have some system of dealing with these based on their own resources and knowledge. The non-existence of extension services and paucity of vital agricultural inputs such as subsidised seeds, credit at reasonable rates of interest and subsidised fertilisers are considered by the villagers as serious constraints. But there is little effort on the part of the community, if at all, to deal with these beyond perceiving that these should be dealt with by the government at the ministerial level. There are certain constraints which are imposed by nature, like uncertainty/irregularity of rainfall and hailstorm, etc., which are way beyond the community's capacity to solve.
8. Diseases, pests and insects that attack crops have increased over time. The growth has been most prolific in weeds. It seems that

the answer to this complex set of constraints lies in integrated pest management, which involves a whole gamut of insect, weed and disease control strategies so inter-woven that not only pests are reduced to satisfactory levels but is sustainable and non-polluting. Integrated pest management is a more complex process than spraying pesticides at regular intervals. It requires a certain level of analytical skill and certain basic training in crop monitoring and ecological principles. Farmers have to be trained as experts and not pressing on with the conventional top-down extension services (though currently dysfunctional for all practical purposes). And farmers are capable of rapidly acquiring and applying principles of integrated pest management. In training the farmers, we may not try to teach them new technologies and knowledge, for, one, they probably know better than us, and two, such technology and knowledge can soon be obsolete. The approach should be to develop in the farmers their own capacity to think for themselves and develop their own solutions. These can and are producing substantial reduction in pesticide/insecticide use in several parts of the world including in some parts of India. In the Indian context this has been clearly demonstrated in the case rice (*Kenmore, 1991; Singh and Dash, 1998*) and groundnut (*ICRISAT 1993*).

9. Pollution has increased. Leaf injury is also visible. But the co-relation between pollution and injury to crops is not perceived. Leaf injury to crops is visible and the insects/diseases, which cause such injuries, are known but that they are due to air pollution, is not established. Even the researchers saw some visible injury on the crops standing in the fields, but their correlation with air pollution was nor perceived by the villagers.
10. There are gender discriminations and gender injustice, and both in terms of agreeableness of work and workload, the dice is loaded against women.

Box 4.6
Functions of Local Institutions

- Organise labour resources for production;
- Mobilize material resources to help produce more (credit, savings, marketing);
- Assist some groups to gain new access to productive resources;
- Secure sustainability in natural resource use;
- Provide social infrastructure at village level;
- Influence policy institutions that affect them;
- Improve flow of information to Governments and NGOs;
- Improve social cohesion;
- Provide a framework for co-operative action;
- Help organise people to use their own knowledge and research to advocate their own rights;
- Mediate access to resources for a select group of people.

Sources: *Uphoff* (1992a and 1992b); *(Cernea* 1991a, 1991b); *Curtis* (1991) and *Norton* (1992).

11. The role of the established state institutions in the life of the community is limited and the villagers also do not seek out these services whatever the reasons. The breaking down of extension service is particularly felt. Our inquiries revealed that the noticeable decline in extension service has been on account of three main reasons. One, the growing volume of technical information has transformed the extension workers (according to one estimate there are 1,00,000 such workers in India) becoming generalists with some knowledge in many areas. This is why in many cases the farmers know more than the extension workers. Two, in times when the fashion is marketisation and downsizing government, public resources are limited for extension work. Three, the back up services for the extension workers to make the impact have vanished.

12. Pollution is perceived to have adverse impact on the state of health in Sagarpur. Those ailments, which hinder agricultural operations, are considered most distressing by the villagers. As in the case of agriculture, the community copes with their health problems and tackle health hazards within the boundary set by their own community and resources.

Figure 4: The Hierarchy of Agrosystems

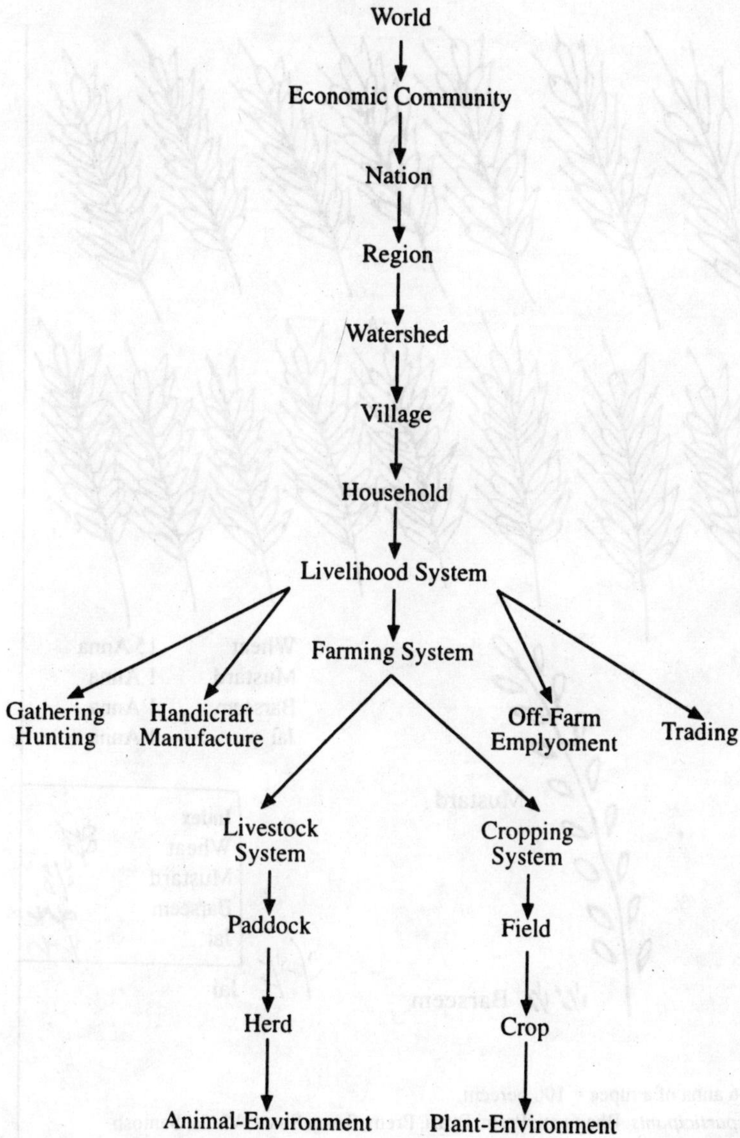

Source: Gordon R. Conway, *The Properties of agroecosystems, Agricultural Systems,* Vol 24, no. 2 (1987), pp. 95-117.

Figure 5: Share of Wheat Crops in Winter Crops, Sagarpur, Faridabad

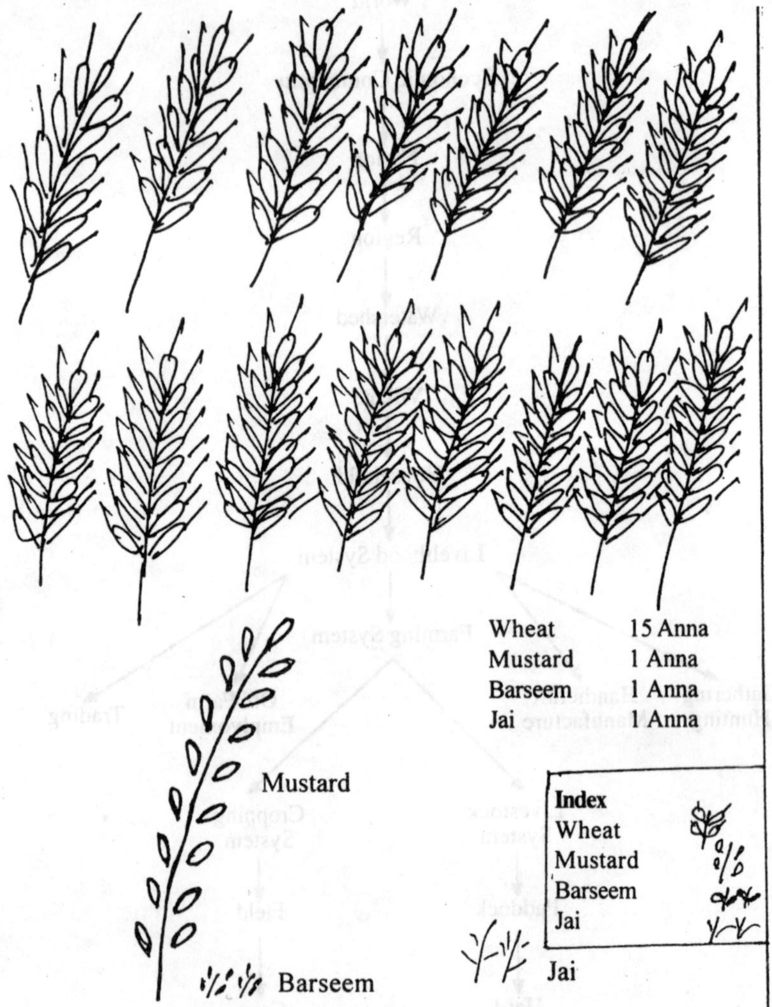

Note: 16 anna of a rupee = 100 percent.
Village participants: Bhagwati, Prem, Pyari, Prem, Saroj, Shant, Vimla, Santosh.
Village: Sagarpur,
Facilitator: Meera Jayaswal
Date: 27.3.99

Figure 6: Causes of Yield Loss: Estimated by Women's Group, Village Sagarpur

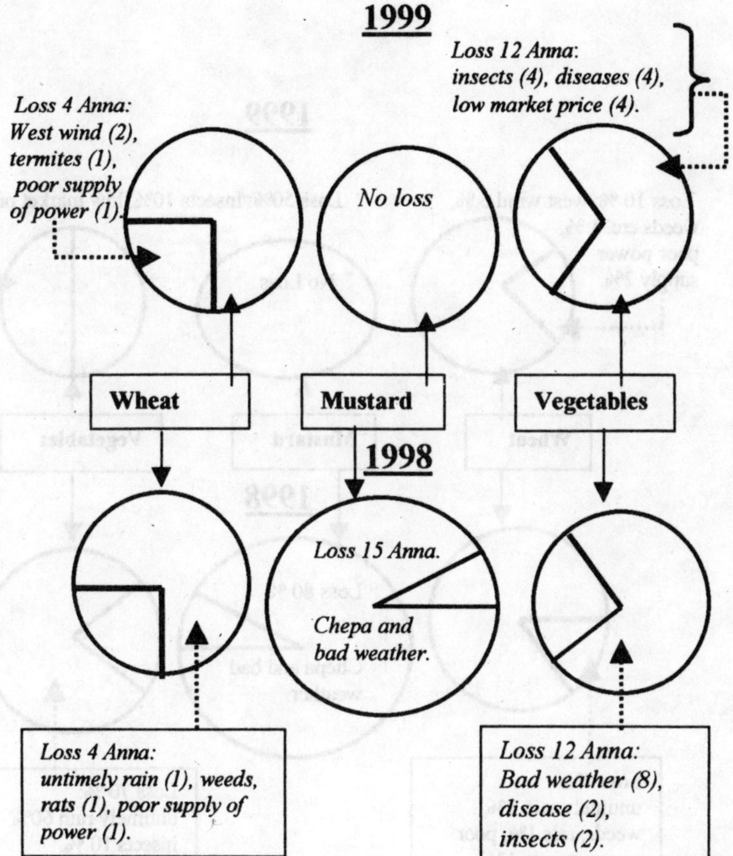

Notes: Village Analysts: Rajwati, Prem, Bhagwati, Pyari, Purandevi, of Hawelliwalla Hamlet.
Date: 5.4.99.
Facilitator: Meera Jayaswal.
16 anna = 100 percent. Figures in parentheses are annas.

Figure 7: Causes of Yield Loss: Estimated by Men's Groups, Village Sagarpur

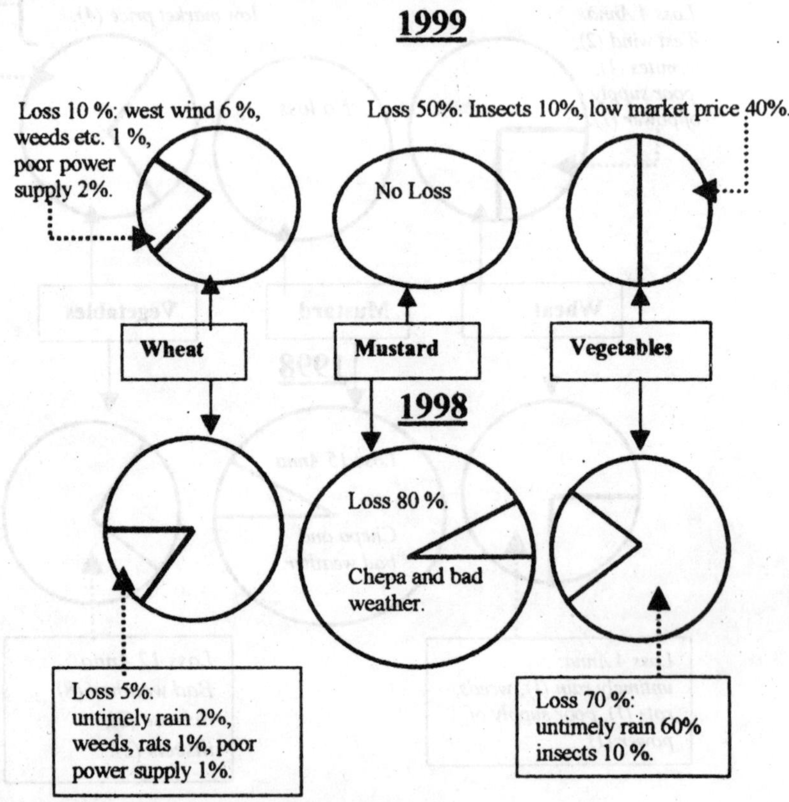

Notes: Portions within thick straight lines indicate losses.
Village Analysts: Nand Kishore Sharma, Karan Singh, Birpal.
Date: 3.4.99.
Facilitator: Meera Jayaswal.

Figure 8: Chapati Diagram on Support System to Help Cultivators to Sustain Wheat Cultivation

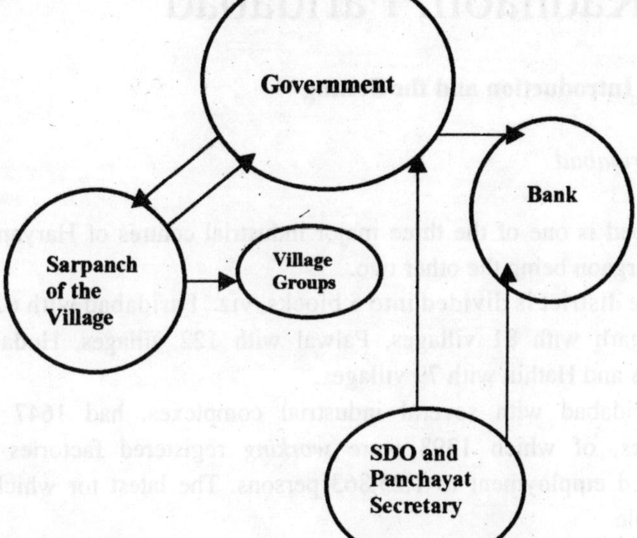

Notes: Village Analysts: Rajwati, Pyari, Kela of Hawelliwalle Hamlet, Sagarpur.
Date: 27.3.99.
Facilitator: Meera Jayaswal.
SDO is Sub Divisional Magistrate. Sarpanch is elected Chief of Village. Panchayat is elected local Self Government.

5 A Minority Community's Perspective from the Green Revolution Heartland: Kadhaoli, Faridabad

Part I. Introduction and the Setting

I.1. Faridabad

Faridabad is one of the three major industrial centres of Haryana, Rewari and Gurgaon being the other two.

The district is divided into 5 blocks, viz., Faridabad with 62 villages, Ballabgarh with 81 villages, Palwal with 122 villages, Hodal with 70 villages and Hathin with 79 villages.

Faridabad with several industrial complexes, had 1647 registered factories, of which 1398 were *working* registered factories and they provided employment to 1,25,863 persons. The latest for which data are available.

Along with industrial development, Faridabad has also made exceptionally good progress in the agricultural sector and lies at the heart of the Green Revolution belt of India. The progress in agriculture has been made possible by huge increases in agricultural production, improved irrigation, flood control measures and the introduction of the "new technology". The total area under high yielding varieties of foodgrain, such as bajra, maize, wheat and paddy during 1989-90 was of the order of 140, 000 hectares. High yielding varieties of wheat are grown in 98.3 per cent of the area under wheat cultivation; and 77.8 per cent of the area under paddy cultivation is under high yielding varieties of paddy. The major Kharif crops are bajra (cultivated over 19.8 thousand hectares) and barley (grown over 5.1 thousand hectares in 1989-90). The major Rabi crops are wheat, cultivated in 119.5 thousand hectares and barley, cultivated in 5.1 thousand hectares, as in 1989-90. Strides in animal husbandry and fisheries have contributed meaningfully to the development of the district.

I.2. Kadhaoli

Kadhaoli is amongst the 81 villages in Ballabgarh Block, Faridabad District and is situated near the Ballabgarh and the Faridabad Industrial Areas, being 4 kms and 7 kms west of the former and the latter respectively. The boundary of Kadhaoli skirts the Ballabhgarh-Mathura Road, with agricultural lands situated adjacent to the road though human settlements are located between half and one kilometer away from the road itself.

The total population of Kadhaoli is 3000, with 1550 male and 1450 females, thus giving it a sex ratio of 935 females per 1000 males, which is not very encouraging. This foreshadows some of the findings in matters of gender justice and gender relations to be discussed later in this study. Of the total population, 6.6 per cent belong to scheduled castes. Most of the inhabitants of Kadhaoli own land, with only 3.33 per cent people who are landless and they are categorized by the villagers as poor. The literacy rate is around 40 per cent, which is disappointing, given that the national average is slightly above 53.6 per cent and Haryana's literacy rate is 55 per cent.

The village is divided into two wards, Aat Bisa and Barah Bisa, the former being the smaller of the two wards. Aat Bisa has a population of 1400, including 200 people belonging to scheduled castes, while Barah Bisa is the home for 1600 people. Aat Bisa is the older part of the village and projects the front facade of Kadhaoli. Barah Bisa forms the interior of the village and is the relatively newer settlement of the two. The total number of households in Kadhaoli is 380, which gives the figure of 7.8 members per household. Aat Bisa has the richer sections of society, comprising large and medium sized farmers, while Barah Bisa comprises small and marginal farmers. The settlement pattern is thus curious: whereas in one ward we have all the rich and people belonging to scheduled castes, in the other we have all the non-rich and the non-poor huddled together.

The village has one Anganwadi and one primary school.

There are in all 4 factories in Kadhaoli and 1 in the adjoining village of Kelly, separated from Kadhaoli by Faridabad-Mathura Road. The factories in Kadhaoli are *prima facie* polluting: Ravi Plastic Factory manufacture polythene bags and emits smoke; G.K.Rubber Factory processes minor rubber products mostly garbage rubber and emits smoke; a second rubber factory with the potential of emitting smoke is in the process of being set up; cement factory manufacturing cement bricks, emits dust; and the pharmaceutical factory (in Kelly) manufacturing medicines , discharges toxic water.

As with almost all villages of India, Kadhaoli has its own story of woes and problems. The general problems of the village are described by the villagers in the Problem Scoring Matrix described below.

Table 1 Problem Prioritization

Problems	**Scoring by Rajma Seeds**	**Rank**
Crisis of hard water	**********10	1
Low voltage and irregular power supply	******6	3
No girls school	********8	2
No boys school	******6	3
No sewing centre for women/girls	****4	4
No latrine for women and girls	******6	3
Mosquitoes	****4	4
Open drains	**2	5
Poverty	********8	2

Analysts: Jamila, Mubina, Phulwati Sabo.
Facilitator: Meera Jayaswal.
Date: 27.3.99.

The villagers view hard water as the most intractable problem faced by the villagers. The local water is so hard that it cannot be used for cooking. Even the buffaloes do not drink it and it is perceived to be the cause of skin diseases. Because Faridabad receives low rainfall and because with increasing pressure on ground water consequent upon industrialization and urbanisation, there is a fall in the water table as well, the problem of drinking water is on the cards. It is interesting that in a state considered prosperous, poverty is seen as the second major problem in the village. This is only a confirmation of the general phenomenon observed throughout India that the Muslims constitute the relatively poorer sections of society. In a traditional community of Muslims in Kadhaoli, non-existence of a school for girl children is deemed a greater problem (ranked at par with poverty) than non-existence of a school for male children. While a male child may travel outside the village, a girl child may not do so: her schooling has to be within the perimeter of the village. As a result, the villagers explained the literacy level was lower among the girls than among the boys.

Non-existence of privacy in defecating is a major problem for the women. And provision for ablating in private becomes crucial in times of conflict and tension, when large landlords refuse permission to women from poorer household to use their land for defecating. Indeed this is an issue of *Right to Excretion*, which is nearly universal, everywhere but grossly under-rated as a problem. Johan Galtung best describes its need in the context of making the need to excretion a right to excretion. "Interestingly, the need for excretion cannot be seen to be covered either" (as a right) "possibly because many believe it is sufficiently well met not to constitute a problem in any society. But the point about need formulations is not necessarily that all needs have their counterparts in rights.....The foreigner in a city without public toilets knows what this means; so do the very poor in a city centre" (*Galtung, 1994*). A women group in Bangladesh during one of the participatory exercise indeed placed the absence of facilities to bathe in private as their best problem (*UNDP, 1996*). This has cultural aspect. The problem of privacy was not raised in any other village analysed in this study. And since in both cases where the issue was raised, the women belonged to the Muslim community, it seems that the need for privacy is greater amongst Muslim women. This is very fair and should be respected.

Part II. Livelihood and Agriculture

II.1. Livelihood in the Village Kadhaoli

The social maps for both Aat Bisa and Ganje Muhalla prepared by the villagers at the first go, reveal the following livelihood structure.

Table 2 Percentage of Population in Different Livelihoods

	Aat Bisa	Ganje Muhalla
Total adult males	159	57
Agriculture	75	91
Industry	8	—
Government service	2	35
Business related jobs	17	50
Labourer	10	54
Unemployed	30	—
Working in gulf countries	30	—
Milk vendors	60	50

It is estimated that 1 per cent of the population is also working in the Gulf countries. The information from the social maps indicate that majority of the inhabitants of the village are dependent on agriculture. Women do not go out to work and are fully dependent on the male members of their households for their needs and upkeep. In the Muslim community in the village women generally are designated to perform tasks inside their households. It is surprising that despite there being 4 factories in the village, only 8 per cent in Aat Bisa and none from Manje Muhalla have been absorbed in the industrial sector.

We may note that in Columns 2 and 3, Table 2, as in case of Table 6 later, the percentages do not add up to 100 per cent, which, data expressed as percentages of total should normally add up to. The reason being, that a large number of villagers have more than one occupation. For instance those who are in milk business are also the cultivators and some also work as agricultural labourers and so on. Hence the percentages show the percentage of total population engaged in these categories of occupation. Clearly villagers pursue multiple occupations.

The villagers mapped their livelihood pattern over a one-year period, starting in Baisakh (the first month of the lunar calendar) through the seasonality analysis. The seasonality analyses were carried out by the men's and women's groups separately in Aat Bisa and Manje Muhalla of Kadhaoli, which are Tables 3, 4, 5 and 6. These Tables, read one with the others indicate the following features:

- Men are required to be in their fields almost every month of the year. Agriculture is part of their life throughout the twelve months. But the nature of the activities described implies that thev are not occupied in agriculture for all the days in all the months discussed. They are required to be in their fields for specific agricultural operations (say, for instance, irrigation) only on some days of the relevant month. This explains why men also have the opportunity to take up other occupations as a secondary means of livelihood, besides agriculture.
- Women also describe (Table 3) agricultural operations month-wise, and their description is consistent with the description of men, but is much more precise and in greater detail. Hark column 4 of Tables 3 and 4. That women are more concerned with food security of the family and that women have the responsibility of processing food inside the home in our rural society, are the traits also visible in the women of Manje Muhalla of Kadhaoli Village. It is this composite approach to ensuring food for the family which enables women in Manje Muhalla to remember and describe to us, in greater detail the steps involved in agricultural operations as they relate to food security at the household level.
- Women are into agricultural activities in all the twelve months in the year. And they are in the thick of it and not operating at the margin. This is interesting. As in the case of men, agriculture forms part of their daily routine for all the twelve months, yet the nature of the activities described implies that they too are not occupied for all the days in all the months. They are engaged in specific agricultural operations (say, for instance, deweeding) only on some days of the month in question.
- Since women do not seek employment beyond the confines of home and family farm/enterprise, they do not seek any secondary source of occupation. Significantly, the women's group generally focused their description on both wheat and fodder, the principal crop and the input to the principal alternative source of income, viz., milk. Men's group detailed activities relating more to other crops: jowar, bajra, paddy, moat, etc. though it outlined timings of irrigating and harvesting of wheat crop.
- People have multiple occupations: agriculture the primary (almost all the people have some land) and some other as secondary. The villagers

thus perceive other sources of employment and income as less important than agriculture but as essential ingredients of Kadhaoli's livelihood system. This despite the fact that agriculture as a commercial venture is less sparkling than some other occupational pursuit, an issue that the villagers raised while evaluating the comparative benefits of agriculture. We need to underscore that those who were met by the research team, are the ones who normally live in the village and more involved in agriculture, with a natural inclination to emphasise the centrality of agriculture in their lives. If the research team could meet some of those who are in service, either with the government or the private firms, a slightly different (and probably a trifle more balanced) picture may have emerged.

Table 3 Seasonality Analysis by Women's Group, Manje Muhalla

Months	Livelihood	Livelihood Constraints	Nature of Agricultural Activity
Baisakh (mid-April-mid-May)	Selling milk, agriculture, labourer	—	Wheat harvesting and storing, arrange for fodder
Jeth (mid-May-mid-June)	Selling milk, agriculture, labourer	40 per cent drop in milk output, summer heat, power shortage, shortage of drinking water and fetching water, traveling long distances.	Preparing land for jowar and bajra, arrange for fodder
Asar (mid-June-mid-July.)	Selling milk, agriculture, labourer	Same as in Jeth	Sowing jowar, bajra, fodder grass, moat, arrange fodder

Months	Livelihood	Livelihood Constraints	Nature of Agricultural Activity
Sawan (mid-July-mid-Aug.)	Selling milk, agriculture, labourer		Deweeding fields, arrange fodder
Bhado (mid-Aug-mid-Sept.)	Selling milk, agriculture, labourer	Power shortage	Irrigating paddy fields, arrange fodder
Kuwar (mid-Sept.-mid-Oct.)	Selling milk, agriculture labourer	Mosquito bite in buffaloes cause a drop in milk yield	Harvest jowar, bbajra and fodder, arrange fodder, prepare land for wheat sowing
Katak (mid-Oct-mid-Nov.)	Selling milk, agriculture, labourer		Water and manure wheat fields, sow wheat, arrange fodder
Aghan (mid-Nov-mid-Dec.)	Selling milk, agriculture, labourer		First round irrigation to wheat fields, arrange fodder
Puus (mid-Dec-mid-Jan.)	Selling milk, agriculture, labourer	Upto 30 per cent fall in milk output due to cold	Second round irrigation to wheat fields and deweeding, arrange fodder
Mah (mid-Jan-mid-Feb.)	Selling milk, agriculture, labourer	Power shortage	Third Round irrigation to wheat fields and collection of fodder
Fagun (mid-Feb-mid-March)	Selling milk, agriculture, labourer		Fourth round irrigation to wheat fields and collection of fodder
Chet (mid-March-mid-April)	Selling milk, agriculture, labourer		Harvesting wheat, storing wheat and collection of fodder

Table 4 Seasonality Analysis by Men's Group, Manje Muhalla, Kadhaoli Village

Months	Livelihood	Constraints to Livelihood	Agricultural Activity
Baisakh (mid-April-mid-May)	Busy harvesting rabi crop, do not work as labourers	Pressure from money lenders, summer heat	Harvesting by some farmers and threshing of wheat, storing of produce, and selling up-to half their harvest, if they have to repay debt
Jeth (mid-May-mid-June)	Agricultural labourer, milk selling.	Extreme summer heat*, heat stroke, acute shortage of drinking water, fetch water traveling 2 kms and buy water at Rs. 150 per week, burning sensation in the eyes, sores and itching, fall in milk yield, shortage of power	Sowing jowar
Asar (mid-June-mid-July.)	as above	Malaria attack*, mosquitoes	Sowing jowar, paddy, bajra, fodder and moat
Sawan (mid-July-mid-Aug.)	as above	Malaria, diarrhea due to impurity in water, some cases of cholera	Deweeding bajra and jowar fields
Bhado (mid-Aug-mid-Sept.)	as above	Malaria, power shortage, joint pains@, cough and some cases of	Irrigating paddy fields

Months	Livelihood	Constraints to Livelihood	Agricultural Activity
		tuberculosis, bang disease in buffaloes affecting their mouth or legs, milk production ceases and can even kill buffaloes	
Kuwar (mid-Sept-mid-Oct.)	as above	Mosquitoes bite buffaloes, reducing milk output	Harvesting jowar and bajra, preparing land for sowing wheat
Katak (mid-Oct-mid-Nov.)	as above	Shortage of credit/loan	In case of no rain, water land, manure lands and sow wheat
Aghan (mid-Nov-mid-Dec.)	as above, take loans for cultivating wheat	Shortage of credit/loan	First irrigation for wheat fields
Puus (mid-Dec-mid-Jan.)	as above	Extreme cold reduces milk yield	Second deweeding of wheat fields
Mah (mid-Jan-mid-Feb.)	Agriculture, milk selling, labourer, private service	Power shortage	Third irrigation of wheat fields
Fagun (mid-Feb-mid-March)	as above		Fourth irrigation of wheat fields
Chet (mid-March-mid-April)		Power shortage	Some farmers harvest their wheat, make bundles for drying

Notes: *Indicates in the last 5-6 years. @Indicates in the last 10 years
Villagę Analysts: Aktar, Abdul Hakim, Chahat, Nishan, Ahmed, Nasib Khan.
Facilitator: Sudipta Roy.

Table 5 Seasonality Analysis by Men's Group in Aat Bisa, Kandhaoli

Months	Livelihood	Constraints to Livelihood	Agricultural Activities
Baisakh (mid-April-mid-May)	Milk, agricultural labour and employment in the private sector	Fever and headache, repayment of loan	Harvesting, drying, threshing of wheat, storing of grains for consumption and selling of surplus
Jeth (mid-May-mid-June)	Same as Baisakh	Summer heat, power shortage, fall in milk output and income, repayment of loans	Preparing land for sowing jowar, paddy, arhar, moong and bajra, along with sesamum
Asar (mid-June-mid-July.)	Same as Jeth	as above	Sowing jowar, paddy, arhar, moong and bajra, along with some sesamum
Sawan (mid-July-mid-Aug.)	Same as Asar	Malaria and cholera, allergy due to parthenium, loss of fodder due to locust	Deweeding the fields
Bhado (mid-Aug-mid-Sept.)	Same as Sawan	as above	Irrigating paddy, jowar, bajra fields
Kuwar (mid-Sept.-mid-Oct.)	Same as Bhado	Fever and boils	Harvesting jowar and bajra, chopping the leaves for fodder, sell surplus, sowing radish and cauliflower

Months	**Livelihood**	**Constraints to Livelihood**	**Agricultural Activities**
Katak (mid-Oct-mid-Nov.)	Same as Kuwar	None	Preparing fields for wheat, harvesting paddy, planting seedlings of cauliflower
Aghan (mid-Nov-mid-Dec.)	Same as Katak	Additional expenditure, and loan for wheat cultivation, burning sensation in the eyes, giddiness and lethargy due to fumes from nearby factories	Sowing wheat, irrigating vegetable fields
Puus (mid-Dec-mid-Jan.)	Same as Aghan	Cough, cold, breathing problem, burning sensation in the eyes, giddiness and lethargy due to fumes from nearby factories	Irrigating fields, selling cauliflower
Mah (mid-Jan-mid-Feb.)	Same as Puus	Same as in Puus plus loan for Ramzaan	Irrigating fields
Fagun (mid-Feb-mid-March)	Same as Mah	Same as in Mah	Irrigating fields
Chet (mid-March mid-April)	Same as Fagun	Same as in Fagun	Irrigating fields

Village Analysts: Hamid, Jakir, Fajruddin, Rashi, Tayab Hussain, Rati Khan, Karim and Yakub.
Facilitator: Sudipta Ray.

The villagers portray a mosaic of livelihoods. Their livelihood patterns are part of the larger hierarchy of agroecosystems shown in figure 4 of Chapter 4 (*Conway, 1987*). If we take the totality of the hierarchy of the agroecosytems, then the villagers gave us an account of the systems from village level and below. In terms of the said figure 4, the villagers were not engaged in gathering hunting and handicraft manufacture. A few opted for off-farm employment and trading. Agriculture remains at the heart of the livelihood system in Kadhaoli, and a fairly large section of the population has more than one source of livelihood. Within the farming system, the inhabitants rely partly on livestock system in its paddock variety (but they are no herdsmen) and more fully in cropping system, involved in the field and with cropping.

For men in Manje Muhalla, the peak season runs for 5 months from Aghan (mid-November to mid-December) to Chet (mid-March to mid-April). Baisakh is a partially busy month (see Table 4). For the women of the same Muhalla, there is no respite. Their work schedule outside home is busy all through the twelve months (see Table 3), notwithstanding their schedule of work inside the household. For the men of Aat Bisa, there is nothing like peak and lean seasons: it is the same, working as agricultural labourers, selling milk and working in private sector establishment (see Table 5). This difference crops up from the occupational structure and caste composition of the two localities. Since Aat Bisa is a habitation of small and marginal farmers and of people belonging to scheduled castes, their small pieces of land cannot tie them to their farms for long. In case of the large and medium farmers of Manje Muhalla, their large farms keep them busy for long stretches of time.

II.2. Role of Agriculture in Kadhaoli

With such a livelihood system, there can be no prize for guessing right how people in Kadhaoli view agriculture: the perception of the impact of agriculture on their life is very positive. First, agriculture makes it possible for the cultivators to ensure that their families get clean and fresh food. Both men and women of Manje Muhalla were categorical that they usually store the best quality food for their household consumption. Agriculture ensures that there is an abundance of food in the system and that the food available has high nutritional value. Second, agriculture is for Kadhaoli an insurance against poverty. It is a source of assured income, which enables them to repay their loans by selling a part of their main crop, wheat. Men in particular view agriculture as a source of assured (read constant) income and hence imparts a sense of stability to their families, otherwise in the mire of uncertainty. This partly explains why the women told us that agriculture is a strong support base for the family. Agriculture also ensures that the farming households have a relatively larger disposable income as they are required to expend only a small proportion of their income on food, which is a uncharacteristic of developing societies. Thirdly, agriculture provides a secure supply of fodder for the households. Grass, chaff, straw and other forms of bio-mass that agriculture generates enables the households to feed their livestock without any additional expenditure. Men's group in Manje Muhalla frankly told us that it would not have been possible for them to maintain their livestock but for fodder supplied by agriculture. Without fodder from agriculture, they said, households could not have maintained their bovine wealth at their current number and would have resulted in a fall in their income from sale of milk. Fourth, it provides a vital source of employment, though not necessarily income, for the women. Because of religion, customs and traditions, women practice pardah, which disables them from working outside their homes. However, they can join their families in the field. Agriculture, therefore, by providing partial employment to women, is an empowering mechanism, however feeble. Finally, agriculture is a source of employment for men for at least four months in a year.

Yes, in the life at Kadhaoli the importance of agriculture cannot be over-emphasized.

II.3. Cropping Pattern in Kadhaoli

Crops Grown There are two cultivating seasons in Kadhaoli: Rabi and Kharif. During Rabi, the principal crops grown are wheat, mustard, and a sprinkling of vegetables like cauliflower and radish. During Kharif season, paddy constitutes the main crop, with bits of bajra, moong, arhar, dhencha and sesamum. Jowar is grown for fodder. For the farmers explained that for them, rabi is by far the more important of the two seasons.

Cropping Pattern Paddy is cultivated on approximately 15 per cent of land; jowar, bajra and sesamum on about 5 per cent of land and wheat is cultivated in over 80 per cent of land. There are two varieties of wheat: an early variety which is sown in 75 per cent, and a late variety which is sown in 25 per cent of the land earmarked for wheat cultivation. Clearly wheat is the cornerstone of the arch of Kadhaoli's agriculture. This is also corroborated by Tables 3, 4 and 5 which depicts the life of a majority of the villagers as revolving around agriculture, and in agriculture where wheat is overbearing. Later in the study we will have occasion to examine the role of wheat in the economy of Kadhaoli. The cropping pattern has been moulded by changes in technology, water availability, the returns from different crops and experience in cultivation of the crops.

Table 6 Historical Transect by Men's Group in Aat Bisa

	Occupational Structure	Industrial Establish -ment	Farming System	Cropping Pattern
1940	99 per cent in agriculture and rest in traditional caste related occupation	Nil	Irrigation with bullock and rehant; manure; ploughing with bullocks; rainfed; traditional harvesting; seeds from own field	Barley and gram as main crops, jowar, bajra, moong, arhar, sugarcane, pulses, chora, mustard, sesamum, horse bean
1950	98.5 per cent in agriculture and others as in the 1940s	Escorts and Bata	Same as in 1940s	Barley and gram main crops, jowar, bajra, moong, arhar, sugarcane, pulses, chora, mustard, sesamum, horse bean

	Occupational Structure	Industrial Establish -ment	Farming System	Cropping Pattern
1960	98 per cent in agriculture and others in private service/non-agricultural labour		Manure and traditional seeds continue, electrification leads to use of tubewells for irrigation, tractors used for ploughing and harvesting	Barley and gram as main crops but area under wheat fell, jowar, bajra, moong, arhar, sugarcane, pulses, chora and mustard, area under sesamum and horse bean reduced
1970	90 per cent in agriculture; 40 per cent in milk business; 7 per cent works as labourers; 1 per cent in government service; 2 per cent in private service		Fertiliser; hybrid seeds; electricity use for tubewells to irrigate, tractors used for ploughing and harvesting, insecticides and pesticides formed part of inputs	Wheat cultivation increased, gram discontinued, paddy and jowar introduced
1980	85 per cent in agriculture; 50 per cent in milk business; 8 per cent labourers; job in private sector 3 per cent; Government Service 2 per cent; and 2 per cent in Gulf and other business	Kelly's Pharma-ceutical Company	Fertilisers; hybrid seeds; electricity use for tubewells to irrigate; tractor used for ploughing and harvesting	The cropping pattern of 1970s continued but mustard cultivation reduced

	Occupational Structure	Industrial Establish -ment	Farming System	Cropping Pattern
1990	Agriculture 75 per cent; gulf 2 per cent; government service 2 per cent; private service 4 per cent; business 2 per cent, labourer 15 per cent; in milk business 60 per cent	Brick kilns, plastic and rubber factories, iron melting	Fertilisers; hybrid seeds; electricity for tubewells; tractors for ploughing and harvesting, insecticides and pesticides used	Wheat is main Rabi crop, main kharif crops: paddy, jowar (for fodder) vegetable cultivation as commercial crops on land near canal

Village Analysts: Haji Karim Khan, Karim, Hamid, Jakir, Fajruddin, Rashi, Tyab Husain, Rati Khan, Yakub.
Facilitator: Sudipta Ray.

II.4. Changes in Agriculture in Kadhaoli

The kind of cultivation currently in place in Kadhaoli is what can be called "annual cropping" in the sense that land is left uncultivated for several months, between the harvest of one crop and the planting of the next. And in some lands multiple cropping has been initiated in the sense that the same plot of land bears two or more successive crops every year. The planting of a new crop takes place shortly after the harvesting of the preceding one and the fallow period is short or even negligible. Changes in agriculture in Kadhaoli has to be viewed in the larger context of other changes that were taking place in Kadhaoli over the years. The historical analysis by men's group in Aat Bisa puts all the changes in Kadhaoli in total perspective. Reference is invited to Tables 6 and 7.

In Column 2, Table 6, as in case of Table 1 earlier, the percentages do not add up to 100 per cent because a large number of villagers have more than one occupation. The percentages show the percentage of total population in these categories of occupation.

Table 7 Changes in Agricultural Output by Men's Group, Aat Bisa

	Wheat Yield	Size of Wheat Grains	Taste of Wheat	Colour of Wheat
1940	4 quintal per acre	*Fat and Long*	Nutritious and tasty (sweet)	Golden yellow
1950	Same as in 1940s	*Fat and Long*	Same as in 1940s	Same as in 1950s
1960	7-8 quintal per acre	*Fat and Long*	Same as in 1950s	Same as in 1960s
1970	16 quintal per acre	*Relatively Smaller*	Less tasty and make bad chapatis	Reddish yellow
1980	Same as in 1970s	*Relatively Smaller*	Same as in 1970s	Reddish yellow
1990	13-15 quintal per acre	*Relatively Smaller*	Same as in 1980s	Reddish yellow

Village Analysts: Haji Karim Khan, Karim, Hamid, Jakir, Fajruddin, Rashi, Tyab Husain, Rati Khan, Yakub.

Facilitator: Sudipta Ray.

If we analyze Tables 6 and 7, there is a discernible change in the occupational structure of the population. From 99 per cent of the population engaged in agriculture in 1940s, it fell to 85 per cent in 1980s and then steadily came down to 75 per cent in 1990s. Milk as a source of livelihood entered Kadhaoli in the 1960s but picked up momentum in 1970s and continued to increase in popularity thereafter. Service either in the private sector or in the government, emerged as an option in 1960s but caught on significantly in 1970s. The opportunities offered by Gulf opened up in 1980s, long after our men and women from Kerala had made for the promised land. It is an apparent paradox that though agricultural income is on the upswing, people are still moving out of it. The solution to the paradox was indicated by the farmers: though income is rising it still remains a losing venture; the opportunity cost is high; the alternative forms of occupation are less risky and less riddled with uncertainties.

These changes are in consonance with the economic changes that hit Kadhaoli. Milk vending appeared as an occupation in 1960s after escorts and bata came in the vicinity of Kadhaoli. These companies brought people from outside, as factory workers, technicians, engineers, specialists etc. who could not maintain cows and buffaloes at home, because of lack of space, time and technology. Such of these people who were non-tinned milk consumers, created a market for milk and it flourished, as these establishments grew and as newer ones came in. It was also the era of increasing cost of living and people were finding it difficult to make both ends meet. Consequently milk vending was taken up as an occupation in Kadhaoli to earn supplementary income. This was necessary for the villagers to keep pace with the high cost of living. In so doing they took full advantage of the demand created for milk by the new 'immigrants'.

Then in 1970s, job opportunities in government establishments and private agencies were created. The rapid pace of industrialisation of the area, warranted many new government offices to be opened, and the new industries as also the new population that came with it, required many new and complementary services, which the private firms could provide. This also enlarged the scope for working as labourers outside of agriculture, from 1970 onward. The number of people absorbed in milk vending and government jobs, private sector jobs and casual labour market in the village, increased markedly with the growth in industrialization and it intensified in 1990s, when Kadhaoli was swamped by factories.

II. 5. Changes in Cropping Pattern

Let us take 1950s as the point of departure. In 1950s, a large number of crops were cultivated, though the villagers did not specify on what percentage of arable land each crop was grown. The crops were a mixture of staple, coarse cereals, lentils, pulses and condiments and sugarcane (for jaggery). The main crops were coarse grains (barley and bajra) and grams. Most of the crops grown were for consumption in the households in the village. By growing this diverse mosaic of crops, the farmers not only diffused their risk of failure, on account of pests, insects, drought, flood, disease or whatever, but also ensured that their households consumed a basket of balanced food which contained fibre, nutrition and protein: carbohydrates, cereals and pulses.

In 1960s, winds of change had begun to hit Kadhaoli. Some of the crops started being looked at with less of interest. Wheat, horse bean and sesamum got pushed out a bit. By the time Kadhaoli reach 1970s, wheat is back with a vengeance, paddy is introduced, but several of the other crops fall by the way side. As of now (1990s) farmers in Kadhaoli are left with wheat, a dash of mustard, and some vegetables like cauliflower and radish, as principal Rabi crops. During Kharif paddy constitutes the main crop, with bits of bajra, moong, arhar, dhencha and sesamum. Jowar is grown for fodder. In terms of variety and diversity, there is a marked reduction, to which extent, the capacity of the farmers to diffuse risk is pruned. This trend is in keeping with the trends seen worldwide as we have mentioned in case of Sagarpur (*See Pimbert, 1993; FAO; 1993, Soetomo 1992; Fowler et. al. 1990*).

This fall in diversity of crops signals a movement away from polyculture towards bi-culture. It signals reduction in palate and nutritional value of the food produced in Kadhaoli. The crop grown in the farms can provide basically only carbohydrates and some fibre in terms of some vegetable, as most of it is for sale. It also indicates that whereas in 1950s and 1960s much of agricultural operations in Khadhaoli were for ensuring self-sufficiency in *food*, in 1990s the emphasis seems to be on self-sufficiency in *income* from sale of agricultural produce. There is a movement from growing crops to meet food requirements of households and of the community, to growing crops for the market's consumption and for money.

II. 6. Changes in Agricultural Practices and Reasons for the Changes

Changes in cropping pattern have been influenced by a chain of dynamic changes in farming practices. In 1940s and 1950s, agriculture was wholly rainfed. Farming was carried out with all traditional practices in regard to seeds, water harvesting structures, soil nutrients and implements. It was basically a household affair. The farmers and the community were in total control of the inputs, barring rains where they were fully dependent upon nature's bounties. There was none of any inputs required to be imported from outside the village.

In the 1960s mechanisation and electrification of agriculture took roots: electrified tubewells and tractors were deployed. In the 1970s we see evidence of agriculture in Kadhaoli exposed to full blown "new technology": hybrid or HYV seeds replacing traditional varieties; chemical fertilisers crowding out manure, insecticides and pesticides replacing naturally pest-resistant and insect-resistant seeds. We see tractors substituting for the bullocks and the wooden plough, and electric pumpset for irrigation in place of the old bullock and burrow. Dependence on the vagaries of nature for water was surely curtailed, but independence from the clutches of human beings was surrendered. The farmers of Kadhaoli, like the farmers of Sagarpur, are dependent upon seed companies/farms for their seeds; pesticide and insecticide companies (and their dealers) for tackling their pests and insects; Haryana state electricity board for their power and hence for irrigation; tractor companies and their dealers for ploughing and the fertilisers companies and their dealers for replenishing soil nutrients. The control of the farmers and the community on inputs vital for their survival is out of their hands. If the process of globalisation proceeds at the current pace and the WTO Agreements are implemented (which will be the case) the control of input to agriculture will shift to multinational corporations.

This shift in farming practices has several ramifications. This shift at the first instance, means that farming is now a High External Input Agriculture (HEIA) from Zero External Input Agriculture (ZEIA) and then Low External Input Agriculture (LEIA). This is what Chambers call "unimproved" agriculture (*Chambers et. al. 1989*) or what Pretty calls "forgotten agriculture" (*Pretty, 1996*). In the 1940s and 1950s agriculture was based on what the farmer and the community had: seeds, labour, bullocks, plough and the wooden hoe, manure and rains. In the 1980s and 1990s, agriculture has come to be based on inputs more from outside the households and the community: HYV seeds, pesticides, insecticides, chemical fertilisers, electricity, tractor power, tubewells and pumpsets. This is a copy book case confirming the framework of "internal resources vs. external resources" provided by *Francis and King (1988)*. We have compared the sourcing of resources in the 1940s and 1950s vis-a-vis 1980s and 1990s in case of Sagarpur. This applies to Khadaoli as well.

As farming in the 1980s and 1990s has become more dependent on "sourcing" from outside Kadhaoli, farming has come to use resources that are not always renewable. Internal resources are "inherently renewable and thus have the potential to be used on a 'sustained' basis, indefinitely, through ecologically sound methods of farming" (*Conway and Barbier, 1990*).

Since agriculture in Kadhaoli has become dependent on external resources, much of it is not provided as a "free good", implying that the farming households must buy them and hence must generate a surplus of production, cash or whatever else of value to exchange for external resources. And the cost of acquiring these resources and their supply channels are rarely controllable always by the farmer household. This has at least three cost implications in terms of open costs, hidden costs and real costs.

In high external input agriculture, it is important to note entails a lot of *real costs*. Even where there is no direct monetary outgoing to acquire a resource, there may be real cost incurred by the farming household. The issues of hidden cost, real cost and open cost as applicable to Sagarpur also applies here in the case of Khadaoli.

The farmers also pointed out that the smaller farmers are constantly squeezed in a cost-price wedge, which promotes higher production using more and more of external inputs and encouraging part-time farming. It is a squeeze that encourages farmers to be the first to maximise production from their resources.

And then this transition also means chemicalisation of agriculture. Cultivators apply to their plots of land fertilisers according to their gut feeling. They generally have no training and there is no extension service. The Agriculture Department is not helpful in matters of fertiliser, pesticide and insecticide uses and even on HYV seeds. They usually experiment a good deal. In case of a new pest/disease attack, the cultivators use whatever they think would stop the disease or pest. If it works, others follow suit, though they themselves have pointed out that there is no guarantee that a "medicine" which has worked in one plot of land will do wonders elsewhere as well. Nevertheless Schumpeter's classical "herds mentality" to follow the innovator operates. Thus right from different kinds of chemical fertilisers and to a lesser degree the insecticides/pesticides applied directly to the fields and insecticides applied to store HYV seeds, have come to include a range of chemicals in agricultural inputs. The impact of these on soil conditions are not currently perceived as important in Kadhaoli.

II. 7. Changes in Yields and the Reasons

Have such dramatic shifts had any impact on yields? We have to return for a while to Table 7. Since wheat is the principal crop grown and the world of farmers in Kadhaoli (as in case of Sagarpur), revolves, as it were, around wheat, it is best to discuss variation in the yields in terms of how yield of wheat has varied. During 1940s and 1950s, output wheat per acre was 4 quintals only. In the 1960s, once electrified pumpsets and tractors for irrigation and ploughing respectively, came into use, yield jumped up by almost 100 per cent: from 4 quintals an acre to 7-8 quintals an acre, between 1950s and 1960s. In the 1970s, when Kadhaoli got the taste of full blown "new technology", yield jumped up by another 100 per cent from the level reached in the 1970s: yield per acre moved up to 16 quintals per acre. And it remained at that level in the 1980s. This was the high noon of the Green Revolution, when HYV seeds, fertilisers, other chemicals, and assured irrigation did the trick. These are the also the decades when government of India began providing price incentives to farmers of wheat (and paddy). Each year, as we know, the government would declare a *minimum support price* and a *procurement prices.* Thus yield was responding to both change in technology as also to the farmers' inclination to grow more in sympathy with price incentives offered by Government of India. This response was similar to those in modernised agriculture in the north and contradicts the belief that the tradition bound "rural producers—especially farmers—would have basically different patterns of decision making and behaviour as compared to the farmers in modernised agriculture in the West" (*Rao, 1990*). But the yield of the 1980s could not be sustained in the 1990s. Yield per acre fell by as much as 20 per cent, to reach 13-15 quintals per acre.

During the years under review, not only did the villagers perceive substantial yield change, but the intrinsic quality of the produce itself was perceived to have changed. Wheat changed in colour from golden yellow to reddish yellow, at the time HYV seeds were introduced. The shape of the grains changed from 'fat and long' grains to relatively smaller grains in the seventies. The good taste of the traditional variety gave way to less tastier stuff, and the grains which the present crop yield, the villagers think, also do not make good *chapatis*. There is a division of opinion on the cause of these changes. While some of the villagers attribute these changes to the shift from traditional variety to HYV seeds, others felt (equally strongly) that these changes were on account of other causes or due to causes unknown.

Box 5.1
How Companies Warn us Against Pesticide Use

"Pesticide manufacturers claim that their responsibility ends with giving instructions on the precautions to be taken while using the insecticides. Most of the container labels (in English in a largely illiterate country) state that the sprayers should not be washed near wells and streams and that all residues should be carefully buried and not thrown into the nearest *nalla.* But the majority of the impoverised farmers wash directly into water sources which get polluted and kill or harm people, fish or other wild life. And the empty tins are sold for re-use which means that they could be used for storing somebody's food or carrying someone's water. Consider the following. Thimet (Cynamid India Ltd.) is second highest in toxicity among all pesticides being currently used. Yet cynamide does not even mention what its chemical composition in its leaflet "Thimet 10-G to Protect Your Cotton Crop" and there is no mention of its hazards, or the safety precautions to be taken in its use. In another leaflet, "Grow More Paddy with Cyanamid Insecticides", it is stated : "Do not use Thimet 10-G when fish are cultivated in paddy fields". Are the manufactureres ignorant of the fact that fish live in nearly all paddy fields and that field water overflows or infiltrates into rivers?"

Extracted from "Technological Interventions" by *Winin Pereria and Jeremy Seabrook* WWF

II. 8. Reasons for Preponderance of Wheat

In the second round of the study the farmers of Kandhaoli were requested to explain why they preferred wheat to any other crop. They explained their reasons in comparison to the other crop grown, viz., mustard, and the alternative means of livelihood, selling milk.

Firstly cultivating wheat provides secured return vis-à-vis mustard. They remember the *procurement price* and the *minimum support price* for wheat and paddy of the government of India. Secondly wheat is a low risk venture: *Khadwa* (disease), weeds (like *jai, mundi* and *bhatus*) and insects cause only minor crop damages of no more than 6 per cent (expressed by villagers as 1 Anna loss), 12 per cent (or 2 Annas loss) and 6 per cent (or 1

Anna loss) respectively. This means that the outgoing on herbicides, insecticides and pesticides in cultivating wheat, is low and wastage on account of these factors is minimum. In the ultimate analysis this shows up as a higher net return to the farmers. Thirdly, it is less time consuming and is less labour intensive, leaving enough time for the men to take up supplementary occupation(s) and the women to take care of the buffaloes, leading to increased household income from the sale of milk. Because wheat cultivation is less labour intensive, farmers do not need to employ labourers beyond what is available within the family. This saves resources and reduces cost of production. Fourthly, by farming wheat on 2 kila of land, a family of 6-7 members would have sufficient harvest of wheat to meet their needs for the whole year. And the husk from the wheat grown on a piece of land measuring 2 kila is enough to meet fodder needs for 2 buffaloes for the whole year. Finally, farmers said they were familiar with the technology of wheat cultivation. Even the soil in Kadhaoli is suitable for growing wheat and the crop is resistant to hard water, which is what is available for irrigation.

As against this, mustard is a picture of contrast. It is a high-risk crop and prone to damage due to frosts and extremely susceptible to what the villagers called *chepa* (a disease) which causes upto 90 per cent loss to crops. To ward off *chepa,* farmers use "medicines" which are very expensive and therefore, cut into their farm profitability. Because of the crop's susceptibility to chepa it requires constant supervision and as such, is labour intensive, sparing little time for the farmers to pursue supplementary occupation to supplement their farm income. For a community with so many buffaloes as a source of livelihood, mustard is unattractive as it gives no fodder, making it incumbent upon the farmers to buy fodder to feed their animals, thus reducing their net return from selling milk. And the last straw on the camel's back is the uncertainty of return: if there is no *chepa* and if the "weathergod" is merciful, sparing Kadhaoli of frosts, the return is very high. But once either infestation of *chepa* or frosts visit mustard, it's all over. Thus, though the soil and water conditions of Kadhaoli do not militate against mustard, the farmers strongly disfavour the crop.

When it comes to vegetable cultivation, the farmers explain, they are labour intensive and needs an enormous amount of supervision. The hard water of Kadhaoli is an added problem as it is unsuitable for vegetable cultivation. Finally, the technology of vegetable cultivation is unfamiliar to our farmers in Kadhaoli. Vegetable cultivation is the last option for Kadhaoli farmers.

Table 8 Preference Ranking of Crops by Women of Village Kadhaoli

Criteria	Wheat	Mustard	Vegetables
Susceptibility to diseases	** (2)	******* ***(10)	***** ***(8)
Susceptibility to frost, west-wind, hailstorm	***(3)	**** ****(8)	**** ****(8)
Suitability of hard water in its cultivation	****** ****(10)	******* ***(10)	*(1)
Utility of by-products	******* ***(10) Husks	*(1) Stem	*(1) Leaves
Long time required to grow	**(2)	**(2)	****** ****(10)@
Income in normal times	********(8)	****** ****(10)	******* ***(10)
Income in abnormal times	******(6)	*(1)	**(2)
Familiarity with farming process	**********(10)	********(8)	None

Note: In the above table, a high score on a negative attribute indicates the intensity of its disutility.

@But it is also capital intensive.

Village Analysts: Jamila, Mubina, Phulwati, Saboo.
Facilitator: Ms. Meera Jaiswal.
Date: 27.3.99.
Validated by: Jubeda, Sajida, Rasidan and Mubina on 5.4.99.

The preference ranking of crops in Table 8 summarizes the discussion.

The villagers substantiated their position by citing the example of their experience of 1998 which is instructive: following the cue from government's dream of the "Yellow Revolution", farmers in Kadhaoli cultivated mustard on land previously earmarked for wheat in the hope of better return. There was an attack of *chepa,* which virtually wiped out the entire mustard crop. The consequence of this has been that been that those who cultivated mustard could not recover even the expenses incurred; they had additionally to buy husks for feeding their buffaloes, making inroads into the profitability of selling milk as well. On top of it, attempts at grounding the "Yellow Revolution" left the farmers with no option but to buy wheat to feed themselves, as all their wheat fields were diverted to growing mustard.

The negative preference for mustard vis-à-vis wheat stems from its susceptibility to pests, natural events like frost, hail and west-wind; and the low value of its by-product.

Part III. Spatial Dimensions

III. 1. Are there Spatial Differences in Yield or Crop Quality?

The two parts of the village have differences in category of farmers but there is no evidence of their being spatial differences in yield. All of the farmers being Muslims, and in terms of customs, usage, practice, tradition, culture, literacy, awareness and indeed religion, they are a homogenous group and hence any likelihood of these factors causing any difference in yield in different segments of the village is ruled out. Most important, the area and the state where Kadhaoli is situated in the heartbelt of the "Green Revolution" that swept Punjab and Haryana, and later Western Uttar Pradesh. Hence the fertilisers, the insecticides, the herbicides, the pesticides and the HYV seeds that the farmers use are of the same brand, quality, potency and procured from the same sources. The terrain and the geomorphologic characteristics of the land within the village are the same. The technology used is the same; the level of mechanisation is almost

Table 9 Agricultural Process and Involvement of Men and Women

Activities	Months	Men's Work	Women's Work	Time (Hrs.)	How do Men manage time	How do Women manage time
Ploughing and leveling (*Mej & Jot*)	Kartick and Aghan (winter)	Plough with tractors	Supervise whether whole field covered	8-10	Men take leave from scheduled work	Additional to daily work schedule
Irrigation and puddling (*Palewat*)	Kartik and Aghan (winter)	Handle pumpsets	Supervise flow of water to all parts of field	4-5	Men take leave from scheduled work	Additional to daily work schedule
Apply fertilizer and sowing	Aghan	Apply fertilisers	Supervise*	4-5	Men take leave from scheduled work	Additional to daily work schedule
Irrigation at 6 inch plant	Poosh (very cold)	Handle pumpsets	Supervise*	4-5	Additional work during night	Additional to daily work
Irrigation on ear of corn formation	Magh (very cold)	Handle pumpsets	Supervise*	4-5	Additional work during night	Additional to daily schedule of work

Irrigation on formation of ear of corn	Magh (very cold)	Handle pumpsets	Supervise*	4-5	Additional work during night	Additional to daily schedule of work
Irrigation on grain formation	Fagun	Handle pumpsets	Supervise*	4-5 during night	Additional work schedule of work	Additional to daily
Irrigation on grain hardening	Chait (hot)	Handle pumpsets	Supervise*	4-5	Additional work during night	Additional to daily schedule of work
Harvesting grains	Baisakh (very hot)		Only women harvest	6 women harvest one acre		Additional work**
Making bundles	Baisakh (very hot)		Only women	1-2 days		Additional work
Threshing	Baisakh (very hot)	Men by tractors	Women help by arranging bundles	4-5	Take leave	Additional work
Transport -ing Grains	Jeth (very hot)	Men by tractors	At home	1 day	Take leave	Additional work

Note: *Supervision, according to the women, include ensuring the flow of irrigation water to all parts of the field. **If land is large enough, local women are employed on daily wage basis or contract basis.

Village Analysts: Fajuri, Rasidan, Sahira, Nasim, Nisia. *Facilitator*: Ms Meera Jaiswal. *Date:* 6.4.99.

uniform. It would have been surprising if the villagers had pointed out any spatial variations in yield.

Part IV. Inputs

IV. 1. What are the Inputs to Agriculture and the Cultivation Process?

It is best to start with the cultivation process and then summarize the inputs to agriculture. Reference is invited to seasonality analysis of agricultural activities done by men and women in Kadhaoli. Table 9 is a reproduction of the same.

Table 9 tells us that the basic inputs to agriculture are: ploughing (tractor time), seeds, fertilisers, irrigation in several rounds, and therefore water and pumpsets; family labour; hired labour; and of course land. There is no mention of any kind of pesticides, insecticides or weedicides.

The process of agriculture, in a normal year, not hit by disease and pests etc., is fairly straight forward, as is evident from column 1 of Table 8. Starting in the month of Kartick and Aghan (mid-October to mid-December) when land is ploughed and leveled, successive steps go on for 6 months in a row. Land is then irrigated during the same period and puddles made. In Aghan (mid-November to mid-December) fertilisers are applied and seeds are sown. Then for five months, fields receive five rounds of irrigation, at the rate of one round per month, except Magh when two rounds of irrigation are required. With each of the first three rounds of irrigation, successive doses of fertilisers are also applied. Baisakh (mid-April to mid-May), is the harvesting month: crop is harvested and bundles made, in preparation for threshing. It is then threshed which occupies farmers for most of Baisakh. In Jeth (mid-May to mid-June), wheat is stored for household consumption and the surplus taken to the market (called "Mandis") for sale either to the government at the procurement prices declared or to traders at the prevailing market price. It is significant that farmers, both women and men, did not mention either use of pesticides or insecticides as a major activity. We may recall in this regard that robustness of the crop against pest and weed attacks was cited by the farmers as one of the reasons for choosing wheat as the most preferred crop, and even where such attacks come, the loss is relatively small which the farmers can absorb.

IV. 2. How Does the Economics of Input Work Out?

The economics of the inputs can be worked out by comparing the yield mentioned in Table 6 with the price of inputs. However, the villagers themselves provided estimates of returns from wheat, mustard and milk, which influenced their decision on the choice of crops. Their estimates are in Table 10.

In Table 10 the cost of green fodder is included. But since farmers do not need to buy green fodder and husk, as these are generally obtained as bye product of farming, their cost of production in case of milk, is reduced by Rs. 30 and hence return from maintaining a buffalo increases by Rs. 30 per day. That is, net return is Rs. 50 per day per buffaloe. Since it takes about six months to raise either mustard or wheat, in order to make comparisons easier, the villagers explained, we have to work out the net return per buffalo for six months. This works out to be Rs. 50 multiplied by 30 times 6, that is, Rs. 9000, without accounting for the imputed cost of labour of the household. Thus selling milk is the least profitable of the three options. It is best described in the words of a woman: "If the cost of our labour and fodder are imputed, even the dung do not remain as our return".

But agriculture is *per se* is not profitable either. Within agriculture, the preferred option is wheat. For a household (family of 5-6 persons as women, men and children contribute all their labour in agriculture) the return is Rs. 7460 over a 6 month period per acre, without adding the imputed cost of family labour, on an outlay of Rs. 6040. That is, the return from wheat cultivation is Rs. 1243 per month per acre. But if labour cost is factored into it as additional outlay, even at the rate of Rs. 80 per day for 60 days (i.e., 33 per cent of 6 months, assuming that farmers would work for no more than 2 months in agricultural operations during a farming cycle) which works out to be Rs. 4800 for one person, there is a reduction in net return to Rs. 2600 per acre per year. And if this estimate is further refined by adding the cost of credit or the foregone interest on the outlay of Rs. 6040, at the rate of 5 per cent per annum (the rate of interest paid on savings bank account in banks and in the post offices), and the land tax, cess and other exaction payable to the state, a further cost escalation is inevitable, on to the outlay already estimated. (Here we are assuming that the farmers have the resources and only the opportunity cost of an alternative channel has been imputed.) A farmer, thus, succinctly lamented: "Landowners do not have money; cultivation eats all of it".

Table 10 Estimate of Cost and Returns from Different Crops (Per Acre) and One Buffalo Per Day (Men and Women)

Wheat		**Mustard**		**Milk**	
Items	*Costs (Rs.)*	*Items*	*Costs (Rs.)*	*Items*	*Costs (Rs.)*
Ploughing	1000	Land preparation	1000	Fodder	16
Leveling					
Softening and	300	Irrigation twice	400	Husk (10 Kgs.)	10
irrigation	1200	Seeds 2 kgs	40	Green fodder	20
Fertilizers	1200	Harvesting++	640	Wheat 2 kg	14
Seeds (60 Kg.)	600	Loading for			
		threshing	200		
Harvesting	200	Threshing	200		
Threshing @	800				
Transportation	200	Transportation	200		
Yield 18 Qtls.	$11700	"Medicines"	1000		
Yield 18					
Quintals (husk)	#1800	Yield 7 Quintals	14000	Milk yield 8 liters	80
Total cost	6040	Total cost	3680	Total cost	60
Total return	13500	Total return	14000	Total return	80
Net return	7460	Net return	10320	Net return	20

Notes: @ Labour cost is Rs. 30 a quintal. Hence 30 times 18 = Rs. 540.
$ indicates 18 quintals wheat multiplied by Rs. 650, the rate at which Wheat is sold.
# Indicates 18 quintals of husk multiplied by Rs. 100, the going market price of Husk.
++ 2 days multiplied by 4, multiplied by Rs. 80, the cost of labour per day.

Village Analysts: Jamila, Mubina, Phulwati, Saboo on 5.4.99.
Validated by: Jubeda, Sajida, Rasidan, Mubina on 5.4.99.
Facilitator: Meera Jayaswal.
Information Received from: Kasam, Dhup Khan, Almuddin and Ibrahim on 7.4.99.

However, if the farmers do not find employment in half of the six months required to grow one crop of wheat, from *Mej* to pulling the grains into the households, then the net profit would be Rs. 7460 over a six month period. Since in Kharif, the other crops paddy, grams, moong etc. are on smaller tracts and are less profitable, the annual income for a farmer from agriculture would be about just above Rs. 11500 per annum, which defines the "poverty line" for India. Poverty small wonder has been listed as a high priority problem in Kadhaoli, scoring 8 points. (See Table 1).

The estimates of yield given by the combined group of women and men of village Kadhaoli in Table 10, differs from the current yield estimate given by men's group of villagers, of Aat Basti in Table 7. If the estimate of Table 7 is taken, the loss to the farmers from wheat cultivation, would be even more. We have not pursued this issue further, because the general point is well taken by the villagers, that wheat cultivation is not a profitable venture for the farmers of Kadhaoli.

If farmers opt for mustard, in place of wheat, the outlay is less than the outlay on wheat cultivation, and the return better. But the uncertainty and high risk associated with mustard cultivation is so great that farmers are thoroughly deterred from venturing into growing mustard in lieu of wheat. Not that they have not tried, but with bitter consequences, which we mentioned earlier. And as Bismilla, a farmer who attempted mustard cultivation put it, a return of Rs. 10320 in six months from mustard is a very rare fortunate gift of "Allah" (God). "Last year", Bismilla rued, "not even Rs. 2000 was returned (from mustard cultivation) because of heavy loss due to frost and *chepa* infestation".

These experiences and non-profitability of agriculture, have impressed upon villagers of Kandhaoli the importance of serving either the government or the private sector. The women in particular pointed out that to be in service is a guarantee of a profitable and secure means of livelihood. Even serving in establishments for earning a daily wage of Rs. 50, is looked upon as a better alternative means of livelihood. In the words of Nagina, "a rich person is the one who has a service also. Even private employers pay Rs. 50 per day, which ensures a secure income". This provides at least a partial answer to the question of why people in our village pursue multiple occupations.

The foregoing may seem somewhat contradictory to what farmers said earlier (described in Part-II), where income from agriculture is conceived as a fixed source of income. There is in reality no contradiction. The sense of "fixity" of income is in the sense that they will get a certain floor level of prices for their produce whatever else happens from the *procurement prices* and *support prices* declared by the government. It is this mind set of certainty that plays a crucial role in farmers' satisfaction.

IV. 3. Who Supplies the Inputs and Who Provides the Extension Services Regarding New Seeds and Fertilisers?

Inputs in case of wheat cultivation in Kadhaoli like in Sagarpur, are tractors, seeds, fertilisers, irrigation in several rounds, and therefore water and pumpsets; family labour; outside labour; and of course land. As we saw the year long agricultural operations are carried out by family labour. Hiring of labour is limited and is confined to labour available in the village itself. Tractors are owned by farmers and there is inter-household hiring of tractors. The case is similar with pumpsets for irrigation. Farmers access other inputs, such as seeds, fertilisers, pesticides, etc., from the open market, which is why they lament that there is no subsidy on fertilisers, seeds etc. The existence of extension service in nowhere noticeable which is why some farmers attributed changes in taste, colour and size in wheat to erroneous use of fertilisers and incorrect use of seeds etc., all of which reflect absence of extension support. We will have more to say when we come to the constraints.

It also has implications for the farmer's friends. HEIA has ensured that the "farmers friends" have also changed. There are now four categories of such "friends". (1) Agro-chemical industries, which provide fertilisers, herbicides, pesticides, insecticides, fungicides, aphicides. (2) Seed producers who would soon be multinational companies with incomes exceeding the GDP of several countries taken together. (3) Equipment and energy companies who provide farmers with machinery (tractors, pumpsets, threshers etc.) and fuel. And (4) probably in the foreseeable future when WTO has its way, Biomedical companies as well who would supply drugs for prophylactic use in intensive farming for vaccination and curative purpose (*Tansy and Worsley,1995*). This means that farming is moving away from depending upon the goodwill and support of households and community in the village based on long term (often multi-generational) personal relationship to "friends" in far corners of the globe based on short-term impersonal and commercial relationships. This makes it even more important to look at the hierarchy of agro-ecosystems (discussed elsewhere in this book) for development to proceed.

Part V. Class Issues

V. 1. Who are the Landowning and Landless Groups?

The division of the village into landowning and landless groups is relatively easy. In the general description of the village in the introductory section it came out fairly well that most of the people own land. Only 3.33 per cent of the people do not own land and they are the ones who belong to scheduled castes. That is, the Muslims are the landowning group, and a portion of the Hindus (scheduled castes) is the landless group. The ownership as also occupation in Kadhaoli are mostly by inheritance and bequest. This is why the Muslims who inherited land have stuck on to it as cultivators (even if part time) and the scheduled castes who are the service providers, like sweepers, cobblers and so on, the traditionally non-cultivating classes, have stuck on to their traditional occupations or work as labourers. And within Muslims there aren't people who have different occupations, like weavers and fishermen, which could have stratified the community on the basis of landownership. Thus while most of the people are landowning, who are Muslims, a small landless class of scheduled castes live in Aat Bisa. There is a class location: small farmers live in Barah Bisa and the large and medium sized farmers live in Aat Bisa. The relatively richer farmers live nearer to the road, while the relatively poorer keep up the rear.

15. Are There Variations In The Types Of Land Used By Different Farmer Groups?

Firstly, in Kadhaoli, farmers showed no signs of stratification in terms of who cultivated which crop. Generally all the farmers cultivated, or were potential cultivators of, all the crops that can be grown in the environment, depending on several factors, including weather, soil conditions, resource availability and opportunity. The villagers did not mention (nor were they probed) that some farmers exclusively grow wheat whereas others grow only vegetables and so on. Farmers are not divided along caste or religious lines either. It is, therefore, difficult to identify different groups of farmers on an objective basis, except on the basis of landholdings: large farmers, medium sized farmers and small farmers.

If we look at the profile of the crops grown, it is clear that wheat is the principal crop grown. And the village land is perceived as being most suitable for cultivating wheat as well. There is no direct evidence on the subject but, given the relative homogeneity of the farming community and the cropping pattern being what it is, variations in different in types of land used by different farmer groups are remote.

V. 3. Is there any Overlap between Landownership with Produce Ownership?

The issues of landownership and produce ownership are not very critical in Kadhaoli. We have seen most of the people have land. Agriculture is for the most part a family enterprise, with outside contribution in the shape of hired labour only at the margin. Those who own the land are the producers as well. There is no system of tenancy. Even those who work outside the village return to the village whenever they are required to be in the village for agriculture. If we recall Table 9, men take leave during cultivation (for *mej, jot and palewat*). For irrigating their fields, they join their families at night to bear the additional burden of watering. And during threshing and marketing of their produce, they proceed on leave from their regular employers.

Land is the farmers' primary asset and is considered by the farmers of Kadhaoli like in the other villages of the study, as the biological basis for agriculture, against the backdrop of its immense utility as the established basis of power. As an asset its value determines how much the farmers can borrow from the Gurgaon Grameen Bank. The fact that the farmers are from the minority community, viz., Muslims also plays a role in this regard. In order to establish their right, title and possession on lands, most of which is inherited, these farmers, prefer to till their own land and not lease them out.

The most overwhelming reason for there being no tenant, the villagers explained, is the economics of farming itself. They recall the estimates of return from alternative crops grown, shown here as Table 10, and the discussion surrounding it. If wheat cultivation results in net loss to the farmer, after factoring in cost of credit and imputed cost of labour, what incentive will the tenant have if he can retain only half of the produce, after putting in as much resources and labour? Given the general principle of sharing of produce between landlords and tenants, the gross return to the tenant cultivator would be half of Rs. 7460 for a 6 month period. That is, the tenant will make Rs. 3730 on an outlay of Rs. 6040, without including imputed labour cost (or wages foregone) of Rs. 9600 plus imputed cost of credit, Rs. 302. The "diseconomies" of tenancy plays a big role in deterring leasing-out and leasing-in of land.

If we take the case of mustard cultivation, the picture is the same. Half of the gross return to the tenant cultivator will be Rs. 5160 (God willing!!) against an outlay of Rs. 3680 plus imputed cost of capital and labour of Rs. 9784. There is no way a rational cultivator will sign up for such a tenancy arrangement. The economics of it all does not work out.

V. 4. Migrant Labourers in Agriculture and Migrant Leases

Let us look at Tables 9 and 10 once again. Most of the steps in cultivation are performed by the farmers themselves and their families. There is very little input of labourers from outside the family. In case some farmers own very large farms, the villagers pointed out while describing the agricultural cycle, shown here as Table 9, they hire labourers from within the village for *harvesting* operations only. The other major activity in the village is selling milk. As we shall see from Table 11 below, the women within the household manage most of it and men partake the responsibility of milking large herds and in selling milk whether in the village or at Ballabhgarh.

There is no scope for employing labourers. Hence migrant labourers are non-existent in the agricultural sector. Similarly in case of migrant leases and we have discussed the issue in the previous paragraphs. There are some 2 per cent people who work as migrants in the Gulf countries but they always leave behind their families to take care of the farms and animals and hence they too do not resort to leasing-out farmland. To top it all, the village itself suffers from an unemployment rate of 20-25 per cent (see Table 1). On a larger plane, throughout India, the evidence suggests that migration is from rural areas to the urban areas in search of better prospects of employment, and rarely intra-rural area migration and none from urban to rural areas. The reason being, the poverty of one village is hardly attractive enough to those who live in poverty in another area, to migrate. Our villages, dependent on land and agriculture, do not offer employment opportunities of the kind and scale that appears reasonably good to induce influx of migrants from other villages. In fact in most of agriculture, there is disguised unemployment, particularly in villages dominated by small and marginal farmers. Therefore, from first principles, migration into a poor village like Kadhaoli is unlikely.

Part VI. Gender

VI. 1. Are There any Differences in the Tasks Carried out by Men and Women?

In Kadhaoli, where we are learning about a Muslim community and in Haryana, the boundaries of what women and men can do (and cannot do) are celebrated facts, as in Sagarpur. An unfailing characteristic of this dichotomy is the "inside-home" and "out-side home" distinction. Recall what the villagers said in Table 9 and read it with ergograph prepared by the women, reproduced as Table 11.

The ergograph at Table 11, makes it manifest that the tasks performed by women in rearing of buffaloes and selling milk are very conveniently fitted into the traditional role of women, viz., collecting fodder and carrying out household chores. Men are involved generally in selling milk in the village and in the nearby town and in some cases help the women in milking the buffaloes. If we look at Table 9, the tasks assigned to women are also demarcated. In cultivating and harvesting wheat, the mainstay of agriculture in Kadhaoli, women supervise the activities from ploughing, leveling and puddling (*mej, jot and palewat*) to several rounds of irrigation. The tasks of 2 months of harvesting, and making bundles for threshing, are under the charge of women. Even when men are engaged in threshing with machines, the women stay on to make the smaller bundles out of the larger bundles, to facilitate threshing.

Table 11 Tasks Performed (Ergograph) by Women in Selling Milk

Who Performs	Steps	What Time/Duration
Women	Prepare feed and dither	1 hr. (5 a.m. to 6 a. m.)
Women*	Milking	15-20 minutes for 1 buffaloe (7 a. m.)
Men	Selling milk	20 minutes in the village and 2 hrs. in Ballabhgarh (7.a. m. to 9 a. m.)
Women	Collect fodder	4 hour (9 a.m. to 1 p. m.)
Women	Bathing/cleaning buffaloes	30 minutes (around 1 p. m.)
Women	Chopping green fodder	30 minutes by machine or 1 hour manually (?)
Women	Removing buffalo dung Make dung cakes	1 hour (4 p.m. to 5 p. m.)
Women	Preparing feed and feeding animals	30 minutes (6 p.a.)
Women	Milking	10-20 minutes per buffaloe
Men	Selling milk	20 minutes in village and 2 hours in town.

Money Goes to Men

Notes: *If there are more than one Buffalo, women and men work.

Village Analysts: Fajuri, Rasidan Sahira, Nasim and Nisia.
Facilitator: Ms. Meera Jaiswal.
Date: 6.4.99.

It is quite remarkable that the agricultural activities under women' charge are in addition to their traditionally assigned responsibilities or what the villagers call the "daily schedule of work". They include as is the case elsewhere, but are not restricted to, fetching water, collecting fuel and fodder, feeding animals, cleaning and washing, bearing and rearing children, processing and cooking food for the households and even caring for the sick and the disabled. In case of men, for irrigating their land they work during night but for other operations like *mej, jot and palewat*; for threshing and for taking the produce to the *mandi* (market), they take leave from their normal work. If one were to talk of workload of men and women on a comparative basis, women are not only overloaded, their workload has increased with the introduction of new technology.

The division of labour amongst women and men, in Kadhaoli, as in case of sagarpur, can also be categorize as being manual and mechanised. Most of the tasks assigned to the women require them to "soil their hands" as it were. Most of the task assigned to women can only be manually performed, starting from supervising irrigation (which at the ground level; or better still at the field level, is making sure that water reach all parts of the field) to harvesting and making bundles for threshing. This is sharp contrast to the tasks performed by men, viz., ploughing, irrigating, threshing and transporting, all of which are mechanised. In terms of effort and disagreeableness, women clearly shoulder a more arduous set of tasks.

Women are engaged inside their homes and if they work in their own fields, most of the time they are there along with male members of the households. Men on the other hand are primarily concerned with such of these activities which warrants interface with outsiders and movement outside their homes/fields. Arranging tractors, arranging irrigation pumpsets, selling milk, threshing wheat and selling wheat both inside the village and in Ballabhgarh town, are tasks assigned to men. This has a serious economic implication as well which, we wish to say as an *obiter dicta,* is seemingly unfair. Because men sell the produce created out of family resources including labour, the proceeds of the sale from such produce go to the men. Though women and men and children all cojointly participate in generating household output, the destination and custody of income arising out of such output, in the last analysis, rests with the men.

Box 5.2
Gender Dimension of Disempowerment

The presence of poverty is linked to unequal access to and distribution of resources, a lack of control over productive resources and limited participation in political and economic institutions. Where such factors are determined structurally, by laws and culture for example, or transiently, by macro-economic policy, their gender bias is clear. Women face institutional obstacles to controlling …..productive resources.

Lourdes Beneria and Savitiri Bisnath in Gender And Poverty (New York: UNDP)1996.

This general sense of women being designated to be in their homes, hearth and fields, is reflected in other spheres of their endeavour as well. For example, the education that the villagers seek for their girl children within the village is a mirror image of this attitude. Girl children, the villagers perceive, must be educated within the limits of the village boundary and hence they rank non-availability of school for the girl children in the village as a major problem (at par with the problem of poverty), ahead of the problem of School for the male children.

VI. 2. Is there any Variation Noticeable with Age or Caste Group?

There is apparently no noticeable variation with age or caste group, barring that those belonging to scheduled castes who are partially landless. People belonging to scheduled castes are not farmers and hence they have an altogether different economic and societal role cut out for them, as distinct from the role of the farming community. Though caste has no correlationship with landownership, as there are many villages where scheduled caste households own land, but in the particular situation of Kadhaoli, the scheduled caste households are landless. The fact that they are landless also means, however, that they are poor.

Part VII. Significance of Agriculture

VII. 1. What is the Significance of Agriculture in Urban and Peri-Urban Areas in Terms of

- Employment
- Food Security
- Income
- Others

Employment: The significance of agriculture in the life of Kandhaoli has been dealt with at length in Part II earlier. Suffice it to say here that agriculture is a source of income, it is a source of employment and it is a source of food and fodder as well. As many as 75 per cent of the people in Aat Bisa and 95 per cent of the people of Manje Muhalla depend on agriculture (Table 1). Employment generating potential of agriculture for women is critical. But for agriculture many of the women in Kadhaoli would not have been employed.

However, people pursue alternative means of livelihoods within the village and outside. There are farmers like in other villages, who also sell milk. There are farmers who work in establishments outside the village but attend to cultivation and harvesting whenever required. There are people serving in the Gulf, but the general pattern is that their families remain at home.

Food Security: In terms of food security, the data in terms of the seasonality analyses at Tables 3, 4 and 5 done by the different groups as well as the problem prioritization in Table 1 do not indicate availability of food as a problem or as a constraint to livelihood. Even the historical transect of the village (at Table 6) nowhere indicates that insufficient food or hunger ever visited the community. In Part II on the significance of agriculture, we noted that people were categorical about first storing their best produce for household consumption and then selling the remaining surplus, if any, in the *Mandi*. Therefore, there are reasons to believe that food has nutritional value, whether adequate or not is anybody's guess. Recall that on the significance of agriculture, Section 4 above, it was mentioned that farmers had a tinge of pride in citing their ability to provide fresh and nutritious food to their households as one of the reasons for believing that agriculture was critical to their existence. The twin perspectives of storing their best produce for household consumption and of having the ability to ensure fresh and nutritious food for their families indicate a concept of food security. Not only is food grown in the system, it is made accessible and there is at least the intention to ensure that it is of adequate nutritional value.

The cropping pattern indicates that Kadhaoli has migrated from ZEIA to HEIA and the diversity of crops has been on the decline. Nevertheless, the principal crops grown are food crops, whether for household consumption or for marketing surplus. The only minor exception being vegetables.

Income: Agriculture is not a profitable venture. However, stability and certainty of assured prices for their crops is not in doubt, particularly when they are assured every year of a *minimum support price* and of a *procurement price* for wheat and paddy. Selling milk and growing mustard are either not profitable or fraught with high risk of failure, without any price cover like wheat and paddy. Agriculture provides valuable fodder, for the buffaloes, making cost of producing milk less expensive and return from selling milk that much higher. Since much of agriculture is based on family labour, agriculture as a source of employment to those whose services are on offer from outside of farming households, is limited.

Food production is part of the overall life support system in Kadhaoli as in any other Indian village. Tasks assigned to women in the cycle of growing and processing food, either by convention or consent, are carried out by the women, in addition to their daily schedule of work. Men too have their roles set out, within the intra-familial distribution of work. They discharge their share of the responsibilities, by eithering work at night or taking leave from their place of employment, if they are employed elsewhere. Both women and men and children work hard in order to fulfill their respective obligations in making agriculture work for their families. Admittedly some work harder than others. Nevertheless food production is perceived as an integral part of household activities and as a necessary condition for holding the household together. In the absence of food, the other household activities, in the villagers' perception, will fall out of place.

Part VIII. Constraints to Agricultural Production

VIII. 1. The Constraints to Agricultural Production

A glimpse of some of the constraints to agriculture was provided by the villagers in their discussion on choice of crops etc. Here we will explore the issues raised in greater depth.

The constraints the community faced in agriculture in the 1950s were none except *Baroo* (weed) in wheat and bajra fields. In the 60s, the period when tubewells and tractors were introduced, the group recalled attack from small white dot sized pests on sugarcane, which dried the whole sugarcane fields in the village. After the introduction of hybrid seeds and fertilisers no major constraint was faced, at least in the 1970s. However, by 1980s termites, weeds, pests and weather fluctuations became serious problems. The cultivators were unable to deal with the situation and hence by 1990s, the damage caused by these pests, weeds, insects and diseases, got prominently reflected in the lower yields in wheat. This also had the effect of consequently downgrading the rating of agriculture as a means of livelihood, in the perception of the villagers. In the 1990s, new problems in the form of pests (locust, *chepa*) and hardening of water, added to their worries. The villagers did not know how to tackle the situation and sought government support. Ranking of constraints in Aat Bisa and Manje Muhalla are detailed in Tables 12 and 13.

A comparison of Tables 12 and 13 discloses both similarities and dissimilarities, where the latter abounds and the former is a rarer commodity. The villagers not merely catalogued the constraints but also ranked them and made a distinction between the constraints and their proximate causes.

In Table 13, women have categorized all the constraints into three clear classes: shortage of power, menace of nilgais, locust, hail and *chepa,* are in one category that inflicts most of the damages. They are all assigned a score of 10 as they all cause losses or damages ranging from Rs. 2000 to Rs. 5000 per acre and more. The second category comprises *sati, asi, rat,* termites, *katali* and *bhatua,* all of which has been assigned a score of 5. The estimated damage or loss caused by these range from Rs. 100 to Rs. 1250 per acre. Then we have category three of constraints, viz., rain and congress grass, which were awarded a score of unity. According to the villagers' perception, there is no estimate possible of the loss or damage to crops caused by these constraints. The rationality is clear: where they cannot estimate the loss or damage, they just recognize the gravity of the constraint but do not rank it based on subjectivity, for that may over-estimate or under-estimate the status of the constraint in a graded catalogue of constraints.

Men have ranked the constraints also in descending order of the magnitude of the problems created, without clear breaks: there is a continuum of gravity. And it is difficult to discern any logic underlying this gradation, because men did not provide any estimate of damage or loss in most of the cases. Thus the estimates of loss by women's group have greater quantification and greater details, perhaps because their lives revolve around producing and processing food, in the fields and in their homes and hearths, and hence more sensitive to loss or damage to food crops.

The list of constraints ranked in descending order of magnitude of damage/loss they cause, by the women of Manje Muhalla, Barah Bisa includes, *inter alia,* only 4 of the constraints indicated by men of Aat Bisa (and vice versa), viz., *nilgai, locust, chepa and termites,* as the ones that cause most damage. Of the remaining constraints ranked by the women, the majority are weeds (5 out of 9), whereas most of the constraints ranked by the men are insects and pests (6 out of 11). Women are the key actors in deweeding during both Rabi and Kharif, and therefore, they are quick in recollecting and articulating names of weeds, as constraints to agriculture. Men on the other hand, because they have responsibilities of "outside-home" work, interact with outsiders and fetch "medicines" to deal with pests. They are, therefore, better placed to talk about pests than weeds and they do so in full measure. Women also find nature's contribution in the form of hail and rain as constraints but men mention none of these.

Table 12 Constraint Ranking by Men's Group in Aat Bisa

Constraints	Crops attacked	Effect	Cause and Relation-ships	Estimated loss (In Rs.)	Score	Stage when attacked	Measures
Locust (insect)	Kiwar and maize	Eats away leaves 2-3	Late rain	3000/acre	***** *** (8)	All stages	Spraying though ineffective, serial spraying sought, various medicines like DDT
High cost	All crops	Affects return, fertilizer must@	Govt. responsible	No estimate	****** ** ** (10)	All stages	
Termites (pest)	Wheat and mustard	Weakens crops and destroys grains	Dry winter and black soil	No estimate	**** **** (8)	All stages	None
Lalrri (pest)	Vegetables	Eats away leaves	Unknown	1000/acre	**** *** (7)	Younger plants	Melathine (sic)
Safed moondi (weed)	Wheat	Looks like wheat, prevents growth of wheat. 3	Unknown, grows naturally	500/acre	*****(5)	Infant stage	None, application of medicines affects the crop too

Jai Rani (weed)	Wheat	Compete with wheat for soil nutrition. 3	unknown. Grows naturally	200/acre	*****(5)	Infant stage	Deweeding but in the process wheat are also uprooted
Chepa (pest)	Mustard, bajra and sugarcane	Dries leaves and then the stems	Unknown	No estimate	*****(5)	Young plants	None
Green Locust (insect)	paddy	Pods are rendered grainless		No estimate	*****(5)	Matured plants	Fenneicate (sic) by large farmers only
Hard water	All crops	Reduces yield, vegetable cultivation not possible. 5	Caused by NTPC plant		*****(5)	Matured plants	
Nilgai	Wheat, jowar, maize and mustard	Aggressive grazing in herds & sits on crops	Ban on killing and no check on animal population	500/acre	****(4)	Any stage	
Soondi (pest)	Paddy	Destroys leaves		No estimate	*****(5)	Young plants	Dimscron (sic) by large farmers only

Notes: @Use of Fertilisers have rendered soil unsuitable for cultivation without Fertilisers. The numbers occurring in column 3 indicate the vintage of the constraints.

Village Analysts: Haji Karim Khan, Hamid, Jakir, Fajruddin, Rashi, Tayab Hussain, Rati Khan, Karim, Yakub.
Facilitator: Sudipta Ray.

Table 13 Constraints Ranking Women's Group, Barah Bisa

Constraints	Crops attacked	Effect	Cause and Relation-ships	Estimated loss (In Rs.)	Score	Stage when attacked	Measures
Power shortage	All crops	Reduces irrigation	Power to industry	70 per cent crop	***** ***** (10)	All stages especially infant	No solution
Nilgai	Wheat bajra, jowar	Grazes/ destroys crop	Deforestation	2000/acre	***** *****(10)	All stages particularly matured stage	No solution
Locust (pest)	Jowar, bajra	Eats away leaves	Dry weather	5000/acre	****** ****(10)	Young stage	No solution
Hail	All crops	Damages crop	Natural	5000/acre for Wheat	****** ****(10)	Infant stage	No solution
Chepa (pest)	Mustard, bajra	Leaves dry up	Natural	2500/acre	****** ****(10)	Youth stage	No solution
Sati (weed)	Jowar, arhar, paddy, vegetables	Crops do not grow	Fertilizer	500/acre	***** (5)	Infant stage	Uprooting but difficult

Asi (weed)	Wheat	Stunts growth	Natural	100/acre	***** (5)	Infant Stage	Uprooting but difficult
Rat	Wheat and paddy	Eats grains and drills hole in the fields	Natural	200/acre	***** (5)	Any stage	No solution
Termites	Wheat, jowar, bajra	Eats roots	Less rain	1250/acre	***** (5)		No solution
Kateli (weed)	Wheat	Stunts growth		Natural	1250/acre	*** ** (5)	Uprooting but difficult
Bhatua (weed)	Wheat	Stunts growth	Natural	1000/acre	***** (5)	Any stage	No solution
Uncertainty of rain	Wheat, mustard, jowar, bajra	Decelera -tes growth of wheat	Natural	No estimate	* (1)	Any stage	No solution
Congress grass (weed)	Wheat, mustard, jowar,bajra	Stunts growth of crop	Natural	No estimate	* (1)	Any stage	No solution

Notes: Village Analysts: Nishar, Mubina, Abruna and Hazrai.
Facilitator: Ms. Meera Jaiswal. *Date*: 7.4.99.

Box 5.3

The Concept of Human Security

- **Human Security has two aspects:**
- **Safety from such chronic threats as hunger, disease and repression.**

Protection from sudden and hurtful disruptions in the patterns of daily life—whether in homes, in jobs or in communities. Such threats exist at all levels of national income and development.

The many threats to human security, differing for individuals at different times, fall into seven main categories:

- Economic insecurity
- Food insecurity
- Health insecurity
- Personal insecurity
- Environmental insecurity
- Community and cultural insecurity
- Political insecurity

Extracted from UNDP: *Human Development Report* 1999 (New York: Oxford University Press) 1999.

Though estimates vary, both the estimates place locust as the most damaging constraint and there are a host of animals and pests which cause damage running into thousands of Rupees. The major constraints are pests, animals and shortage of power. The loss inflicted by weeds, rats and termites are all comparatively lower in order of magnitude. A rational response should, therefore, have been emphasis on removing the constraints caused by locusts, animals and pests. Weeds, rats and termites should have been lower down in the response agenda. If we see the responses (last column of Tables 12 and 13) it is surprising that farmers have tried to tackle basically the weeds. True, they did try for serial spraying of fields for locust, because individual action do not yield the desired result (for if one field is sprayed the locust moves on to the next and so on) but to what extent it was pursued to its logical conclusion and to what effect are not reflected in these exercises. The measures taken to confront the problems caused by locust, animals and pest leave one wondering why these did not enter in the farmers' calculation in Kadhaoli.

The farmers also mentioned that they face shortage of credit since last 8-9 years. In addition the women painted a rather gloomy picture of their future, marred by increasing difficulties and greater poverty. Because the joint family system is on its decaying phase and population is increasing, fragmentation and sub-division of land are imminent, leading to diseconomies of small farms and low output and income. The Haryana urban development authority is contemplating acquisition of land from the village, for constructing Sector 29 of Ballabgarh Township. HUDA in one stroke has instilled a sense of fear and uncertainty in the minds of farmers: fear of displacement and consequent hardship; uncertainty about what future holds for them and when the axe will fall. In such an environment the people in Kadhaoli are experiencing, in so many words, "Human insecurity". This has set some farmers thinking of selling off their land at a higher price in Kadhaoli and migrating to UP and buy land at a relatively lower price there. The general environment, the women perceived, did not call for cheers.

Table 14 is consistent with Table 12 and 13. It adds elements like lack of subsidy, paucity of credit, poor state of health during the cultivation season, and westerly winds as constraints especially for wheat cultivation. While the last was peculiar to wheat, the others were not. The villagers added these new factors in the second round of analysis as they have greater applicability to wheat cultivation. Wheat being cultivated in as much as 80 per cent of the cultivable land, the requirement of resources and power are much greater than for any other crop. Naturally, they said, it is during wheat cultivation that they garner all their mite and it is then that they face the brunt of resource constraint. Their realization of the help that appropriate and properly targeted subsidy and availability of credit could render, is at its highest. On constraints imposed by fragile state of health, the farmers explained, health problems crop up mostly in the period between December and April, and is primarily during Rabi, the period when wheat is grown. In consequences, constraints imposed by health are articulated up front while analyzing constraints wheat farming faces than in other cases.

Table 14 Constraints Faced by Farmers in Wheat Cultivation Depicted by Women's Group in Barah Bisa

Constraints & their Score	Months	Damage	Estimate of Loss	Vintage	Measures Taken
Yield Related					
Westerly wind (6)	March-April	Dries green crop and grains leading to loss in yield	2 quintals per acre approximately	10-12 years. Particularly severe in 1999	Early harvesting of crops
Kadwa (disease) (1)	January-March	Ear of corn becomes black and grains do not form	Varies. In 1999, 50 kgs per acre lost	10-12 years	None
Weeds (jai, mundi, bhatua, katail) (2)	November-April	Grow faster than wheat and absorb soil nutrients	This year 50 kgs per acre	15-20 years	Medicines are used but saves crop partially
Termites (2)	November-April	Roots eaten up and plants dry up as a result	Varies according as number of termites vary	8-10 years	Plants are irrigated which kills termites
Birds (1)	November (sowing season) and March-April (when grains ripen)	Eat wheat seeds sown and grains before harvesting	10-15 kgs per acre of ripe grain 2-3 kgs of seed per acre	—	None
Nilgai (2)*	January-March	Graze crops	Marginal	10-15 years	Vigil
Rats (1)	January-March	Eats grains	1 quintal	Many years	None

Resource Related					
Lack of money (3)	October-March	Cuts out essential expenditure in agriculture	2 quintals per acre	8-10 years	Loan from money lender
Bad Health					
sickness like najla, fever, diarrhea and body-ache (4)	December-April	Prevents performing at peak levels of efficiency	—	8-10 years	
Government					
Fear of land acquisition (8)	Throughout the year	—	—	—	—
Power shortage (5)	December-April	Reduces irrigation, most harmful	2 quintals per acre	4-5 years	Generator has to be arranged
No subsidy on seeds, fertilisers and medicines (5)	November-April	Buying from open market, increases burdens	—	—	—

Notes: *indicates Nilgais are a species of Deer, which is endangered, and hence killing them is prohibited by law.

Village Analysts: Fajuri,Rasidan, Sahira, Nasim and Nisia. *Facilitated by*: Meera Jayaswal. *Date*: 6.4.99.

These additional constraints do not alter the general tenor of the inquiry, because these constraints are generic in character and would be found in any farming system of a poor community. But they are real and are policy related and we will deal with them in the next section.

VIII. 2. Factors that Influence the Constraints

Details of factors that influence the constraints are somewhat limited. Attack of locust, according to the men in Aat Bisa, is influenced by timings of the monsoons. In the event of a delayed monsoon, leading to late rains, the danger of locust infestation looms very large. Termites, for them, flourish by dry winter. This was confirmed by scientific people in September 1999 at New Delhi (See the *Indian Express,* 24th September, 1999). They perceive the problem of hard water to be associated with high tension underground cabling by NTPC (National Thermal Power Corporation). Presumably the two occurrences have coincided. They consider all other constraints to be imposed by nature.

According to the women's group, appearance of locust in larger numbers, coincided with years in which Kadhaoli received less than their normal quota of rainfall. *Sati* weed has been the singular contribution of fertilisers. Termites, they think like the men's group, were more visible during dry weather. Nilgais, grown as they have due to their "protected-animal status", stray into human habitation and hence cropping fields in search of food as deforestation has robbed them of their natural source of food. And shortage of power, the women thought, is caused by undue demand on power put by industry, who enjoy more clout, leading to farmers' needs being sidelined. Like their men counterpart, women ascribe a large number of the constraints to nature.

There are three constraints, viz., power shortage, paucity of credit and absence of subsidy, whose origin can be traced to either faulty or wrong policies or to wrong implementation of policies. Giving subsidy for fertilisers and other external inputs to popularize them and then withdrawing them or targeting them so badly that the money does not go where the mouth is, has indeed been as good as suicidal. The non-availability of credit is a sad commentary on the banking system's ability to reach the needy, despite decades of efforts at migrating from class banking to mass banking and despite the network of nationalised banks, scheduled banks and the regional rural banks, maintained at considerable social cost. Power shortage that has plagued every sector of our economy needs to be corrected, and in particular special attention has to be paid in making sure that it does not at least affect food production.

Probably the farmers realised but did not articulate that growing crops in continual mono-culture or bi-culture leads inevitably to much greater pest, weed, disease, fertility and soil erosion problems than the mixed cropping systems (*Francis, 1994; Edwards et. al., 1993*). Though agriculture has not turned mono or bi-culture but the tendency is towards that limiting case and there is an increase in the number of pests, weeds, insects etc., that constrain agriculture. This has to be taken care of or else tackling pests, weeds, etc will be a nightmare.

Part IX. Injury to Crops

IX. 1. Visible Injury to Crops

The constraints spelt out in Tables-12 to 14, *ipso facto* indicate that visible injury to crops is noticeable, but none of them in particular is perceived by the farmers as being caused by air pollution. For instance, grazing by nilgais leaves brazen marks of injury on the crops. Locust attack, *chepa* infestation and hailstorm imprint visible signs of injury on the leaves and the crops visited by them. During the first round of study the researchers did look out for injuries and they saw some jowar fields badly damaged due to locust invasion in both Aat Bisa and Manje Muhalla. The ridges of fields in Barah Bisa had plenty of congress grass. The researchers found yellow tinge on jowar leaves not mutilated by locust, which the farmers said is due to poor rain and lack of water. Red spots were seen on bajra leaves. While some farmers said these spots are due to locust excretes, others thought it is nothing to be alarmed about. They were normal. Yellow spots on Arhar (a kind of lentil) leaves were noticeable, but the farmers thought of it as the general renewal process where leaves dry up and new ones grow in place.

Lalrri while eating away the leaves, termites in nibbling away the plant roots, and *soondi's* sucking away green juice from the paddy leaves, all leave scars on the leaves/crops.

The fumes emitted from the factories mix with dew-drops, during winter, especially during January and February and settle on the wheat crops. Where crops are exposed to such deposits for one month continuously, which generally is the case, the grains of wheat becomes smaller in size, which in turn reduces the price at which they could be marketed.

However in one instance presumably the researchers were not shown any field. Some of the men in Aat Bisa mentioned to TPRT during the first round of study about blackening of crops in the fields at the entrance of the village, facing the factories but other participants disagreed. On the request of the TPRT, the men who disagreed that blackening of crops is a reality, started drawing a field map and sat separately. Discussion proceeded with the others in the group to probe blackening of the crops but not with much success as apparently "the onlookers kept on disturbing and misleading the participants". Consequently the TPRT requested the participants to physically show them standing crops with black stains which they initially agreed. But by that time the field map was ready and the other section, which drew the field map objected to TPRT physically verifying the veracity of their statements. Some elderly citizens from amongst the onlookers also took unkindly to a physical verification of facts. Those who had earlier volunteered to show the researchers around, now retracted on the ground that they had to respect their elders. The TPRT had to be satisfied with the details provided by the participants in the group discussions and saw the fields pointed out in the field map where damage to crops is indeed visible.

IX. 2. To what extent is Leaf Injury Perceived to be Caused by Air Pollution?

There seems to be no perception amongst the people of Kadhaoli that any of the list of injuries to plants and crops are indeed caused by air. Tables 12 and 13, which specify the causes of the injuries do not include air pollution as one of them. Most of them are natural or policy directed. The only exception perhaps is the case of fumes emitted from the factories, which mix with dew-drops, during winter, especially during January and February and settle on wheat crops.

26. What Happens to Injured Crops: consumed, Sold, used as Fodder or Dumped?

Crops injured are differentially treated in Kadhaoli, pretty much in the same way as in Sagarpur. Insect infested and disease infested crop plants, which are likely to perpetuate the pest or the disease are uprooted and dumped; insect or disease infested crops whose grain quality has deteriorated are sold in the markets of Ballabgarh. Only the best produce is stored for household consumption. Crops affected by locust, *jai rani, sati* and *asi* and *katali* weeds are uprooted and dumped. Crops affected by nilgai, *chepa* pest, hail and green locust are sold in the market for whatever remains of them. Generally injured crops are not consumed.

IX. 4. What are the Perceived Impacts of Air Pollution on Agriculture?

The villagers pointed out that they are exposed to three kinds of pollution: pollution from vehicular traffic, pollution in the air and poisonous water they use. There are four air-polluting factories in their environment as well. During summer and winter months, a few of the villagers mentioned that people do smell rubber smoke. They also indicated that while passing by cement brick kilns, the air they breathe smells "dusty" and the dust emitted out of these kilns create visible layers on the green leaves of standing plants.

The women were not aware of air pollution caused by industries. The second research team tried to enrich the discussion by a leading question, on whether they are aware about the emissions from the industries, to which they did specify three types of emission: hot air, smoke and poisonous water. Hot air emanating from the factories has led to increasing the temperature in the vicinity of the village within a radius of one-two kilometers but, in their perception, it has no impact on Kadhaoli. Smoke causes health hazards to factory workers, but again has no impact on Kadhaoli. Dust that comes out of the factories causes itching eyes and coughs and dust residue on crops reduces yield, but its impact on Kandhaoli is marginal as it affects only those fields which adjoin the cement brick kilns.

On the whole, the problem of air pollution is not perceived as a mentionable problem.

The presence of water-pollutants leading to deteriorating water quality (problem of hard water) caused by NTPC, is perceived as a major problem. The farmers also explained that, that portion of cultivable land which is adjacent to the pharmaceutical factory in Kelly receives liberal quantities of contaminated (read poisonous) water, that in addition to destroying their crops, causes death to their animals which drink or lick the water. Even water from the irrigation canal, is no longer fit for irrigation as it has since been converted into a sewer.

The interaction that the second research team had with the men's group provided some reasons to ponder over on why awareness on air pollution is so low among the women. Insignificant progress in enhancing literacy rates among women, little interaction between men and women, even within the family, women being over-burdened with daily schedule of work (discussed earlier), absence of any community group engaged in awareness building and finally, land buying spree of neighbouring factories, have contributed towards making the community as a whole totally averse to listening anything to do with these factories.

IX. 5. What Changes in Types of Pest, Pest Population and Past Damage have been Perceived Spatially and Historically?

There is a general feeling that the number of pests and weeds is on the rise over the years. Since the analysis is in terms of constraints, the discussion focused on constraints. Refer to Tables 12 and 14. In column 4, Table 12, men of Aat Bisa had indicated by assigning a number, the vintage of the constraints. Locust, *safed moondi* and *jai rani* have plagued agriculture for the last 3 years. Nilgais give farmers nightmares since last 10 years or so. Hard water hit them 5 years ago. Rest of the problems, according to the villagers, are with them since long. In Table 14, column 5, the women of Barah Bisa, specifically spell out that most of the problems are in Kadhaoli for 8-10 years or more. The weeds, according to this group, like *jai, safed mundi, bhatua* and *katail,* have acquired prominence over last half a decade or little more than that. Historically speaking then, there is an increase in the number of constraints that farmers in Kadhaoli face.

If we consider Aat Bisa and Manje Muhalla (Barah Bisa) as two separate geographical entities, there are some minor differences in constraints faced by the two locations. But these differences are more in terms of details and crop specific, and not specific to location. For instance the nilagis have started visiting Aat Bisa for the last 8-10 years whereas they are with Barah Bisa farmers for 15 years or so. On this divergence, the farmers clarified, nilgais visit the interior of the village, Barah Bisa for a longer time and initially avoided Aat Bisa as it is nearer the road that disturbs them in their meals. However, once farmers at Barah Bisa started taking precautions, however simple, these animals found Barah Bisa fields less attractive and made forays into Aat Bisa fields as well.

Part X. How Do People Deal With Constraints to Agricultural Production?

X. 1. How do Farmers Tackle Perceived Constraints: Through Changed Practice? Organized Action/ Through Existing Organizational Structures?

We have dealt with the responses of the communities to the constraints in Tables 12, 13 and 14 above and the recital of farmers' response gives an account of the nature and content of such responses. There is scant systematic response. There has been no change in practices, which the villagers think is worth indicating and there is none of the organised action, which we see in other parts of the country. The villagers themselves point out the latter fact in the context of awareness about air pollution and its effects. Given the fact that most of the farmers are small, they are very large in number and dispersed and do not take organised action.

There are organizational structures to assist farmers, but none come to help these farmers of Kadhaoli, whether poor or not, despite substantive public money being spent on maintaining them.

There is no sign of the villagers approaching higher authorities to remove the constraints faced by them in carrying out agriculture. In many cases the farmers have made no attempt to remove the constraints at all. They have solved whatever they could with their resources and suffer the consequences of constraints that are beyond their means. The fact that

Haryana Urban Development Authority (HUDA) is trying to acquire land in the village for sector 29 of Ballabgarh, has disheartened Kadhaoli villagers no end. It has actually instilled a fear of dislocation in them. There have been, in a few cases attempts to see if it helps to move higher authorities but the outcomes have not encouraged them to move on. This is moreso because approaching higher authorities is a costly affair. The deprivation that stalks the poor farmers of Kadhaoli certainly makes them diffident in approaching higher authorities to seek redressal of their problems. The low level of literacy, is another major impediment to approaching authorities for remedy because they need to write letters, petitions and complaints, and do seemingly endless paperwork to get things moving. Who is going to do that? A wild goose chase!!

X. 2. What are the Resources on which Basic Attempts to Influence are Executed: Money, Caste/Kinship, Information/Knowledge, Legal Rights, Public Trusts, Political Friends?

The only basic resources on which changes are sought to be made is the effort and resources of the farmers themselves. Given the politico-economic environment in which the farmers operate, they do not have the money to exhaust on influencing public policy; they are politically powerless to exercise any clout in terms of caste/kinship and indeed in Kadhaoli Caste is not a factor, most of the villagers being Muslims. Their knowledge base and levels of literacy is low, which together with limited financial resources make accessing legal rights, if there are any, impossible. They have no political friends, except during perhaps elections when Muslims in Kadhaoli, as in other parts of India, are seen as a vote bank to woo.

Part XI. Impact on Health

XI. 1. What are the Impacts of Industrialization?

Impacts of pollution and agricultural practices have been perceived as having bearing on the status of health in humans and animals, in Kadhaoli.

Burning sensation in throat, eyes and nose have been mentioned. The villagers perceive that pollution causes throat irritation and cough and when ignored results in TB. Weakening of eye sight due to fumes from near-by pharmaceutical factory and giddy feeling caused by fumes emitted from rubber and pharmaceutical factories have been marked as important health problems. Villagers also mentioned the impact of pollution on animal health. Mysterious death of buffaloes during the last two years in monsoon is attributed to air pollution. These issues have been the subject matter of the participatory sessions. The health map at Table 15 gives a good account of the status of health and other relevant details, in Kadhaoli in a summary form.

The range of diseases suffered varies from serious to common ailments. To ascertain how the villagers assessed the gravity of the diseases a health problem ranking was also attempted. The villagers first wrote down the health problems they face throughout the year. They were then requested to place 10 seeds of Rajma against the problem they considered most acute and then one less against the next most important problem and so on. They placed 10 seeds against "cough, cold and najla" and 8 seeds against "severe pain in palms" and "fever during wheat harvesting". The result is at Table 16.

This paints a curious ranking. TB and cholera are at the bottom of the scale, whereas "cough, cold and najla", are at the top. They ranked those health problems as being gravest, which interferes with the agricultural operations most; not necessarily their killing potential. Thus ailments that restrict their capacity to cultivate or harvest their crops are most distressing for them: cough, cold and najla, fever during harvesting and severe pain in palms experienced during wheat harvesting. TB, asthma and cholera are less restrictive in their immediate impact on the capability of the farmers to carry out their tasks in the fields and hence are placed at the lower end of the ranking.

Table 15 Health Map of Village Khadhaoli

Health Problem	Annual Incidence	Trend	Expenses incurred in treatment	Perceived Causes	Treatment
Eye problem	Many women; few men	10-12 years	Minimum Rs. 100 per occasion	Hard water and dust particles in air	Medical help sought if condition is acute
Fever during harvesting	Many women and children; fewer men	8-10 years	Minimum Rs. 100 per occasion	Hot sun during summer and cold wave	Medical help sought if condition is acute
Cough, cold and najla	Many women and children; fewer men	8-10 years	Minimum Rs. 100 per occasion	Hot sun during summer and cold wave	Medical help sought if condition is acute
Diarrhoea	Many children and some women	Incidence on the rise in recent years	Minimum Rs. 1000 per hospitalisation	Heat and hot sun during harvesting season	Medical help sought if condition is acute
Sever pain in palms	Many women	8-10 years	—	The rough surface of wheat stalk	Medical help sought if condition is acute.
Bai	Men and women	Many years	Unlimited	Caused by *Bai* wind	No medical help sought

Tuberculosis	More men than in women	Many years	Unlimited		No medical help sought
Cholera	Children and women	Many years	Minimum Rs. 2000	Dirty environment	Treatment in Ballabhgarh
Asthma	Men	Many years	Minimum Rs. 1000		Treatment in Balabhgarh
Malaria	Men and children	Many years	Minimum Rs. 2000	Because of mosquitoes	Treatment in Balabhgarh

Village Analysts: Fajuri, Rasidan, Sahira, Nasim and Nisia.
Facilitated by: Meera Jayaswal.
Date: 6.4.99.

Table 16 Ranking of Diseases by Villagers, Kadhaoli

Problems/ Diseases	No. of Rajma Placed	Score
Eye problem	*****	5
Fever during wheat cultivation	********	8
Cough, cold and najla	**********	10
Diarrhoea	******	6
Severe pain in palms	********	8
Bai	****	4
Tuberculosis	**	2
Cholera	**	2
Asthma	**	2
Malaria	******	6

Village Analysts: Fajuri, Rasidan, Sahira, Nasim and Nisia.
Facilitated by: Meera Jayaswal.
Date: 6.4.99.

Part XII. Conclusions

From the above discussion the following broad conclusions are possible.

1. Agriculture is an important source of livelihood for the people but may not be categorized as the single most important. It provides stable village income and provides employment and ensures food availability for the village. The crops grown are mostly food crops, and a moderate amount of cash crops in the form of vegetables. It is important to recognise that we are only dealing with the agro-ecosystems from village level and downwards.
2. Villagers generally have a diversified means of livelihood and do not depend upon any one means of livelihood for sustenance and survival. For example, those who are engaged in agriculture are also engaged in some alternative means of livelihood like working in government or engaged in petty trade. Though there is some element of polyculture still visible, the extent of diversity in the crops grown, has over the years dwindled. There is no apparent

food insecurity in the village.

3. Agriculture has become High External Input Agriculture, from Zero External Input Agriculture, even as late as in the 1940s. Though agriculture is still polyculture, crop diversity has declined markedly and is moving towards bi-culture. These changes have made the farmers vulnerable to both external shocks and to internal risks.
4. As agriculture gradually graduated to high external input agriculture in the 1960s, 1970s, 1980s and the 1990s, it has led to making agriculture a high cost operation (in terms of all real cost, open cost and hidden cost) and the vulnerability of the farmers to external shocks so much more. Indeed the farmers did rank the high cost of agriculture as one of the major problems of the sector, giving it a score of 10. Reference is invited to Table 12. This high cost of agriculture, deters others from entering the sector and induces those who are in the sector to move out of it.
5. There is an increase in productivity over the years. There is no comparison of yields obtaining in 1990 with what were obtaining in the 1950s. Yields were at the highest in the 1960s. The high growth in yield achieved in the 1960s, could not be sustained in the 80s though they did hold on in the 1970s. The exceptionally high level of yield in the 1960s achieved was by the use of "new-technology", viz., use of fertilisers, improved variety of seeds and irrigation. This village being in the agro-climatic zone with low to medium rainfall and served with assured sources of irrigation, reaped the maximum impact of the new-technology, because such areas are "most suitable for profitable application of new seed-fertiliser technologies" (*Rao, 1989*).
6. The factories near and in the village have opened up job opportunities for the job seekers, but these job opportunities could not absorb all those who were willing to work. Large number of people are still unemployed.
7. There are a plethora of constraints faced by the villagers in their agricultural operations, including pest and insect attacks. While pests, insects and diseases have caused more damage than weeds, most of the measures taken by the farmers to counter the constraints have been directed towards weeds and a bare minimum

towards controlling pests and animals. The cultivators have a limited system of coping with some of these constraints based on their own resources and knowledge.

8. Agriculture is not seen as a profitable venture by many villagers in Kadhaoli. Since we are concerned here with the perception of the villagers, one may not probe the issue further, but it has to be noted that a part of the problem lies in approaching agriculture as a profit oriented institution as opposed to life oriented structure, an attitude of mind which is understandable in an age when profits, privatization and globalisation are the key words. As such it is placed in the field of competition on this very narrowly defined basis. It has to be recognised that this is a partial analysis which is not cognizant of the vital aspects of sustainability of resource use, reproduction of competent personnel and maintenance of biodiversity. There is need to relook at this perspective of agriculture.
9. The non-existence of extension services and paucity of vital agricultural inputs such as subsidy on improved variety of seeds, credit availability and subsidy on fertilizers as also pesticides and weedicides are considered by the villagers as serious constraints but there is little effort on the part of the community to deal with these beyond what is possible within the community. There are certain constraints like uncertainty/irregularity of rainfall and hailstorm, etc., which are way beyond the community's capacity to solve.
10. The number of diseases, pests and insects that attack crops have increased over time. It seems that the answer to this complex set of constraints lies in integrated pest management, which involves a whole gamut of insect, weed and diseases control strategies so inter-woven that not only pests are reduced to satisfactory levels but is sustainable and non-polluting. Farmers have to be trained as experts and not pressing on with the conventional top-down extension services (though currently dysfunctional for all practical purposes). The approach should be to develop in the farmers their own capacity to think for themselves and develop their own solutions. These can and are producing substantial reduction in pesticide/insecticide use in several parts of the world including in some parts of India. In the Indian context this has been clearly

demonstrated in the case of rice (*Kenmore, 1991; Singh and Dash, 1998*) and groundnut (*ICRISAT 1993*). The same is true of diseases afflicting human beings.

11. Pollution has increased. But a co-relation between pollution and injury to crops is not perceived. Leaf injury to crops is visible and the insects/diseases, which cause such injuries, are known but that they are due to air pollution, is not established. Even the researchers saw some visible injury on the crops standing in the fields, but their correlation with air pollution was neither suggested nor perceived by the villagers. The issue of crop injury due to air pollution should be further investigated. Because at least the possibility of fluoride pollution is significant given that brick kilns, amongst others, emit smoke, which generally has hydrogen fluoride. Hydrogen fluoride enters principally through the leaf stomata, though soluble forms penetrate the leaf cuticle directly. This damages crops and trees (*Agarwal and Garrity, 1987*).
12. There are gender discriminations and gender injustice, and both in terms of agreeableness of work and work-load itself, the dice is loaded against women.
13. The role of the established state institutions in the life of the community is limited and the villagers also do not seek out these services whatever the reasons. This is unhelpful for agriculture to be sustainable. There has to be a convergence of appropriate technologies (read resources conserving technologies), village level institutions and groups, and enabling external institutions, like the extension workers, panchayats, and other development institutions. If each of these is conceived as circles, then there has to be an overlap of these three circles. The larger the area under overlap, the better the chances of agriculture being sustainable.
14. Pollution is perceived to have adverse impact on the state of health in Kadhaoli. Those ailments, which hinder agricultural operations are considered most distressing by the villagers. As in the case of agriculture, the community copes with their health problems and tackle health hazards within the confines of their own community and resources.

6 A Perspective from a Municipal Township: Uncha Gaon, Faridabad

Part I: General Information

I. 1. Faridabad

Faridabad is one of the three industrial centres of Haryana, Rewari and Gurgaon being the other two. The district is divided into 5 blocks, viz., Faridabad with 62 villages, Ballabgarh with 81 villages, Palwal with 122 villages, Hodal with 70 villages and Hathin with 79 villages.

Along with industrial development, Faridabad has also made exceptionally good progress in the agricultural sector and lies at the heart of the Green Revolution belt of India. The progress in agriculture has been made possible by huge increases in agricultural production, improved irrigation, flood control measures and the introduction of the "new technology". The total area under high yielding varieties of foodgrains, such as bajra, maize, wheat and paddy during 1989-90 is of the order of 140, 000 hectares. High yielding varieties of wheat are grown in 98,3 per cent of the area under wheat cultivation; and 77.8 per cent of the area under paddy cultivation is under high yielding varieties of paddy. The major Kharif crops are bajra (cultivated over 19.8 thousand hectares) and barley (grown over 5.1 thousand hectares in 1989-90). The major Rabi crops are wheat, cultivated in 119.5 thousand hectares and barley, cultivated in 5.1 thousand hectare, as in 1989-90. Strides in animal husbandry and fisheries have also contributed significantly to the development of the district.

I. 2. Uncha Gaon

Uncha Gaon is situated approximately 4.3 kms South East of Faridabad old industrial area and 1.34 from Ballabgarh industrial area. It came under the Faridabad Nagapalika (Municipality) in 1985, the year in which land was acquired by Haryana Urban Development Authority for the Ballabgarh residential complex.

Uncha Gaon is spread over a very large area. It is exposed to vehicular traffic and dust pollution due to its location right on the road. Uncha Gaon has the look and feel of a town as well as of a village. On both sides of the road you have rows of shops including liquor shops (called wine shops), hotels, chemists and studios. Most of the people living in Uncha Gaon proper are engaged in non-agricultural occupations, largely ignorant of what goes on in the various hamlets around the township. Most of the houses in Uncha Gaon are more than one storied, and are brick houses.

The inner area of Uncha Gaon, called *Gola Neem*, resembles a village and is divided into smaller hamlets. The inhabitants have knowledge of agriculture and many of them are agriculturists and have considerable experience of cultivation. Uncha Gaon is divided into five hamlets or Muhallas:

- Ahir Muhalla with 10 households.
- Gujar Muhalla with 10 households.
- Saini Muhalla with 400 households.
- Harijan Muhalla with 250 households.
- Sahupura Roadside Muhalla with 50-55 households.

Inhabitants of Ahir, Saini and Sahupura Roadside Muhalla, have agricultural lands and cultivate their own land. Quite a few of the inhabitants work as agricultural labourers. Generally the *Malis* of Saini Hamlet grow vegetables and the *Ahirs* of Ahir Muhalla cultivate wheat during Rabi season and Jowar during Kharif season.

I. 3. Developing the Bond in a Tea Stall

Uncha Gaon was chosen as the area of study, in which the researchers had no role. The area was given to them as they were given to study Sagarpur and Kadhaoli. They arrived at the locale, Uncha Gaon, expecting pretty much of what they experienced in their earlier forays. They were in for a big surprise. Not only was Uncha Gaon no village, but the social and economic environments were markedly different. The small open tea stalls that greeted them in Sagarpur and Kadhaoli were replaced by restaurants, with formal furniture, notwithstanding their unseeming looks. They found it difficult to locate any group which had more than two people and who were at once knowledgeable about agriculture. Though fields were visible, cultivators were not. Ultimately one of the residents helped the researchers to reach Saini Muhalla, the oldest ward or hamlet of Uncha Gaon, hoping to locate some farmers. They were led to a small tea stall where a few elder citizens of the ward were sitting. The researchers, as usual, introduced themselves and explained to the group the purpose of their visit. The group of senior citizens introduced themselves and disclosed that they have been farmers since their childhood.

The senior citizens gave some idea to the researchers about Saini Muhalla: there were about 500 people in 150 households, around 80 per cent of whom were engaged in agriculture. The researchers wanted to streamline the discussion and so enquired of the villagers present at the tea stall whether they could join them for a group discussion on a voluntary basis about agriculture. This did not go down well with the villagers present there. Discussing agriculture with outsiders was a felony. They refused to co-operate and got agitated that agriculture was sought to be discussed. It was soon discovered that because Haryana Urban Development Authority was on a Land-acquisition spree, the villagers mistook the researchers as being government functionaries, out to elicit information for use by the government. This was not acceptable, since the villagers had little land for cultivation and any further intrusion was not acceptable to them. The researchers ultimately succeeded in pacifying the group. In the meanwhile younger people joined the group and this helped ease the situation. To avoid further dislocation the group was divided into two: one of the researchers sat with one group in the tea stall and the other went out to the fields with a second group. Both the groups had a mixture of young and old alike, though the number of people participating in the discussion kept on changing, with fresh entrants and exists.

Part II. Livelihood Systems

II. 1. Livelihood Systems

The groups were separately led into discussing their livelihood systems, through seasonality analysis. Since the group inside the tea stall had difficulty in discussing a monthwise seasonality analysis, as they thought it boring, the group decided to change their discussion to per annum basis from the monthwise analysis. The method was also changed from verbal (group discussion) to visual. The group was, thus, provided with postcard sized cards, with a request to jot down the names of months separately on the cards provided. The group wrote down the names of the months, according the lunar calendar, and then arranged them on the floor, starting with Baisakh (the first month in the lunar calendar). They then recollected the livelihood they pursued in each month, wrote them separately on another set of cards and placed them alongside the name of relevant month. They were then requested to write down the constraints they faced in the pursuit of their livelihoods, against each month, on another set of cards and place them against the livelihood to which the relative constraint was most relevant. This was executed with precision.

The group also indicated the nature of agricultural work done by them during these months and the constraints they face in agriculture in different months. They then wrote down these two sets of information on two sets of cards and placed them against the name of the month to which they relate. The "document" that was generated on the floor, was then "interviewed". In the course of the interview the group brought live pests/insects (such as *gandars, lalrii,* locust) from the fields to explain the nature of the constraints faced. A similar exercise was carried out with the women group as well. The resultant output is transcribed as Tables 1 and 2.

The women's group mentioned that agriculture, selling milk, working as labourers and working in industry were their livelihood activity throughout the twelve months. And the constraint that they faced was repayment of loan in Baisakh. They did not outline any coping mechanisms.

Tables 1 and 2, indicate that the main occupation of the inhabitants of Uncha Gaon is agriculture. A much smaller number of people are self employed in small business and petty trade, employed in government service, and working as labourers. Selling of milk is a secondary occupation of a large number of villagers. We juxtaposed the data with the data from Column 1 of Table 10. The exact livelihood structure of Uncha Gaon in 1990s consists of 80 per cent agriculturists; 60 per cent milk vendors; 7 per cent private small businessmen and petty traders; 2 per cent Government employees and 5 per cent labourers.

There are no visible variations either on a month to month basis or seasonally, in the nature of "employment" available to the people. That neither agriculture nor industry is any longer able to absorb all those who are willing to work has resulted in 5 per cent of the people remaining unemployed. A 5 per cent rate of unemployment is significant in an industrial area, lying in the heart of the Green Revolution belt, of a relatively prosperous state of Haryana.

The present livelihood structure has evolved over the years. From a purely agrarian economy in 1940s when 100 per cent of the people were agriculturists, Uncha Gaon experienced a 5 per cent reduction in the number of people dependent on agriculture in 1950s and then another 5 per cent reduction in the decade of the 70s. Between 1980 and 1990, agriculture lost another 10 per cent people embracing agriculture as their source of livelihood. Thus in 1990s, 80 per cent of the inhabitants of Uncha Gaon are agriculturists. This 80 per cent is still very high, given that 70 per cent (give or take 2 per cent) of Indians depended on agriculture, all through the 20th Century. At least 60 per cent of villagers generally pursue more than a single occupation.

Clearly most of the inhabitants of Uncha Gaon have some land except for the 5 per cent landless. The village is predominantly a village of the agriculturists class.

Tables 1, 2 and 3 show that within the agriculturists class there are two notable features: one, there is a great deal of emphasis on growing vegetables, large in variety and significant in the number of times they are grown, and not on food crops like wheat and paddy; two, the agriculturists primarily comprise of only small and marginal farmers; there being very few large or medium sized farmers. The urban base of the village and the nearness of the industrial areas of Ballabgarh as well as Faridabad, provide

Table 1 Seasonality Analysis of Livelihood and Constraints by Men's Group, Saini Muhalla

Months	Means of Livelihood	Constraints Encountered
Baisakh	Agriculture, private and government service, selling milk, labourer, truck, petty business like brokerage, shops	Stomach ache and diahorroea due to consumption of new wheat, milk yield declines, prices increase marginally; hence net loss, repayment of loans to money lenders
Jeth	Same as in Baisakh.	Acute shortage of water, irregular power supply, extreme heat, increase in mosquitoes, milk yield falls, prices rise marginally; hence total loss
Ashar	Same as in Jeth	Fever and malaria, threat of cholera, farmers and daily wage earners find it difficult to go out for work
Sawan	Same as in Ashar	Fever and malaria, threat of cholera, farmers and daily wage earners find it difficult to go out for work, forced to cut expenditure, no income from agriculture. excess humidity, *Gulguta* in buffaloes due to eating new grass
Bhado	Same as in Sawan	Fever and malaria, threat of cholera, farmers and daily wage earners find it difficult to go out for work, forced to cut expenditure, no income from agriculture, excess humidity, insects attack foot of buffaloes, burning sensation in eyes from Thermocol factories' smoke, allergy due to congress grass
Kuar	Same as in Bhado	Same constraints as the ones faced in Bhado
Katak	Same as in Kuar	Getting loans, cough, cold and headache, repayment of loans

Months	Means of Livelihood	Constraints Encountered
Aghan	Same as in Kartick	Same as Kartick
Poosh	Same as in Aghan	Pneumonia in children
Magh	Same as in Poosh	Same as Poosh
Fagun	Same as in Magh	Repayment of loan, cold and fever (no serious health problem), milk yield starts falling, resulting in loss
Chet	Same as in Fagun	Same as in Fagun

Village Analysts: Balbir, Bansi, Harish, Omprakash, Bhagawat, Krisen, Mahesh, Babloo.
Facilitator: Sudipta Ray

Table 2 Seasonality Analysis of Agricultural Activities and Constraints by Women's Group

Months	Livelihood	Agricultural activities	Constraints
Bais-akh	Agriculture, selling milk, working as labourers and in industry	Harvesting wheat and threshing, selling lobia (beans), ridge gourd, radish and brinjals	Power shortage, hailstorm lalrii eats leaves of vegetables
Jeth		Irrigating vegetable fields, sowing bajra, jowar, chilies, bottle gourd etc. selling lobia, bitter gourd, onions, lady's finger, bottle gourd etc.	Power shortage, locust on jowar
Ashar		Sowing bajra and jowar, seeds of cauliflower, lady's finger, bottle gourd, spinach, selling pumpkins, green chilies, onion, lady's finger	Low rainfall, moriya in chilies, chitli young vegetable plants

Months	Livelihood	Agricultural activities	Constraints
Sawan		Paddy transplantation, applying fertilizers, transplanting spinach and cauliflower seedlings, selling bottle/ bitter gourd, onion, lady's finger etc.	Same as Ashar
Bhado		Selling spinach	Same as Sawan
Kuar		Planting cauliflower, radish and potatoes	
Katak		Harvesting paddy, planting cabbage and cauliflower, selling cauliflower, brinjals, spinach, chilies and radish	Sundi infestation in vegetables
Aghan		Sowing wheat, sowing potatoe, selling carrots, cauliflower, lobia, chilies, gourd, lady's finger	Same as Kartick
Poosh		Irrigate wheat fields, sow onion and chili seeds, sell carrot, cauliflower, lobia, potatoes (earlier stored), cabbage	
Magh		Irrigate wheat field (twice), apply fertilizers, sell brinjals, carrot, lobia, cauliflower, sow bitter gourd, cucumber, onion, ridge gourd, chilies, radish etc.	
Fagun		Irrigate wheat fields, selling chilies, potatoes, cabbage, cauliflower, spinach, swing seeds of lobia, ridge gourd, bitter gourd	Rust in wheat

Months	Livelihood	Agricultural activities	Constraints
Chet		Harvesting and threshing of wheat, selling of bitter gourd, onion, cucumber, brinjals. sowing spinach	

Village Analysts: Tarawati, Kamala, Lali, Sarbir.
Facilitator: Ms. Meera Jayaswal.

Table 3 Landholding Pattern in Uncha Gaon

Category of Villagers	Landholding Pattern
Landless	5 per cent
Less than 1 acre (marginal farmers)	60 per cent
Between 1 and 3 Acres	35 per cent

the vegetable growers good access to a market for vegetables, all year round; not just in any particular season. And secondly, the small pieces of land owned by the villagers, make growing of paddy and wheat less feasible than growing vegetables. Thus the composition of agricultural produce, is determined by the size of landholdings, availability of markets and the economics of growing vegetables vis-à-vis growing paddy and wheat (the last we will discuss later in this chapter).

If we take all the livelihood systems pursued in Uncha Gaon, they form part of the larger hierarchy of agrosystems shown in figure 4 of Chapter 4 (*Conway, 1987*) and the villagers gave us an account of the agro-systems from village level and below. Villagers in Uncha Gaon as in the case of Sagarpur and Kadhaoli, are not generally engaged in gathering-hunting and handicraft manufacture; only a few are in off-farm employment and trading systems. Agriculture remains at the heart of the livelihood system in Uncha Gaon, though a fairly large section of the population has more than one source of livelihood. Within the farming system, the inhabitants rely partly on livestock system and more fully in cropping system, involved in the field and growing crop.

However, not unlike Sagarpur and Kadhaoli, farmers in Uncha Gaon grow primary commodities, mostly vegetables, for sale. These commodities may be eaten, used in preparing drinks, turned into paper or clothes or used as drugs. The farmers are unconcerned. Only a portion of what these farmers grow is used to feed themselves and their family. Agricultural trade (read vegetable trade) is a significant factor in the trading system of Unchao Gaon. But in this game the farmers are price takers, not price makers, which makes their life a little more insecure and uncertain.

II. 2. General Problems

A village comprising landless people, marginal and small farmers, is likely to have several general problems. In the general discussion both men and women spelt out a litany of problems and it became difficult to put the discussion to some order. The women among the group volunteered to sit down to isolate their "best problems" and then rank them in descending order of their severity. This was agreed. The women listed their best problems first and then indicated the severity of general problems faced by the community, by placing Rajma seeds against each of the identified "best problems". The principle followed is larger the number of seeds placed against a "best problem", the more severe it is, 10 indicating the severest problem and 1 indicating the least severe problem. The outcome of the exercise is at Table 4. The group also indicated the hardship caused by each of their best problems.

Clearly acquisition of land by the government in the Haryana urban development authority, is ranked as their foremost problem. Loss of land is the gravest threat to their means of livelihood. It foretells the pains of impending hunger. For the farmers, growing crops is the source of life itself. Even a small piece of land, with the irrigation potential and the suitability of growing and marketing vegetables help people avert the pangs of starvation. Thus a legal action by the state, apparently in public interest, is about to push the farming households to starvation. This seems to be a vindication of what Sen beautifully wrote, nearly two decades ago, as the concluding line of his famous work, *Poverty and Famines* (1981): "Starvation deaths can reflect legality with a vengeance". Alcoholism is ranked only next to land acquisition as a general problem of Uncha Gaon. It is as much a social problem as it is an economic problem. Recognizing the problems created by alcoholism, the government of Haryana had in 1996-97 imposed prohibition in the state along with other states like Andhra Pradesh. However, in a patriarchal society, where higher echelons of government and bureaucracy are dominated by men, prohibition was

Table 4 Scoring and Ranking of Problems of Ahir Muhalla Village by Women's Group

Problems	Hardships caused	Rank/ score	Since how many years
Power shortage#	Fodder cutting and irrigation hampered	Score: 6 Rank: 4	5-6 years
Land acquisition by Govt.	With limited employment opportunity, households threatened by land acquisition face prospects of starvation	Score: 10 Rank: 1	Anticipated from 1999
Unemployment	Poverty in households	Score: 7 Rank: 3	10-12 years
Drinking habit of men	Loss of household income, violence and spousal battery	Score: 8 Rank: 2	5-6 years
Poverty#	Cut in consumption of essential commodities	Score: 6 Rank: 4	6-7 years
Outsiders employed in local industry*	Local person gets displaced from the labour market. Increased theft, robbery etc.	Score: 4 Rank: 5	10-12 years
No training centre for women*	Women remain unskilled	Score: 4 Rank: 5	— —

Notes: #Power shortage and poverty ranked at par as the 4th severest problem.
*Outsiders grabbing employment opportunities and lack of training centre ranked at par, as the 5th severest problem.

Village Analysts: Kela, Vidya and Bhagwati.
Facilitator: Meera Jayaswal.
Dated: 10.4.99 at Ahir Muhalla.

repealed in 1998, on the ostensible grounds that it was difficult to implement the prohibition, leading to illicit brewing and "smuggling" of liquor, and that the state exchequer was losing out valuable excise revenue, which could have been utilised for development projects. Where the revenue from sale of liquor has gone, no body has any clue, either in the government or outside it, but the villagers, particularly women, like the women of Sagarpur know what consequences flow from abolition of prohibition, namely, domestic (and social) violence and loss of peace rests ultimately. It has more severe implications. Alcoholism is not only an evil in itself but it also causes loss of household (scarce) income, indicating that irrespective of who creates, or how household income is created, the end control is with the male members of the household. It sadly mirrors an iniquitous distribution of intra-familial power, loaded against women.

Villagers comprising landless people, 60 per cent marginal farmers and 30 per cent small farmers, where men revel in expending scare resources on alcoholism, the experience in suffering poverty is telling. And their sense of deprivation is much more painful as they are exposed to and aware of the luxuries enjoyed by the "haves", due to the nearness of Uncha Gaon to much richer urban areas of Ballabgarh and Faridabad, and access to TV programmes crammed with crash consumerism. This pain of deprivation is heightened by the reality that the employment opportunities created at considerable cost to the villagers, subserve the interest of outsiders, most of whom are not the 'have nots'. Getting a job in the government or in industry requires several qualifications: technical, non-technical and supra-technical. The last one is the trickiest and includes connections, capacity to bribe, caste affiliation and of course the "spit and polish" (like a glossy annual report of an organisation, notwithstanding its niggardly contribution) which the "have-nots" of Uncha Gaon do not have. Thus the villagers face the twin realities: of land, the vital source of life itself, being taken away by the state (which ironically is supposed to protect them) and of employment opportunities being taken away by outsiders, not infrequently, the 'haves'. This is a setting ideal for deterioration of social capital and for breeding anti-social elements. The resultant scenario is increase in theft, robbery and spousal battery. How much of alcoholism is on account of social pressure and how much of it is on account of habit, could not be determined but both have their own roles to play.

II. 3. Crops Grown and the Cropping Pattern

There are two kinds of crops grown: food crops and cash crops. Jowar (in Kharif season) and wheat (in Rabi season) are the principal food crops grown. The cash crops are vegetables: during Kharif, tomatoes, brinjals, lady's finger, spinach, field-ridge, ghiya and cucumber are principally grown. During Rabi, potatoe on the one hand and cauliflower, mustard saag, cabbage, spinach, bitter gourd and bottle gourd etc., on the other, are the principal crops grown. It has been pointed out that with improved variety of seeds, some of the vegetables like cabbage and bottle/bitter gourd are beginning to be grown round the year. However, unlike Sagarpur and Kadhaoli, food crops are grown on a much smaller scale than cash crops in both absolute and relative terms.

The cropping pattern of Uncha Gaon is fairly straight forward: a wide variety of vegetables, jowar and wheat are grown. The researchers in fact saw numerous vegetable crops at various stages of their maturity: untied cabbage, prematurely dried onion leaves; ready and healthy vegetables, like brinjals, tomato, cucumber, spinach; young vegetable seedlings, also sold for profit; and carrot,"sauf" plants. The distribution of wheat, jowar and vegetables are best described by Table 4, prepared by women of Sahupura road side Muhalla.

Land is partitioned into two sectors: the food crop sector and the cash crop sector, each occupying approximately 50 per cent of cultivable land.

In the food crop sector jowar and wheat are the principal crops grown. The entire land earmarked for food crops is utilised for jowar cultivation for 5 months, from Jeth to Kuar, including land preparation in Jeth and harvesting in Kuar, or may be in some years spilling into Kartick. The same land is utilised for the next 7 months, from Kartick to Baisakh for growing wheat, including preparation of land in Kartick and harvesting of wheat in Baisakh. Almost 80 per cent of the wheat sown are late varieties, viz., 1553, 2339 and 2338.

In the cash crop sector, the principal crops are vegetables of every description and potato. During the 5 month period (from Jeth to Kuar) when jowar is grown on the land earmarked for food crops, on the entire land earmarked for cash crops, vegetables like tomato, brinjal, lady's finger, spinach, gourd of various kinds and cucumber are grown.

Table 5 Cropping Pattern in Uncha Gaon

Months	***On 50 per cent of Cultivable Land***	***On 50 per cent of Cultivable Land***	
Jeth	*Land Preparation*	Cultivation of tomatoes, brinjals, lady's finger, spinach, cucumber, ridge gourd, bottle gourd etc.	
Asarh	Jowar cultivation	Ditto	
Sawan	Jowar cultivation	Ditto	
Bhado	Jowar cultivation	Ditto	
Kuar	Jowar cultivation	Ditto	
		On 25 per cent of Land	**On 25 per cent of Land**
Kartik	*Land Preparation*	Vegetables like cauliflower, spinach, cabbage, radish, chilies, onion, bitter gourd etc.	Potato
Aghan	Wheat cultivation	as above	Potato
Poosh	Wheat cultivation	as above	Potato
Magh	Wheat cultivation	as above	Potato
Fagun	Wheat cultivation	as above	Vegetables
Chait	Wheat cultivation	as above	Vegetables
Baisakh	Wheat harvesting	as above	Vegetables

Village Analysts: Amarwali, Bhagwati, Umraon and others.
Facilitated by: Ms. Meera Jayaswal.
Date: 27.3.99.

During the 4 month period of Kartik, Aghan, Poosh and Magh, only 50 per cent of the land set apart for cash crops (that is, only 25 per cent of total cultivatable land) is utilised for growing vegetables like

Table 6 Seasonality Analysis of Agricultural Activities and Food Consumption by Men's Group Saini Muhalla

Months	Food Consumption	Agricultural Activities
Baisakh	Chappatis with pickle or chili chutney, vegetables from their own fields	Harvesting of wheat and selling the produce, brinjal, melon and onion sold, sow seeds for lady's finger, bottle gourd, torai, chili, pumpkin, cucumber, bitter gourd, income from agriculture is 50 per cent
Jeth	Chappatis with pickle or chili chutney, occasionally vegetables, fruits, dalia, lassi or milk and tea, 3 meals plus an evening meal of tea/ milk	Irrigation and weeding in the fields, collection of fodder, like cutting grass and harvesting jowar, sowing of jowar and maize seeds, selling cucumber, kakri and melon
Ashar	Same as Jeth	Irrigating fields, cutting fodder, selling vegetables sown in baisakh, income 25 per cent, sowing bajra
Sawan	Two meals of chappatis with pickle or chili chutney, home grown vegetables **H**	Seedling of cauliflower and brinjal raised, cutting some jowar for fodder
Bhado	Same as Sawan **H**	Cutting jowar, sowing radish, carrot, spinach cabbage seeds, transplanting cauliflower brinjal seedlings
Kuar	Two meals of chappatis with pickle or chili chutney, some vegetables **H**	Irrigating and weeding fields, cutting some Jowar

Months	Food Consumption	Agricultural Activities
Katak	Chappatis with pickle or chili chutney, occasionally vegetables, fruits, milk tea, 3 meals plus an evening meal of tea or milk	Harvesting jowar and bajra, selling spinach, cauliflower, fenugreek, coriander, brinjal, radish, income is upto 20 per cent
Aghan	Same as Kartick	Sowing wheat seeds, selling spinach, cauliflower, coriander, brinjal, radish, cabbage, income upto 40 per cent
Poosh	Bajra chappatis with sarson da saag, pickle or chili chutney, occasionally vegetables, 3 meals plus an evening meal of tea/milk	Irrigating land, selling spinach, cauliflower, fenugreek, coriander, brinjal, radish, cabbage, income upto 45 per cent
Magh	Same as Poosh	Selling spinach cauliflower, fenugreek, coriander, brinjal, radish, cabbage, income upto 40 per cent, irrigating fields, sowing cucumber and melon seeds
Fagun	Same as Magh	Selling cauliflower, potato, brinjal, fenugreek, spinach, carrot, radish. Income is 45 per cent, irrigating and weeding fields
Chet	Same as Magh	Fenugreek, spinach, coriander, carrot and sarson da saag sold, income is 35 per cent, irrigate fields

Notes: **H indicates hunger periods.**

Village Analysts: Balbir, Bansi, Harish, Omprakash, Bhagawat, Krisen, Mahesh, Babloo.
Facilitator: Sudipta Ray.

cauliflower and cabbage etc., and on the balance 50 per cent of the land set apart for cash crops (that is, 25 per cent of total cultivable land) potatoe is cultivated. In the following three months of Fagun Chait and Baisakh, the segmentation of land set apart for cash crops, between growing vegetables and raising potatoes, seen in the earlier four months is done away with. The entire 50 per cent of cultivable land meant for cash crops, is devoted to growing vegetables of all kinds.

In the process farmers practice crop rotation: land on which jowar is grown in the first instance, is then utilised to grow vegetables and potatoes. And land on which vegetables are grown in the first place, is then devoted to growing wheat. This means that the same plot of land is cultivated alternately for growing jowar and wheat on the one hand, and vegetables and potatoes on the other. Such rotation, the villagers perceive, replenishes soil nutrients and residues from one kind of crop helps manure land for growing the other kind of crop. It is pointed out that in Table 5, though the villagers have shown that they grow vegetables on all the 12 months, yet the nature of the activities varies from month to month and growing and selling of vegetables also includes rearing and selling seedlings of vegetables like cauliflower, onion and cabbage. This is made clearer in the seasonality analysis done by men in saini muhalla, which is presented in Table 6. Attention in particular is drawn to Column 3.

There are in virtually all the months of the year something to harvest/ gather/collect, something to sow, something to transplant and something to sell. It absorbs the energy and resources, including time of the farmers and their households all through. The farmers' households are in the field from 7.00 - 8.00 a.m. in the morning till 6.00 - 7.00 p.m. in the evening (with a margin of about an hour or half an hour on either side to make adjustment for sunrise and sunset during winter and summer months) with an hour of break in the afternoon, for midday meals. This is one reason why apart from selling milk, the farmers in Uncha Gaon have no secondary occupation. This confirms what we have learnt from the villagers of Kadhaoli and Sagarpur earlier, that growing vegetable is a highly labour intensive venture, and which is why those villagers prefer cultivating wheat to vegetables.

A look at the total cropping scenario tells us that Uncha Gaon is still in some form of what Boserup calls "multiple cropping" unlike Sagarpur and

Kadhaoli which are inching towards an annual cropping agriculture (Boserup, 1993 has identified several stages in agriculture). With the existing irrigation potential of the village and the availability of markets, more rounds of vegetables could have been grown but the fall in water table to below 85 feet has prevented the farmers from increasing the number of cropping rounds.

II. 4. What is the Intensity of Cultivation

From the discussion we had with the villagers and from what is articulated in Tables 5 and 6, the intensity of cultivation is fairly high. Each plot of land is cultivated several times over. And there are several doses of fertilisers applied, for each round of crops grown. If we see Column 3 of Table 6 and read it with Table 5, it clarifies that the same land is cultivated several times in a year. Though in Table 5 the villagers have shown that they grow tomato, lady's finger etc. from Jeth to Kuar (four months) it does not mean that the crop cycle of each of these crops is of four months duration. There is a good mix of fast growing and late varieties of vegetables. Cauliflower has a longer gestation period while spinach and cabbage yield crops faster. They also pointed out that they grow some vegetables once, but reap harvest several times over. For instance, spinach can be harvested upto 7 times. If they find that due to excess supply a vegetable is unlikely to fetch a good price, they do not harvest it at all and leave it to flower, so that they can gather the seeds and sell them instead; or plough them back into the fields as manure. Similarly for ridge gourd, bitter gourd and bottle gourd: the creepers are raised once and the fruits (for want of a better word) they bear are plucked several times. In fact at any point in time, after these plants reach fruit bearing stage, they will have fruits of varying maturity.

All farmers also do not grow all the vegetables concurrently: different farmers grow different vegetables, with considerable overlaps as well. Similarly farmers grow various combinations of early and late varieties of several of these vegetables in order to ensure that there is something to sell all the time and the cash flow of the household is maintained in all the months. As one farmer poetically told us: "wheat is like the moon: it vanishes after some time. Vegetables are like streams, always flowing".

Similarly it does not take 7 months (from Kartik to Baisakh) to grow cauliflower, spinach etc. For instance the land on which potato is cultivated (between Kartik and Magh) is used for vegetable cultivation from Fagun to Baisakh (see Table 5, last column).

The facts that most of the farmers are small and marginal farmers, and are owner cultivators, also contribute to increase the intensity of cultivation. This is particularly so because the farmers have their small and marginal farms as their basic (and in many cases, the only) source of livelihood. That is why as we stated earlier, men and the women of the village are in the field from 7.00 - 8.00 a.m. in the morning till 6.00 or 7.00 p.m. in the evening (give or take approximately an hour or half on either side for variations in sunrise and sunset during winter and summer) with an hour of afternoon break for partaking of their midday meals. The amount of labour applied to land is another indication of a high level of farming intensity. There is no data, however, to exactly pinpoint and say precisely how many times the farmers cultivate their plots of land.

Part III: Agricultural Practices

III. 1. Uncha Gaon and Agricultural Practices that have Taken Place

The group of men who went out of the tea stall to tell us the story of their livelihood system, was asked by the facilitator, if it was possible for them to provide some insight into the story of the livelihood pattern as it has evolved over the years, now that they have told us what their agricultural practices are at the current point of time. The facilitator first prodded them to recall the significant events of their lives over the last 50 years or so. The group responded remarkably well and told us that in the 1940s the wells were *Kuccha* (unbricked), India won independence and punjabi refuges from Pakistan were allotted land in Faridabad for resettlement and rehabilitation. In the 1950s, they recalled, the *Kuccha* wells were all brick laid as the government gave incentives for so doing and bata shoe factory came to be established. In the 1960s, tractor and electricity were first used in cultivation, and fertilisers were used too. It was not until the 1970s that the HYV seeds came to Uncha Gaon. This was the historic decade when the state of Haryana was carved out of Punjab. The group recalled that in the 1980s, Uncha Gaon became a part of Nagarpalika (municipality). They then went about drawing the Historical Transect at Tables 7 and 8.

Table 7 Historical Transect of Farming System and Crops by Male Group, Saini Muhalla, Uncha Gaon

Decade	Occupation	Cropping Pattern	Farming System	Constraints
1940	100 per cent agri-culture	Wheat, jowar, bajra, barley, gram, maize, moat, henna	Irrigation by rehant and rains, organic manure, seeds from previous year's harvest, ploughing with bullock, cart for transporting produce	None
1950	95 per cent in agriculture, rest in industry, government and labourers	as above	as above	None
1960	95 per cent in agriculture, 2 per cent labourers, 3 per cent service and 50 per cent milk	Same as in 1950s but pulses reduced	Late 1960s HYV seeds introduced, tractor for ploughing, electric pump for irrigating	Increase in nagfal (weed)

Decade	Occupation	Cropping Pattern	Farming System	Constraints
1970	90 per cent agriculture 55 per cent milk, rest as in 1960	Vegetables started to be grown on a commercial basis	Hybrid seeds in full force, pesticides, tractor for ploughing, electric pump for irrigation, fertilisers are the in thing	Jai and Mundi appear in wheat field, kanduwa in wheat field
1980	Same as 1970 except 60 per cent in milk vending	Onion added to the list of items grown on a commercial basis	as above	Termites emerge, nilgais start grazing crops
1990	80 per cent agriculture, 60 per cent milk, 5 per cent private service, 7 per cent petty trade/ business, 3 per cent labourer and 2 per cent in government	Wheat, jowar mustard, cauliflower, potatoes, cabbage, brinjals, chili, gourds of all variety	as above	Termites increase, nilgais continue grazing, weeds: doob grass, motha, zinzri, makra, sati and congress grass, green tidda in lobia and cauliflower, increase in incidence of gandar (caterpillar), water table has gone below 85 feet, moriya in chilies

Facilitator: Sudipta Ray

Table 8 Historical Transect of Changes in Farm Produce by Men's Group, Saini Muhalla, Uncha Gaon

Decade	Yield of Wheat	Size of Wheat Grains	Colour of Wheat Grains	Industrial Growth
1940	3-4 quintals/acre	Long and fat	Golden	Nil
1950	3-4 quintals/acre	as above	as above	Bata and escorts
1960	16 quintals/acre	Relatively small and thin	Orangeish red	Steel factory
1970	16 quintals/acre	as above	Yellow	Ajit rubber and thermocol factories
1980	13 quintals. Yield started falling in late 1980s	From late 1980 less grain per ear of corn and small in size	From the late 1980s, creamish	Khanna thermocol factory
1990	Wheat yield 13 quintals/acre, yield of ladys finger, cucumber, small melon and onion falling since last 4-5 years	Small in size and less grain	Creamish, height of standing wheat crop has declined, wheat corn size has fallen by 1 per cent	

Notes: The villagers also indicated that bottle gourd no longer tastes as good as it used to be. Cauliflower since last 10-12 years develop black stains, which when washed turns creamish, spoiling the white colour of cauliflower, considered a mark of its good quality.

Facilitator: Sudipta Ray

By examining Tables 7 and 8, one could read a few general trends indicated by the villagers.

Agriculture, which absorbed 100 per cent of the total population of Uncha Gaon in the 1940-50, has gradually lost its pre-eminence. It now supports no more than 80 per cent of the population, though it is above the national average of 70 per cent. The economy of Uncha Gaon, thus, remains greatly dependent on agriculture for its survival and sustenance.

As agriculture declined in importance, selling milk gained in prominence: from none in the business of selling milk, in the 1940-50, it now engages almost 60 per cent of the total population of Uncha Gaon, as a secondary source of employment and a supplementary source of income.

With the flux of time as new industries moved into the vicinity of Uncha Gaon, people to some extent diversified their livelihood pattern: from a purely agrarian economy in the 1950s, Uncha Gaon has moved into an economy where service sector has gained in importance, small industry and petty business have given livelihoods to quite a large number of the people, and demand for pure labourers has increased.

This diversification in livelihood and demand for labourers as also services could not absorb all the additional hands that were added to the labour force, because the villagers perceive that outsiders have come in to fill in the job vacancies created. The mechanisation of agriculture also prevented these people being absorbed into the agricultural sector. This shows up as 5 per cent of the people being unemployed.

Having summarised the general trends indicated by the villagers, we might now turn to what villagers perceive as changes in cropping pattern, agricultural practices and yield and crop quality. Let us take the decade of the 1940s as the point of departure and Tables 7 and 8 as reference data. Refer to first column of Table 7 and last of Table 8. In that decade, a large number of crops were cultivated, though it is difficult to reconstruct the exact percentage of arable land on which each crop was grown. The crops were a mixture of staples, coarse cereals and pulses and henna for use as cosmetic, usually worn as intricate designs on palms/hands and feet during weddings. The main crops were coarse grains (barley and bajra) and cereals (wheat, jowar and maize). All the crops grown were for household consumption in the village. Farming was both subsistence and sustenance activity. The variety of crops grown gave the farmers not only the opportunity to diffuse their risks of failure, due to pests, insects, droughts, floods, disease or whatever, either singly or in some combination, but also ensured that consumption basket of the households had a combination of food which contained fibre, nutrition and protein. In the 1950s the position remained largely the same.

In 1960s, winds of change began to sweep Uncha Gaon. Pulses were reduced. By the time Uncha Gaon reached 1970s, vegetable was introduced, as a commercial crop and it is important to recognise this fact. In the next decade, as HYV seeds took ground, wheat remained the only main Rabi crop and bajra held on as the main Kharif crop. Cultivation of gram stops. In the 1980s mustard and onion took roots as a cash crop in the hope of a high return.

As of now (1990s) farmers in Uncha Gaon are left with wheat and jowar as principal Rabi and Kharif non-commercial crops respectively, with a sprinkling of bajra. Food crops are grown in 50 per cent of the gross cropped area of the village. Wheat is grown for household consumption as also for sale in the market. Cash crops are grown on the other 50 per cent of arable land, which are mainly vegetables and grown, in the main, for sale.

As we move from the 1940 into the last decade of the last century, Tables 7 and 8 brings us near the truth that the mosaic of crops grown in Uncha Gaon is also becoming boring in terms of nutrition and palate: from several crops of different values and uses and nutrition, the present days crops grown, are basically three: vegetables, wheat and jowar (as fodder). This reduction in diversity of crops signals a movement away from poly-culture *towards* standard mono-culture. It signals reduction in palate and nutritional value of the food consumed in farm households of Uncha Gaon. Additionally, whereas in 1950s and 1960s much of agricultural operations were for ensuring self-sufficiency in *food*, in 1990s the emphasis seems to be on generating *income for self-sufficiency in income*. Thus, in a sense and certainly partially, production in Uncha Gaon has shifted from catering to the needs of the "have nots" of the village to the needs of the "haves" outside the village, by exhausting the natural resources meant to serve the essential needs of the "have nots". This has serious inter-generational questions and somebody needs to address them. Recall that the villagers have mentioned the falling of the water table to below 85 feet which makes irrigation difficult. This may be interpreted to mean that water resources are being used up beyond sustainable (read replenishable limits), to cater to the needs of "haves" of the present generation living outside the village at the expense of conserving resources for future generations.

III. 2. Changes in Agricultural Practices and Reasons for the Changes

With the changes in cropping pattern witnessed by Uncha Gaon, there has been other changes as well, some influenced by it, others influencing it. A chain of dynamic changes in farming practices has influenced the changes in cropping pattern shown to us by the villagers. In 1940s and 1950s, we were told agriculture was wholly rainfed. Agriculture was all about traditional practices in regard to seeds, water harvesting structures, soil nutrients and implements. The farmers and the community were in total control of the inputs, barring rains where they depended on nature. None of the inputs were imported from outside the village.

During 1960-70 mechanization of agriculture starts taking roots: tubewells and tractors come to their own. In 1970-80, we see agriculture in Uncha Gaon adopting "new technology" in its full form: hybrid or HYV seeds replacing traditional varieties; chemical fertilisers crowding out manure (nitrogen-fertiliser consumption in Ballabgarh increased from 625 kg in 1989 to 1857 kg in 1994-95; phospherous consumption has increased from 40 kgs in 1989-90 to 383 kg in 1994-95), insecticides and pesticides put in operation in place of seeds known to be naturally pest and insect resistant, and tractors substituting for the bullocks and the wooden plough. The last remnants of the traditional practice is crop rotation: land on which bajra/wheat is grown in one round is then used to grow vegetables and vice-versa. Dependence on rains for water is eliminated as pumpsets provide water for farming, but the farmers have at once, surrendered their independence from the clutches of the powerful elements in the economy. The farmers are dependent upon seed Companies/Farms; Pesticide and Insecticide Companies through their dealers; Haryana state electricity board; tractor companies and the fertilisers companies. The control of the farmers and the community on inputs vital for their survival is out of their hands. (Tractorisation increased cultivable land size to double with 14 years between 1972 and 1986: from 7.91 acres in 1972 to 14.91 acres in 1986.)

This shift in farming practices also means that farming is now a High External Input Agriculture (HEIA) from Zero External Input Agriculture (ZEIA) during 1940-50 and then Low External Input Agriculture (LEIA) in 1960-70, as we travel through time. In the 1940s and 1950s agriculture was based on what the farmer and the community had: seeds, labour, bullocks, plough and the wooden hoe, manure and rains. In the 1980s and 1990s, agriculture has come to be based on inputs more from outside the households and the community: HYV seeds, pesticides, insecticides, chemical fertilisers, electricity, tractor power, tubewells and pumpsets. Thus whereas in the 1940s and 1950s the farmers could be comfortably in cultivation and farming, buying virtually nothing from outside his/her household or at best the community, in the 1990s we are in Uncha Gaon where farmers buy virtually everything except family labour from outside the household. This transition from ZEIA to LEIA and eventually to HEIA, that the villagers of Uncha Gaon show us through Tables 7 and 8, is a copy book case confirming the framework of "internal resources vs. external resources" provided by Francis and King (1988). See chapter 4 for a discussion on the issues.

Except for energy required for photosynthesis drawn from sun, in the 1980s and 1990s, farming in Uncha Gaon relies primarily on external sources for accessing inputs into farming, including knowledge. Water, nitrogen, other nutrients, seeds, machinery, weed and pest control, extension and credit are all accessed, in the main, from outside. Accessing inputs from outside the households and community results in a net outflow of resources from the households/community. In a sense, increasing agricultural activity could be a mechanism for immiserisation of farmers. For a more definitve assessment of this dimension, we need to work out the terms of trade faced by agriculture which is beyond the scope of this document.

A concommitant development is unsustainable use of resources. When farming in the 1980s and 1990s has become more dependent on sourcing agricultural inputs from outside Uncha Gaon, farming has come to use resources that are not always renewable as in case of Sagarpur and Khadaoli. Internal resources are "inherently renewable and thus have the potential to be used on a 'sustained' basis, indefinitely, through ecologically sound methods of farming" (*Conway and Barbier, 1990*). Water, nitrogen, other nutrients, seeds, machinery, weed and pest control are made available by using resources that are no longer renewable.

Since agriculture in Uncha Gaon has become dependent on external sources for inputs into farming, much of it is not provided as a "free good", unlike farming in the 1940s and 1950s. This implies that the farming households of Uncha Gaon must now buy the required inputs and hence must generate a surplus of production, to exchange for external resources. And because the cost of acquiring these inputs and their supply channels are rarely controlled by the farming household, the farmers are most of the time "price-takers". Just as in cases of Sagarpur and Kadhaoli, this has at least three cost implications in terms of direct costs, hidden costs and real costs. We will analyse the monetised impact of these on the economics of agriculture in Part V and concentrate now on the dynamics that this cost escalation has created, to which we shall now turn.

The transition from ZEIA to LEIA and eventually to HEIA, has made agriculture a high direct cost because the farmer has to buy the inputs. There is little of agricultural inputs required which is available free of charge. Farmers have to buy seeds, fertilsiers, tractors, threshers, pumpsets (or hire them), weedicides, pesticides, capital and so on. Thus the cost of farming operation has gone up so much so that it has put sustainability of peasant agriculture in doubt. The high cost of external inputs is pinching the farmers lately.

The transition from ZEIA to HEIA has also made a noticeable impact on the *hidden* cost of operation. The increase in fossil fuel use to keep outputs high, also means more energy consumption. The hidden costs rise as a result. Shift from ZEIA to HEIA has led to substitution of manual labour and animal power by tractors, threshers and pumpsets (either diesel or electric) that we saw, which implies that external energy sources have substituted energy sources found in the household and the community. All this along with use of fertilisers, which is mostly NKP, agriculture has become very energy intensive in Uncha Gaon.

High external input agriculture entails a lot of *real costs*, in addition to direct and hidden costs. Even where there is no direct monetary outgoing to procure an input, there may be real cost incurred by the farming household.

The farmers also pointed out that the smaller farmers are constantly squeezed in a cost-price wedge. It is a squeeze that encourages farmers to be the first to maximise production from their resources. This promotes higher production using more and more of external inputs and encouraging part-time farming.

True in all these developments output has also increased but costs have also increased. And as we shall examine a little later, the increase in cost has outstripped the benefit of increased output. Small wonder the villagers assigned high cost of agriculture as a reason why they want to migrate out of the sector (reference is invited to columns 4 of Tables 10 and 11). In such a situation, HEIA always puts sustainability of agriculture in doubt.

HEIA in the process has changed the composition of the farmer's friends. HEIA has ensured that the "farmers friends" are spread all over the place. There are now four category of such "friends": (1) Agro-chemical industries who provide fertilisers and "cides"—herbicides, pesticides, insecticides, fungicides, aphicides; (2) Seed producers; (3) Equipment and energy companies and (4) probably in the foreseeable future biomedical companies as well who would supply drugs for prophylactic use in intensive farming for vaccination and curative purpose (*Tansy and Worsley, 1995*). This means that farming instead of depending upon the goodwill and support of households and community in the village based on long term (often multi-generational) relationship, depend on "friends" in far corners of the globe worked out on the basis of short term impersonal and commercial considerations.

III. 3. Changes in Yields and the Reasons Therefore.

Have such dramatic shifts in agricultural practices had any impact on yields? We have to return for a while to Tables 8 once again. Since wheat is the principal food crop grown since 1940s, it is best to discuss variation in the yields in terms of how yield of wheat has varied for a temporal survey of yields. During the 1940s, output of wheat per acre was 3-4 quintals only. During 1950s the yield remains the same. In the late 1960s, the yield increased to about 16 quintals per acre, once tubewells and tractors, came into use and HYV seeds replaced the traditional ones. That is, within a decade, yield jumped from 3-4 quintals an acre to around 16 quintals an acre, a jump of 400 per cent. In the 1970s this increase in yield got entrenched with "new technology" coming full circle: fertilisers and pesticides being the latest addition to the basket of agricultural inputs. It was also the time when government of India started providing price incentives to farmers of wheat (and paddy) in terms of *minimum support price* and *procurement prices*. Thus yield increase in Uncha Gaon was responding, as elsewhere, to change in technology and to the price incentives offered by government of India. And it remained at that level in most of 1980, but during the late 1980s yield started falling. It came to 13 quintals per acre and remained at that level in the 1990s. In effect, is the high yield per acre, of the 1970s and early 1980s was not sustained in the late 1980s and 1990s. Yield per acre fell by almost 19 per cent, to reach about 13 quintals per acre during the last decade.

During the years under review, not only did the villagers of Uncha Gaon, like those of Sagarpur and Kadhaoli, perceive yield change but the intrinsic quality of the produce itself is perceived to have changed, in looks, shape, size and taste. Wheat change colour from golden to reddish orange in the 1960s, at the time HYV seeds are introduced. Its colour now is creamish. The shape and size of the grains change from 'long and fat' grains to "relatively small and thin" grains in the sixties, and then to "small and thin" grains in the 1980s. The good taste of the traditional variety also gives way to less tastier stuff during 1970-80.

III. 4. Are there Spatial Differences in Yields or Crop Quality

If we look at Tables 8 and 9, we have a fairly good idea of how decadal yield of the principal crop has behaved over the last 50 years or so. Both in Saini Muhalla and Ahir Muhallas the yield have been about the same

In terms of the texture, shape, colour and size of the grains, in both the localities, there is no variation. From long, fat and golden coloured grains in 1940s, to relatively smaller sized orange reddish coloured grains in 1960s and then to small sized thin grains in late 1980s, are common to both the localities. The perceived changes in the taste of wheat they grow also include deterioration in tastes. Wheat no longer tastes as good as it used to in the earlier decades.

Part IV. Constraints to Agricultural Production

IV. 1. The Constraints Faced by Agriculture

The villagers of Uncha Gaon like farmers of Sagarpur and Kadhaoli, perceive that farmers are at the riskiest end of the food system. Farm production depends on a wide range of factors, many of which are far beyond their control (moreso after farming has become HEIA). They point to climate and vagaries of nature as the elements which make them throw their hands up, in despair. Good weather—good rainfall, no frost, no hailstrom—can produce large harvests but for which there are insufficient markets. A big harvest will depress prices so much that it may not be worth taking the crop out of the ground. Indeed the farmers did plough back their carrots in 1998 into the fields, as carrot prices had crashed so much that it would not have even paid for the cost of their extraction and transportation to the market. In case the weathergod failed the farmers, harvests are reduced. Consequently there are huge shortfalls in supply. Prices rise and the high prices allure the farmers and encourages them to grow more of the crop for the following year. This in turn will then produce another glut in that crop and the vicious circle starts all over again. Such gluts and surpluses and shortages are endemic to farming. These have added to the instability of farming and insecurity of the farmers.

A review given by the villagers in Tables 7 and 8 above, of the sweep of changes that agriculture of Uncha Gaon has seen, points to certain crops being dropped from the agricultural map. This has been due to various reasons including falling size of landholdings etc. It did mean that agriculture has faced constraints of different kinds over these years. The rationale for dwindling interest in agriculture set forth by the villagers also point to certain negative features of agriculture perceived by the villagers. It faces constraints even now. Constraints faced by agriculture are perceived differently by different stakeholders. In this study the perceived constraints have not been classified as those seen by men and women separately. The last column of Table 9, the second column of Table 10 and the first column of Table 11, give an account of the problems faced by agriculturists.

First, the constraints were listed and then, scores were given by the group, using Rajma seeds. Fixed scoring of ten was done. The group placed ten seeds against the constraint they perceived as their "best" problem and one seed against the constraint that is considered least harmful. Two to nine seeds were kept on the basis of the severity of the remaining problems. Then they ranked the constraints in descending order of the magnitude of the problem, rank 1 being assigned to the severest of the constraints, scoring 10 points designated by 10 Rajma seeds. The biggest constraint is shortage of power, followed by *sundi* (a pest) and termites. Congress grass is ranked 7th (the lowest) in the ranking of constraints.

There thus is a continuum of gravity of the problems the constraints pose. The logic of the ranking as explained by the villagers is like the following: the ranking is not based on the extent of loss suffered on account of the constraints alone. The probability of the constraint showing up and the crop they are likely to affect, taken with the extent of damage caused that informs the ranking. Thus though locust can damage upto 80 per cent of the crops it is ranked 5, for it destroys jowar and maize which are not high value crops. As against that shortage of power is capable of inflicting only 30 per cent loss, as against 80 per cent by locust, it is ranked as the number 1 constraint because it affects all crops, is certain to occur and is certain to adversely affect production.

The constraints are a mixture of weeds, pests, animals, insects and infrastructural failure. The major constraints faced are power shortage that hampers irrigation, *sundi* (pest), termites, *moriya* (pest), *lalri* (red coloured fly), *chittli* (pests) and *nilgai*. The major constraints are, therefore, pests, animals and shortage of power. The loss inflicted by weeds and pollution are all comparatively lesser and they are, therefore, ranked lower in the graded list of constraints. The major infrastructural constraints are power shortage and falling water table (at this point in time, it is placed at 85 feet below the ground level). A rational response should, therefore, have been emphasis on removing the constraints caused by animals and pests, and to a more limited extent shortage of water. If we see the responses (last Column of Table 10), the farmers have tried to tackle basically the weeds. There is on the whole very little effort on the part of the farmers to tackle the other constraints *per se*.

It is interesting that land acquisition which was ranked as the number 1 general problem, was not mentioned as a constraint to agricultural production, by the men's group of saini muhalla. The villagers of sahupura roadside Muhalla, however, listed land acquired by the government as a major problem. When we tried to reconcile this difference in perception with the villagers of Saini Muhalla, they explained that in their ranking and scoring of the constraints they have accounted for only the current constraints that visit agriculture. They have avoided including potential constraints. Hence though they are fully alive of the problems their livelihoods will encounter once land acquisition is completed, they have not listed it as one of the constraints.

The other constraints mentioned by the farmers of Sahupura roadside Muhalla are shortage of power, west wind, untimely rain, *fall in market price*, nilgai, insects, diseases, weeds, lack of cold storage (post-harvest technology), hybrid seeds for vegetables, theft of vegetables, increasing cost of agricultural inputs (seeds, fertilisers and "medicines"). Except for stealing (which started 2-3 years ago); power shortage, untimely rain and high cost of inputs (the three which are pronounced since last 4-5 years), all other constraints are with them for more than 6 years. And the responses of

Table 9 Seasonality Analysis of Agricultural Constraints and Coping Strategies by Men's Group, Saini Muhalla

Months	Agricultural Constraints	Coping Strategies
Baisakh	Unseasonal rains and hailstorm can damage crops	None
Jeth	Water and power shortage, dry heat damages crops like cucumber, melon, bottle gourd, *motha* (weed) damages cucumber, kakri (increased in the last 6-7 years), *sati* (weed) hits jowar (increased since 5-6 years), *sundi* attack	None against heat wave, generators for power shortage, uprooting of *motha* and *sati* affected crops, pesticides against *sundi* (effective upto 25 per cent)
Ashar	Threat of hailstorm, *sati* in jowar, *sundi* in vegetables, *moriya* (disease) in chili fields, in 1998, 80 per cent crop loss	For *sati* and *sundi* affected crops, same as in Jeth, none against others
Sawan	*Sati* in jowar, *sundi* in vegetables, drying of cauliflower leaves, excessive rain, grazing by nilgai	*Lithon* and *dimacron* applied to cauliflower, without success, vigil against nilgai, none for others

Months	Agricultural Constraints	Coping Strategies
Bhado	*Sati* in jowar, *sundi* in vegetables, *gandar* (caterpillar) in brinjal, mosquitoes on green leafy vegetables, like spinach	*Sati* and *sundi* is dealt with as in Jeth, DDT for mosquitoes, none against others
Kuar	*Kana* (fungus) on fruits and cauliflower (disfiguring the produce), *gandar* (caterpillar) in brinjal, nilgai attack	Experimentation with *lithol*, dimacron to control *Kana*, vigil against nilgai, even erecting temporary huts near fields
Katak	Same as Kuar	Same as in Kuar
Aghan	Same as kartick plus jai and *mondi* (grasses) impede growth of wheat	Same as in Kuar No response to *jai* and *moondi*
Poosh	Same as aghan, additionally, rain and hailstorm, *chepa* (pest) attack on cabbage, green and black *gandar* attack, nilgai and cattle grazing	None against rain and hail, *paramol* or *malathine* sprayed once every fifth day for *gandar*, None against *chepa*, vigil against nilgai, erecting temporary huts near fields
Magh	*Gandar* on vegetables, frost, excessive cold prevents grain ripening, excessive rain, *chepa* attack on leafy vegetables	Pesticides against *gandar* (25 per cent success rate). None against *Chepa*, rain and cold.
Fagun	*Choori* (pest) eats away roots of plants like cucumber, *lalrri* (insect) eats leaves of cucumber and kakri, *chepa* attack mustard flowers, cabbage, cauliflower and fenugreek	None
Chet	Same as Fagun	None

Village Analysts: Balbir, Bansi, Harish, Omprakash, Bhagawat, Krisen, Mahesh, Babloo.
Facilitator: Sudipta Ray

the farmers of Sahupura were a shade or two better than those of Saini Muhalla: uprooting, some sprinkling of "medicines" and representation to government authorities, without any success of course. But that is another matter.

How interesting that though agriculture is HEIA since the last two decades and more, the high cost of external inputs is pinching the farmers since the last 4-5 years. The only explanation for this sudden upward rise in input costs, it seems to us, lies in the implementation of the structural adjustment programme, consequent cut in subsidies (real or virtual) to agricultural inputs and the general rise in prices.

IV. 2. Factors that Influence the Constraints

Details of factors that influence the constraints are somewhat limited. Attack of locust, according to men and women in Uncha Gaon, is greatly influenced by timings of the monsoons. Delayed monsoon, leading to late rains, increases the danger of locust and termite infestation considerably. *Sati* weed is again perceived as caused by late arrival of rains and use of chemical fertilisers. What the farmers said is confirmed by a group of technical people who met in September 1999 in Delhi (See the *Indian Express,* 24th September, 1999).

Nilgais have strayed into human habitation, and hence to cropping fields, the villagers explained, because deforestation has robbed them of their natural source of food. And shortage of power, the villagers perceived is caused by Government's faulty policy of meeting industry's undue demand for power at the cost of agriculture. The fall in the water table is on account of the area receiving less than their normal rainfall and overuse of ground water. This is confirmed by the secondary data on rainfall made available by the meteorological department of the government of India. In 1988, Haryana received 1108 mm of rain per annum, which fell to 736.5 mm per year in 1991. This has further fallen to 489 mm in 1994, when the all-India average is approximately 750 mm.

All groups consider all other constraints to be imposed by nature or the causes are unknown to them. None of the groups considered paucity of funds (credit) as a constraint to agriculture, though they had counted poverty and unemployment in the village as two of the major general problems of the village.

Part V. Economics of Agricultural Operations

V. 1. What are the Inputs to Agriculture and the Cultivation Process?

It is best to start with the cultivation process and then summarize the inputs to agriculture. Reference is invited to seasonality analysis of agricultural activities done by villagers in Uncha Gaón. Table 12 is generated out of the same. From Table 12, the basic inputs to agriculture are: ploughing (tractor time), seeds, fertilisers, irrigation in several rounds and pumpsets; labour and of course land.

The process of agriculture, in a normal year, that is, a year not hit by disease and pests etc., is fairly straight forward, as is evident from a remark made by Umbrao to one of the researchers, whose English translation is: "Wheat cultivation is simple. Only west wind, if blows early, harms it".

Let us look at wheat cultivation first. It all starts in Uncha Gaon as elsewhere, the months of Kartick and Aghan (mid-October to mid-December) when land is ploughed for five times, of which two are wet ploughing, and then leveled. This is followed by successive steps that go on for 6 months in a row. Land is then irrigated during the same months and puddles made. Aghan (mid-November to mid-December) is for fertilisers application and seeds to be sown. For four months, thereafter, from Poosh to Chait, fields receive five rounds of irrigation, at the rate of one round per month except the month of Magh when fields are irrigated twice. Each of the first three rounds of irrigation is accompanied by a dose of fertiliser. In Baisakh (mid-April to mid-May), when wheat is harvested and bundles made. Threshing occupies farmers for most of Baisakh. Jeth (mid-May to Mid-June) is the month for storing wheat. The surplus is then taken to the market (called "Mandis") for sale either to the government at the procurement prices declared, or to other buyers and traders at the going market price.

Growing cauliflower and potatoe is different and less organised, in that it does not follow a calendar of months. It has its own calendar. Let us take up cauliflower. First a nursery is raised, for which a nursery bed is prepared of rows and either 1 kg of Kisan Khad or manure (costing Rs. 250 per 50 kg) is provided as additional nutrients. Approximately 1 kg of seed (bought at a price of Rs. 1000) is sown, out of which only 500 grams germinate. As

Table 10 Ranking of Agricultural Constraints, Saini Muhalla, Uncha Gaon

Constraint	Crops Affected	Effects	Crop Loss	Score	Rank	Affects When	Measures
Power shortage	All crops	Irrigation hampered	30 per cent	***** *****	1	May, June, July	None
Sundi (pest)	Cauliflower and cabbage	Eats leaves spoils flowers	40 per cent	***** ****	2	November December	None
Termites	All crops	Eats roots Wheat yield falls	40 per cent	**** ****	3	All Year Round	None
Moriya	Chilies	Leaves dehydrate	50 per cent	*******	4	July and August	None
Lalri	Vegetables	Eats leaves	40 per cent	******	5	March, April, May	None
Chittli (pest)	Vegetables	Eats cauliflower roots, brinjal, cucumber Leaves dry	20 per cent	******	5	July and August	None
Nilgai	All crops	Grazes	40 per cent	******	5		None
Low rainfall	All crops	Crops dry up	20 per cent	****	6	July and August	None
Locust (pest)	Jowar and maize	Eats leaves	80 per cent	****	6	July and August	None

Sati (weed)	All crops	Impedes growth	20 per cent	****	6		Uprooting‡
Mosquito	Spinach	Eats leaves	20 per cent	***	7	All months	DDT @
Smoke (pollution)	cauliflower and spinach	Cauliflower becomes creamish in colour. Spinach leaves turn blackish green	10 per cent Cauliflower and 5 per cent spinach	***	7	May, June	None except washing spinach
Rust disease or kandhwa	Wheat	Grains turn black and leaves yellow and then decay	20 per cent	***	7	February	None
Congress grass (weed)	All crops	Impedes	5 per cent growth. Perceived cancerous	*	7	Uprooting	

‡Expensive and time consuming.
@Spurious DDT is an added problem.

Village Analysts: Lala Ram, Mulchand, Mit Ram, Balak Ram and Girija.
Facilitator: Ms. Meera Jayaswal.

a second step, deweeding is done and at intervals of 10 days, the nursery bed is watered either manually by sprinklers or by rain. The third step is to plough the field where the seedlings are transplanted. A minimum of five rounds of ploughing are essential, at a cost of Rs.1000 per round. It takes the seedlings about 4-6 weeks to be ready for transplantation. The fourth step is to apply DAP (costing Rs. 150 per 50 kg) to the fields and then transplant the seedlings. As the fifth step, between 2 to 3 weeks, deweeding is essential and after another 2-3 weeks the first round

Table 11 Agricultural Process and Involvement of Men and Women

Agricultural Operations	Months	Tasks handled by Men	Tasks handled by Women	Time taken (Days)
Ploughing and leveling (Mej and Jot)	Kartik Aghan	Plough by using tractors	Supervision and help	Week to ten days
Irrigation and puddling (palewat)	Kartik Aghan	Irrigate with pumpsets	Supervision	6 days or so
Apply fertilizer, sow seeds	Aghan	Apply fertilisers	Supervision	4-5 days
First irrigation at 6 inch plant	Poosh	Irrigate with pumpsets	Supervision	4 days or so
Second irrigation	Magh	Irrigate with pumpsets	Supervision	4 days or so
Third irrigation on ear of corn coming out	Magh	Irrigate with pumpsets	Supervision	4 days or so

Agricultural Operations	Months	Tasks handled by Men	Tasks handled by Women	Time taken (Days)
Fourth irrigation on grain formation	Fagun	Irrigate with pumpsets	Supervision	4 days or so
Fifth irrigation on grains maturing	Chet	Irrigate with pumpsets	Supervision	4 days or so
Harvesting	Baisakh		Harvest	A Week
Making bundles	Baisakh		Make bundles	2
Threshing	Baisakh	Using tractors		4-5
Transporting to home and market	Jeth	Using tractors		1

Note: * Supervision means making sure that irrigation water reaches all parts of the field. Compiled from group discussion with men and women's group by the Participatory Assessment Researchers.

of irrigation is due. The fifth step is to deweed the fields again, before the next round of irrigation. This is followed by another round of deweeding. The sixth step is application of fertilisers, which in Uncha Gaon is Kisan Khad. The seventh step is irrigating the land again and for the last time. The flower are ready for sale within the next 2 weeks or so.

In order to keep the pests at bay, at intervals of every 15 days, "Trigen" (sic), as pesticides is sprayed. *Trigen* costs Rs. 50 per 50 kg.

V. 2. How Does the Economics of Input Work Out?

With all these inputs, cost of agriculture is fairly high. The economics of the inputs can be worked out by comparing the yield mentioned in Table 6 with the price of inputs. The villagers themselves provided estimates of returns from wheat, mustard and potatoe, which influenced their decision on the choice of crops. Their estimates are in Tables 13 and 14.

Through these tables the villagers clearly tell us that cultivating cash crop is far more profitable than cultivating their land for growing food crops. The tables also tell us how returns will behave if farmers grew only the particular crop per acre throughout the year. The cost of cultivation is not in the above tables inclusive of the cost of credit. Men borrowed money, particularly during the months of Bhado, Kartick and Kuar, for sowing of winter vegetables, preparing land for cultivating wheat, mending "animal shelter roofs", treatment of illness etc. Loan upto Rs. 5000 is borrowed from friends, relatives and local businessmen (money lenders) if it is to meet expenses for treatment, to defray costs of meeting social obligations like marriage in the family etc. Loans for agriculture, buying buffaloes, tractors and threshers are availed of from the Gurgaon grameen bank and the local land mortgage bank. This distinction is made on the basis of the collateral required. For loans which can not be backed by collateral security, resources are raised

Table 12 Return from Agriculture in Kharif Season Per Acre (in Rupees)

Crops	Expenditure	Income	Gross Return
Spinach	8000	50000	42000
Cauliflower	6000	50000	44000
Cabbage	6000	50000	44000
Cucumber	4000	30000	26000
Brinjal	8000	50000	42000
Potatoes	6000	50000	44000

Village Analysts: Kamalawali, Samantara, Rani and Umraon.
Facilitator: Meera Jayaswal.
Date: 27.3.99.

from informal sources at a usury rates of interest; for loans which can be backed by collateral security, credit is sought from formal purveyors of credit, who charge regulated interest rates. That is why though the gross return from farming is very high, the monthly net income is modest. The villagers gave us the data in Table 15 to illustrate the point.

Table 13 Return from Agriculture in Rabi Season Per Acre (in Rupees)

Crops	Expenditure	Income	Gross Return
Wheat	3000	8000	5000
Vegetables	12000	34500	22500

Village Analysts: Kamalawali, Samantara, Rani and Umraon.
Facilitator: Meera Jayaswal.
Date: 27.3.99.

Table 14 Cost and Returns from Agriculture to Households Per Acre (in Rupees)

Months	Income	Input Cost	Savings
Baisakh (Veg)	6000	1500	4500
Jeth (Veg)	4500	3000	1500
Asard (Veg)	6000	3000	3000
Sawan (Veg)	6000	3000	3000
Bhado (Veg)	6000	3000	3000
Kuar (Veg)	7500	4500	300
Kartck (Veg)	6000	4500	1500
Aghan (Veg)	4500	1500	3000
Poosh (Veg)	4500	1500	3000
Magh (veg)	4500	1500	3000
Fagun (Veg)	7500	3000	4500
Chet (Veg)	7500	3000	4500
TOTAL from Vegetables per annum (p.a.)	**70,500**	**33000**	**37500**
TOTAL from Wheat p.a.	**8000**	**3000**	**5000**
TOTAL from Jowar p.a.	**3000**	**1000**	**2000**
TOTAL from sale of milk p.a.	**86400**	**24000**	**62400**

The craze for vegetable cultivation is for its commercial value. Wheat is cultivated as a food crop and jowar is grown for fodder. The cropping pattern is so devised that agriculture provides food, cash and fodder. In Sen's terminology, for wheat, farmers have endowment entitlements and for other consumption needs including other kinds of food, the farmers depend on trade entitlements (*Sen, 1981*). The returns from vegetables incidentally are reaped over a period of 12 months, whereas returns from wheat and jowar are reaped after putting in 6 months of labour.

Of the three main occupations (growing vegetables, growing wheat and selling milk) apparently selling milk is most lucrative and is assisted by farming for it provides fodder and labour, managed by household labour perceived as free. The villagers explained that profitability of the three livelihoods needs to be qualified. With the flux of time, the value of land increases, their asset appreciates in value and the farmers do not have to worry about its replacement cost, or provide for depreciation. In case of selling milk, on the contrary, the value of their bovine wealth is depleted every year and replacement cost often becomes relevant. Loss of assets due to death of buffaloes has to be taken cognisance of as well, which is not the case with land. Hence, the return from selling milk requires mid way corrections. According to the farmer's perception, cultivating vegetable is their best bet.

The villagers in working out the economics of farming and agriculture did not factor in the imputed cost of labour of the household. Assuming that only adults work, a minimum of 2 adults spend one year in generating the income. If we assume that they are required to put in only 180 days of work and the wages they could earn in the next best alternative employment is Rs. 60 per day, they would have earned Rs. 21600. If we notionally deduct this cost from the net returns from agriculture seen in Table 15, the picture become less cheerful.

V. 3. Who Supplies the Inputs and Who Provides the Extension Services Regarding New Seeds and Fertilisers?

As we discussed above agricultural inputs for cultivating wheat are tractors, seeds, fertilisers, irrigation in several rounds, and therefore water and pumpsets; family labour; outside labour; and of course land. As we saw the year long agricultural operations are carried out by family labour. Tractors, and pumpsets are owned by farmers, and there is inter-household hiring of tractors. In some rare cases generators are also used to energise the pumpsets for irrigation, which is also accessed from the market. Farmers access other inputs from the open market. The existence of extension service is weak which is why farmers do not respond to a host of constraints though they are aware of them, which reflects absence of extension support. The steady decline in and ultimately breaking down of extension service is particularly felt.

Part VI. Class Issues

The division of the village into landowning and landless groups is relatively easy. There are only 5 per cent landless people. The majority of the people are Jats. But land is owned by all classes of people.

Uncha Gaon farmers showed no signs of stratification in terms of who cultivated which crop or land. Generally all farmers cultivate, or are potential cultivators of all the crops (wheat being the dominant food crop and vegetables being cash crops with potatoe the single largest produce) depending on several factors, including weather, soil conditions, resource availability and opportunity. Farmers *inter se* are not divided along caste or religious lines.

The issue of land ownership and produce ownership does not seem to be relevant in Uncha Gaon, as it is in some other villages. Most people are engaged in agriculture, except the landless. Agriculture is for the most part a family enterprise, except in case of very few large farmers. Those who own the land are the producers as well. There is no system of tenancy. Even those who work outside the village return to the village whenever required in the interest of farming.

Like Sagarpur and Kadhaoli, Uncha Gaon farmers prefer to till their own land. Most of the farmers in Uncha Gaon being small and marginal farmers, they have no land to lease out. Since vegetable cultivation is a highly labour intensive business, there is little slack capacity with the farmers to lease-in other farmers' land.

On the question of migrant labourers in agriculture and migrant leases, let us look at Table 12 once again. Most of the steps in cultivation are performed by the farmers themselves and their families, with very little hired labour inputs. Where very few large farmers owning very large farms, the villagers pointed out, require additional person power, they hire labourers from within the village from amongst marginal farmers who have spare "cultivating capacity". As the women within the household manage most of other activities like looking after animal etc. there is hardly any scope, if at all, to employ hired labourers. Hence migrant labourers are non-existent in the agricultural sector.

Similar is the case of migrant leases and we have discussed the issue in the previous paragraphs. However, migrant labourers in the industrial establishment in and around Uncha Gaon has an important presence, but a discussion of he same is beyond the scope of this paper.

Part VII Gender

VII. 1. Is there any Difference in the Tasks Carried out by Men and Women?

In Uncha Gaon, we are talking about a community comprising Jats, where women's and men's domains are clearly demarcated. Jats are a community of farmers, generally landowning class and politically exceptionally vocal. Jats have been classified, by government of India, as belonging to other backward castes *(Times of India,* 22nd October 1999). The dichotomy of "inside-home" and "outside-home" jobs, in this schema is distinct.

Reference is invited to Table 12. The picture is the same as we found in case of Kadhaoli and Sagarpur: tasks cut out for men and women are well demarcated. Let us take the case of wheat cultivation. Women supervise ploughing, leveling and puddling and several rounds of irrigation. Everything relating to harvesting, and making bundles from harvsted crops for threshing, are under the charge of women. Even when men are engaged in threshing with machines, the women make the smaller bundles to facilitate the process.

The next picture is also familiar. Tasks entrusted to women's care are in addition to their traditionally assigned responsibilities, viz., fetching water, collecting fuel and fodder, feeding animals, cleaning, washing, bearing and rearing children and cooking food for the households. They have to deal with their men folk, in some cases in drunken state. In case of men, for irrigating their land they work additional hours at night but for other operations like for threshing and for taking the produce to the *Mandis* (markets), they take leave from their normal routine. If one were to compute the workload of men and women on a comparative basis, women are obviously overloaded.

Most of the tasks assigned to the women require them to work with their hands (as they can only be manually performed, using simple implements like a sickle for harvesting) starting from supervising irrigation to harvesting and making bundles. The tasks performed by men on the contrary, viz., ploughing, irrigating, threshing and transporting, are all mechanised. Tractors, pumpsets and threshers are their aids. Thus if we now compare the two sets of activities, it further reveals that most of what women do is confined within the household and their fields, and most of what men do require them to interface with the outside world: arranging tractors, looking around for pumpsets and transporting the produce for sale.

That men sell vegetables and crops produced by the entire farming household has a serious economic implication. In case of Uncha Gaon, because men *sell* the vegetable produce created out of family resources, the proceeds of the sale from such produce, go to men. Though women, men and children all conjointly participate in generating the output, custody of income arising out of such output eventually goes to the men. And decisions regarding appropriation of the household incomes also rests with men, which gives them the extra room to decide the pattern of expenditure, including the capacity to accommodate the cost of their drinks.

Box 6.1
Women Carry a Disproportionate Burden

Women have the primary responsibility for household chores, activities that keep them inside the house most of the time. As the household food preparers, women are often exposed to high levels of smoke for long periods. Small wonder that the majority of the 2.2 million deaths every year from indoor pollution occur among women. They also take the responsibility for obtaining water and washing the family clothes—activities that can be hazardous when sanitation is poor, washing facilities are primitive and water used is contaminated. And women are usually responsible for caring for sick children, increasing their exposure to disease-causing organisms.

The kind of employment that women have access to often puts them at risks as well. In rural areas many women work in agricultural fields, where they are exposed to toxics from fertilisers and pesticides.....Another common source of income for women is piece work done at home...which can involve the use of dangerous adhesives and other inflammable or toxic materials.

In poor households women have the responsibility of collecting fuelwood and cow dung to meet family's energy requirements. In an environmentally degraded setting that may mean long hours of walking to collect fuel. These activities significantly reduce women's time for other activities as well as exposing them to health risks. Moreover, girls often help their mothers fetch water and fuelwood, depriving them of education.

Source: World Resources Institute: *World Resources 1996-97* (New-York: Oxford University Press) 1996.

Part VIII. Significance of Agriculture

VIII. 1. What is the Significance of Agriculture in Urban and Peri-Urban Areas in Terms of:

- Employment and Food Security
- Income
- Others

Employment The significance of agriculture in the life of Uncha Gaon has been dealt with at length. In each of the Muhallas of the village, baring the Harijan Basti, 80 per cent of the people depend on agriculture on an average. It is not only a source of income, it is also a source of employment, food and fodder. The role of agriculture in providing employment to the women is particularly important. Where women do not seek employment outside their community, agriculture is a vital source of utilising their labour power. However, it is not the only source of employment and income. As in many other similar villages in Faridabad, people pursue some alternative means of livelihoods as well within the village and outside, most prominently, selling milk. Since much of agriculture is based on family labour, and demand for labour in agriculture at best of times is only seasonal, agriculture as a source of employment to those who depend solely on sale of their labour power is limited.

Food Security The importance of agriculture for food security in a poor agricultural society, can not be overemphasized. Food security means that there is enough food in the system, that people have the purchasing power to access the food so available, that people have the ability to access such food, that the food available is culturally acceptable and that the food so available has adequate nutritional value for a healthy life.

The data in terms of the problem prioritization in Table 4 does not indicate availability of food as a problem or as a constraint to livelihood. Even the historical transects of the village nowhere indicates that insufficient food or hunger ever visited the community. However from the seasonal analysis of agricultural activities by men's group in Saini Muhalla, reproduced in Table 6, elements of food insecurity are clear. We reproduce in Table 15, the food consumption pattern as depicted by the said seasonality analysis.

Sawan, Bhado and Kuar are hunger months for the people at large. We have marked Column 1 of Table 15, with the letter 'H' to denote months, which could be hunger months. During these three months the typical diet of a farm household consists of chappatis and pickle or chili chutney, twice a day. The story is about the same in Baisakh, with addition of vegetables from their own fields, which would be some brinjals and onions. Though people at large do not face starvation, there is hunger and

Table 15 Seasonality Analysis of Agricultural Activities and Food Consumption by Men's Group in Saini Muhalla

Months	Food Consumption	Agricultural Activities
Baisakh	Chappatis with pickle or chili chutney, vegetables from their own fields	Harvesting of wheat and selling the produce, brinjal, melon and onion sold, sow seeds for lady's finger, bottle gourd, torai, chili, pumpkin, cucumber, bitter gourd, income is 50 per cent
Jeth	Chappatis with pickle or chili chutney, occasionally vegetables, fruits, dalia, lassi or milk and tea, 3 meals plus an evening meal of tea/ milk	Irrigation and weeding in the fields, collection of fodder, like cutting grass and harvesting jowar, sowing of jowar and maize seeds, selling cucumber, kakri and melon
Ashar	Same as Jeth	Irrigating fields, cutting fodder, selling vegetables sown in Baisakh, income 25 per cent, sowing bajra
Sawan H	2 meals of chappatis, pickle or chili chutney, some veg	Seedling of cauliflower and brinjal raised, cutting some jowar for fodder
Bhado H	Same as Sawan	Cutting jowar, sowing radish, carrot, spinach cabbage seeds, transplanting cauliflower brinjal seedlings
Kuar H	Same as Bhado	Irrigating and weeding fields, cutting some jowar

Months	Food Consumption	Agricultural Activities
Katak	Chappatis with pickle or chili chutney, occasionally vegetables, fruits, milk tea, 3 meals plus an evening meal of tea or milk	Harvesting jowar and bajra, selling spinach, cauliflower, fenugreek, coriander, brinjal, radish, income is upto 20 per cent
Aghan	Same as Kartick	Sowing wheat seeds, selling spinach cauliflower, fenugreek, coriander, brinjal, radish, cabbage, income upto 40 per cent
Poosh	Bajra Chappatis with Sarson da Saag, pickle or Chili chutney Occasionally vegetables. 3 meals plus an evening meal of tea or milk	Irrigating land, selling spinach cauliflower, fenugreek, coriander, brinjal, radish, cabbage, income upto 45 per cent
Magh	Same as Poosh	Selling spinach cauliflower, fenugreek, coriander, brinjal, radish, cabbage, income upto 40 per cent. Irrigating fields, sowing cucumber and melon seeds
Fagun	Same as Magh	Selling cauliflower, potato, brinjal, fenugreek, spinach, carrot, radish, income is 45 per cent, irrigating and weeding fields
Chet	Same as Magh	Fenugreek, spinach, coriander, carrot and sarson da saag sold, income is 35 per cent, irrigate fields

Notes: H indicates hunger periods.
Village Analysts: Balbir, Bansi, Harish, Omprakash, Bhagawat, Krisen, Mahesh, Babloo.
Facilitator: Sudipta Ray

the variety and palate of the meals is very boring. The nutritional component of food intake is suspect. During the remaining 8-9 months people do not starve and the consumption basket is varied. It has cereals, fibre, protein and dairy products. And the frequency of meals is generally the standard 3 meals a day, with a fourth meal in the form of a light supper of milk or tea.

Because farmers of Uncha Gaon have migrated from agriculture for sustenance and subsistence (in their broadest connotation) and from food self sufficiency to income self-sufficiency, hunger stalks the villagers whenever income dips. If we see Column 3, of Table 15, in all those months where the villagers have something to sell, they eat well. In the three months of Sawan, Bhado and Kuar the farmers have nothing to sell, and hence are cash-strapped. They, therefore, hack back consumption. This is also the period, the villagers explained, when diseases are at their full fury: malaria, diarrhea and dengue, apart from the chronic ones in the form of najla, headache, gastritis and white discharge amongst women. (We will discuss the problem of health later.) This means that farmers are forced to spend sizeable portions of their income on treatment during these months, making further inroads into their resource base and forcing them in turn to cut their consumption basket. Food security for Uncha Gaon is, thus, a function of cash sales and incidence of disease. Uncha Gaon's food security is jeopardised, for at least three months, because the farmers have migrated from endowment based entitlement to food in favour of exchange based entitlement.

The redeeming feature is the cropping pattern. Though cash crops have the primacy, wheat as a food crop is still cultivated. The cropping pattern also indicates that despite Uncha Gaon having migrated from ZEIA to HEIA and the diversity of crops is on the decline, nevertheless, a variety of vegetables are grown. And there are overlaps. This helps in distributing the risks that farmers face. In the event of one crop failing, for whatever reason, they can fall back on the other vegetables that they grow. As a village women Umraon remarked: "The price of carrots fell tremendously. As a result, we did not dig out the carrots. Instead we ploughed the land. But potatoes and cauliflower saved us".

Income Agriculture as a profitable venture is in no doubt in the villager's perception. However, instability and uncertainty of assured prices for their crops are in doubt. The stability of prices for wheat is imparted by the minimum support price and procurement price for wheat (and paddy) declared by the government. This helps reduce risks involved in farming. There are thus two kinds of agricultural produce: vegetables which, are moie profitable and food crops which are less lucrative. But the crops, which are more lucrative are the ones with higher risks of price volatility, and the ones which are less lucrative are the ones that have price stability. Stability and returns are the two objectives that a wise farmer must reconcile.

Since 80 per cent of the people in Uncha Gaon depend on agriculture, it is one of the principle sources of income. The other principal source is sale of milk. From one acre of land, the total return from agriculture per household is about Rs. 44,500. That is, the income of the household is about Rs. 3700 per month. Tables 13 and 14 give an idea of the kinds of money that farmers make from agriculture in Kharif and Rabi respectively. It will be seen from Table 13 that except for cucumber, the returns from all other vegetables in Kharif are about the same. But farmers grow potatoes on 50 per cent of their land under vegetables, because potatoes have a long self life and can be stored for almost a year, obviating the need to sell them off when the prices are lowest immediately after the harvest. This is not the case with other vegetables. In Rabi, though vegetables give a far better returns than wheat, the other crop grown during the season (Rs.22500 as against Rs. 5000), yet farmers grow wheat along with vegetables, to make sure that they have enough of staple foods in their granary without depending on the market. There is an attempt to have partial self-sufficiency in food at the household level.

Part IX. Injury to Crops

IX. 1. Any Visible Injury to Crops?

Constraints set out in the two tables, being Tables 10 and 11, spell out that visible injury to crops is noticeable. Grazing by nilgais, which featured in the constraints listed by all the groups, leaves brazen marks of injury on the crops. Locust attack and *chepa* infestation imprint visible signs of injury on the leaves and the crop. When crops are smothered by dry west wind , it is there for all to see. Leaves partially mauled by *sundi* look ghastly. Spinach leaves with holes created by mosquitoes are noticeable. The drying up of the leaves of brinjal plants due to *chittli* attack is prominent. The researchers did notice for themselves visible leaf injury.

Neither the researchers saw nor the villagers of Uncha Gaon perceived leaf injury due to air pollution. Damage to crops, in terms of change in colour of cauliflower and spinach, due to smoke and dust was specifically mentioned, which will be discussed separately.

IX. 2. To What Extent is Leaf Injury Perceived to be Caused by Air Pollution?

The story of air pollution affecting agriculture in Uncha Gaon reads something like the following. Black deposit (assumed to emitted from local thermocol factory) falls on cauliflower and spinach, which is more prominent during winter, leading to the cauliflower turning creamish and the spinach turning blackish. The taste also changes and becomes salty. Tomatoes also turn blackish due to smoke emitted from the neighbouring factories, though not resulting in financial loss. Flowers of brinjal, tomato and chili get wasted, when the ashes mixed with smoke fall on them. As per men's group, *moriya* disease in chili is assumed to be due to some pollution in the air. Water also turns black when stored overnight, due to air pollution.

The people of Uncha Gaon, therefore, do not perceive that any of the leaf injuries is indeed caused by air. Tables specifying the causes of the injuries do not include air pollution as one of them. The constraints are either animal attack, pests and insect infestation, or induced by nature such as hailstrom, dry west wind, none of which admit of linking with air pollution. Most of the underlying causes of the constraints faced by agriculture are natural, or connected with rainfall and/or policy induced.

IX. 3. What Happens to Injured Crops: Consumed, Sold, Used as Fodder or Dumped?

Crops injured are differentially treated. Insect infested and disease affected crops, which are likely to perpetuate the pest or the disease are uprooted and dumped. Crops affected by locust, *sundi* are uprooted and, some of it is used as inferior quality fodder. Crops infected with *sati* are uprooted and discarded, for even animals refuse to consume them. Grains affected by nilgai, *chepa* pest, locust are sold in the market for whatever remains of them. Generally injured crops are not consumed by human beings.

IX. 4. What are the Perceived Impacts of Air Pollution on Agriculture?

During the first phase of the study, air pollution did not figure in any of the discussions, diagrams, analysis and mapping. The first phase of the study indicates that women are apparently not aware of air pollution caused by heavy vehicular traffic and factories.

During the second phase of the study, the research team requested them to remember if they had any problem with dust or smoke. They could only remember that tender flowers of guava and lemon wither away due to dust before bearing fruits and those, which survive, to bear fruits yield fruits of uneven shapes and sizes. The women's group did mention that dust and thick smoke emitted from nearby factories cause marginal loss to vegetables. Smoke is harmful during winter only, when the thick air does not allow smoke to rise up. A mixture of thick smoke and dew, deposit on vegetable leaves and cauliflower and tomatoes. While washing these vegetables with water takes off the stain most of the time, cauliflower changes its white colour to creamish, despite the washes and this reduces its value by 25 per cent in terms of prices. In effect the impact of air pollution is perceived as being restricted to deteriorating the quality of cauliflowers.

IX. 5. What Changes in Types of Pest, Pest Population and Past Damage have been Perceived Spatially and Historically?

Agriculture has traditionally been free from pests and pest damage in the 1940s and 1950s. Since the introduction of the HYV seeds and mechanised agriculture, pests and insects have made a major appearance, as would be apparent from the vintage of these pests and insects from Tables 10 and 11. Add to this the fact that the prevailing perception is that the number of pests and weeds are on the rise in recent years. Refer to Tables 10 and 11. Locust, *sundi, chepa* and *jai rani* have plagued agriculture for the last 3 years or so. Termites have come in over the last 4-5 years. Nilgais are farmer's nightmares since last 10 years or so. Shortage of power is creating problems since 5-8 years. Rest of the problems, according them, has been with them from before, and in many cases the villagers did not specify the vintage as well. It is not possible to reconstruct the past damage spatially and historically, with the available data base.

Part X. How Do People Deal with Constraints to Agricultural Production?

X. 1. How do Farmers Tackle Perceived Constraints: Through Changed Practice? Organized Action/ Through Existing Organizational Structures?

We have dealt with the responses indicated by the groups to the constraints in Tables 10 and 11. The recital of farmers' responses gives an account of the nature and content of such responses.

There is no systematic response. Farmers have not changed agricultural practices. There was none, which the villagers indicate and there is nothing visible of the organised action, which we see in some parts of Haryana, like the agitation by farmers for power supply at subsidised rates. As a matter of fact the response *per se* of the farmers to tackle the constraints has on the whole been itself feeble.

There are organizational (read institutional!) structures to support agricultural activities, but none apparently come to the help of these farmers. Most of these have become dysfunctional.

X. 2. If Constraints can not be Removed at the Local Level, Whether Farmers Approach Higher Authorities?

There is no sign of villagers approaching higher authorities to ameliorate their condition. In many cases, farmers have made no attempt to remove the constraint at all. They resolve whatever is possible within their ways and means. And behave rationally in doing nothing in redressing the constraints that can not be removed solely with their own resources. The fact that Haryana urban development authority (HUDA) is trying to acquire land in the village, has disheartened Uncha Gaon villagers. It has instilled a fear of starvation, consequent upon loss of their land, the source of their livelihood. They have made some attempts at petitioning higher authorities to dissuade HUDA from acquiring their land but to no avail. It cost them time and money and they could not deal with the endless paper work. The problems that stalk the poor farmers of Uncha Gaon certainly do not encourage them to approach higher authorities in seeking redressal of their problems. This is more so because the bureaucracy is known for its insensitivity to the problems of the poor and the disadvantaged.

Part XI. Impact on Health

XI. 1. What are the Impacts of Industrialization?

Health is a matter of concern in all our villages. The impact of pollution and agricultural practices both have bearing on the status of health in humans and animals, in Uncha Gaon. There has been increased incidence of burning sensation in the eyes and TB for the last 10-15 years. Air pollution, according to men group, has led to increased incidence of heart attack and cancer. Women attribute increased incidence of breathing problem and coughing due to air pollution. Emissions from rubber and thermocol factory led to bad odour and feeling of nausea. Men group felt that the pollution from Thermocol factories might be affecting the health of their buffaloes though no visible symptoms have been noticed. The women, however, do not think in similar fashion.

These issues were explored at the participatory sessions. The Women's Group of Ahir Muhalla catalogued 9 health problems or the village and ranked them as well. The scoring and ranking is shown in Table 17.

Table 16 Graded Scoring of Health Problems in Ahir Muhalla by Women's Group

Health Problems	Scoring	Rank	Treatment	Expenditure
Malaria	******** 8	1	Only in severe cases	400-500
Gastritis	********8	1	No	—
Headache	********8	1	No	—
Diarrhea	********8	1	Only in severe cases	400-500
Najla	******6	2	Only in severe cases	200-300
Dengu	******6	2	Yes	400-500
Bai	*****5	3	No	—
Stomach Ache	****4	4	No	—
White Discharge	****4	4	No	—

Village Analysts: Kela, Vidya, Bhagwati.
Facilitator: Ms. Meera Jayaswal.
Dated: 10.4.99.

The villagers first listed the problems, without any ordering. Then against each problem they placed Rajma seeds as indicators of the score they assign to each of these. The severity of the diseases is shown by the number of Rajma seeds placed against the name of the disease, shown in Table 16 by asterisk marks in Table 16. These are the scores. Thus the disease which has the highest score is the severest, and ranked 1 and so on.

There are three categories of diseases that villagers suffer in Uncha Gaon. Malaria, gastritis, headache and diarrhoea are ranked 1 and are perceived as causing the severest problems. Najla and Dengu are placed at number two, followed by Bai. The least problematic are stomachache and white discharge. It is also apparent that the villagers seek the advice of private practitioners, which is why their outgoing on treatment of ailments is so high. They do not apparently use the health service outlets provided by the state in terms of the public health centre (PHC), maternity and child health centre (MCH) and referral hospitals. None of the diseases are due to air pollution.

The villagers of Uncha Goan, like the villagers of Sagarpur and Kadhaoli, apparently did not perceive any adverse impact of pesticides, herbicides etc. (called "medicines" in local parlance) upon the farmers' health, both from being exposed to them while spraying and sprinkling them in their fields and from consuming food laced with these "medicines".

Part XII: Conclusions

There could be several minor and major conclusions drawn from the above discussion, some of which have been pointed out in the main text itself. These general conclusions are quite similar to the conclusions we have drawn for Kadhaoli and Sagarpur. Nevertheless it would be useful to draw the following broad conclusions.

1. Agriculture is an important source of livelihood in Uncha Gaon but may not be categorized as the single most important source of livelihood. Only cultivation of wheat provides stable village income to some villagers. Because large parts of agricultural lands are dedicated to growing vegetables, the volatility of income is high because vegetables prices are subject to fluctuations in the short and very short run.
2. Agriculture provides fodder for the animal population of Uncha Gaon, which helps the farmers in sustaining the milk business of the village.
3. Agriculture ensures food availability for the village through exchange entitlements. The crops grown in Uncha Gaon, are mostly cash crops, and that too vegetables, predominantly potatoes in Rabi season. Within the general category of vegetables, both late and early varieties of vegetables are grown in different combinations, to ensure, as far as possible that the cash flow of the household does not dry up. Only a moderate acreage 25 per cent of arable land is deployed for food crops in the form of wheat. Most of the vegetables grown are for sale in the market and not for consumption by those who produce them. This has resulted in drawing more ground water beyond sustainable limits set by the parameters of agro-climatic zone in which the village is situated. Food is being produced in Uncha

Gaon in response to demands of those who can pay for it in the market outside Uncha Gaon. This, in some feeble sense at least, raises the question the rationality of the system of markets and prices in allocating resources. If food is to be grown such that those who can pay for it are freely able to get such food, irrespective of its impact on natural resources, then there could be problems down the road. Since vegetable cultivation requires considerably more water than alternative crops, there is an inter-generational question. Is the present generation of farmers and vegetable consumers using up resources that are rightfully the asset of future generations?

4. Villagers generally do not have a diversified means of livelihood but at least 60 per cent of them do not depend upon any one means of livelihood for sustenance and survival. For example, though 80 per cent of the people are dependent on agriculture, 60 per cent also are into selling milk.
5. Though most of the crops are cash crops, there is some element of poly-culture still visible, despite dwindling diversity in the crops grown witnessed over the years.
6. There is no apparent food insecurity for 8-9 months in a year, but for 3-4 months, people suffer hunger. The consumption basket during the hunger months is less nutritious and lacks palate. The consumption basket during the non-hunger months is deficient in proteins and other nutrients as they comprise only of chappatis and some vegetables.
7. Agriculture is today High External Input Agriculture, and has moved to its current state in the 1960s and 1970s, from Zero External Input Agriculture, even as late as in the 1940s. This change has increased the farmers' vulnerability to both external shocks and to internal risks.
8. As agriculture gradually graduated to High External Input Agriculture in the 1960s, 1970s, 1980s and the 1990s, it has resulted in making agriculture a high cost operation and the vulnerability of the farmers to external shocks so much more significant.

9. There is a dramatic increase in productivity in 1990 over the level obtaining in 1950s. Yields are seen to reach their highest in the 1970s and 1980s but the high growth rates in yield were not sustained in the 1990s. The exceptionally high level of yield in the 1970s was achieved by adopting "new technology", viz., use of fertilisers, improved (HYV) variety of seeds and irrigation.
10. The rapid industrialisation of areas around Uncha Gaon is opening up job opportunities for job seekers, but these job opportunities are not going to the villagers. The unemployment rate in Uncha Gaon is rather high and people listed outsiders usurping job opportunities denying the local youth their fair share of the livelihood market, as a major problem confronting the community.
11. There are a large number of constraints faced by the villagers in their agricultural operations, including pest and insect attacks. None are, however, related to pollution in general and air pollution in particular. While pests, insects and diseases have caused more damage than weeds, most of the measures taken by the farmers to counter the constraints are restricted to eliminating weeds and bare minimum towards pests and animals. The cultivators have some system of coping with some of these constraints based on their own resources and knowledge. The non-existence of extension services and paucity of vital agricultural inputs are considered by the villagers as serious constraints. But there is little effort on the part of the community, if at all, to deal with these, except perceiving that such constraints should be dealt with by the government. There are certain constraints which are imposed by nature, like uncertainty/irregularity of rainfall and hailstrom, which are way beyond the community's capacity to solve. There are, then, constraints imposed by living beings (indirectly) such as grazing their crops by nilgais due to deforestation, which again lies beyond the capacity of the farmers.
12. Diseases, pests and insects that attack crops have increased over time, more so over the last 3-4 years. The growth has been most prolific in weeds.

13. Pollution has increased. But the co-relation between pollution and injury to crops is not perceived. Leaf injury tc crops is visible and the insects/diseases which casue such injuries are known but that they are due to air pollution, is not established. Even the researchers saw some visible injury on the crops standing in the fields, but the villagers did not correlate these injuries with air pollution.
14. There are gender discriminations and gender injustice, and both in terms of agreeableness of work and workload proper, the dice is loaded against women. There is evidence which reflect intra-familial disparity in distribution of power.
15. The role of the established state institutions in the life of the community is limited and the villagers also do not seek out these services whatever the reasons.
16. The role played support institutions established to assist farmers and boost agriculture leaves much to be desired. There is need to look at these seriously.

7 Comparative Picture of Pollution, Agriculture and Livelihood in Varanasi and Faridabad

I. Introduction

Varanasi and Faridabad are the two districts selected for the study on the impact of air pollution on agriculture and livelihood in the peri-urban areas. Results emanating from the study of the villages have been documented in two forms: one, a report distilling peoples' perception on a wide range of issues having bearing on agriculture, livelihood and pollution, in particular air pollution; two, indepth studies of five villages in the two district. This chapter will deal with a comparative picture of people's perception on the issues at hand in respect of the villages covered by the indepth study.

Varanasi and Faridabad are located in two vastly contrasting settings both politically, economically and agro-ecologically.

Varanasi is in the largest and one of the poorest states of India, namely, Uttar Pradesh, and then in the poorer part of the state, Eastern Uttar Pradesh. Uttar Pradesh is predominantly an agricultural economy and is well endowed in terms of environmental resources. It receives one of the highest rainfalls in the country, particularly Eastern Uttar Pradesh where Varanasi is located. It is fed by two of the major river systems in the country, that of the mighty Ganges and Yamuna. Varanasi is blessed with fertile alluvium soil and is the home of all major religions in the country. Green revolution has caught on in western Uttar Pradesh only; the rest of the state generally hinging on to traditional agriculture, with Green Revolution catching on. Poverty is the hallmark of Varanasi.

Haryana is one of the newer and smaller states of India. It was curved out of erstwhile Punjab in 1966. Faridabad is a major industrial center in Haryana. Haryana and Faridabad lie in the heartland of green revolution. It is one of the richer states in India. Faridabad receives lesser rainfall than Varanasi. Prosperity all round is an unmistakable characteristic of Faridabad.

It is against this backdrop that we will compare people's perspective on pollution, livelihood and agriculture.

II. Organisation of the Chapter

We will divide this chapter into nine sections. Section III will deal with livelihood. Section IV will be a comparative picture of livelihood and agriculture. Constraints to agriculture and coping strategies will be described in section V. Section VI will deal specifically with air pollution and its perceived impact on agriculture. In section VII we will look at the institutional issues and section VIII at health problems confronting the two communities. Finally we will have a fleeting glimpse of the quality of life in Varanasi and Faridabad.

III. Livelihood. Agriculture and Constraints to Agriculture

III. 1. Patterns of Livelihood

Patterns of livelihood were analysed in villages of both the districts, by men and women separately. In most villages studied in Faridabad and Varanasi, agriculture is very important. From 60 to 90 per cent of the people in different villages are dependent upon agriculture. It is the principal source of food in all the villages. It provides endowment entitlements or exchange entitlements of food to almost all the households. It is the major employer, in both the districts. It is the major source of fodder, either from straw and residues of foodcrops cultivated or from fodder grown as livestock feed, in all the villages studied. It creates effective demand for a whole range of allied ancillary activities like running barbers shops, petty trade, cart pulling, local transportation, tailoring and daily labour.

Box 7.1
Livelihood Pattern in Faridabad Villages

- **Kadhaoli village**—Agriculture is the main occupation for almost 75 per cent of villagers, though the importance of agriculture is declining over the years.
- **Sagarpur village**—Agriculture is an additional source of income; it is a part time-occupation. Around 95 per cent of villagers are engaged in selling milk and 60 per cent are engaged in agriculture.
- **Uncha Gaon village**—Vegetable cultivation is the principal agricultural activity. There is uncertainty in pursuing agriculture as a livelihood due to recent acquisition of land by Haryana Urban Development Authority.

Source: Based on field reports of PA researchers on Faridabad.

Rearing of milch animals and selling milk is a very popular economic activity in both the districts, in which men and women all participate, with separate roles curved out in which men sell the milk. Most of the animals in Faridabad villages are water buffaloes, whereas in Varanasi, there is a mixture of buffaloes and cows. The quality of milk produced in the two districts is different and they are used for different purposes, generating different income levels.

Women in most of the villages do not work outside their households, but the rigidity is more pronounced in the villages in Faridabad. At least in one of the Varanasi villages, Tikri, women do go out to work outside their village, but they belong to lower castes and that is rare. Women uniformly have the responsibility of cooking, cleaning, collecting or preparing fodder, collecting fuelwood and drinking water, bear and nurse children. The classical dichotomy presented by "inside home" and "outside home" syndromes operate: men are mostly engaged in work outside the households and frequently even outside their village, but women are generally given to work inside their households and village. Even when they migrate out of their village, women and children stay back in the villages to take care of their agricultural land, bullocks and ploughs.

Generally men are the ones who take household produce for sale, either in the Mandis, nearby towns or within the villages themselves.

Box 7.2
Livelihood Pattern in Varanasi Villages

- **Tikri**—Agriculture is the primary occupation for 90 per cent of the population, in which both young and old are engaged. Apart from agriculture, some educated youth are employed in the local university while many work as wage labourers. Among the land-owning classes of Tikri, very from older generation are engaged in agriculture, while others have leased-out their land and are either in business or in service.
- **Chandpur**—In Chandpur, main livelihood activities consist of agriculture, livestock, service and wage labour. Role of agriculture is limited since the proportion of cultivable land has declined and people have diversified their livelihood from agriculture to services in both private and government (around 7 per cent of total villagers engaged).

Villagers in most of the villages have multiple occupations, particularly men. The range of occupations, outside of agriculture and allied activities, in which people are engaged, is wide, in both Faridabad and Varanasi but farming, livestock rearing, milk selling and working as agricultural labourer, constitute the core occupations. The difference is that the sources of other secondary occupation are different in the two districts. In case of Varanasi, the secondary occupations are more in the service sector and in self-employment ventures in unskilled sectors like running grocery shops, retailing, plying auto-rickshaw and vegetable vending. Whereas in the case of Faridabad, secondary occupations are predominantly in the defense services, police force, government offices, private sector establishments and in skilled or semi skilled sectors. The secondary occupations of the people in the two districts also reflect the huge differences in cultural traits of the inhabitants. Whereas the Haryanvis, particularly the Jats of Haryana, are known for their ruggedness, valour and gallantry and enterprise, the people of Varanasi are religious, docile, quiet, risk-averse and more attached to their home and hearth.

Box 7.3

Comparative Livelihood Pattern in Varanasi and Faridabad

Livelihood in Varanasi	*Livelihood in Faridabad*
Farming	Cultivation of land
Working as agricultural labourer	Livestock rearing
Raising livestock	Selling milk
Selling milk	Working as agricultural labourer
Service sector workers	Government service
Masonry work	Private service
Shop keeping	Military service
TV repairing	Police service
Electric repairing	Goldsmithy
Tailoring	Running shops
Stitching	Carpenters
Tractor lending	Weavers
	Barbers

III. 2. Changing Role of Agriculture

The composition of the farming community in Varanasi is different from that of the farming community in Faridabad. In Varanasi there is considerable influence of caste in the farming community, in as much as some landowning castes do not cultivate their own land. They lease-out their lands to lower caste people for cultivation. For instance the landowning Brahmin and the Bhumiars. There is, therefore, a high incidence of tenancy in Varanasi. Since law prohibits tenancy in Uttar Pradesh, most of such tenants are concealed. In Faridabad on the other hand, there is no such trend. There are only class difference designated by size of land holdings. There is absence of tenants. The landowners are also cultivators.

The practice of agriculture in the two districts, mirror a broad similarity but there are basic differences. In the case of Varanasi, the impact of the

Green Revolution is a later phenomenon and has just about caught on. In Faridabad villages, the Green Revolution is present in its full-blown form and they are probably entering the "yellowing phase of the Green Revolution". In both the places, agriculture has become high external input agriculture, moreso in Faridabad. The cost of cultivation has also increased in both the districts but it is much more perceptible in Faridabad. Faridabad villages have also experimented with the "Yellow Revolution" (cultivation of mustard) with disastrous consequences but none of it is seen in Varanasi villages (may be again reflecting risk averseness). There is a shift towards cash crops in both the districts but the move is distinctly visible and more down the road in the villages in Faridabad.

In all the villages, the position of agriculture as a means of livelihoods, with all its merits and contribution to community life, is on the decline. In Varanasi and Faridabad, the principal reasons for this phenomenon are increasing constraints, rising costs and greater risks involved in farming; alternative employment opportunities have become available in manufacturing and service sector, and acquisition of agricultural land for non-agricultural purposes, such as construction of houses, industrial and commercial establishments. In Faridabad villages, fragmentation of land due to land-man ratio deteriorating and reluctance on the part of the present generation to soil their hands are additional reasons why acceptability of agriculture as a source of livelihood is on the decline.

There is a clear difference in the approach to agriculture between the older generation of farmers and the younger generation *per se* in Faridabad. The young villagers in Faridabad, who are educated (the literacy rate in the villages is as high as 90 per cent in some cases), the costs and labour and boredom involved in farming is not worth the cause. They perceive agriculture more from a commercial perspective than anything else. The older generation perceive agriculture as a link between land, livestock, family life and quality of life. To the older generation and women, agriculture provides food, fodder and fuel; land under agriculture is a potential collateral to raise loans; agriculture is a source of employment, for the landless and women; it is a source of income from the sale of cash crops and vegetables. They also see agriculture as a possible hedge against unemployment of their children. This difference in inter-generational perspectives is not there in Varanasi, possibly because the level of industrialisation in and around the Varanasi villages and literacy levels (around 52 per cent) are much lower.

Box 7.4
Reasons for Decline in Agriculture in Faridabad and Varanasi

Varanasi	*Faridabad*
Increasing constraints (power shortage, no extension)	Increasing constraints (power shortage, no extension)
More pests	New pests
More insects	New insects
More weeds	New weeds
More risks (erratic and uneven rainfall, new diseases)	More Risks (erratic and uneven rainfall, sudden climatic change)
Alternative employment available	Alternative employment available
Conversion of agricultural land for construction	Conversion of agricultural land for industrial and construction purposes
Increasing costs and falling returns	New diseases
	Fragmentation of land
	Younger generation unwilling to soil hands
	Falling returns

III. 3. Farming Practices

Throughout the villages farming practices have changed. There are three agricultural seasons in Faridabad, namely, Kharif (Monsoon), Rabi (Summer) and Jayad (Winter). In Varanasi there are only two cultivation seasons, namely, Kharif and Rabi.

Box 7.5.
Cropping Pattern and Crops Grown in Varanasi and Faridabad

Varanasi		Faridabad		
Kharif	*Rabi*	*Kharif*	*Rabi*	*Jiyad*
Paddy (main crop)	Wheat (main crop)	Jowar (main crop)	Wheat (main crop)	
Maize	Radish	Paddy	Vegetables*	
Jowar	Cauliflower	Vegetables*		
Arhar	Peas			
Cauliflower	Potaoes/onion/garlic			
Brinjals	Jowar			
	Methi (fenugreek)			

*These include spinach, cabbage, cauliflower, onion, bottle gourd, bitter gourd, snake gourd, brinjal, lady's finger, fenugreek, coriander, radish etc.

In Varanasi villages, the main crops are paddy in Kharif and wheat in Rabi, with land under wheat considerably less than land under paddy. Kharif is the principal cultivating season. In case of villages in Faridabad, the situation is reverse: Rabi is the principal cultivating season and wheat is the principal crop, grown for consumption. Paddy is cultivated only on a small portion of cultivable land during Kharif, jowar for fodder being the main Kharif crop. Vegetables are grown in a big way throughout the year mainly as a cash crop. Livestock rearing and milk vending being a very important activity for the Faridabad farmers and they grow jowar as fodder as their main crop.

Improved *irrigation* has played a significant role in both the districts in influencing the cropping pattern. Whereas in Varanasi, with improved, though deficient, irrigation facilities, farmers have substituted growing millets by paddy and wheat, in Faridabad villages, with better irrigation, farmers have abandoned growing grams and other coarse grains, in favour of vegetable cultivation. Similarly, changing over from manure in favour of chemical fertilisers for replenishing soil nutrients has also impacted upon crops grown. Because of chemical fertilisers, land in Varanasi can no longer support cultivation of barley and gram. According to the farmers in

Faridabad, due to use of fertilisers (and pesticides), soil conditions have deteriorated. These changes in cropping pattern have their impact on food security, which we will discuss separately.

The intensity of cultivation is high. In both places there is the system of multiple cropping. For instance, during Rabi season (from Aghan to Baisakh) in some of the villages of Varanasi early varieties of vegetables are grown. Once these are harvested for sale in the market, wheat is cultivated for household consumption. Over the years the number of crops grown has declined very considerably.

III. 4. Seasonality of Activities.

Amidst all the fury of living lives under non-optimal conditions, there is a pattern in the lifestyles of farmers in Varanasi and Faridabad. There is drudgery and hard work but variations as well which may be one of the contributory factors leading to their staunch perseverance. The seasonality of activity in the two districts is shown in Box 7.6.

Information from Box 7.6 paints a landscape where the farmers seem to be very busy. They are engaged in some form of agricultural activity or the other in every month: ploughing, preparing land, manuring/fertilising, irrigating, sowing, harvesting, and threshing, selling etc. These are all true for the farmers of Varanasi and Faridabad. These activities do not however, keep the farming households busy on all the days of each month, particularly where we are dealing with small and marginal farmers predominantly. They are in their fields on some days, which allows them to either work in government, public sector and private sector establishments and come home to cultivate on the days they are needed, or they take up secondary employment when not working in their fields.

And within these months there are differences in the intensity and pace of the activities. For Varanasi, the principal agricultural season is Kharif and the principal crop is paddy (wheat being a relatively minor crop). Hence farmers are extremely busy during the months from Jeth to Ashar (cultivation and post-cultivation activities) and then again in Kuar and Katak (harvesting and post-harvesting efforts). For Faridabad, on the other hand, the principal season is Rabi and the principal crop is wheat, not paddy (indeed paddy is a very minor crop for farmers in Faridabad). The farmers in Faridabad villages enjoy a rather lean period from Ashar to Bhado, but start having a gruelling time from Katak when wheat cultivation starts, till Chet-Baisakh, when wheat is harvested. Thus both the principal cultivation season and the principal crops are different for Varanasi and Faridabad. From this it follows, that the nature of the agricultural operations are different for the farmers in the villages in the two districts: for farmers in Faridabad, a lot of effort and resources are expended in irrigation for wheat cultivation, because it is an irrigation-intensive crop. But farmers in Varanasi, the principal crop is rainfed and though there is some irrigation, it is limited. A reference to the activities in Columns 2 and 3 of Box 7.6 is invited.

A noticeable difference is that vegetable cultivation occupies a small space in the life of the Varanasi farmers; it is catching on. But for farmers in Faridabad, they are into vegetable cultivation in a big way and both in range and frequency of vegetable cultivation they are further down the road than the Varanasi farmers. The rapid growth of Haryana's economy and the pace of industrialisation in Ballabgarh have created an environment conducive to vegetable cultivation. Vegetable cultivation is also extremely labour intensive and therefore, leaves little time for the farmers in Faridabad for leisure and recreation. Indeed, some Faridabad villagers indicated their preference for cultivating wheat to vegetable, for the one reason that the latter required a lot of labour and personal attention of the farmers.

Box 7.6.
Activities Related to Agriculture: A Comparative Picture

Month	Agricultural Activity-Varanasi	Agricultural Activity-Faridabad
Jeth-Asar (15 May-15 July)	Sowing and transplanting paddy, harvesting and selling vegetables; harvesting and threshing of wheat, and selling surplus; sowing jimikand,	Preparing land, sowing jowar, bajra, paddy, moong, etc; irrigating vegetable fields; selling vegetables

	turmeric, pigeon peas, bajrar, some vegetables, and moong; jimikand is harvested and fields cleared	
Sawan (15 July-15 August)	Vegetable, maize and paddy are cultivated, paddy transplantation continues, deweeding of paddy fields, sowing soya, maize, moong and jowar, and vegetables	Deweeding fields, arranging fodder (women), sowing of dhencha, cutting of jowar, preparing seedlings, irrigating land, if there is no rain, applying pesticides and fertilisers, transplanting and sowing paddy, planting of vegetables, selling vegetables, spraying "medicine" for locusts, deweeding fields
Bhado (15 Aug-15 Sept)	Deweeding paddy fields, fertiliser application planting of paddy saplings, sowing cauliflower, bajrar and mustard, harvesting maize	Irrigating paddy and jowar fields, cutting leaves for fodder, planting vegetables, harvesting jowar and
Kuwar-Katak (15 Sept-15 Nov)	Ploughing, sowing vegetables, pea, and gram, harvesting bajra and paddy, harvesting and selling vegetables, harvesting moong (in Kuwar,), maize and jowar, in kartick, ploughing fields for next season	harvesting, stocking seeds, preparing land, irrigating and manuring field, sowing wheat and other minor crops, cutting for fodder, sowing and planting vegetables, harvesting bajra in Kuwar and drying it for 3-4 days
Aghan-Pus-Mah-Phagun (15 Nov-15 March)	Harvesting of paddy (and threshing, parboiling, pounding and dehusking of paddy), mustard and pigeon pea. Sowing	Irrigating wheat fields several times and spraying of fertilizers, in Aghan, sowing crops

	vegetables, grams, peas, wheat, sugarcane and melons. Ploughing field several times, applying fertilisers, irrigating fields with vegetables and wheat, preparing field for sowing potato, tilling of potato fields and second round of irrigation, second round of irrigation, deweeding and application of urea for wheat, harvesting and washing vegetables	and vegetables. Irrigating vegetable fields, applying fertilisers, harvesting and selling vegetables and deweeding wheat field, collecting grass and barsan leaves for fodder, harvesting of mustard, small farmers extract oil from mustard, collecting seeds for further processing,
Chet-Baisakh (15 March-15 May)	Mainly spinach and *ninwa* together with other vegetables like gourd, radish, etc. are sown, wheat and tomatoes are harvested; fertiliser application, threshing of wheat begins, winter vegetables, grams, mustard and pigeon pea are harvested, tilling takes place in onion fields; 2-3 rounds of irrigation applied	harvesting, threshing, storing, drying and selling wheat, collecting fodder, irrigating fields, selling vegetables, cutting of barsan and white jai for fodder, in Chet, preparing field for kharif crop; tilling, ploughing, manuring and irrigating fields

Notes: (i) This is a general seasonal calendar as described by women groups and men groups from selected villages of Varanasi and Faridabad. Not all households of all the villages are engaged in all activities mentioned above.

(ii) There are different crops and vegetables sown in different villages and the above table provides a general picture of the agricultural activities undertaken in the villages of Varanasi and Faridabad, under study. For village-specific activity see field results related to the villages.

(iii) Information Source: Field reports of PA researchers on Faridabad and the Draft Interim Project Report on "Impact of Air Pollution on Agriculture in Urban and Peri-Urban Areas".

(iv) The data included in the Box do not include purchase of inputs and marketing of outputs (at least not in most of the cases). Ancillary activities like tending the buffaloes/oxen for the plough and maintenance of agricultural implements have not been shown.

The seasonal activities also indicate that women in Faridabad and Varanasi have different activity sets. For Varanasi, the months of Ashar and Sawan, are for paddy transplantation. In the post harvest period in Aghan-Pus-Mah-Fagun, women put in a lot of effort in harvesting paddy, threshing, winnowing, parboiling, dehusking and pounding paddy. For the women in Faridabad, these activities are on a low key. Their post harvest activities in Chet-Baisakh is threshing and grinding wheat, though with the advent of aata chakki (flour mill) the last activity has become lesser arduous. Deweeding and helping in irrigation, and preparing fodder for the households animals are additional agricultural tasks handled by women.

IV. Constraints to Agriculture and Coping Strategies

IV. 1. Constraints

Agriculture faces a large number of constraints. The constraints can be variously categorised. For Varanasi and Faridabad, we have categorised these in terms of problem clusters. Thus for Varanasi, the constraints are: (i) weather related, (ii) weed related, (iii) pest and insect related, (iv) animal related, (v) pollution related, (vi) disease related, (vii) land and external input related, (viii) water related, (ix) infrastructure and credit related and (x) institutional arrangement related. In Faridabad the constraints can be categorised as falling under: (i) weather condition related, (ii) weed related, (iii) pest and insect related, (iv) disease, (v) pollution related, (vi) animal related (viii) infrastructure, (ix) external input and output related. The details are given in Boxes 7.7 and 7.8.

Several features of the constraints in both the districts are noticeable. They warrant a few comments. First, the number of weeds in Faridabad are far more than the number of weed related problems of Varanasi villages, though the number of pests and insects are about the same in the villages of the districts. The number of diseases affecting farming in Faridabad villages in lower than the number of diseases affecting farmers in Varanasi. It is possible that higher doses and higher frequency of insecticides and pesticides applications in Faridabad villages may have kept at bay diseases but in the process have also destroyed insects and plants which naturally keep weeds under check. In Varanasi, lesser number of pesticides and insecticides application have allowed insects and plants that keep a check on weeds, to survive but in the process the farmers have lost out in contending with a larger number of diseases. This requires further examination. Second in almost all the villages, the use of external inputs have risen though more in Faridabad villages than in Varanasi villages, where "modern methods" co-exists with semi-traditional methods of cultivation. In all the villages constraints are posed by external inputs, but with a difference. In case of Faridabad villages, the external input related constraints relate more to high costs involved, non-availability, or non-availability in time, of the inputs, while in case of Varanasi villages the external related constraints relate additionally to poor quality, spuriousness and adulterated external inputs. The difference in literacy levels and difference in availability of extension services (howsoever poor), have something to do with this variation in the nature of the constraints posed by external inputs. Third, in all the villages, pollution of different kinds—air and water pollution as also pollution caused by use of chemical fertilisers/pesticides/insecticides—are perceived as damaging crops. The impact of air pollution is more evident in Faridabad villages than in the Varanasi villages. Probably the higher level of industrialisation in areas around the Faridabad villages than in areas in the vicinity of the Varanasi villages offer some explanation for this difference. Fourth, in villages in both the districts, there are constraints imposed by state policies, which are matters that lie in the domain of public action. Supplying power to agriculture for free may be good but the uncertainty of power supply has done more damage to crops than the good done by the provision of free supply. Similarly, acquisition of land from farmers for different non-agricultural purposes has made inroads into agricultural production and injected elements of uncertainty in farmers' mind, which is detrimental to higher productivity. Finally, when men and women have separately ranked the constraints in the two sets of villages, the perception of both men and women are about the same in Varanasi. But in case of Faridabad villages, there are considerable divergences in perception on the constraints. Men rank constraints to agriculture on account of infrastructure and external input related problems as their "best set of problems", women rank constraints posed by weeds and pests as their greatest problems. Generally though there is a broad agreement and views of both women and men groups of villages in Faridabad and Varanasi are found to more or less converge in identifying infrastructure and external input-related set of problems as one of the priority set of problems.

Villagers everywhere find it difficult to cope with bureaucratic inefficiency and lackadaisical attitude, particularly so, of the extension department and state support system. Sadly enough, such problems have intensified over the years, adding to the worries of the farmers. In consequence all over the two districts, production and livelihoods, returns from and cost of farming, both direct and indirect, have all gone from bad to worse for the farmers, who are at the riskiest end of agricultural production. The second prioritised set of problems for women groups relate to crop disease and the adverse impact of pollution. Problem of crop disease is third in priority for men. Farmers have to cope with a variety of crop diseases, some of which are relatively new while others, which are prevalent since long years. The constraints posed by animal related problems are similarly viewed in all the villages of Varanasi and Faridabad: nilgais, stray cows and buffaloes are as much a problem in Varanasi as they are in Faridabad.

Box 7.7
Constraints in Agriculture, by Problem-Clusters in Varanasi Villages

- **Weather condition related problems**: Hailstorm, frost, dry wind and fog; recurring flood; insufficient, uneven, unseasonal and erratic rainfall; crops getting damaged due to weather fluctuations.
- **Weed related problem**: Crops damage by *genhu ka mama*.
- **Pest and insect-related problems**: Too many pests; pests attack at the flowering stage; pest attack in paddy; attack by different pests like *katui, tikuli, macchi* (pest fly), *bhurila* (hairy caterpillar).
- **Animal related problems**: Crops grazed and damaged by nilgais and stray livestock and rats.
- **Pollution related problems**: Fields damaged by polluted water from factory; decrease in level of fruit production; yellowing of wheat crop; lemon trees do not bear fruits for many years; smoke as pollution.

- **Diseases**: Incidence of agricultural disease on the rise in the last 4 years; lack of treatment. Crop diseases like *safra, hardwa, gurchawa, jhulsa, oktwa, tunki, angarwa* etc. damage crops; disease in arhar and paddy are specially mentioned.
- **Water related problems**: Inadequate irrigation facility and high cost of irrigation at times leading to lands lying fallow; lack of tube well; forced to fetch drinking water from a distance; no tube well installed by the government; reservoir of water getting contaminated.
- **Land and External Input related problems**: Small size of cultivable land; cultivable land far from home; constraint of land ceiling act; high cost of share cropping; constraint of scattered land; lack of animals/tractors for ploughing; shortage of electricity; high costs of seeds and fertilisers; supply of poor quality and adulterated fertilisers and pesticides; non-availability of good quality seeds; high price of fertilisers and seeds; non-availability of insecticides/seeds in time forces farmers to buy them at higher price; problem of getting insecticide and seeds at right price; seeds of potato and onion were very costly; shortage of wage labourers and heavy workload.
- **Infrastructure and credit related problems**: Improper roads cause difficulty in transporting fruits/vegetables; non-availability of agricultural loan and crop credit in time; acute shortage of credit and cash; complex process of getting loans; absence of institutional facility for getting loan; high cost of loan; lack of knowledge of scientific cultivation; lack of knowledge of proper selection and use of seed; absence of agriculture-related training and extension services.
- **Organisational arrangement related problems**: Communication gap between villagers and officials; local cooperative centre closed down due to corruption and bankruptcy; officials related to village institutions corrupt; no service delivery of Kisan Sewa Bank; prices of farmers' produce not decided by farmers: they are price takers.

Box 7.8

Constraints in Agriculture by Problem-Clusters in Faridabad Villages

Weather Condition-related: hailstorm damages all crops and its maximum damage is to crops in their infant stage; unseasonal and heavy rain accelerates the growth of weeds amongst crops like wheat, mustard, jowar and bajrar at any stage; excess rain damages the standing crops; lightning damages mustard flower.
Weed-related: *Sati*, a variety of local grass, arrests the growth of jowar, arhar, vegetables and paddy. It originates from fertiliser use and is mostly active at the infant stage of the crop. It competes with the crop for nutrients and absorbs all the fertilisers. There is a rise in incidence of *sati* during the last 10-12 years. However, if it rains before the crop grows then *sati* dies and has minimal impact. Uprooting the weed is quite difficult; it is used as fodder. *katoll* affects wheat crop and stunts its growth; it is quite difficult to uproot. It is used as fodder and does not create health problem. *Bhatua*-stunts the growth of wheat at any stage. Congress grass/*gajar grass* (parthenium) stunts the growth of crops like wheat, jowar, bajrar, arhar and mustard. It can occur at any stage and it grows faster than the crop and turns into bushes. *Congress grass* creates smell and allergy and can lead to respiratory problems. It grows throughout the year and affects all the crops. It can host a number of poisonous insects in its bush. For the last ten years it has become rampant; once uprooted it re-grows quickly. Incidence of *safed moondi* has increased in recent years and it affects wheat by competing with crop for nutrients mostly at the infant stage. Incidence of *rani jai* has increased over last 8 years, which stunts the growth of wheat mostly at the infant stage and it has to be uprooted at regular intervals to protect the crop. Like *safed moondi*, it competes with wheat crop for nutrient. *mundi, gehun ka mama,* are commonly found in wheat fields and have close resemblance to wheat crop. They sucks the nutrients from the field and overpowers wheat crop and can lead to massive loss in crop yield. The local view is that such grass came with hybrid Mexican seed of wheat. There are no effective measures available against parthenium (congress grass in all fields), *rani jai* (in wheat), *sati* (more in millets); *safed moondi* (in wheat) etc.
Pest and insect related: *Chepa* occurs naturally and damages crops like mustard and bajrar, mostly at the youth stage; leaves of the crops becomes sticky and dries; covers and eats the mustard flower and dries the flower. *Sundi* pest sticks to the leaves of paddy and sucks the juice out of it. *Kanduwa* attacks matured wheat. *Geddar* attacks young vegetables. *Lairri* eats the

leaves of vegetables. *Locust* attack has increased over the last 3-5 years (first seen 4 years back) in Kharif season. They eat leaves of jowar, bajrar and dhencha crops at their growing stage. Aided by dry weather, *termite* eats up roots of wheat, jowar and bajrar. *Other small insects* of different varieties are found at the root, on the leaves, stem, twigs of crops, some of which eat away tender leaves, flowers and thus prevents grain formation. Their incidence has increased over the last ten years, which is attributed to growing use of fertilisers, high yielding seeds and cropping patterns leading to loss in crop diversity.

Pollution related: Yellowing of leaves is a common occurrence in vegetables and wheat, a disease noticeable in the last 10 to 20 years, leading to premature drying of plant, adversely affecting crop growth. Incidence of such disease is attributed to factors like smoke and dust from near-by factories, use of chemical fertilisers and pesticides in large quantities. Curling of leaf (blight), affects potato, chili and brinjal. It leads to twisting of leaf and affects yield. It is commonly prevalent in crops grown with improved variety of seeds.

Disease related: Blast disease affects paddy, especially musthar basmati. When crops are affected by this disease different parts of the plant dry up and crop gets destroyed. Local people fear that the disease can spread to other crops. Leprosy affects sugarcane at its joints and dries up the plant. This disease occurs in improved variety of sugarcane. Smoke from nearby thermocol factory gets deposited on the vegetables like cauliflower, spinach etc.

Animal-related problem: Nilgais, an endangered species of deer protected under wild life protection, move in herds of 10 to 15, destroying crops of jowar, bajrar, wheat and mustard by grazing, trampling and sitting on them. They enter the mustard field the mostly in winter, for it makes them feel warm. They also destroy the flower and premature crops of lintel, peas and sugarcane. This has made some farmers to stop growing these crops. They attack more when the crops mature. Wheat crop is hard for them to consume and thus are spared of their attack. Field rat is generally problematic for wheat and paddy; eat grains and bores holes in the fields. Rats can attack the crop at any stage.

Infrastructure related: Because of erratic supply of electricity, tube wells cannot be operated for irrigation and farmers are unable to irrigate land; they are forced to depend on rain and tractors for irrigation. Water has turned hard in the past 5 years, which leads to crop getting wasted. Hardness of water has increased due to boring of electric polls by national thermal power corporation 4-5 years back. Acquisition of agricultural land by HUDA is impacting on their livelihood.

External Input and Output related: Ground water level is falling rapidly. There is little or no water in government canal; farmers are using water from sewage canal. Fertilisers are not released in time by the government and hence problem of crops not getting nutrients in time. Non-availability of good quality seeds in time; high prices of input and low selling prices of outputs; the cold winter nights and thick fog posing problems in irrigating fields, are the other constraints.

Box 7.9

Prioritised Problem Indices (PPIs) of Agricultural Constraints/Problems

Problem/Constraint Criteria	**Faridabad** *Rank by Women*	*Rank by Men*	**Varanasi** *Rank by Women*	*Rank by Men*
1. Weather/climate and natural resource conditions-related	3	6	5	5
2. Weed-related	2	3	7	6
3. Pest and insect-related	1	2	3	2
4. Animal-related	4	4	4	4
5. Disease and pollution-related	6	5	2	3
6. Infrastructure/external input-related	5	1	1	1
7. Organization-related	-	7	6	7

Then there are differences in how the farmers perceive the constraints in Varanasi from how farmers perceive problems in Faridabad. Of the set of 7 constraints ranked, organisational related problems posing constraints are ranked low down on the priority list of constraints by almost all the groups, and almost all groups consider that infrastructure/external input related problems presenting the most important set of constraints. All groups rank pests and insect related constraints as a very important set of constraints as well. That is, in villages everywhere have similar perception about the boundary set of constraints. There are differences in perception with regard to the remaining intervening constraints.

It must be mentioned that the constraints faced by the villagers in the villages in Faridabad and Varanasi, have a seasonal character and not all the constraints afflict the villages all round the year. For instance, power shortage, creating problems in irrigating fields, impact on farming throughout the year. Pest and insects appear only during seasons when individual pests and insects thrive. Unseasonal rains come in Cheth and Baisakh and they are therefore to be tackled only during these months.

IV. 2. Coping Strategies

How do our villagers in Varanasi and Faridabad cope with the volley of constraints to which their principal livelihood is subject? How interesting that in both the districts, the coping strategies of the farmers remain almost the same as would perhaps be in all similar rural areas in India. They were rational and villagers have attempted to sort out the problems which, they can sort out at their level, through personal effort. These included substituting or avoiding crops like chickpeas, sugarcane and lentils, certain kinds of vegetables, and cash crops like mustard, which are vulnerable to pests, weeds and disease; fencing and guarding fields to ward off nilgais and stray animals; poisoning rats; a tendency or inclination to move out of agriculture; selling off agricultural lands and migrating to other areas; hunting for supplementary sources of income to finance high cost agriculture and/or hedge against crop failures; application of pesticides and "medicines" based on experimentation of fellow farmers and advice from dealers and even hiring generators for ensuring power supply at times when irrigation is needed.

Everywhere farmers perceive and recognise the importance of the state as manifested in the block development officer, the agriculture department, electricity department, panchayat pradhan, seed farms and even the minister in one case. They are aware of the support that their agriculture can receive to their overall wellbeing, but they lament that these institutions are either non-existent or non-functional. They are in some cases too far removed from the psyche of the farmers for them to even think of approaching them. Some farmers have tried to bring to the notice of these support institutions/ departments, their problems but to little avail. There is no forum to listen to their complaint, like the consumers redressal forum or the forum for listening to problems of bank customers and even insurance policy holders. The insensitivity of the support institutions and government functionaries to the problems of the farmers comes out quite convincingly. As a result, in many cases, farmers rely more as the next best alternative, on the traditional support structures like the village money lender, the shopkeeper who sells insecticides and pesticides, the seed supplier and the like, despite the knowledge that they often get spurious and adulterated inputs. The support that farmers get from these sources may be at exorbitant costs (nominal and real) but they are reliable in terms of their timing and flow of supply.

V. Impact of Air Pollution

Different kinds of pollutants are present in Varanasi and Faridabad as described by the local village communities. Such pollutants are basically air and water.

Air-pollution is linked to industrial estate in near-by towns of Ballavgarh and Faridabad for villages in Faridabad, vehicular-related, local factory-related. Ballavgarh and Faridabad industrial belts are close to the villages and the smoke and different pollutants from the factories pollute the air and settle on crops and affect crop yield. The air pollution has increased due to considerable increase in the number of vehicles in that area over the last 20 years. This has led to smoke and dust in the air; it has also affected crop production. Pollution through local factories and industrial units like those of brick kilns, thermocol, plastic and cement pipe factories have affected crops and health of both human beings and animals. Box 7.10 is a summary of the perception of villagers about air pollution and its perceived impact on agriculture.

Though not related to air pollution yet given the importance of the pollutant, contaminated water from industrial units, found in some villages is perceived to have negatively affected crops, health of human beings and animals.

The women and men groups in Varanasi villages described the sources of local pollution as industrial estate, industrial units, domestic coal stoves, garbage and vehicular pollution. The women and men groups are aware of selected impacts of air pollution upon village communities, as shown in Box 7.11. In general, the villagers relate the direct impact of air pollution on their health and less so on crops and agricultural production, unless it is an impact of pollution quite close to their field, like the ones caused by brick kiln near-by. Scientifically, though there is evidence of one to one relations between certain pollutants and certain kinds of disease, weeds, pest attacks adversely impacting on crop yield and growth, the village communities have different perspective in this regard. The participatory appraisal researchers have observed that the incidence of pest, insect and weed are noticed more in those villages, which are situated in the ozone pollutant zone, where dependence of people on farming is greater than on other means of livelihoods.

On the whole, the sources of and impact of air pollution are perceived more in the villages of Faridabad than in the villages of Varanasi. There could be several reasons for this, including higher industrialisation in areas around and in the vicinity of Faridabad villages, more green cover and natural vegetation, and the overall level of awareness, consequent upon higher literacy rates of the villagers. It is also to be underscored that though there has been general agreement on the pollutants and their impact, in some cases perceptions did vary and there apparently was no reconciliation.

Box 7.10
Pollution—Sources and Impacts in Faridabad

Village	*Pollutants and their Effects*
Khadaoli	1. The fumes emitted from the factory mixed with due in winter, especially in January and February falls on wheat and gets deposited. In years when this continues for a month the size of wheat grain reduces, which affects its price.
	2. Water becomes hard due to pollution.
	3. Wastes from the acid factory thrown into the adjoining canal burns crops in the nearby field and affects fertility of the soil.
Sagarpur	1. Length of wheat crops has shortened. There is also less number of grains per wheat crop, which are relatively thin. This is because dust from brick kiln falls on the crop.
Uncha Gaon	1. Black deposit (assumed to come from local thermocol factory) falls on cauliflower and spinach, which is more prominent during winter. This leads to the cauliflower turning creamish and the spinach turning blackish. The taste becomes salty.
	2. Tomatoes were also turning blackish though not resulting in financial loss.
	3. Flowers of brinjal, tomato and chili get wasted when the ashes along with smoke fall on them.
	4. As per men group, moriya disease in chili is assumed to be due to some pollution in the air. The water also turns black when kept overnight.

Note: As described by women groups and men groups from selected villages of Faridabad

Source: Based on field reports on Faridabad by PA Researchers

VI. Institutional Issues

We have already detailed the institutional issues while discussing the constraints, suffice it to say for the present that a lot needs to be done.

In Varanasi, dysfunctional or non-existent institutional facility for supply of credit; lack of support mechanisms for imparting knowledge of scientific cultivation; lack of knowledge of proper selection and use of seeds; absence of agriculture-related training and extension services, are serious problems. Communication gap between villagers and officials; closing down of the local institutions such as the cooperative centre in one village, due to corruption and bankruptcy are some of the institutional problems farmers face. The absence of any institutional mechanism to ensure that farmers get a fair price, is a big institutional problem. In Faridabad, acquisition of agricultural land by Haryana urban development authority and absence of water in government canal are complex issues. For instance, lack of water in government canal has forced farmers to using water from sewage canal. This means that lack of canal water is tantamount to directly channeling pollutants into otherwise fertile cultivable land of farmers, for entirely avoidable reasons. Fertilisers are not released in time by the government and hence crops do not get nutrients when at the right time. Supply of fertilisers is not a problem. Demand for fertilisers exists. There is need to have a bit of co-ordination, driven by institutions and systems, not people. Similarly non-availability of good quality seeds is no mean problem that can be easily rectified by simple changes in institutions.

At present the existing support system is clearly not that responsive. There are no NGOs working in the villages at present and community-based organizations like local panchayat are not that effective. The villagers of Kadhaoli actually complained that lower level of awareness amongst the villagers about pollution and low level of literacy, is partly due to the absence of any NGO. The Sub-Divisional Agriculture Office at Ballavgarh caters to 192 villages. Visits of extension officials are not regular and do not help in solving local problems. Visits of officials from other relevant departments are few, which benefit generally the well to do farmers who have some clout, while others remain unaware of such visits. Indifferent attitude of the local state departments related to agriculture is a major stumbling block. Irregular supply of fertilisers and pesticides results in crop loss. Credit agencies also do not respond adequately to farmers' needs.

Box 7.11

Pollution: Sources and Impacts in Varanasi

Village	Pollutants and their Effects
Chandpur,	1. In Chandpur, though the brick kilns have closed, fruit production has dropped and soil is damaged. 2. Chemical effluent, in the form of wastewater from industrial estate and saree printing units, has turned 10 bighas of land barren. 3. The villagers are aware of the adverse effects of emissions from the brick kiln (Chandpur village) on mango (blackening in colour, lessening of its sweetness etc.), on papaya (lessening of its sweetness) and on neem tree (making the leaves yellowish and weakening its twigs and small branches). 4. There is little or no awareness of the adverse effects of air pollution in the hamlets of Chandpur, possibly because there was no primary pollutant near-by.
Tikri,	1. Villagers reported loss in yield of fruit from the orchard (mango) due to smoke coming from brick kiln. Loss in mango and berry yields due to the deposition of smoke etc. from the brick kiln in the neighbouring villages. 2. Pollution from brick kiln was the only identified source of pollution. 3. Vehicular pollution was not identified as a source of pollutant in villages due to less frequent vehicular traffic in absence of roads, open space and greenery in the villages. 4. Pollution due to garbage was identified as one of the areas of concern in the villages of Tikri. It was reported to be the causal factor for poor health of human and livestock.

Note: As described by women groups and men groups from selected villages of Varanasi

Source: Based on field reports on Varanasi by PA Researchers

It is sad that after expending so much of political effort and resources to amend the constitution to provide for panchayats as the third tier of government, these institutions have not taken roots, either in Varanasi or in Faridabad. And that too even after five years of arduous march on the road. The panchayat samitis in the villages in Varanasi were perceived not fulfilling their duties/responsibilities fully. The village Panchayats apparently could not perform as they received only 60 per cent of the total grant from the government. Most of the villages in the jurisdiction of Panchayat Samities were deprived of the various schemes undertaken by it. People in general felt that the Samities had failed miserably to perform its welfare activities in the areas of providing medicines in wells, conducting immunisation programme, family planning and other related programmes. If it is argued that Panchayat Samities are enjoined to perform any of these functions, it only shows that the people are not even made aware of the roles of Panchayats.

The picture is not very different in Faridabad. For many villages, the local Panchayat is not that effective for lack of funds, and hence authority to take decisions. For instance, there are cases where these institutions were unable to take action, even where formal complaints were lodged with them, against pollutants being released by brick kilns in one case and themocol factory in another. While, probably because of higher literacy levels, the people in Faridabad do not have high expectations of the Panchayats, they do perceive that these important local level institutions operate only at the margin in their scheme of things.

Thus in both Varanasi and Faridabad villages, people look upon Panchctas as important local level institutions. In Varanasi these institutions are seen as not fulfilling their developmental roles; in Faridabad people have negative experience with Panchayats in fulfilling their protective or regulatory roles.

VII. Comparative Picture of Health Status

The health status of the people in the villagers in the two district is compared in Boxes 7.11 and 7.12. In both the districts villagers suffer from a large number of diseases, symptomatic of a situation where health infrastructure is as bad as the institutional arrangement for supporting farming. The common diseases in the villages of Varanasi are coughs and colds, T.B., skin diseases, eye diseases, stomach problems and "enlargement", malaria, jaundice, gastritis, frequent body ache and mild fever among the elderly, asthma, frequent brain fever amongst children, increased incidence of pimples all over body of children, diarrhea, ear disease and pus flowing out of ear amongst children and sores on different parts of the body.

In Faridabad in addition to the diseases mentioned by farmers in Varanasi, villagers mentioned cancer, heart attack, nose burning, headache and dizziness, blood pressure, heart ache, "baye" (arthritis??), pain in appendice, allergy, weakening of eye sight, dengue (incidence for the first time two years back), acidity and pain in stomach, young women have serious cases of leukorria (white discharge), pain in the waist, tooth decay among children and breathing problems.

It is apparent that there are three kinds of health problems in the villages. *One*, diseases that are chronic in nature which, affects large sections of the population irrespective of season; *two*, diseases that are specific and affects only some people, and *three*, diseases which, afflict the general population during certain times of the year, and relate to public health. For example, stomach problems, cough and cold, asthma, body ache and fever, headache, arthritis, weakening of eyesight and sores are general ailments and are chronic in nature. We may categorise them as falling in the first category. Heart attacks, T.B. and problems of blood pressure and such other ailments are people specific, and fall in the second category. Then dengue, diarrhea, malaria, jaundice and brain fever come in spurts and during certain parts of the year to which the entire population is vulnerable, is in the third category. These diseases are matters that lie in the domain of public health. The fact that all three kinds of diseases affect people in our villages points to the need to have preventive health interventions, promotive health interventions and curative health care. While curative health can be left to individual initiative, the need for preventive and promotive health forming the core of health strategy of the government in both the states (and districts) can not be overemphasized.

If the two lists are considered, then it seems that the number of diseases perceived to be present in Faridabad are higher than the number of diseases in Varanasi. Since there is no data on how many people actually suffer from these diseases, we can not conclude either way whether people in one district are healthier than the other.

Villagers' perceptions about the status of health in the two districts are different and they are significant. Farmers in Varanasi articulated the problems of child health better than problems of the general population. While the villagers in both the districts gave a long list of diseases, the Faridabad villagers related the deteriorating health status to industrialisation, which the farmers of Varanasi did not. The villagers of Varanasi emphasized the problems of mal-nutrition amongst children, which was seemingly not an issue in Faridabad, probably because of better food security situation in the latter than in the former. The farmers in Faridabad villages related some of their ailments clearly to increased local emissions, villagers in Varanasi related some of the diseases suffered by them to consumption of foodgrains grown by using chemical fertilisers and pesticides and changes in climatic conditions. This may be partly explained, prima facie, by the fact that the level of industrialisation is higher in and around the area adjoining the villages in Faridabad than in Varanasi. The differences in villagers' perceptions in the two districts are tabulated in Box 7.13.

VIII. Quality of Life

Quality of life is an issue which did not figure on a separate plane of inquiry but every element discussed is interwoven into the fabric of quality of life: pollution, crop yields, health, employment, livelihood and food security. In both Varanasi and Faridabad villages, majority of people felt that the process of local industrialisation has helped them by offering more employment, a larger market for their product and labour, and higher prices for their products such as milk and food grains.

Industrialisation and urbanisation have been perceived as a mixed blessing by the villagers in both Faridabad and Varanasi, despite differences in their respective levels of industrialisation. In the villagers' perception, in the villages in both the districts, though they have derived benefits, the costs of industrialisation have been quite considerable. The women groups were particular, in the Villages of Faridabad, in pointing out the costs of urbanisation and industrialisation.

But the costs were different. For Villagers in Faridabad, the major costs were scarcity of grazing land, loss of village identity, health complications due to pollution, increased cost of living, congestion, decline in the quality of soçial environment and damage to crops. They have also indicated deterioration in the quality of water and actions by Haryana urban development a uthority to acquire land, particularly agricultural land, for non-agricultural purposes, as costs of industrialisation. The major costs perceived by villagers in Varanasi were cultivation of market-driven commercial crops, higher doses of external inputs and high accompanying risks in agriculture and higher pest problems. Migration of men in search of jobs created special problems for women. Increased pollution negatively affecting food and fruit production and falling sanitation standards with industrial waste and higher crime rate, were the other problems for Varanasi.

Box 7.12
Health Issues: Varanasi

Chandpur

- Increased incidence of cough, skin disease, stomach enlargement, and eye disease in children in last 15-20 years.
- Increase in incidence of skin disease, TB, gastric ulcer in adults, especially women.
- In Chandpur, rise in incidence of malaria due to mosquitoes.
- In Chandpur, the women group said that pneumonia had become endemic for the last 7 to 8 years and at least 100 children were affected last year, of which 10 children died.
- In Chandpur, health problems relate to cases of jaundice; gastritis supposedly due to contaminated food; frequent body ache and mild fever among the elderly; asthma; frequent brain fever amongst children; increased incidence of pimples all over body of children; diarrhea; ear disease and pus flowing out of ear amongst children; and nagging cold and cough affecting many villagers.

Tikri

- **Groups from Tikri perceive poor health of the villagers, especially the younger group, because of increased consumption of fertiliser-based crops and poor food intake.**
- **Some villagers of Tikri village thought that TB and asthma were hereditary.**
- **A moderate increase in respiratory problems was reported from Tikri.**
- **In Morya hamlet of Tikri village, health problem related to stomach trouble due to consumption and handling of grains to which insecticides and pesticides have been applied.**
- **In Morya hamlet of Tikri village, some villagers get sores on different parts of the body, such as hand, head, face, stomach, legs etc., reasons for which were attributed to changes in atmospheric temperature and weather.**
- **In Morya hamlet, the participants thought that they were getting weaker due to consumption of food grown with the help of fertilisers and pesticides, lacking in nutrients, unable to provide strength. Consumption of such grains by livestock also led to weakness in livestock; the milk yield of livestock got adversely affected and the quality of milk had low level of nutrients.**

Note: **As described by women groups and men groups from selected villages of Varanasi.**

Source: **Based on field reports on Varanasi by PA Researchers.**

Box 7.13
Health Issues: Faridabad

Villages	Type of Disease/Illness identified
Kadhaoli	• Burning sensation in throat, eyes and nose; pollution causes throat irritation and cough and when ignored results in TB; weakening of eye sight due to fumes from near-by pharmaceutical factory; giddy feeling due to fumes emitted from rubber and pharmaceutical factory.
Sagarpur	• Eyesight getting affected amongst others by brick kiln emissions; rise in cases of TB and cancer; lethargy, greying of hair, breathing problems and fever especially among children.
Uncha Gaon	• There has been increased incidence of burning sensation in the eyes and TB for the last 10-15 years. Air pollution, according to men group, has led to increased incidence of heart attack and cancer. Women attribute increased incidence of breathing problem and coughing due to air pollution. Emissions from rubber and thermocol factory lead to bad odour and feeling of nausea.
	• Men's group felt that the pollution from thermocol factories might be affecting the health of their buffaloes though no visible symptoms have been noticed. The women, however, do not think in similar fashion.

Note: As described by women groups and men groups from selected villages of Faridabad.

Source: Based on field reports on Faridabad by PA Researchers.

Box 7.14

Comparative Status of Health in Faridabad and Varanasi

Health Status in Varanasi (1)	*Health Status in Faridabad* (2)
1. Both women and men groups have listed a number of diseases and illness, which they and their children suffer from, but did not relate them to any phenomenon.	1. The community members are aware of the deteriorating health conditions in recent years with rapid industrialisation at local level.
2. There is increased incidence of cough, respiratory disease, stomach-related disease, skin disease, eye infection, TB and malaria, most of them amongst children.	2. There has been a rise in respiratory diseases, breathlessness, burning sensation of throat, eyes and nose and headache, with higher incidence in winter months and higher pollution.
3. Many children are also victims of nutrition related problems.	3. The health expenses have gone up for local communities since home medicines hardly work. Health of their livestock is also affected by air pollution causing indigestion, diarrhoea and death.
4. The village groups relate the diseases to a mix of factors such as increased use of fertilisers and chemicals in agriculture causing stomach-related disease/illness and respiratory diseases due to change of weather.	4. It was not difficult for many village groups to draw one to one emissions and physical discomfort and illness, which they suffer.
5. However, not many villagers perceive any impact of air pollution causing serious impairment of health.	5. Community perspective on general health status indicates adverse impact of air pollution apart from other common diseases.

IX. Concluding Remarks

Thus in the villages of Faridabad and Varanasi, there are clearly indications that villagers are aware of the ongoing industrialisation, benefits from it and the costs involved. The increase in the number of pollutants, and levels of pollution have been recognised. Their effect has been identified, but it has been linked better with health status of the villagers than with the health of their agriculture. The constraints to agriculture have been identified and they too are perceived as increasing. In general there are similarities in the perception of the villagers about the broad trends both in Faridabad and Varanasi. There are differences, which are space specific and gender specific. These differences have lessons for policy making.

8 A Synthesis of Villager's Perceptions and Conclusions

I. The Setting

This study covered villages in the two states of Uttar Pradesh and Haryana. In Uttar Pradesh, the villages are clustered around the urban agglomeration of Varanasi, and in Haryana, the villages are clustered around the industrial hub of Ballavgarh, in Faridabad, one of the fastest developing urban centres in the country. The villages in Varanasi (being in Eastern Uttar Pradesh) are at the fringes of the Green Revolution belt, while the villages in Faridabad are in heartland of Green Revolution. The two sets of villages offer lot of contrast in terms of culture, attitude, social environment, human capital, economy, ecology and natural resource base. A study of the impact of air pollution on the agriculture in these two sets of villages has, therefore, been a rewarding exercise and has not only generated policy issues but also lessons from "people's participation". We will presently turn to summarise some of these in the paragraphs to follow.

We have divided the discussion into 12 sections. Each section will deal with analysis of people's perception on each of the critical issues examined in this study, namely, livelihood and agroecosystems, farming practices, variations in cost of farming and the transition from ZEIA–LEIA–HEIA, changes in crop diversity, changes in agriculture and food security, constraints to agricultural production, gender equity and gender justice, pollution in relation to industrialisation and urbanisation, impact of pollution on health, coping strategies and finally people's perception of well being. We begin with livelihood.

II. Livelihood and Agro-ecosystems

The livelihood option exercised by a majority of the villagers, within the hierarchy of agroecosystems, is biased in favour of the farming system. If we refer to figure 9, then the livelihood of a minority, may be a significant minority, of the people who fall under off-farm employment and trading. There is none of gathering/hunting and handicraft/manufacture systems. Within the farming system, the dependence is more on the cropping system than on the livestock system. And within the livestock system, they are confined to the paddock system only (there being no herdsmen). Thus in operational terms most of our village folks are either into growing crops or into raising herds of milch animals and selling milk. Amongst the villages studied, some villages like the 3 villages of Kadhaoli, Sagarpur and Uncha Gaon from Haryana and Chandpur from Uttar Pradesh are m^ deeply involved in the farming system, than other villages. But nearly everywhere, agriculture is a critical livelihood, irrespective of whether farmers have a secondary source of income, or agriculture partakes the nature of a secondary source of income, or not. Agriculture is carried out on land handed down from one generation to another as bequest.

In Uttar Pradesh, villagers are too poor to buy land; in Haryana the market for land has flourished, with the prosperity ushered by Green Revolution and the rapid urbanisation/industrialisation of the areas in the vicinity of the villages, such as around Kadhaoli, Sagarpur and Uncha Gaon. Land prices have shot up and they are high enough, to induce villagers to sell off their land and emigrate to the neighbouring Uttar Pradesh, where with the same resources they believe, they would be able to acquire larger plots of land and afford bigger farms. In the villages under study there is virtually no land, which the present day cultivators have purchased. With the flux of time, and with the dismantling of the joint family system and growth in population, the villagers pointed out, the land-man ratio has deteriorated. The pressure on inherited land which they till are on the rise, resulting in a steady decrease in size of landholdings and small size of farming plots. This with the high cost of cultivation has disillusioned the farmers with farming: in most of the villages, the villagers displayed a clear loss of interest in pursuing agriculture as a means of livelihood. If this continues unabated, farm and farm workers will become something of an endangered species, like what has happened in the developed countries (*Tansey and Worseley, 1995*). The variations in climatic conditions has increased the risks borne by the farmers in growing crops, which as it is, forms the riskiest end of the farming system. As even a large farmer, Dr. Ajaipal Singh, a farmer of Faridkot put it : "Farming is a high-risk, low return profession" (*Indian Express, 7th April 2000*). And the growing list of constraints, man-made and nature-bestowed, like shortage of power, lack of credit, falling water table, pests, insects and weeds, taken one with the other, have added several folds of burden on the farmers. It is true that agricultural prices have grown and so have yield, but the high cost of farming and living have outstripped the resource generated by the farms.

The livelihood systems currently in vogue in these villages have evolved over the years. We have data of the last six decades for our study as provided by the villagers. Whereas in the 1940s, most of the villagers were into farming; the situation remained nearly the same during the 1950s as well. Changes started in the 1960s. By the time we enter the 1980s, villagers started diversifying their livelihood: milk vending, serving the government (in case of Haryana most of it was either in the police or defense services) and private industry, self-employment, petty trade, transport and working as pure labourer. A diversification of occupational option of this nature has to be contextualised. Given the time and era through which these villagers were passing, there were two forces at work. One, as we mentioned earlier, agriculture was losing its lusture as a lucrative means of livelihood, and two, with the burgeoning state, the employment opportunities out side of agriculture including self employment through credit from the formal system (nationalised banks and grameen banks) was opening up. A feature that came out in some of the villages in Uttar Pradesh, like in Chandpur and Tikri was that agriculture could no longer absorb all the people available for employment. This is in part, because natural growth in labour force has outstripped growth in demand for labour in the sector, the State having one of the highest fertility rates in the country. And partly because people were displaced from agriculture due to its mechanisation, at least partial, and alternative means of employment had to be sought.

Thus for the farmers the "mantra" is "diversify or perish". The findings in these villages are abundantly corroborated by events overtaking agriculture elsewhere as well. Even medium and large farmers have launched a spectrum of paralell non-agricultural ventures to beef up their dipping incomes. Indeed today, almost half the shops in Asia's largest grain market in Khanna, are owned by farmer-cum-commission agents. A veteran "artiya" (grain dealer) in Khanna, Sri Prem Chand remarked: "Agriculture is a side business now, most farmers are into the transport or cloth trade" (*Singh, 2000*).

Within the villages there are inter-State variations. In U.P, the diversification of livelihood was *mostly in and around* the village. For instance, in Chandpur, the diversification led to farmers scouting around for options within the village, like setting up powerloom and handloom weaving, stitching, earning daily wages, farm and agricultural work, working in transport sector or in self-employment like running auto rickshaws, vegetable hawking, setting up of petty shops and electric repairing outlets and so on. In Tikri, the diversification led to "agriculture plus": agriculture along with another source of income. For instance, agriculture and selling milk; agriculture and working as labourers, agriculture and working in the service sector like shops etc. Some emigrated out of the village in search of work retaining their land and property in the village. In Haryana, the diversification was *outside* the village. For example, in the two villages of Sagarpur and Uncha Gaon, working in the police and defense forces, working for the government departments, serving in the industrial complexes, and selling milk in the industrial townships of Ballabgarh and Faridabad were the options. In Uncha Gaon agriculture in growing cash crops, backed up by selling milk provide bulk of the employment. In Kadhaoli, working in government offices or in private sector employment is highly valued. These variations are a reflection of both the mindset of the people as also the opportunities available. In case of Haryana villages, the prospects of agricultural lands being acquired by the government, has also set the farmers thinking on exploring alternatives to agriculture. Returns from agriculture seem to be an overriding consideration in continuing in farming and in judging the importance of agriculture.

Box 8.1
Agriculture is Just Side-Business for Farmers, Money is Elsewhere

Sukhmani Singh, *Faridkot, April 6*

Agricultural expansion, the acid test for the land-addicted Jat-sikh farmer is now strictly taboo.

Economic exigencies clearly dictate otherwise. "While the cost of inputs has been soaring—diesel and fertiliser costs have risen by 30-40 per cent and labour cost almost doubled in the past five years, the returns are even lower than the bank rate of return."

Sample the facts. In a weird paradox, while agricultural prices continue to soar, the returns remain constant. Says S. S. Sibis, 50, one of four brothers collectively owning 100 acres in Ramnagar near Sangrur, "Although the value of my land is Rs. 50 lakh per acre, my annual returns from it are a mere Rs. 15000 per acre". So canny instincts dictate that a farmer ploughs his surpluses, if any, not into development of his land but into commercial property in cities like Chandigarh or Ludhiana. Compared to farmland, the returns are substantially higher—a small shop brought at Rs. 15 lakh yields a monthly rent of Rs. 9000…

Sibia diversified many years ago into poultry farming, wisely followed by a chicken speciality take-away restaurant … The most recent is an agreement with Baskin Robbins for operating an icecream parlour … So while wheat and paddy cultivation gives him his bread, other businesses provide the butter and jam.

G. S. Kalkat, Vice Chancellor of Punjab Agricultural University dispels popular myths about farming in Punjab. "The concept of the millionare farmer is mythical. Farmers are in bad shape. Those who are well-off have other sources of income. . ."

While the marginal farmer has no alternative but to perish, choking in debt trap, even medium farmers are under pressure to invent ways and means of beating inflation and meeting expenses.

Take the example of Sunder Singh, 34, a 24 acre farmers in Alwalpur near Jalandhar, who switched from wheat-paddy to potato and sunflower six years ago but still didn't manage to reap a good harvest…. "Farming is only lucrative if you have the money to get into trading and storing as

> well. Potatoes (sic) was a ruinous gamble. Free power meant no power. I spent more on generating power to run my tubewell. While being a farmer makes no sense today, I lack the business acumen to get out of it totally". Others are not even as fortunate as Singh. To sell off land and switch entirely to a new business is too risky a proposition".
>
> Apart from side business, some of the larger ones have switched over to new, more profitable crops. But these form a minority. Estimate Kalkat, "Only a very small percentage of farmers, farming around 10,000 acres annually are switching to what we advocate—fruit and vegetables rather than cereals."
>
> *The Indian Express,*
> New-Delhi, 7th April 2000

In this connection, it has to be underscored that in the process of agricultural production, the social and economic roles are intertwined. The fact that farmers' are willing to abandon agriculture, because of falling returns, caused *inter alia* by high cost of external inputs, indicate that in an environment where money alone matters, importance of only half of this relationship is being recognised. Because subsistence agriculture is still prominent, there is difficulty in understanding the need for efficiency, which becomes more important when the product enters the market place. In an age where privatisation and globalisation are buzz words, market alone matters. This explains partially the current attitude of some of the farmers. While efficiency in farming must be encouraged, nonetheless policy makers and social engineers have a special role in emphasizing that the concept of efficiency in agriculture, must include the efficient way in which it discharges its social goals and that agriculture needs to be valued for its social roles as well and pursued without regard for efficiency in terms of nominal returns. Paul Thompson, the distinguished philosopher beautifully puts it which, bears repetition here:

> These economic goals are real goals to be sure... But we will never find complete salvation merely in the right set of economic policies. To make an agriculture that will serve our need for a spirit of community and self reliance in the future, we must first accept the need for community and self reliance once again as social and moral goals for agriculture (*Thompson, 1986, p.41*).

Policy changes are required to ensure that agriculturists and farmers remain in agriculture. It is also important to appreciate that since agriculture in the villages form an integral part of a whole gamut of agro-ecosystem hierarchies, we have to discover the behaviour of the higher systems which is not readily discovered simply from a study of the lower systems and vice versa. This has consequences for agricultural policy and planning. It follows that each level in the agro-ecosystem hierarchy has to be analysed, and developed both in its own right and in relation to the other levels above and below. This totality of understanding has to be used as the basis of development (*Conway and Barbier, 1990*). Since in this study we have attempted at a "comparative-static" partial analysis of the farming sub-system and livelihood sub-system within the village system, leaving out by the nature of our study the other systems, such as the household and watershed, further work is necessary for policy prescriptions.

Nevertheless, despite all its "sham, drudgery and broken dreams" (*Desiderata*, undated), agriculture still holds an important place in the lives of the villagers, for intangible and tangible reasons. The need to hold on to land is very strong. The villagers see land not only as the biological basis for growing food, but also as the source of power and social standing. It is perceived as the basis for accessing other inputs like credit, as a hedge against inflation and as an avenue to increase their net worth, because land prices are on the rise, particularly in the Hayana villages. That agriculture provides food (as one farmers called it "nutritious and good food"), that it provides a certain amount of money to access other commodities, that it provides the much needed fodder for feeding and maintaining their milch animals at a tolerable cost, that it provides employment, particularly to women, are not lost on the villagers. In one sense, the unique position that agriculture enjoyed in the 1940s and 1950s is not undiminished in importance, but it still supports a majority of the villagers in India's villages (ranging from 70 to 80 per cent). The pride in the farmers' eyes as being the custodian of land as a family heirloom, handed down to them for generations, is no less satisfying for them.

III. Farming Practices

If agriculture still is such an important part of the village life, it merits a few more comments. The Indian economy has gone a radical change since the implementation of the WB–IMF designed structural adjustment programme since July, 1991. Privatisation, deregulation, globalisation and freeing markets, have characterised policy making, at least in the rhetoric, since then. The villages under study have certainly not been immune to the tumultuous changes that the Indian economy underwent. Being urban and peri-urban areas they have significant interface with the urban events and processes, and are abreast of the happenings around them. Agriculture in these villages did not remain insulated from these developments.

In 1940s and 1950s, agriculture was wholly rainfed. Farming was carried out with all traditional practices. Seeds, water harvesting structures, soil nutrients and implements were all of the traditional variety and accessed from local resources. It was basically a household affair. The farmers and the community were in total control of the inputs, barring rains where they were fully dependent upon nature's bounties. There was no input required to be imported from outside the village.

Two decades later mechanization and electrification of agriculture took roots: electrified tubewells and tractors were deployed, with different degrees of intensity in the villages, more in Haryana and less so in Uttar Pradesh. In 1970s we see evidence of agriculture in all the Villages exposed to full blown "new technology" but their absorption was more pronounced in Haryana villages than in the Uttar Pradesh villages. The induction of hybrid or HYV seeds replacing traditional varieties; chemical fertilisers crowding out manure; insecticides and pesticides in place of pest-resistant and insect-resistant plants were common. This despite the fact that more than 300 plant species have been traditionally used for pest control in India and a large storehouse of knowledge verified by continuous practice, is available (*Pereira and Seabrook, 1990*). Tractors substituting the bullocks and the wooden plough, and electricity driven irrigation facilities in place of traditional irrigating methods, are distinctly noticeable in almost all the villages with some variations according to local conditions, more in Haryana and less in Uttar Pradesh.

Cultivators apply to their plots of land fertilisers according to their gut feeling. They generally have no training and there is no extension service. The Agriculture Department is not helpful in matters of giving information to the farmers on use of fertiliser, pesticide and insecticide and even on HYV seeds. The farmers usually experiment a good deal. In case of a new pest/disease attack, the cultivators use whatever they think would stop the disease or pest. If it works, others follow suit, with the full knowledge that there is no guarantee that a "medicine" which has worked in one plot of land will do wonders elsewhere as well. For instance a farmer in Uncha Gaon found out the hard way that DDT mixed with urea in the chilli fields to tackle *moriya* did not work though it has worked for another farmer. Farmers also go by the advice they receive from the dealers, which is reduced, for practical purposes, to a single line advice: "spray as long as the pests/insects persists" (see Box 8.4). The experimentation based on pure gut feeling of others and the advice of shop keepers, fail more often than succeed. This entails therefore, waste of resources and time.

In all the villages, dependence on nature for water has surely declined but the downside of it is that at once dependence on human beings has increased. Farmers are more dependent now upon seed companies and government seed farms (and the attendant bureaucracy) for their seeds; pesticide and insecticide companies (and their dealers) for their pesticides and insecticides; the respective state electricity boards for their power and hence for irrigation; tractor companies and their dealers for ploughing and the fertilisers companies and their dealers (and the attendant bureaucracy) for replenishing soil nutrients, than they were ever before. The control of the farmers and the community on inputs vital for their survival, as a consequence, is out of their hands. If the process of globalisation proceeds at the current pace and the WTO agreements are implemented (which will be the case) the control of inputs to agriculture will further shift to a larger domain, may be even a global domain, not accountable to any one.

Box 8.2

The Food We Eat: Interconnections of Violence

"Food grown using synthetic fertilisers and pesticides has a higher content of harm than food grown organically. Synthetic pesticides are particularly violent because they kill not only the target pest but also millions of other helpful insect species. Some of these pesticides will persist in the environment for hundreds of years."

.......Winin Pereria and Jeremy Seabrook
ASKING THE EARTH: Farms, Forestry and Survival in India

This shift at the first instance, means that farming is now a High External Input Agriculture (HEIA) from Zero External Input Agriculture (ZEIA)/ Low External Input Agriculture (LEIA). That is, agriculture is in the process of abandoning Chambers' *"unimproved" agriculture (Chambers et. el. 1989)* or Pretty's *forgotten agriculture* (*Pretty, 1996*) as we travel through time from 1940s to 1990s. In the 1940s and 1950s agriculture was based on what the farmer and the community had: seeds, labour, bullocks, plough and the wooden hoe, manure and rains. In the 1980s and 1990s, agriculture has come to be based on inputs more from outside the households and the community: HYV seeds, pesticides, insecticides, chemical fertilisers, electricity, tractor power, tubewells and pumpsets. This is a copy-book case confirming the framework of "internal resources vs. external resources" provided by Francis and King (1988). We have compared the sourcing of resources in the 1940s and 1950s vis-a-vis 1980s and 1990s and the picture looks something like the following Table 1.

Except for receiving energy from Sun for plant photosynthesis, and a portion of family labour, the farmers are buying a whole lot of inputs from outside. In the process, since farming in the 1980s and 1990s has become more dependent on sourcing inputs from outside the villages, farming has come to use resources that are not always renewable. Internal resources are "inherently renewable and thus have the potential to be used on a 'sustained' basis, indefinitely, through ecologically sound methods of farming" (*Conway and Barbier, 1990*). The external inputs in the 1990s are

Table 1 Comparative Picture of Farming

Farming in the 1940s and 1950s	**Sourcing of Resources**
Sun	Sources of energy for plant photosynthesis.
Water	Rain and small/or small local irrigation schemes.
Nitrogen	Fixed from air, recycled in soil organic matter.
Other Nutrients	From soil reserves recycled in cropping system.
Weed and Pest Control	Biological, cultural and mechanical.
Seed	Varieties produced on farm save from previous year.
Machinery	Built and maintained by farming households or in the community.
Labour	Most work done by family members.
Capital	Source is household and community, reinvested locally.
Management	Information from farmers and local community.
Farming in the 1980s and 1990s	**Sourcing of Resources.**
Sun	Sources of energy for plant photosynthesis.
Water	Large dams, centralised distribution, pumpsets, deep wells.
Nitrogen	Primarily from applied chemical fertilisers.
Other Nutrients	Applied from outside.
Weed and Pest Control	Chemical insecticides, herbicides and weedicides.
Seeds	Hybrid, HYV or certified varieties purchased annually.
Machinery	Purchased and replaced frequently.
Labour	Family labour and hired labour. Labour hired for fixing pumpsets/tractors/threshers etc. included.
Capital	External indebtedness to banks, money lenders; resources leave the community.
Management	From input suppliers, extension workers, agricultural experts.

in most cases not renewable. HYV seeds, machines, soil nutrients, fertilisers etc. are either not renewable or use resources which are not renewable.

The movement away from our traditional system of LEIA actually started as a part of the erstwhile colonial policy of replacing agriculture by a system that is market driven. The Director of Agriculture, Bombay Presidency wrote as far back as 1913:

> The old self-sufficing agriculture by which each tract, each village and each holding supplied its own needs is now largely a thing of the past... The Bombay Presidency draws much of its food supply from outside, while it exports large quantities of cotton and oil;-seeds. Its agriculture has become commercialised (*Keatinge, 1913*).

And this according to one commentator results in transfer of resources from the impoverished to those who already have enough (*Pereira and Seabrook, 1990*).

The fact that agriculture has come to depend on external inputs now as against internal inputs in the recent past best illustrates the movement of agriculture from the natural ecosystem to a "human subsidized agro-ecosystem". In the natural ecosystem, the principal source of energy is the sun (the left-hand side of Table 1). Farmers in India have always sought innovations in farming: new seeds, newer plant varieties, improved methods of cultivation, improved techniques of farming and better machinery for adaptation and integration into the ongoing farming systems. But the current situation of agriculture has been carried to an extreme with integral dependence on outside subsidies. There is thus implicitly less importance now being given in the 1980s and 1990s to the knowledge and skill of the farmers than has been the case in the 1940s and 1950s in Indian agriculture. Actually the "traditional knowledge" of agricultural production in all parts of the world, at the same time as it is being passed down through generations, is continually being adopted to change conditions, incremented and reformed. The possibility of more intensive management applied to the "human subsidized" situation does still offer hope for the recognition of traditional knowledge and skill. Steps to stimulate the recycling of nutrients within the system and minimising wasteful inputs and optimising nutrient outputs are renewed methods of improvement in agriculture which policy interventions must ensure.

IV. Cost of Farming and the ZEIA—LEIA—HEIA Continuum

Since agriculture in the Villages has become more or less dependent on external resources, much of it is *not* provided as a "free good". This implies that the farming households must buy most of the inputs and hence must generate a surplus of production, cash or whatever else of value, to exchange for external resources. And the cost of acquiring these resources and their supply channels are all controlled by institutions or individuals which, are outside the farming household/community.

The transition from ZEIA to LEIA and eventually to HEIA, has made agriculture a high *open* cost operation, because as we stated in the previous paragraph, the farmers in the villages under study have to buy most of the inputs. There is little of the resources required which is free of charge, as virtually nothing is a free good. Thus the cost of farming operation has gone up so much so that it has put sustainability of peasant agriculture in jeopardy. The high cost of external inputs is pinching the farmers since the last 4-5 years. This is best illustrated by what Sanjay Singh a farmer from Rewala Village who owns 50 bighas of land said: "Our cost has doubled in trying to protect our crops. I have spent as much as buying Rs. 15,000 in buying pesticides" *(Indian Express*, 25th September 1999).

Box 8.3
Warli Adivasis Speak

"The Adivasis used chemical fertilizer because it had been given free to them by the government. After a time, they simply stopped using it or used as little as possible with as much organic manure as they could get; they said chemical fertilizer was ruining the soil. They had also been given seedlings of high yielding varieties of paddy. They use these, but rotate them with traditional varieties, to prevent the former from impoverishing the soil. What we learned is that you must also go in for inputs that don't cost a lot of money—organic manures, organic pesticides—and a whole scheme of self reliant village development, whereby you don't export the richness of land."

One explanation for this sudden upward rise in input costs, according to us, lies in the implementation of the structural adjustment programme of the IMF-World Bank, consequent cut in subsidies (real or virtual) and the general rise in prices. It is anticipated that with globalisation and full implementation of the TRIPS Agreement of the WTO, which is lurking round the corner, the cost of these inputs will rise further (*Third World Network, 1999*). Since a Patent Holder will have patent rights for 20 years, those who wish to use, imitate or modify such patented "technology"/ inputs, will have to pay royalty to the patent holder. This will increase the cost of adopting new technology and/or new inputs, and hence put further incremental pressure on input prices to spiral. Moreover, those firms or individuals, which would take out patents will not change the technology for as long as they could. And this bodes ill for the farmers so keen to adopt new technology: technology will remain stagnant for a long time. The several fold increase in yield seen in the 1970s due to affordable technological change, will no longer be possible.

The transition from ZEIA to HEIA has also made a noticeable impact on the *hidden* cost of operation. The increase in fossil fuel used to keep outputs high, also means more energy consumption. Shift from ZEIA to HEIA has led to substitution of manual labour and animal power by tractors, threshers and pumpsets, which implies that external energy sources have substituted sources of energy found in the household and the community. All of these along with use of fertilisers, which is mostly NKP, have caused agriculture to become highly energy intensive activity now. Although we have no estimates of how much is the total energy inputs to agriculture due to the use of fertilisers (NKP), pumpsets and tractors, in the villages, but in third world countries these amongst themselves consume more than 90 per cent of total energy inputs for farming. For India as a whole there is one estimate that 10-20 per cent increase in yields following mechanisation, costs an additional 43-260 per cent more in energy consumption. In Punjab, the neighbouring state of Haryana where we have studied 3 villages, farms in a class 14-25 hectares use three times as much direct energy per hectare as farmers smaller than 6 hectares, the large farms being mechanised and smaller farms still adhering, at least in some respects, to traditional methods of cultivation (*Singh and Miglani, 1976*). Note the figures in Table 2, which corroborates the above.

Table 2 Energy Consumption for High Input Agriculture in West Bengal and Uttar Pradesh

Low External Input comparison	High External Input comparison	Amount of extra yield for High External Input	Extra Energy Consumption for High External Input
	State of West Bengal, in Eastern India		
Bullock, rice	Power tiller, rice	+ 8 per cent	+ 200 +
Bullock, rice	Tractor, rice	+ 13 per cent	+ 43 per cent
Bullock, wheat	Power tiller, wheat	+ 12 per cent	+ 74 per cent
Bullock, wheat	Tractor, wheat	+ 6 per cent	+ 89 per cent
	State of Uttar Pradesh in North India		
Bullock, rice	Mechanized rice	+ 20 per cent	+ 45 per cent
Bullock, wheat	Mechanized wheat	+ 29 per cent	+ 138 per cent

Source: *Singh and Singh,* 1976.

In the above table, the transition of the two states, West Bengal and Uttar Pradesh, from producing both rice and wheat with bullock power to mechanisation of different degrees have resulted in extra yield being added, but the additional energy requirements have gone up way beyond the increase in extra yield.

For example, in West Bengal, by transiting from a system of agriculture where bullocks and wooden plough were used to plough paddy fields to the system of tilling land with power tillers, the gain in yield for high external input was 8 per cent. But the additional energy consumption needed for the high external input was 200 per cent. Similarly as the farmers in the state transited from bullock-wheat to power tiller-wheat, extra yield for high input reaped by them was 6 per cent, whereas the increase in extra energy they had to expend in the process was 89 per cent. For Uttar Pradesh, movement from bullock-wheat to mechanised-wheat led to a yield increase of 29 per cent as against extra energy consumption of 138 per cent. Similarly for other forms of cultivating rice and wheat. The point we are driving at is that as farming moves from traditional methods of low external input cultivation to mechanised or partially mechanised high external input agriculture, yield increases, and at once, energy consumption also increases and often at a steeper rate. In percentage terms, the increases in energy requirements far outstrip the increases in yield. The differentials in yield increase and extra energy requirement depends on local conditions and micro-level environments. Since we do not have data specific to all the villages on the issue, we can only say broadly that the movement from ZEIA to HEIA has increased the energy intensity of farming for farmers. And this has happened in many parts of the world,. including the United States, whenever such transition has been operationalised (*Ikerd et. al, 1992*).

High external input agriculture, entails a lot more increases in *real costs*. Even where there is no direct monetary outgoing to acquire a resource, there are steep hikes in real cost incurred by the farming household. The most obvious examples are the time and energy spent in procuring seeds and other inputs from local distributors in nearby towns or block office; time expended in fetching diesel for pumpsets (in case the pumpsets are not electricity operated); chasing the state electricity board employees for restoration of power when power failure occurs etc. Add to this the loss in terms of crops lost or land left fallow, owing to non-availability or untimely availability of any of the inputs. The waste of time, energy and paper required to obtain credit from formal purveyors of credit is oppressive. And the farmers can scarcely do anything about it because the control over prices and supply of inputs does not rest with the farmers and their community. The farmers are price takers and supply of inputs follow business considerations and not needs of the farming community.

The smaller farmers are always caught up in the jam between rising input costs and volatile output prices. They are, thus, constantly squeezed in a cost-price wedge which promotes higher production using more and more of external inputs It is a squeeze that encourages farmers to be the first to maximise production from their resources. There are no inbuilt inducements and there is no structural arrangement which, promote sustainability of such agriculture. We saw how farmers have migrated from producing for self sufficiency and food security at the household level to self-sufficiency in income.

This system of costs and prices and markets, is also encouraging part-time farming. Either farmers are in employment, trade, business in and around the village, or are emigrants serving in the military, police and other employers in private/public sector. In the former case, the farmers treat agriculture as their primary means of livelihood and the "other" employment as their secondary source of income. In the latter case, they impose the burden of farming on their families or they return to the farms during cultivation and harvesting, considering agriculture as their secondary source of income. Within the village when farmers take to rearing milch animals and selling milk, there is some element of complementarity. But when they engage themselves in other occupations, such as petty trade or military service, there is a loss to the farming system and attrition from the stock of peasant agriculturists.

And then this transition also means chemicalisation of agriculture. The different kinds of chemical fertilisers and to a lesser degree the insecticides/pesticides applied directly to the fields and insecticides applied to store HYV seeds, means that agricultural inputs have come to include a whole range of chemicals. Since much of it is applied without the necessary technical details being available with the farmers, they disturb the chemical balance of the soil. As a matter of fact the Government of India (*Economic Survey, 1995-96*) suggests that the ideal average NPK ratio for the country as a whole is 4:2:1. (Of course the optimum ratio depends upon the soil type and other agro-climatic characteristics.) Against this the proportion at the all India level of NPK ratio was 5.9:1.9:1 in 1981. In 1992-93 this ratio has deteriorated to 8.9:2.8:1 (*Ranade and Dev, 1997*). The impact of these chemicals on soil conditions may not be currently perceived as important in the villages studied, but agricultural history in several parts of the country, including Haryana, is replete with instances where such a transition has caused damage to land leading to fall in productivity, a phenomenon poetically called "Yellowing of the Green Revolution". Even the father of India's Green Revolution (read rice revolution) has urged for curbing "Green Revolution" and promoting an "evergreen revolution" (*Swaminathan, 1999*). The impact on the health of soil may be even worse, because the farmers complained that the dealers short change them by supplying spurious "medicines". Indeed the farmers often approach the dealers with the name of the pest or disease and request them for a remedy. There being no extension, they feel obliged to take to their fields whatever the dealers "prescribe" as the remedy. Experts believe that what is worrying is the amount of spraying of pesticides and insecticides done to the crops. In another context a farmer of Rewala village confessed: "With normal rain, one or two spraying (sic) are enough, but now I have already done seven-eight and the crop is just mid-way". Little wonder that most of the pesticides are just "bought off the shelf with the shop keeper giving them advice on how much to use it and in what combination. 'There is no limit to how many times it can be used as long as they can see the worms', said a local shopkeeper selling seeds and pesticides in Najafgarh giving advice to a farmers of the area" (*Jain, 1999*).

The foregoing phenomena tell us a story similar to what happened in developed countries in the not so distant past. The high cost often leads to people leaving agriculture and we have seen that people on the balance, in many villages, would opt out of agriculture should the option arise. "Between 1945 and 1952, the number of regulars hired and family workers on farms in England alone fell from 478000 to 135000. In the past decade" (the 1980s), "there have been dramatic falls in the numbers of most classes of people engaged in farming activities throughout Britain....Fewer people make a living from the land and, of course, they understand it less" (*Pretty and Howes, 1995*). The villages under study paint an almost similar picture. And as we can see that in HEIA most of the technology promoted is labour saving, which was exactly behind their unsuitability for use in countries like ours, with large labour reserves and lack of capital to put them to work.

V. Diversity: Whether Poly Culture?

The cropping pattern and crop diversity have also seen a sea change. In 1950s, a large number of crops were cultivated, though the villagers did not specify on what percentage of arable land each crop was grown. The crops were a mixture of staple, coarse cereals, lentils, pulses, beans of different kinds and condiments and sugarcane (for jaggery). The main crops were coarse grains and cereals: barley, jowar and bajra, grams, maize and so on. There were wheat and paddy of different varieties. Most of the crops grown were for consumption in the households in the villages. By growing this diverse mosaic of crops, the farmers not only diffused their risk of failure, on account of pests, insects, drought, flood, disease or whatever, but also ensured that their households consumed a basket of food which contained fibre, nutrition and protein: carbohydrates, cereals and pulses.

In 1960s, winds of change had begun to hit the villages. Some of the crops started being looked at with less of interest. In the 1990s, farmers in the villages are left with wheat and mustard, and some vegetables like cauliflower and radish, as principal Rabi crops. During kharif, paddy constitutes the main crop, with bits of bajra, moong, arhar, dhencha and sesame. Jowar is grown for fodder. As a matter of fact the principal Rabi crop in Kadhaoli and Sagarpur is wheat, and in Uncha Gaon the only food crop grown during the year is wheat in 50 per cent of arable land during Rabi. In case of Uncha Gaon the principal crops are vegetables of different variety grown throughout the year. As much as 75 per cent of agriculture in Uncha Gaon is apportioned to vegetable cultivation for commercial purposes. In the 1980s some attempt at promoting "Yellow Revolution" to grow more mustard, was made but the revolution died in its infancy. The risks associated with growing of mustard despite the prospects of high return left the villagers in Haryana, unpersuaded into believing that swapping wheat for Mustard was a judicious option. Sugarcane was abandoned as a commercial crop in Sagarpur because the sugar mill at Palwal within whose catchment area the village fell was shut down and there were no takers of sugarcane for commercial use.

A large menu of factors determines the crops chosen for cultivation. Water requirements and water availability, size of the landholdings, experience the farmers have gathered in growing the crop, time required to grow the crop, its labour intensity, cost of cultivation and return and finally the risks involved, all enter the decision making process of the farmers. The principal trade-off is between cost and return on the one hand and risks involved on the other. The farmers, in Haryana at least, are willing to err on the side of caution: they are risk averse, that has resulted in the "battle" between the "Yellow Revolution" and Green Revolution, being won by the latter. It is not that all the decisions regarding cropping are a function of all of the above factors, but most of the decisions about growing crops are generally affected by these factors. In case of wheat the additional factor has been the response of the farmers to price incentives in the form of minimum support price and the procurement price declared by the government of India. The decision regarding choice of crops to grow is, thus, influenced pretty much by the same factors that influence small

Box 8.4
Loss of Diversity in Different Countries

India
Once 30,000 rice varieties grown; now it is expected that just 10 varieties rice will soon cover 75 per cent of rice area.

Phillipines
Before the modernisation of early 1970s, 3500 varieties of rice existed; now only 3-5 are grown in irrigated areas.

Europe
Half of all breeds of domestic animals (horses, cattle, sheep, goats, pigs and poultry) have become extinct since the beginning of the 20th century; a third of the remaining 770 breeds are in danger of disappearing by 2010.

France
30 per cent of bread wheat from 2 varieties and 70 per cent from 10 varieties. In the SE, the provencal diet contained 250 plant species at the beginning of the 20th century; now it comprises only 30-60.

The Netherlands
A single potatoe variety covers 80 per cent of potatoe land; 90 per cent of wheat planted to 3 varieties; 75 per cent of barley planted to 1 variety.

UK
68 per cent of early potatoes planted to 3 variety; 4 wheat varieties account for 71 per cent of wheat area.

USA
71 per cent maize area planted to 6 varieties; 96 per cent pea area planted to 2 varieties; 65 per cent rice area planted to 4 varieties; 76 per cent snap bean area planted to 3 varieties.

6121 apple varieties (85 per cent), 2354 pear varieties (88 per cent), 516 cabbage varieties (95 per cent), 394 field maize varieties (91 per cent), 329 tomato varieties (81 per cent)and 295 sweet (95 per cent) corn varieties, are all lost.

Source: *Pimbert*, 1993; FAO, 1993; *Soetomo*, 1992; *Fowler, Vellve* and *Mooney*, 1990 as quoted in *Pretty*, 1995.

farmers in other parts of the world. In other countries crops "are commonly distinguished by farmers by such characteristics as color of different plant parts, yield, culinary quality, resistance to diseases or pests, storage properties, altitude for optimum growth, and growth habit. Unlike selection and breeding criteria applied to modern crop varieties, yield may or may not be an overriding concern in the selection of traditional varieties by farmers" (*Merrick, 1990*). It has to be underscored that considerable amount of the changes in the cropping pattern has been on account of the farmers' response to technological changes. That is why in almost all the villages, the changes in seeds used, in technology of production, in application of chemical fertilisers and in yield increases were observable during the mid 1960s onwards.

The impact of costs and returns deciding on what crops to grow warrants a few more comments. In one of the villages studied, Uncha Gaon, vegetables grown are grown primarily for sale in the market where there is a demand for vegetable. Vegetable cultivation is a highly water intensive activity and with erratic and insufficient rainfall, much of this agriculture depends on irrigation by drawing ground water. In the absence of any water market and extension service, this has resulted in drawing ground water beyond sustainable limits set by parameters of the agro-climatic zone in which the village is situated. The water table has predictably fallen below 85 feet. Food is being produced in Uncha Gaon by using natural resources beyond sustainable limits in response to demands of, not the villagers but those who can pay for it. This, in some feeble sense not only questions the infallibility of the system of markets and prices in allocating resources but also makes us think whether sustaining and scaling up such agriculture is leading to an alarming rate of natural resource depletion and in the last analysis posing a definite threat to long term survival of agriculture. If food is to be grown such that those who can pay for it are able to freely get such food, not because of societal needs, irrespective of its impact on natural resources, then there could be problems down the road. Shall we ask: are we using now resources of future generations to satisfy the demands of those who can now pay for it presently?

What about variety and diversity? In terms of variety and diversity, there is a marked reduction in almost all the villages, to which extent, the capacity of the farmers to diffuse risk is pruned. This is not peculiar to these villages for this trend has been with us for many years and this trend is in keeping with the trends seen worldwide, as pointed out by *Pimbert* (1993), *FAO* (1993), *Scetomo* (1992), and *Fowler et. al.* (1990) amongst others. As a matter of fact a noted agricultural economist pointed out to me that in the world there are 1,20,000 weeds and plants that are edible of which we now cultivate only 50 and of these only 3 provide 75 per cent of our food. In India once more than 30,000 varieties of rice were grown, whereas now it is anticipated that soon only 10 varieties will be grown in 75 per cent of the area under paddy cultivation (*FAO, 1993*).

This fall in diversity of crops signals a movement away from poly-culture towards bi-culture or mono-culture. It signals reduction in palate and nutritional value of the food for the villagers in all the villages. The crop grown in the farms can provide basically only carbohydrates and a modicum of fibre in terms of some vegetable, as most of it is for sale. It also indicates that there is a movement from growing crops to meet food requirements of households and of the community, to growing crops for the market's consumption and for money. Importantly enough, this marks a shift in the rural mindset and this shift in the mindset has a bearing on the social and political environment in the village.

In terms of Boserup's classification of agriculture, the villages under study are moving further away from multiple cropping to annual cropping (*Boserup, 1993*). We have to add here that as we have stated earlier, it is no one's position that a mixture of crops is better than mono/bi-cropping. Much depends upon the local conditions and the characteristics of the crops themselves. However there is evidence that pest infestation frequently gets reduced in inter-cropping, because of various factors (*Risch, Andow,* and *Altieri 1983*). "Host plants are more widely spread and so harder to find; one species may trap a pest or one specie may repel a pest; and/or predators may be attracted. Weeds are more likely to be suppressed by mixtures" (*Pretty, 1995*). In fact after examining Asian countries that adopted Green Revolution seeds and methods, *Edwards et.al.*, arrived at the conclusion that "Growing crops in continual monoculture or bi-culture leads inevitably to much greater pest weed, disease, fertility and soil erosion problems than mixed cropping systems common in mixed cropping..." *(Edwards et. al., 1993).* Inter cropping also leads to replenishment of soil nutrients without outside intervention.

VI. Changes in Agriculture and Food Security

Households in the villages produced their own food directly and also brought food from the open market. In 1998 and 1999, the period of this study, harvests were normal and yields were not dispersed. There was therefore food security ensured mostly by direct entitlements and partially through exchange entitlement (*Sen, 1881*). Though earnings out of wages were low in almost all the villages, the villagers complained, not of fluctuations, but irregularity, in that those who offered their services did not always find employment even on a daily wage basis.

The basic diet is chappatis and rice eaten with Dal. Chilli chutney (paste) was found the more frequent accompaniment of Chappatis for the poorer farmers. Vegetables and milk were rarer occupants of their plates and mostly during seasons when they were harvested. The villagers as a part of their daily intake of food did not mention animal protein. In some villages they had meat (goat meat) once a month or so. Poultry and fish were conspicuous by their absence from the villagers' menu of what they eat. Families frequently ate a mixture of water and leafy vegetables (spinach, sarson da saag, cabbage, tender pumpkin-creepers and tender bottle-gourd creepers, fenugreek plants etc.) with chilies and salt. The high fibre diet and malabsorption, as evidenced especially from bout of diarrhoea that all villagers complained of, probably results in low digestibility (*Das Gupta and Ray, 1990*), which may be further reduced in summer and rainy season. Assessed against local standards, many families in the villages were eating a diet, which, indicated household poverty (*Kabeer, 1989; Kynch, 1994*).

The constraints to agriculture pointed out by the villagers have a large number of insects and pests, like caterpillar, locust, termites and other predators. These ravage crops frequently and though the loss in all cases are not large in value and volume terms, yet these losses had perceptible impact on the diet which the villagers ate. For instance, pulses when attacked by any of these predators not only robs the villagers of a source of income, it also means that the villagers would consume so much less of pulses (Daal) and hence so much less of protein.

The changes in cropping pattern could have also led to changes in consumption pattern. Since in the days of the ZEIA most of what was produced was for sustenance and subsistence, it is not hard to imagine that the consumption basket had a variety of food stuff. The food which villagers consumed was both nutritious and palatable. With reduction in the number and kinds of crop grown, there is no way that the same variety and palate would be maintained. The quality of the villagers' staple diet, wheat, had lost some of the good tastes it had in the days of the yore. And at least in Sagarpur and Kadhaoli, villagers were categorical that taste of wheat was still deteriorating and that the wheat that they are now growing no longer makes good "Chappatis".

In most of the villages, there is food insecurity. The intensity and duration of hunger varies. Food insecurity is more in Uttar Pradesh than in Haryana. The intensity of food insecurity is higher in Uttar Pradesh, the poorer of the two States. This lends some credence to the widely held theory that the overall growth of the economy is an important component of the composite mechanism for eliminating poverty and hunger.

In some villages in Uttar Pradesh people suffer hunger for long months. For example in Chandpur, villagers silently bear hunger for five months from Baisakh till Bhado. They generally have one meal of chapatis with chilli paste and occasionally some cheap vegetables. It is only (in Kartick) after the first flush of harvests comes, that people's food intake improves. In Tikri people suffer hunger for five months from Jeth to Kuar, when they have a single meal of chappatis and chilli paste. This is particularly damaging because these are the months when people, particularly women work their hardest as it is the main cultivation season for Uttar Pradesh. And this is the season when employment outside their farms are hardest to get (*Alagh, 1999*).

Even in villages where the thrust of agriculture is commercial agriculture and despite these villages being in peri-urban areas, people suffer food insecurity in some form or the other, all round the year. And they suffer hunger during the months of Sawan, Bhado and Kuar. In other months their diet lacks nutrition, is deficient in calorie intake and there is no variety. For example, in Sagarpur, 75 per cent of the people being marginal farmers (as defined by the villagers owning less than one acre of land), they suffer from food insecurity for most part of the year. And of the remaining 25 per cent we can only say that food is available but the nutritional content, calorific value and the quantity of food consumed are unclear.

Since many of these villages have no secondary source of food, like food from common property resources, micro-environment and forests, any option of reducing their hunger from hunger foods is closed. In at least one case, there is direct evidence that contamination of a pond and destruction of mango and guava orchards, have robbed the poor of a natural source of nutrition and diet. The pollution of Ganges has added to the misery of Malhas in Tikri, as marine life has been damaged by pollutants in the river, robbing them of a vital source of food and income to access food.

Men in most of the villages studied control the income and expenditure, to which we will come later in Section VIII below. But this has impact on food security. Because men in the villages control the income generated by the household, most of the time collectively, and expenditure in a "single household accounting system", individuals within the households do not keep and dispose off some or all of the product of their labour. Because as we shall see later, women have little access to resources or markets, they have no alternative but to seek and keep "the protection of their men: though the adoption of attitudes of submissiveness, propriety and self sacrifice" (*Kandiyoti* as quoted in *Kabeer, 1991*).

In the villages women did the domestic tasks and their activities affected food production—especially marketable milk from the buffaloes and/or cows they keep at home. Milk production and care of livestock are closely bound to the home. Women and girl children made fuel from dung, collected fuelwood and engaged in deweeding fields, processed, prepared and cooked food at home.

As a general rule men do buying and selling at markets, being in a privileged position vis-à-vis women when deciding what and how much to buy, including not infrequently liquor. Women generally act as dependents, probably stating their household demands inside their homes rather than wielding effective demand in the market place. Men thus exercise basic control over the supply of food to the family through deciding on the crops for cultivation on household land (direct entitlements) and market transactions (exchange entitlements). Women on the other hand affect the quantity of provisions through the "domestic economy", as it were, and the quality of food through processing.

The gender division of labour in food production and distribution and processing influence the nutritional needs of the households. Women in the villages have a long and arduous routine of domestic and household farm work, but may have more opportunities than some men to adopt to lower food intakes, either through the basic metabolic rate or ergonomically. In 1998 and 1999, women rarely ground wheat, a highly energy consuming task, as most of the villages were near a Township where "Aati Chaakis" (flour mills) are available, and indeed none of the women's group in their seasonality analysis of activities included grinding of wheat as a part of their daily schedule.

From the employment picture painted by the villagers, it is apparent that the opportunities for employment for women are severely constrained. The overall burden and energy needs, for women may be actually lower than men, something similar to what *Kabeer,* 1991 articulated. There are caste differences in women's employment. However, if we add to this the different "scheduled activity of women" and their "self-employment" inside their homes to supplement household income, the workload of women is substantially higher. Women's hours of leisure and sleep are so much less. Different activity levels of men and women and compulsions to provision the household with commodities or to reproduce the family, loaded against women do result in lower output capacity and risk of ill health in women.

VII. Constraints to Agricultural Production

Agriculture like any other economic activity in India is beset with a host of problems. The constraints faced by agriculture in the village under study can be classified like the farmers of Chandpur as under:

- *Environmental and Situational Constraints* Tyranny of the raingod: uncertainty, irregularity and maldistribution of rainfall; frosts and hailstorms; small size of holdings, paucity of water and non-availability of irrigation in time; effluent discharge from the industrial establishments, floods etc.

Agro-Biological Constraints non-availability of manure/fertilizers and good quality seeds; attack by nilagis; weed, pest and insect infestation; menace of the rats and the locust, white ants and termite attacks and the like.

Socio-Economic Constraints non-availability of credit in time and high rate of interest, high irrigation charges, lack of animal power and machines (read tractors) for use in agriculture, shortage of electric power, lack of extension and training, non-availability of seeds and fertilizers at fair prices, etc.

Administrative and Managerial Constraints: distance between agricultural lands and human habitation, lack of co-ordination amongst government functionaries connected with agriculture, breakdown of extension services, dysfunctionality of the agriculture department and agriculture related departments etc.

The introduction of new technology and planting into the agricultural system, HYV seeds, chemical fertilisers, pesticides, insecticides and herbicides, leaving the farmers to fend for themselves, has done agriculture no good. The cost has been very high and wastage of resources as painful. In this, farmers were particularly incensed by the absence of extension support. The decline in extension service has been for two apparent reasons. One, the expanding volume of technical information has resulted in extension workers becoming generalists with some knowledge in many areas, unable to better serve the farming community. Two, in current times of economic recession and downsizing of government public resources are limited for extension work. Voluntary educational programmes typically lose priority and are cut back and eventually eliminated. A very senior functionary of government of India told us that there are in all 1,00,000 extension workers of all varieties taken together for India as a whole. But the bankrupt state governments can neither pay for their skill upgradation nor for their travel to reach the farmers. This has very serious policy implications. It is a sad commentary on our fiscal management that reportedly even an agriculturally advanced and otherwise prosperous state like Punjab had to mortgage (literally) its markfed building in chandigarh to pay for the salaries of its employees in September 1999.

Table 3 A Sample of Constraints Faced By Different Villages

Chandpur	Sagarpur	Uncha Gaon	Sagarpur	Kadhaoli Men	Kadhaoli Women
Jhulsa	Power shortage	Power shortage	Locust(insect)	Power shortage	Locust(insect)
Angarwar	Nilgai	Land acquisition by govt.	Batti (weed)	Nilgai	High cost
Flies	Locust (pest)	Unemployment	Termites(pest)	Locust (pest)	Termites (pest)
Change in climate		Drinking habit of men	Power shortage		Lalrri(pest)
Insects	Chepa (pest)	Poverty	Safed moondi (weed)	Chepa (pest)	Safed moondi (weed)
Gharroj (Nilgai)	Sati (weed)	Outsiders	Rat	Sati (weed)	Jai rani (weed)
			Employed in local industry		
Rats	Safed mondi (weed)	No training	Chepa(pest)	Safed mondi (weed)	Chepa (pest)
			Centre for women		
Tunki	Rani Jai	Change in climate	Congress Grass (weed)	Rani Jai	Green locust (insect)
Contaminated water reservoir	Termites		Safed kira (pest)	Termites	Hard water
Flies	Congress grass (weed)		Titri (insect)	Congress grass (weed)	Nilgai
	Change in climate		Sati (weed)	Climatic changes	Soondi (pest)
			Nilgai		
			Soondi(pest) Hail		

There has been an increase in the number of weeds, pests and insects and diseases over the years. We present below in a tabular form the constraints mentioned by the villagers in four of the villages, noting that in Kadhaoli, men and women have separately identified their constraints in farming.

For Tikri, the villagers had classified their constraints into three classes and they are not reduced in a tabular form to preserve its "beauty". The classification is this:

- *Environmental and Situational Constraints* change in climatic conditions leading to uncertainty/irregularity of rainfall, small size of holdings, scattered land, etc. The women added scarcity of land as an additional problem.

- *Agro-Biological Constraints*: weeds, diseases like banjh rog, pests (dhola, deemak, machhi-flies) and insect attack on crops (gur chawa-leaf-roll, galwa, jhulsa, maho, ukatha, kabra and khadra), attack by whiteants and rats etc. The women perceive that the problem of attacks by nilgais needs to be addressed.

- *Socio-Economic Constraints* lack of electric power, non-availability of seeds and unadulterated fertilizers, spurious insecticides and shortage of labour. Shortage of money and water for irrigation were added problems indicated by the women.

Of all the constraints identified by the villagers, damage inflicted by locust, termites, nilgais, congress grass (parthenium), power shortage and climate change is a constant refrain. The dysfunctionality of supporting structures and institutions for supporting agriculture is mentioned in almost every discussion, particularly in the villages where "new technology" is deeply embedded. While farmers have abandoned their traditional way of cultivating land and with it, their traditional institutions, support structures and knowledge (in response to technological change and "price incentives"), new structures and institutions are not in place. There is a vacuum and farmers have no wherewithal to fill that vacuum. The situation is very similar to what has happened in a village near Delhi, which is stated below for comparison.

Box 8.5

Shopkeepers as Advisors

"No rain means more pesticides in your subzi"

"......farmers pray for rains, spray more pesticides"

—*Indian Express*, New-Delhi, September 25th 1999.

In Daulatpur village beyond Najafgarh, Ram Singh is busy spraying his field of cabbage with some pesticides. "This kind of bad monsoon happens once in 10 years. My Bajra crop had to be destroyed midway because the grains were too small and they died anyway", he said with desperation evident on his face... "With farmers looking skywards for monsoon rains, the vegetables are just going to be expensive but also heavily laced with pesticides". With no rains, the villagers are trying to save their crops with extra dose of pesticides.... "Our cost has doubled in trying to protect our crops. I have spent as much as Rs. 15000 in buying pesticides", said Sanjay Singh from Rewala Village who owns 50 bighas of land... What is worrying is the number of sprayings that have been done to the crops. "With normal rain, one or two spraying are enough, but now I have already done seven-eight and the crop is just mid-way", said Sanjay Singh....Little wonder then that all farmers reel off names of pesticides—Cartrap, Colt, Monocil and Polytrin. And most of it just bought off the shelf with the shopkeeper giving them advice on how much to use it and in what combination. "There is no limit to how many times it can be used as long as they can see worms", said a local shopkeeper selling seeds and pesticide in Najafgarh giving advice to a farmer of the Area.

There are seven types of local level institutions, which are necessary for the peasant-farmers in the villages to sustain. Community based organisation (CBOs), natural resources management groups, farmer research institutions, extension service agencies, farmer to farmer extension groups, purveyors of credit and consumer groups. The success of agriculture that is sustainable and capable of ensuring the nation's food security, depends not just on the backbreaking labour, motivation, skills and knowledge of the peasant-farmers, but on action taken by institutions or groups and communities as a whole. Unfortunately in the villages studied, most of these institutions, even NGOs, are missing. And they have their impact on agricultural production, pollution and food security. This makes the task of our agricultural reconstruction so much more challenging. The need for revamping the supporting structures and institutions (not necessarily the newer variety) to pay increasing attention to community-based action through local level institutions and user groups, to support the peasant farmers, can not be overemphasized.

While the vintage of almost all of the constraints mentioned has been identified by the farmers, their exact causation is not always recognisable. For instance, the advent of congress grass (parthenium) is linked to import of wheat under P/L 480, from The United States. The increased predation of nilgais is clearly associated with deforestation and consequent loss in their natural source of food. However, the farmers could not point their fingers on why a majority of the weeds, pests, insects and diseases occur. They did not specify why these are on the rise than ever before. For example, there is no answer to why *gandar* (caterpillar) infestation is on the rise or why has frequency of *chepa* increased and so on. The farmers have only identified the conditions in which some of these thrive: locust increases in seasons that receive delayed monsoon, white ants thrive in dry soil and so on.

The extent of loss from some of these constraints have been estimated by the farmers. The estimates vary within the village and across the villages. In some cases the loss could be as much as cent per cent loss of crops, while in others it could run into few hundreds of Rupees. In some cases, crops affected by pests, insects and diseases are used a inferior quality fodder of whatever remains of them but in a majority of the cases such damaged crops are uprooted and discarded. This tells us that one of the major responses of the community towards removing these constraints is uprooting. In all the villages, the major damage to crops and consequent loss is inflicted by pests, insects and diseases (barring "Raingod"). But the majority of the farmers' responses have been to deal with weeds. They did try to spray and sprinkle "medicines" to tackle the pests, insects and diseases, but they were never concerted and never well orchestrated, as some of them will need. Lack of information both about the predators and the remedial measures, has contributed to imparting the copying mechanisms its emaciated outfit.

A few issue which find no place in the prioritised list of constraints have cropped up time and again during the discussions deserve mention. The small farm and plot sizes, lack of credit or paucity of money and absence of adequate provision for education are the more important ones. They are all related to matters of policy and should be dealt with at that level.

VIII. Gender Equity and Gender Justice

The separate job descriptions, for women and men exist virtually everywhere. In practically all the villages, the tasks performed by women in rearing of buffaloes and selling milk are very conveniently fitted into the traditional role of women, viz., collecting fodder and carrying out household chores. Men are involved generally in selling milk in the village and in the nearby town, and in some cases help the women in milking the buffaloes. In cultivating and harvesting wheat, the mainstay of agriculture in a majority of the villages, women supervise the activities from ploughing, leveling and puddling (*mej, jot and palewat*) to several rounds of irrigation. Harvesting, and making bundles for threshing, at considerable physical pain (in one village pain in the palm during harvesting is listed as a major health problem by the women) are women's responsibility. Even when men are engaged in threshing with machines, women stay on to make the smaller bundles out of the larger ones, to facilitate the process.

Agricultural activities under women's charge are in addition to their traditionally assigned responsibilities (villagers in one village called the "daily schedule of work") viz., fetching water, collecting fuel and fodder, feeding animals, cleaning and washing, bearing and rearing children, processing and cooking food. In case of men, for irrigating their land they work during night but for other operations like *mej, jot and palewat*, for threshing and for taking the produce to the *mandi* (market), they take leave from their normal work.

The situation is worse in the villages in Uttar Pradesh. Women in these villages in addition to their daily schedule of work and discharging their designated responsibilities in agriculture, have to earn to supplement household income by working out of their homes: like making birdis, making necklaces out of artificial pearls, making garlands of rudrakhs etc.. While men rest or enjoy recreation, women more often than not work. They often make these necklaces and birdis when the men folk have gone to sleep late in the night after "supper" if there is one. This is oppressing. Viewed in its totality, workload of men and women on a comparative basis mirror discrimination; women are generally speaking overloaded. If one was to factor in the elements of leisure and recreation the situation is even worse: men enjoy some of it, women have none.

From the foregoing recital one conclusion is possible: poorer the state of the households greater the load on women. For instance, by comparing the workload of women in Tikri and Chandpur, on the one hand, with the workload of the women in Kadhaoli, Sagarpur and Uncha Gaon on the other, there is little difficulty in visualising that the former is decidedly more than the latter. This is more troubling when we consider the fact that the food intake is lower and hunger more severe, in Uttar Pradesh villages than in the villages of Haryana. Poverty *per se* disempowers women more in poorer locations.

Most of the tasks assigned to the women require them to "soil their hands" as it were, for they can only be manually performed. Starting from supervising irrigation (ensuring that water reach all parts of the field) and even at night (in Kadhaoli for instance), to harvesting and making bundles from harvested crops, the use of mechanical device is conspicuous by its absence. Sickle and rope are all that they require. In contrast, tasks assigned to men, viz., ploughing, irrigating, threshing and transporting, are all mechanised. In terms of effort and disagreeableness, women clearly shoulder a more disagreeable set of tasks. The increase in yield over the decades due to "new technology", means increased work for women: they have to harvest larger volume of crops, make more bundles, dehusk more grains and carry more headloads, and store higher quantities of hay/fodder. It has, therefore, been commented that the induction of new-technology into agriculture has led to feminisation of work.

Box 8.6

Contextualising Poverty from a Gender Perspective

"The experience of poverty is both shared and distributed within families. All suffer but some suffer more than others."

Robert Chambers

The division of labour amongst women and men also has the flavour of "inside-family" and "outside-family" syndrome (*World Bank,* 1989). Women are engaged inside their households, and if they work in their own fields, most of the time they serve alongside their male counterparts. They do not step out of their doorsteps to work for others. Men on the other hand are encouraged to take up employment in either the "public" or the private sector; even in the informal sector. Even in major household activities, such as cultivation and harvesting of crops, they are outbound all the time: arranging tractors, procuring irrigation pumpsets, selling milk, threshing crops and best of all, selling the farming household's output, both inside the village and outside it. Because men are engaged in the actual act of selling the produce created out of family resources including labour, the proceeds of the sale from such produce go to the men. Though women and men and children all conjointly participate in producing goods, the destination and custody of income arising from sale of those goods, in the first place rests with the men. This process of disposing agricultural produce disempowers women.

The unequal social relationship between men and women are mirrored both within the family and outside as well. Women have to work more, eat less. They are even constricted (in one case) from talking to men and in one case even with men belonging to their households. The diseases commonly suffered by women are downplayed in importance; discounted in responses (see Box 8.5). They suffer domestic violence occasioned by men's frolicking with alcohol. Women have less to spend on their children's education, because men exchange a big chunk of scarce household income with alcohol. Despite all this, women have devised their own coping mechanisms, feeling safe in the citadel of their belief that much of all this is sanctified by religion, customs, practices, usage and tradition.

Box 8.7

.....Thus Spoke Bisambari, Village Baraoli, a Mother of Two Daughters....

"Dhanae Kanjoosh Hain. Bimari mein bhi nahi dehkhatae. Maroon ya bachun" (They are very miserly. Even in illness, they don't permit us to have doctor's consultancy. They don't care whether I die or remain alive). *"Ladkhi hai. Ladkhi ki karae? Keshnae pauni diye? Aapi ho jaigee. Foot faradk jaigi"* (It is a girl. What to do? Who has ever given her water? Gradually she will be cured).

As told to Ms. Meera Jayaswal, 'Second round of the study on The Impact of Air Pollution on Urban and Peri Urban Agriculture in Areas of Faridabad', 1999.

Thus with the need for women to work for wages/cash income, in addition to the traditional role they play in agriculture and within households, including providing care for those who cannot take care of themselves, as in case of the villages in Uttar Pradesh, women in the villages now have triple burden. The proximity of the villages to urban and peri-urban centres, has provided space for women to earn some money by making Birdis, or garlands of Rudrakhs etc. This is bringing more income and providing some extra cash to supplement sagging finances of cash-strapped households, but it has not meant any change in the perception of women's status nor for their workload in the family. There is thus a sharp rise in the intensity of women's labour, a finding that sounds familiar to the conclusion arrived at by the three studies in India undertaken by CEHAT as part of a multination project (*EPW, 1999*).

IX. Pollution and Industrialisation and Urbanisation

Let us first look at the scientific literature and then turn to the villages studied. The phenomena of industrialisation and urbanisation currently sweeping the India economy have both positive and negative externalities for such agriculture. For one, they increase demand for goods produced in peri-urban agriculture, expand markets, and increase employment and income opportunities; for the other, they adversely affect agricultural production, alternate livelihoods, health and quality of life, including social capital. Most often, industrial and urban growth pose major threats to agriculture by polluting natural environment and spoiling social environment. Rise in levels of air and water pollutants, are characteristic features of industrialisation and urbanisation, often accentuated by non-implementation of anti-pollution laws. Air pollutants that are most damaging to agriculture are sulphur dioxide and the oxides of nitrogen, which are categorised as acid pollutants, and ozone together with other photochemical oxidants. Fluorides are another set of pollutants. According to scientific literature pollution has serious impact on agriculture. Studies in India and in neighbouring countries have documented these effects. For instance Bambawale have found evidence of ozone causing injury to crops in India (Bambawale, 1986). In the Punjab adverse impact of air pollution have been demonstrated both on wheat and rice yields (*Wahid et.al., 1995a and 1995b*).

Air pollution in the peri-urban areas studied comes from both urbanisation and industrialisation. Let us deal with air pollution from urbanistion first. Peri-urban areas are either located along roads which, carry vehicular traffic or are visited by motor vehicles for a wide variety of reasons. As per scientific evidence the following are the likely consequences. As nitrogen oxide is released by the burning of fuel in vehicles, being an unstable compound it instantly combines with oxygen to form nitrogen dioxide, which we are told, in sunlight, gives out an extra molecule of oxygen to from ozone. The suspended particle matter (SPM) provides a convenient platform for chemical reactions, which create a haze like effect, seen mostly in the morning. Ozone is concentrated in the morning because nitrogen oxide reacts with the previous night's ozone to start this chain chemical reaction. By noon when vehicular emission is high, ozone starts forming and some of it escapes because of a rise in temperature. As evening descends and temperature falls, the earth becomes a piston, compressing the pollutants. The ozone starts to drift to areas with lower density. The peri-urban areas are the receptor sites where even if the people are not culprits in contributing to the "smog", they receive the brunt of it. When ozone drifts to peri-urban areas it is said to destroy crops in large quantities. This is extremely dangerous for farming households as well those who are exposed to the outdoors for long hours and who are engaged in hard physical labour.

Industrialisation produces *inter alia* sulphur dioxide by burning fossil fuel containing Sulphur. We are not aware of any data regarding India, but generally 70 per cent of sulphur emission comes from power generating stations. And the areas studied in this research project are in the vicinity of power plants.

It is also well established that the highest ambient concentration of sulphur dioxide occur in and around cities and near centres of industrial activity. The adoption of efficient dispersion mechanisms may reduce the severity of SO_2 pollution close to its sources but this may have been at the expense of increased ambient levels over much larger areas. However, in India as in the case of other developing countries, high levels of SO_2 are not so widely dispersed and they tend to be concentrated in and around urban areas and are usually localised.

The effect of sulphur dioxide can lead to visible injury, which, can take the form of necrosis of plant tissue—typically the leaves died from the tip of the plant downwards. It can also lead to growth reduction in certain plants and decline in yields in certain varieties of crops.

Fluorine is the other major pollutant. Fluorine is typically emitted as hydrogen fluorine from brick kilns and tile works, steel works, potteries and fertiliser factories. Effect of fluorine in reducing yield has been noticed in several countries in food crops and vegetables. Several of our villages studied are near establishments, which, are prone to release fluorine.

A major problem for agriculture is the presence of particles, mainly dust and soot in the air. Coal burning produces very high levels of suspended particulate. Today the effect of deposition of dust from cement works, motorway construction, power stations and quarries and from traffic on motorways, on crops is well documented. Usually though the loss to the farmer arises because high value produce, such as fruit, vegetables and horticultural crops, are rendered unsaleable.

Though the individual pollutants can cause damage to agriculture, polluted air usually consists of a mixture of pollutants, which may adversely affect agriculture in a more complex way. SO2 pollution effects become confounded, for instance, by the presence of nitrogen oxides. The most talked about impact is the health impact of air pollution leading to higher levels of morbidity, premature mortality and cases of chronic bronchitis and other respiratory infections.

There are a number of studies which have linked pollution to crop loss and damage to agriculture but the need for a better understanding of the impacts in the field has also been emphasized (*Varshney et. al.*, 1997 as quoted in *Marshall*, 1997). "Sulphur dioxide assessments were based on dose response relationships determined from a study around a thermal power plant in Uttar Pradesh on wheat" (*Singh et.al., 1990*). Information on power plants was used to estimate the concentrations of sulphur dioxide experienced by crops in other comparable locations. The results showed that "whilst the losses on a district-wide basis are small, farmers within 10 km of the power stations may experience yield losses of 10 to 60 per cent" (*Marshall, 1997*). There is need to look into these aspects in greater details.

Now against the above scientific knowledge, how have the villagers of the villages studied perceived the impact of pollution in agriculture, health, animal and indeed their lives? This is the key question examined.

The impact of pollution on the livelihood and lives of the people has been differently perceived in different villages. Except for the farmers of one or two villages, in the villagers' perception, the main benefit of industrialisation has been creation of job opportunities, both in the industrial plants set up and in the ancillary activities which have grown around these plants. Opportunities in services sector have benefited the villagers most: driving, running auto-rickshaws, renting of tractors, transporting goods, working as labourers and earning a livelihood in government offices. The rise in land prices as a consequence of industrialisation is perceived as bringing benefits by upward revaluation of their assets, land. The increase in demand for fresh milk, which the new industries have helped to generate, has been a boon to the villagers both in Uttar Pradesh and Haryana, helping farmers to create a stable and good supplementary source of income, having complementarity with agriculture.

In one case, at least, expansion of industrial employment has helped in loosening exploitative class and caste relations. Occupations for the Harijans, particularly the women, in Trkri, were restricted to their traditional occupations like cobblers, cleaners/sweepers and tanners. They were looked down upon. Outside of their traditional occupations, employment was restricted to whatever job opportunities existed with non-higher caste households. The upper caste households were unwilling to employ lower caste people in their homes and fields. Things have changed. Because employment opportunities have expanded due to industrialisation, they seek employment outside, in the city and neighbouring industries where caste identities are less pronounced and less cared for. In the process shortage of labour within the village has been created, forcing upper caste households to employ Harijans in their households, which they never did before. Thus upward economic mobility of Harijans has helped in their upward social mobility, in a society still bound by traditions and customs, and in countering exploitation of Harijan women by upper castes, in an environment of unequal power-status structure.

Adverse impact of industrialisation and pollution on agriculture has been perceived by villagers from different dimensions. In Uttar Pradesh the impact has been on destroying fruit bearing trees, robbing the poor of an important source of food and nutrition; pollutants discharged in river Ganges have made serious inroads into the livelihoods of malahs (fisherfolks) and source of food protein in Tikri. In several places (Kadhaoli and Sagarpur) the noticeable changes in shape and size of grains are perceived as being caused by pollution. The changes in colour of crops and vegetables (causing loss in sale value) have been reported. Villagers' perceptions about loss in quality of cereals, pulses, vegetables and fruits due to use of fertilisers, is strong. They establish a clear link between deterioration in water quality (water becoming hard) and industrialisation, including setting up of a thermal plant by NTPC. Increased hardness of water limited the options of diversifying agriculture in the villages of Haryana. The effluent discharge from factories has damaged crops and killed Buffaloes in Kadhaoli. The threat from the Haryana Urban Development Authority of acquiring land has demoralised the farmers and the consequent prospect of losing their source of livelihood and food supply, makes some of the farmers think that they are at the brink of starvation.

X. Health

Ill health is fairly widespread in the villages and discomforting too. Malaria afflicted the villagers from time to time. Cough and cold, fever, diarrhoea, female diseases, tuberculosis, and several other diseases visited the villagers regularly. And these are on the rise.

Industrial development and the resultant pollution have been clearly linked with the added health problems faced by the villagers. Weakening of eyesight, tuberculosis, cough and cold, asthma, diarrhoea and even cancer are perceived as linked to increased pollution. In one village the smoke emitted from the adjoining factories was perceived as causing health problems to the employees in the industries. In Sagarpur, the in-migrants that worked in the brick kilns and stayed in temporary shelters adjacent to the kilns suffered particularly more diseases, during the 9 months of their stay from October to July. The women correlated the higher incidence of disease during these months to pollutants released from the kilns. The contamination of a tank in Chandpur is perceived as a potential health hazard.

Part of the increase in diseases suffered could be on account of poor nutritional status of the people in the five villages covered in this study (*Kynch and Maguire, 1994*). Power to resist disease after exposure—a functioning immune system—is partly altered by poor nutrition and genetic factors (*Thomas, 1992*). Though the villagers do not perceive but to an experienced observer variable immunocompetence, widespread morbidity and deteriorating environment in the villages appear as contributory factors towards synergising hunger and ill-health which are characteristic of deprivation. Though bad health and hunger and malnutrition are often not easy for the villagers to distinguish, nevertheless the link between the two is undeniable. Several symptoms of illness (fever, cough and cold, weakness, diarrhea, deteriorating eyesight etc.) are common in protein-energy malnutrition (*Jelliffe and Jelliffe, 1989; Peel, 1979*). And if we examine the food calendars of the villages, protein deficiency in the farming households' diet is discernible. In better months (or what for want of a better word we may call "non-hunger months") the typical diet of a farming household comprise Chappatis, some vegetables and a bit of Daal (pulses). Milk is occasionally consumed and animal protein is a rarer phenomenon.

In most of the villages, in the exercise of choice by the households between accessing health care facilities and access to food, there is a bias in favour of accessing health care, a finding similar to what Kynch and Maguire found in Palanpur (*Kynch and Maguire, 1994*). Families spending large sums of money to access health care outside the village and outside of the government health delivery system, are common and accepted as part of life. But families spending large sums of money (several thousands at times) to access food for guaranteeing food security, even during hunger months are rare. There are instances where families borrow money during the hunger periods, but such borrowing is just to stave off starvation and not to ensure food security.

The concern for illness is clearly visible, not so for mal-nourishment or under-nourishment. That probably is the reason why in the health delivery system, there is no provision for treatment of mal-nourishment or under-nourishment. Well one may argue that to expect that a system which, cannot even cope with the needs of preventive health and deliver even primary health care to suffering people, could have the fineness to deal with under-nourishment or mal-nourishment is unrealistic. But that is another matter.

However, though the villagers seemingly were more preoccupied with morbidity than hunger, food insecurity and mal-nourishment, they were concerned with the quality of food. Villagers in Faridabad did tell us that they stored their best food for household consumption. In one village the farmers categorised the quality of wheat according to the time of its harvesting. And they stored class 1 wheat (harvested first) for their families; they sold class 2 wheat (harvested next) to the government at the declared procurement prices or in the market; and they used class-3 variety of wheat (harvested last) as fodder. In all the villages, the farmers were categorical in indicating the secular deterioration in the colour, size, culinary quality and taste of wheat, after the introduction of the HYV varieties of seeds. Similar is the case with milk. In one village in Varanasi, milk, which had higher fat content, commanded a higher price in the open market, both within the village and in the neighbouring towns.

XI. Coping Strategies

Arrayed against the formidable catalogue of constraints, human beings generally respond well with appropriate coping strategies. Farmers in our villages have devised their own coping strategies, though not necessarily to circumvent the predators. "Farmers live their day as it comes" (*Ray, 1999*). Villagers in general and farmers in particular are almost overwhelmed by the constraints they face. Constraints to agriculture are just one among the several sets of problems that inhabitants of our peri-urban villages face. The magnitude of uncertainty in their lives makes it futile to think of a future to deal with constraints posed by weeds, pests, insects and "Weathergods". Nevertheless they have made some attempts. The Agriculture Department (read Office) has been posted with developments regarding pest infestation and rampant growth of weeds but to little avail. More than half the farmers think that they hold such a small piece of land that it is neither feasible nor does it serve any purpose trying to find solutions to major problems of weeds, pests, insects and diseases.

Farmers threatened with the prospect of facing eviction from land acquired in public interest, have made up their mind of migrating to interior villages in the State or migrate to other States where land prices are not as prohibitive. They plan to expend the compensation amounts that they are likely to get to buy more land and develop larger farms in the interiors and in the neighbouring state Uttar Pradesh. In Sagarpur, farmers have thought even beyond that: they want to beat the government in its game. They plan to sell their land to private parties before governments notification is issued acquiring their land. This will bring them two advantages. One, since the going price of land is higher than compensation amounts receivable from government (the government always fixes its compensation package at a level lower than market price), they would gain monetarily. Two, if the private buyers set up industrial establishment on lands so purchased, by executive fiat it is enjoined that the erstwhile owner of such land will be given some employment in the new establishment. How far they will succeed, they are a bit uncertain.

It seems that *prima facie* one of the greatest of village resources remains largely untapped in most of the villages. The bargaining and leverage potential of a united group of farmers have not been realised at all. The villages need a catalyst to set in motion the process of participatory development and ignite their imagination to organise and fight for their rights. The village leadership and community cohesion need to be put to good use for encouraging villagers themselves to tackle together the problems they all have in common, and to facilitate linkages with various resources bases, including extension, technical advice and financial assistance.

XII. Perception of Well Being

People's perception of their well being and the indicators to express them, are matters of great interest for development practitioners and social scientists and even the multilateral institutions like the world bank (*PRAXIS,* 1999a, 1999b, 1999c). And the diversity of these indicators of well being has been talked about for quite some time. Several observers have written about it extensively. And people's perception of the indicators of their well being varies greatly with what outsiders perceive as the indicators of the poor person's well being (*Mukherjee,* 1992; *RRA Notes,* No. 15, 1992). The reasons for this are many but the more persuasive of the reasons are chronicled by Chambers in one of his best read book, *Putting the Last First* (*Chambers, 1983*). In this study as well, people's perception about their well being has been of interest. For one set of people, *who are relatively better off,* the indicator of well being is the number and quality of facilities they can provide to their children. This may be interpreted to imply that how much a household values its children, is an indicator of its well being. The number and quality of facilities, which children enjoy, indicate the state of their well being. The facilities are good schools, good health care, good food and good clothes. They are even prepared to sell their land and migrate to "cheaper" places to guarantee better facilities for their children.

Contrast this with a *poor community.* Their ability to work outside the bounds of their traditionally defined roles that is socially demeaning, and the ability to move outside the boundary of their village, beyond the clutches and exploitation of upper castes, to them indicate well being. A silent challenge to the unequal relationship between upper and lower castes is considered a step towards well being. An interpretation of this perception in substance, means that relatively poorer people equate well being with a life led with personal dignity, implying social and political equality and ability to make simple economic choices, basic to their lives.

These two contrasting pictures bring into the play inter-generational issues. While the relatively better off consider improvements in the quality of life for their next generation as the indicators of their well being, the relatively worse-off amongst the poor, consider improvements in their quality of life as indicators of their well being. The poorer sections of society are so distressed by loads of injustices and deprivations that for them the present is all that matters. The future is just too far away.

There is a third set of villagers who link well being to ownership of land. Landless people are categorised as poor straight away. Landless are poor not merely because they have no biological basis for growing crops, they are also disempowered from accessing vital resources to meet their basic needs. And those who possess land and have some form of employment outside household's farms, are "non-poor". They not only have the biological basis for growing crops as a means of livelihood but also have financial backstopping for the livelihood system, to smoothen out possible unevenness in flow of resources into their households.

XIII. Summary

That India is a predominantly agrarian economy is fully reflected at the village level, with shades of variations. But, for better or worse, this agrarian economy has not been static; it has been changing, the change being fastest during the late 1960s and the 1970s. Of the notable changes, emergence of wheat and paddy as the principal crops with jowar and bajra playing only second fiddle is most important. Agricultural yield has increased several fold over the last three decade or so, agriculture has moved away from being the basis of life itself to basis of life *also*. Though food crops are the bulwarks of agriculture, a preference for cash crops is on the rise. In the process agriculture has migrated from low external input agriculture to high external input agriculture, and this in turn has made agriculture a high cost (real and hidden) operation. There are policy implications here. If we as a nation would like to have self-sufficiency in food, it is important that our agricultural policy and food policy make appropriate arrangements to ensure that cash crops do not swamp away food crops. With globalisation and liberalisation, we should not wake up to find that international aid agencies and the WB urging farmers "to change from the production of local food crops to cultivate brussels sprouts, snow peas and broccoli", as Tom Barry found in Guatemala (*Francis,* 1994, p. 93). As Francis further remarked "since these foods have very low acceptance locally, they have no direct effect on local food security, but could provide export earnings; that is if the international commodity prices remain favorable to Guatemalan produce in relation to that from other possible sources. Even in this case there is no assurance that income from exports would be used for food or would be available to those in need of food . . . Information from other central American countries also demonstrate that the production of food itself may threaten food security", unless the food grown is for ensuring food security of the country at the household level.

But it has not been all hunky dory. There are problems all the way. Small size of holdings, shortage of water for cultivation, power shortage, high input cost and high financial risks and all the growing number of pests, weeds, insects and diseases have made agriculture a less attractive proposition than what it used to be in the 1940s and 1950s. "Yield increases alone do not matter", is the message that comes across very clearly. The yield increases initially registered in the 1970s and to some extent even earlier have started coming down from the 1980s.

Lack of institutional support for agriculture has been a common refrain. The virtual dismantling of the network of extension workers have left the farmers in a quandary. Farmers have got used to HYV seeds and fertilisers and all the "cides", that go with it, but they have not been provided with technical details to use them correctly. Gut feeling is all that they have to follow. At best some peer-group counseling, based on random experiences, provide them with the basis to work with pesticides, insecticides and newer varieties of seeds introduced systemically. This can harm the farmers, their land and their health in the long run.

Two perennial problems of rural India persist. One, hunger stalks the villages in most of the cases. Hunger periods are clearly marked and these hunger periods coincide with periods when those who go to bed hungry have to work the hardest. All the good monsoons (last year it was the tenth year in a row that we have had good monsoons) and bumper harvests and burgeoning PDS shops, are apparently not touching the heart of hunger:

hunger at the household level. Two, the traditional roles prescribed for the women continue to hold their sway. The discrimination against them continues unabated, sanctified on different basis and internalized by the women themselves on account of the social constructs within which they have been nurtured. All the invasion of electronic media and the massive explosion of information technology seems have left this dimension of our society untouched.

Pollution has been experienced and perceived all over and of every description: water pollution, air pollution, vehicular pollution, pollution from effluent discharge into rivers and water channels/bodies, dust pollution and so on, including pollution from brick kilns and high tension power cabling by national thermal power corporation. Increased in pollution levels have also been clearly felt. Their impact on human and animal health has been fairly widely perceived. Their impact on crops has been also felt but not severely. Injury to crops from smoke and dust has been registered, seen and perceived, but not extensively. It has been difficult always for the farmers to connect the current spate of crop injuries, diseases and consequent losses with increase in air pollution.

Figure 9: The Hierarchy of Agrosystems

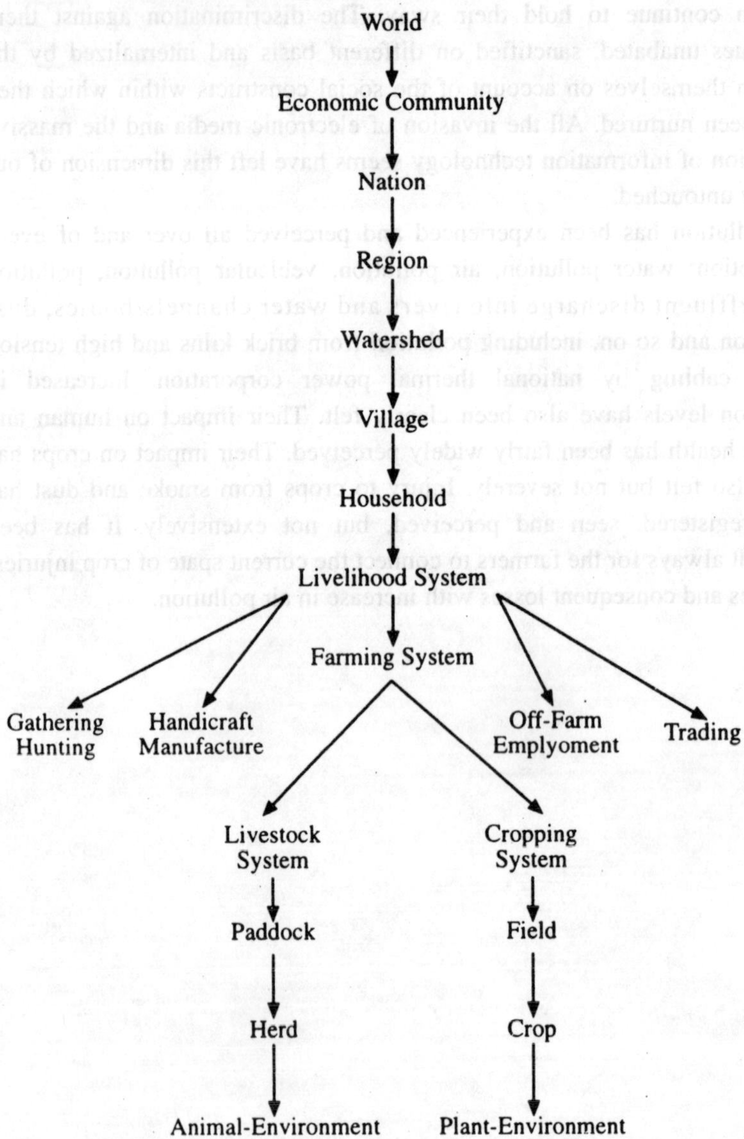

Source: Gordon R. Conway, *The Properties of agroecosystems, Agricultural Systems,* Vol 24, no. 2 (1987), pp. 95-117.

Bibliography

Agarwal, P. K. and D. P. Garrity: "Intercroping of Legumes to Contribute Nitrogen in Low-input Upland Rice-based Cropping System" paper read at the International Symposium on Nutrient Management for Food Crops in Tropical Farming System, Malang, Indonesia, 1987.

Ahmed, Iftikar: "Technology and Feminisation of Work", *Economic and Political Weekly*, Vol. XXIX, No. 18, April, 30th, 1994.

Alagh, Y. K. : "Listen to the Views of the Poor, Grain of Truth", *Indian Express*, New Delhi, 28th September, 1999.

Bambawale, O. M.: "Evidence of Ozone injury to a crop plant in India", in *Atmospheric Environment*, Vol. 20, 1986.

Boserup, Ester: *The Conditions of Agricultural Growth, The Economics of Agrarian Change under Population Pressure* (London: Earthscan) 1993.

Cernea, M.M.: *Putting People First* (Oxford: Oxford University Press) 1991.

Cernea, M.M.: "Culture and Organisation, The Social Responsibility of Induced Development", *Sustainable Development*, Vol.1, No. 2, 1993, pp. 18-29.

Chambers, Roberts: *Rural Development, Putting the Last First* (London: Longman) 1983.

Chambers, Roberts : *Micro-Environment Unobserved*, GateKeeper Series (London: Institute of Environment and Development) 1992.

Chambers, Robert: "Foreward" in Scoones, Ian and John Thompson (eds.): *Beyond Farmer First* (London: Intermediate Technology) 1994.

Chambers, Roberts, A. Percy and L. A. Thrupp: *Farmer First: Farmer Innovation and Agricultural Research* (London: Intermediate Technology Press Ltd.) 1989.

Collins J. J. and D. Harris (1983): "Air Pollution assessment at the international Crops Research Institute for the Semi-arid Tropics, India", *Environmental Technological Letters*, Vol.8, 1983, pp.10785-10787.

Conway, Gordon R.: "The properties of Agroecosystems", *Agricultural Systems*, Vol. 24, No. 2, 1987.

Conway, Gordon R. and Edward B. Barbier: *After The Green Revolution, Sustainable Agriculture for Development* (London: Earthscan Publications Ltd.) 1990.

Conway, Gordon and Edward B. Barbier: *After the Green Revolution* (London: Earthscan), 1990.

Conway, Gordon and Jules Pretty: *Unwelcome Harvest* (London: Earthscan) 1991.

Curtis, Donald: *Beyond Government: Organisations for Common Benefit* (London: Macmillan Education Ltd) 1991.

Das Gupta, Partha and Debraj Ray: "Adopting to Undernourishment", in Jean Dreze and Amartya Sen (ed.): *The Political Economy of Hunger*, Vol. 1 (Oxford: Clarendron Press) 1990.

Dinham, B.: *The Pesticide Hazard* (London: Zed Books) 1993.

Economic and Political Weekly: "Women and Work", *Economic and Political Weekly*, October 9, 1999, p. 2893.

Edwards, C. A., M.K. Wali, D. J. Horn and F. Miller: *Agriculture and the Environment* (London: Elsevier Science Publishers) 1993.

Food and Agricultural Organisation: *Fruit Bearing Forest Tress* (Rome: FAO) 1982.

Food and Agricultural Organisation: *Food and Fruit Bearing Forest Species 1: Examples from Eastern Africa* (Rome: FAO) 1983.

Food and Agricultural Organisation: *Food and Fruit Bearing Forest Species 2: Examples from South Eastern Asia* (Rome: FAO) 1984.

Food and Agricultural Organisation: *Food and Fruit Bearing Forest Species 3: Examples from Latin America* (Rome: FAO) 1986.

Food and Agriculture Organisation: *Harvesting Nature's Diversity* (Rome: FAO) 1993.

Food and Agriculture Organisation: *The State of Food and Agriculture* (Rome: FAO, 1993).

Fowler, C. and P. Mooney: *The Threatened Gene: Food, Policies and the Loss of Genetic Diversity* (Cambridge: The Lutterworth Press) 1990.

Francis, C. A. and J. A. King: "Cropping Systems Based on Farm Derived Renewable Resources", *Agricultural Systems*, Vol. 27, pp. 67-75, 1988.

Francis, David G.: *Family Agriculture, Tradition and Transformation* (London: Earthscan Publications Ltd.) 1994.

Galtung, Johan: *Human Rights in Another Key* (Cambridge: Polity Press) 1994, p 72.

Government of Haryana: *Statistical Abstract of Haryana, 1985-86 to 1996-97.*

Government of Haryana: *Statistical Data Base (1997)*, Sub-Divisional Agricultural Office, Ballabgarh, Faridabad, 1997.

Government of India: *Economic Survey*, 1995-96 (New Delhi: Ministry of Finance) 1997.

Halbwachs, G: "Organisational responses of higher plants to atmospheric pollutants: sulphur dioxide and fluoride" in M. Treshow (ed.): *Air Pollution and Plant Life* (Chichester: John Wiley and Sons), 1984.

Hanumantha Rao, C. H.: "Technological Change in Indian Agriculture, Emerging Trends and Perspectives", *Presidential Address* to The Golden Jubilee Conference of The Indian Society of Agricultural Economics, Bombay, December 1989.

Hobbelnik (eds.): *Growing Diversity: Genetic Resources and Local Food Security* (London: IT Publications) 1992.

ICRISAT: "Will the Pod-borer Become the Farmer's Pall Bearer", Hyderabad, *SAT News*, 7-10.

Ikerd, J., Monson, S. and D.V. Dyne: *Potential Impacts of Sustainable Agriculture* (Missouri: University of Missouri, Department of Agricultural Economics) 1992.

Indian Express: "No Rains Means More Pesticides in Your Subzi", *Express Newsline*. New Delhi, 25th September 1999.

International Institute for Environment and Development: *RRA Notes, No.15* (London: IIED) 1992.

Jain, Onu: "No Rains means more pesticides in your subzi", *Indian Express*, New Delhi, 25th September 1999.

Jaiswal, Meera: *Second Round of the Study on Impact of Air Pollution on Agriculture in Urban and Peri-Urban Areas of Faridabad* (Ranchi: Ranchi University) 1999, mimeograph.

Jeffery, Patricia; Roger Jeffrey and Andrew Lyon: *Labour Pains and Labour Power* (London: Zed Books and New Delhi: Manohar) 1989.

Jodha, N. S.: *Rural Common Property Resources: A Growing Crisis* (London: International Institute for Environment and Development) Gatekeeper Series, 1990.

Joshi, Hema and Sunita Bisht: *Report on Impact of Air Pollution on Agriculture in Urban and Peri-Urban Areas* (New Delhi: National Institute of Urban Affairs), mimeo, 1999.

Kabeer, Naila: "Gender, production and well being: rethinking the household economy", University of Sussex, *Institute of Development Studies Discussion Paper No. 288*, 1991.

Kabeer, Naila: "Monitoring Poverty as if Gender Mattered: a methodology for Rural Bangaldesh", University of Sussex, Institute of Development Studies *Discussion Paper No. 255*, 1989 and *Journal of Peasant Studies*, 1991.

Keatinge, G. F.: "Agricultural Progress in Western India", *Poona Agricultural College Magazine*, July, 1913.

Kenmore, P: *How Rice Farmers Clean Up the Environment, Conserve Bio-diversity, Raise More Food, Make Higher Profits* (Manila: Food and Agriculture Organisation) 1991.

Kerr, John M., Dinesh K. Marothia, Kartar Singh, C. Ramaswamy and William R. Bentley (eds.): *Natural Resources Economics* (New Delhi and Calcutta: Oxford and IBH Publishing Co.) 1997, Chapter 3.

Khoshoo, T.N.: *Environmental Concerns and Strategies* (New Delhi: India Environmental Society) 1984.

Kynch, Jocelyn and Mike Maquire: "Wasted Cultivators and Stunted Little Girls: Variations in Nutritional Status in a North Indian Village", *Discussion Paper 69*, University of Oxford, Institute of Economics and Statistics, 1989.

Lobao, Londa M.: *Locality and Inequality: Farm and Industry Structure and Socio-Economic Conditions* (Albany: State University of New York Press) 1990.

Markhan, Adams: *A Brief History of Pollution* (Earthscan Publications Ltd., London, 1994).

Marshall, Fiona; Mike Ashmore and Fiona Hinchcliffe: *A Hidden threat to food production: air pollution and agriculture in the developing world* (London: International Institute for Environment and Development) Gatekeeper Series No. 73, 1997.

Mehta, Jaya: "Employment and Unemployment in Indian Economy", in *Alternative Economic Survey 1996-1997* (New Delhi: Delhi Science Forum) 1997.

Merrick, Laura: "Crop Diversity and its Conservation in Traditional Agroecosystems" in M.E. Altieri and S. B. Hecht (eds.): *Agroecology and Small Farm Development* (Bosca Raton: CRC Press) 1990.

Mukherjee, Amitava: *Structural Adjustment and Food Security* (Aldershot: Avebury) 1994. Kong etc.: Avebury) 1994.

Mukherjee, Amitava: "Institutional Sanctions, Choice and the Secondary Food System: Incompleteness of Sen's Entitlement and Deprivation Thesis as an Explanation of Hunger" in *Economics, Development and The Quest for Alternatives*, K. K. George et. al. (eds.) (New Delhi: Concept Publishing Company) 1997, and in *Indian Economic Journal*, Vol. 43, No. 4, April-June, 1995-1996.

Mukherjee, Amitava and Neela Mukherjee: "Rural Women's Participation: Food Gathering, Food Insecurity and Hunger Periods: Some Policy Implications from Village Krishna Rakshit Chak" (co-authored) in Agarwal Anil (ed.) *The Challenge of the Balance, Environmental Economics in India* (New Delhi: Centre for Science and Environment) 1997.

Mukherjee, Amitava and Neela Mukherjee: "What The Food Calendars Reveal: A Longitudinal Stdy of Krishna Rakshit Chak", in *Learning to Share Series* (New Delhi: Concept Publishing Co.) forthcoming.

Mukherjee, Neela: "Villagers Perceptions of Rural Poverty through the Mapping Method of PRA", *RRA Notes, No. 15*, IIED, London, 1992.

Mukherjee, Neela (1995 reprint): *Participatory Rural Appraisal* (New Delhi: Concept Publishing Company).

Murakami, Shimpei: *Lessons from Nature: A Guide to Ecological Agriculture in the Topics* (Manikganj, Bangladesh: Proshika) 1991.

NABARD: *Tractorisation in Haryana-An ExPost Evaluation Study*, NABARD, 1994.

Norton, A.: *Analysis and Action in Local Institutional Development*, paper read at the GAPP Conference on Participatory Development, 9th –10th July, 1992, London, 1992.

NSSO: *Sarvekshana*, Vol. XX, No. 3, 70th Issue, January-March 1977.

NSSO: *Sarvekshana*, Vol. XVI, July-September, 1992.

Pereira, Winin and Seabrook, Jeremy: *Asking The Earth, Farms, Forestry and Survival In India* (London: Earthscan) 1990.

Pimbert, M.: "The Making of Agricultural Biodiversity in Europe", in V. Rajan (ed.) *Rebuilding Communities, Experiences and Experiments in Europe* (London: Resurgence Books) 1993.

PRAXIS: *Consultations with the Poor, A Study to Inform WDR 2000-01, Site 1 Synthesis Report* (Patna: PRAXIS) 1999, mimeographed.

PRAXIS: *Consultations with the Poor, A Study to Inform WDR 2000-01, Site 6 Synthesis Report* (Patna: PRAXIS) 1999, mimeographed.

PRAXIS: *Country Synthesis Report, Consultations with the Poor, India* (Patna: PRAXIS) 1999, mimeographed.

Pretty, Jules N: *Regenerating Agriculture* (New Delhi: Vikas and London: Earthscan) 1996, Chapter 2.

Pretty, J.N. and R. Howes: *Sustainable Agriculture in Britain: Recent Achievements and New Policy Challenges*, International Institute for Environment and Development Research Series (London: IIED) Vol. 2, 1993.

Ranade, Ajit and S. Mahendra Dev: "Agriculture and Rural Development", in Kirit S. Parikh (ed.): *India Development Report* (New Delhi: Oxford University Press) 1997.

Rao, V.M.: "Village Studies From The Economic Perspective: Some Priority Issues and Themes", *The Administrator*, Vol.XXXVI, No. 3, 1990.

Rao, V.M., Alakh, N., Sharma and Ravi Srivastava: *Voices of the Poor, Poverty in Peoples Perceptions in India* (New Delhi: Institute for Human Development) 1999.

Ray, Sudipta: *Participatory Field Research Report: Impact of Air Pollution on Agriculture in the Urban and Peri-Urban Areas of Varanasi* (New Delhi) 1999. Mimeograph.

Ray, Sudipta: *Impact of Air Pollution on Agriculture in Urban and Peri-Urban Areas of Faridabad, Field Report-Round II* (New Delhi) 1999. Mimeograph.

Roberts, T.M.: "Long Term Effects of Sulphur Dioxide on Crops: an analysis of dose-response relations", Phil. Trans. Royal Society London, No.305, 1984.

Rodhe, H. and R. Harrera: *Acidification in Tropical Countries* (Chister: John Wiley and Sons), 1988.

Runeckles, V.C.: "Impact of Air Pollutant combinations on plants", in M. Treshow (ed.): *Air Pollution and Plant Life* (Chichester: John Wiley and Sons) 1984.

Sanyal, Manoj K., Pradip K. Biswas and Samaresh Bardhan: "Institutional Change and Output Growth in West Bengal Agriculture", *Economic and Political Weekly*, November 21-28, 1998.

Scoones, Ian and John Thompson (eds.): *Beyond Farmer First* (London: Intermediate Technology) 1994.

Sen, Abhijit: "Economic Reforms, Employment and Poverty: Trends and Options", *Economic and Political Weekly*, Special Number, Vol.31, Nos. 35-37, August 1996.

Sen, Abhijit and Utsa Patnaik: "A Country Study on Poverty in India", *DSA Working Paper*, Centre for Economic Studies and Planning, Jawaharlal Nehru University, New Delhi, December 1997.

Sen, Amartya: *Hunger in a Contemporary World* (London: STICERD, London School of Economics) 1997.

Sen, Amartya: *Poverty and Famines: An Essay in Entitlements and Deprivation* (Oxford: The Clarendon Press) 1981.

Shanker, Kripa: "The Question of Tenancy Reforms" paper read at the National Workshop on Tenancy Reform, Lal Bahadur Shastri National Academy of Administration, Mussoorie, September 24-25th 1999.

Shariff, Abusaleh: *India Human Development Report* (New Delhi: Oxford University Press) 1999.

Shiva, Vandana: *The Violence of the Green Revolution* (Penang, Malaysia: Third World Network) 1991.

Simmons, I.G.: *Interpreting Nature, Cultural Constructions of the Environment* (London: Routledge) 1993.

Singh, J. P. and Alok Dash: "Agriculture" in Alternative Survey Group: *Alternative Economic Survey, 1991-1998, Seven Years of Structural Reforms* (New Delhi: Rainbow Publishers Ltd., Lokyayan and Azadi Bachao Andolan) 1998.

Singh, J. and S. S. Miglani: "An Economic Analysis of Energy Requirements in Punjab Agriculture", *Indian Journal Of Agricultural Economics*, No. 3, July- September 1976.

Singh, L. R. and B. Singh: "Level and Pattern of Energy Consumption in an Agriculturally Advanced Area of Uttar Pradesh", *Indian Journal of Agricultural Economics*, No. 3, July-September, 1976.

Singh, J.S., K.P. Singh and M. Agarwal: *Environment Degradation of Obra-Renukoot-Singhrauli Areas and its Impact on Natural and Derived Ecosystems*, Project Report submitted to the Ministry of Environment and Forests, Government of India, 4/167/84/MAB/EN-2RE, 1990.

Srinivas, M.N. (ed.): *India's Villages* (Bombay: Asia Publishing House) 1955.

Swaminathan, M.S: *A Century of Hope* (New Delhi: East West Books) 1999.

Third World Network: *Third World Resurgence*, Issue No. 108-109, August/September 1999.

Thompson, A: "The Social Goals of Agriculture", *Agriculture and Human Values*, Vol. 3, No.4, 1986, pp. 32-42.

UNDP: *Human Development Report* (New Delhi: Oxford University Press) 1992.

UNDP: *Report on Human Development in Bangladesh, A Pro-Poor Agenda*, Volume 3, (United Nations Development Programme, Dhaka) 1996.

Uphoff, Norman: "Approaches and methods for monitoring and evealuation of popular participation in World Bank-assisted projects", Paper for World Bank Workshop on Popular Participation, 26th to 27th February 1992 (Washington D.C.: The World Bank) 1992.

Uphoff, Norman: *Learning from Gal Oya: Possibilities for Participatory Development and Post Newtinian Science* (Ithaca: Cornell University Press) 1992.

Varshney, B.K., M. Agarwal, K. Ahmed, P.S. Dubey and S.H. Raza: *Effect of Air Pollution on India Crop Plants*, Project report Submitted to Imperial College Centre for Environmental Technology, London, 1997.

Wahid, A., R. Maggs, S.R.A. Shamsi, J.N.B. Bell and M.R. Ashmore: *Air Pollution and its impacts on wheat yield in Pakistan Punjab, Environmental Pollution*, Vol. 88, 1995.

Wijewardene, R. and P. Waidyantha: *Systems Techniques and Tools for Small Farmers in Humid Topics* (Colombo: Department of Agriculture, Government of Sri Lanka and CCGAAP) 1994.

World Bank: *Gender and Poverty in India* (Washington D.C.: The World Bank) 1989.

World Resources Institute, *World Resources, A Guide to the Global Environment*, Oxford, 1998.

Yugandhar, B.N. and P.S. Datta (eds.): *Land Reforms in India, Rajasthan–Feudalism and Change* (New Delhi: Sage) 1995.